SCAVULLO
ON
MEN

Francesco Scavullo

with Bob Colacello
and Séan Byrnes

Random House New York

My thanks to my editor Susan Bolotin and to my personal
assistant Joy Land for her enthusiastic support

Also by Francesco Scavullo
Scavullo on Beauty

Designed by Rochelle Udell
Séan Byrnes: Photo Editor

Library of Congress Cataloging in Publication Data

Scavullo, Francesco, 1929–
  Scavullo on men.

  1. Biography—20th century. 2. Interviews.
3. Grooming for men. 4. Success. I. Colacello,
Bob, joint author. II. Title.
CT120.S333   646.7   77-5965
ISBN 0-394-41934-0

Manufactured in the United States of America
9 8 7 6 5 4 3 2
First Edition

CONTENTS

In memory of John J. McKendry

SCAVULLO

I love photographing men. I like to talk to men and just snap them very candidly. I think men are less nervous than women in front of the camera. And if they are nervous, they don't show it. Women are more insecure in front of the camera because they worry about their lipstick, their eye make-up, their hair, while a man just looks in the mirror before the shooting to see if his hair is in place or his tie is straight.

But I never actually know what I'm looking for when I photograph a man or a woman. I just go into the studio and record what I see in front of me. I do try to put people at ease. I guess I'm really looking for the best moment to freeze. I want my photographs to inspire, not depress. I believe in the dignity of man.

With every person I photograph I always think, If that were me, how would I want to look? So there is something of my own personality recorded in my photographs too.

I chose the men in this book because I was fascinated by them. I like people who are doing something. I think it's important to take this life that's given to us and try to make it better and better, to improve ourselves, to move and grow. I don't like people who sit and watch life pass by, especially those who complain that it's passing them by.

I like to photograph young men if they're beautiful, intense, poetic. Otherwise I would rather photograph older men who have more of a story going on in their face. I think that age helps a lot of men, more than it helps a lot of women.

President John F. Kennedy was my one great, great hero. I admired him tremendously. But I keep meeting more and more men that I admire—not fewer and fewer—which is amazing. As far as leaders go, I would like to feel they care—and not only about themselves. I think we need saints in this world. Where are the saints? They all get martyred. And that makes me very sad.

I think we are in a period of mediocrity. They don't want glamorous women in movies. Everything has to be middle of the road. Of course, there's big money to be made out there in Middle America. But the American people need to be educated so badly by the artists of the world, by intelligent and creative men and women who are able to lift the people up out of what they are. Unfortunately, our so-called cultural, intellectual and political leaders want to make a buck. So they give the people mediocrity.

I hate make-up on men. It's another example of making money off the people rather than educating them and raising their level of taste. The less make-up the better—on men, women or children. If you're using it to cover up something, then find out what you're covering up and attack the problem: don't cover it up; try to get rid of it. I don't think we should cover up anything, from pimples to political scandals—we should find out what's wrong.

I think it's good for men that women are going out and working. Women have to work, for economic reasons, and *emotional* reasons—they want to *do* something with their lives. I think it'll make it easier to be a man because we won't have to carry the whole load.

I think love is the most important thing for any human being, man or woman, whether they accept it or not. Love is food for the soul. But it's very difficult to love; it's very difficult to be loved. It takes more work than anything else in the world.

Beauty in a man? Energy. Cleanliness. Sensitivity. Of course, there are all kinds of beauty in men and women. I would never be able to say what type I liked. I do love clean-looking people, tight, trim people, I don't like sloppy-looking people, loose, flabby people; and I always stare right into the eyes to find out if I'm going to get a message.

I think a man should take care of himself as well as a woman takes care of herself. There's no one special way you can take care of yourself. I, personally, am careful about what I eat, I'm concerned about chemicals, I'm concerned about the environment, I don't like to be in smoke-filled rooms or carbon-monoxide-filled streets. I'm almost too concerned about that, it drives me crazy sometimes. I don't drink a lot, and then I only drink Russian vodka because it's purified over charcoal, like the water I drink. I eat lamb, chicken, fish, rice and vegetables—organic whenever possible. I hate fried foods, greasy foods, highly seasoned foods, olive oil—even though I'm an Italian. No sugar. Very little honey. No coffee. No tea, except herbal.

But that's my own personal way of taking care of myself. In general terms, I think that every human being, male or female, should have a very good doctor—an internist who understands your whole body and who understands you. That is very important. And I think one should have a nutritionist who can examine your body and tell you exactly what your body needs to function well, what it rejects, what makes it sick, what's good for it.

Exercise is terribly important. I don't mean weight lifting, pumping iron. That's not going to help you have a longer, healthier life—it won't put more movement into your life. Exercise should open you up, get your body relaxed as well as strong—it should be like swimming. After all, swimmers' bodies are the most attractive; they have grace and a fluid line. Swimming is the only sport that uses every muscle, that stretches the body to its full potential.

And taking care of your skin and your hair is very important. For a long time men thought it was feminine to care, but that is changing, thank God. I think every man should go to a dermatologist at least once in his life to find out what kind of skin and scalp he has, and therefore what kind of soap and shampoo he should use. I think it's very important to check all these things out: what kind of soap is best for your body, what kind of skin cream to use, how much sun you can take. Too much sun can cause skin cancer, so what I'm talking about is not superficial or frivolous.

Haircuts are important, too. I've found that most men know when they have a bad one. Unlike women, they usually don't get stuck with a bad haircut more than once. They move around and find somebody that's right for themselves. And I think manicures help nails look better and more attractive.

Finally, I'd consider plastic surgery if I had anything that made me look tired or unattractive. I wouldn't expect plastic surgery to make me look twenty years old. But if you feel good, why shouldn't you look good? If gravity is pulling your face down and your spirits are pulling you up, why not go to a doctor to reverse the effects of gravity?

These are, of course, my personal opinions. I have, therefore, interviewed seven experts in their fields who can help all men look and feel healthier, more energetic and more attractive.

GIO

Barber, Bergdorf Goodman Men's Salon

Mr. Scavullo: How do you cut thinning hair, which is a problem for many men?
Gio: The best thing is to cut as short as you can. It looks thicker and it looks as if the person has more hair. Don't let it get long, it gets stringy, and when it starts to get oily you should shampoo it every day. But I cut it short, blunt. I don't use thinning shears, just scissors. In some cases I recommend a hairpiece, but only when you can cover the piece with your own hair. If your hair starts receding in the back, on the crown or in the front, but you can still part it on the side and comb over the piece, it looks fantastic. I only recommend a whole piece, a wig, if the person needs it for business, like theater or movies. The same with hair transplants. People who are almost completely bald think they are going to get a hair transplant and they will look better, but when they finish they have no hair in the back because they have to take it from the back and put it in the front—so it doesn't look good. It's only good as filler to make hair thicker. I think hair is more important for men than it is for women because women can always use make-up or wear a wig and nobody can tell. But for men, the main thing is the hair.
Do you have a lot of men who color their hair?
Yes. For men who start to go gray on the sides, if the gray doesn't look good, I darken it a little bit. But for those who have beautiful gray hair, I think it's a shame to dye it. I may give it a little silver gleam to make it whiter.
Do you shape hair according to the shape of the skull?
Yes, it all depends on the shape of the head. And I can improve the shape of the head—it doesn't matter what shape it is—I can really shape the hair and make a head look almost perfect. But I can't make miracles. Nobody can make miracles. But whether you're called barber or haircutter or hairdresser, you have to know the basics. And then you have to have some imagination, you have to be creative. A haircut is like a sculpture. Some people sculpt in bronze, in wood, in gold. I do my sculpture in hair. And I love my profession, I love what I do. I enjoy it so much when somebody comes to me for the first time and his hair is a mess. And I take that hair and in ten minutes I change it completely. It's a great feeling.

MARIO BADESCU

Skin-Care Specialist

Mr. Scavullo: Is men's skin different from women's?
Mr. Badescu: No, it's not. Structurally, there's no difference between a man's skin and a woman's.
But the care is different.
The care depends on whether a man or a woman is vain or not. But men have problem skin, women have problem skin. Men have dry skin, women have dry skin. Men have acne problems, women have acne problems. The difference between men and women is that we exercise our skin more by shaving it. And when we shave we increase the blood circulation to the skin, which brings oxygen to the face, which is the only thing that can nourish the skin.
Men in their twenties all have good skin, don't they?
No, at twenty you can have dry skin. And when wrinkles come, nothing can be done. But you can prevent wrinkles with a lot of cream and by taking proper care of the skin. While shaving helps the skin as far as exercise and circulation, it can also cause many other problems because most men don't know how to shave—they go up and down against the direction of the root, and this causes ingrown hairs. Also, if you have dry skin, you should shave and *leave the water on the face*; don't dry it, because that dries the skin—*rinse* the alkalinity off the face. Most men don't realize this because they have no education about skin care. They think that by using creams and taking proper care of the skin they lose their masculinity. A woman client of mine said, "My brother-in-law is such a marvelous person, but he has such dry skin." So she bought before-and-after shaving cream from me for him. And when she gave it to him, he threw the cream in the garbage and said, "I'm not going to use cream, I'm a man!"
Is electric shaving better for a man's skin?
Electric shaving doesn't cut as close to the skin, so you don't get as good a shave. But the main difference is that you don't use water. And the most common problem with men is broken capillaries, caused by the hot water which they use to shave.
Is there anything you can do for broken capillaries?
Eat a lot of vitamin C and vitamin E, rose hips and sunflower seeds—that can prevent them.
Are broken capillaries caused by age?
Yes, and also the sun, the wind, not protecting the face, using a lot of moisturizer in the morning in the wintertime because the weather is freezing. You know, every moisturizer contains between fifty and seventy-five percent water, and that freezes in cold weather and breaks capillaries. Also, going from hot to cold breaks the capillaries. You should cover your face or use a protective cream against the cold. There are so many ways to take care of the skin, but first of all, men and women should know the facts about their own skin. After you know your skin, you know the way to take care of it—it's not hard to go to a drugstore and buy cream to protect the skin. And take shaving cream—change until you find the right one. Maybe you are allergic to menthol—so many men are allergic to it. Men, like women, should use cleansing cream to remove impurities because the impurities in the air don't know whether you are man or woman when they fall on your skin. I have fifteen years' experience with skin treatments, mostly for women but also for men. I didn't start in the beauty field. I was a chemist and I was trained in skin chemistry in Paris and Vienna. And I never saw any difference between skin care for men and skin care for women.
Most men like to use soap. Is that bad?
Use soap. But rinse with water, remove the alkalinity. And if you want to be very conscientious, just take some water with lemon because it has a little acid to rebalance the pH on the face. So, use soap, rinse with water, and then apply a moisturizer. And know how to change according to the season. Everybody uses moisturizers for the day, and night cream for the night, which is wrong. Use the night cream in the morning in the wintertime. And reverse it. People think, Why should I use a night cream in the morning? But they don't think about the weather. When you ski, use no moisturizers at all. Protect the skin with lots of suntan cream because the sun is stronger when you're skiing than if you're on the beach. Then in the summer for tennis, swimming, use moisturizer.
Does skin change as you get older?
Absolutely. It depends on your hormones. For example, I told a client twenty-five years ago to use soap because his skin was very oily—but he kept using what I had prescribed twenty-five years before. Your glands don't secrete the same

amount of oil when the skin is twenty-five years older. I couldn't understand a man not realizing this!

Many men get facial treatments at barbers and hairdressers. Is that good for their skin?
I don't believe in hot towels at all. Too hot can break the capillaries and open the pores. And if you use a mask, you have to use one that is suitable for your type of skin, but barbers or hairdressers use the same mask for everybody. It's a mask with a lot of zinc oxide, which if you use it on skin with broken capillaries is very damaging. These treatments are horrible. The operators just want to make money. You should go to a place especially to take care of your skin.

How is steam or sauna on the skin?
You have to protect the skin with cream. If you don't have cream, use oil—on the whole body, or else you dehydrate your skin. I'm not against saunas, I'm not against sun, if you know how to take care of your skin. It's very important that you perspire a lot and get rid of the toxins that you have in your system—this is very good for the body, it gets the blood circulating all over the body, but take care of your skin, too. After the sauna, don't dehydrate your skin; use a moisturizer on your whole body because you're losing water through perspiration, and you lose elasticity. Again, go out in the sun and perspire a lot. But if you use a moisturizer after the sun, you don't burn, and your skin regains its elasticity.

What about swimming in pools?
Chlorine is very bad. Use a protective cream before you go into the pool. Absolutely. A moisturizer on the body, and a cream on the face. Oil is even better than moisturizers because they contain water, and chlorine will dissolve them—but not the oil. You can use any kind of oil, even cooking oil. But the face is more sensitive than the body because the face is more exposed to everything, so use a protective cream like Vita, or a nourishing cream. And, also, don't fool around with sun lamps. They are the worst because they burn the skin.

LUCETTE
Manicurist, L.A.L. Salon

Mr. Scavullo: What types of men like to have their nails manicured?
Lucette: Older men, young men, all kinds of men get manicures because they figure the nails are part of the body, part of the personality.

Do many men have pedicures?
Yes. Men like a pedicure because it's very comfortable.

Do men who have manicures generally have beautiful nails or bad nails?
A lot of men have very bad nails. But a manicure makes the nails look good. It is not only to cut the nails. It is to cut the nails, to cut the cuticles and to give a good buff because nails look beautiful just buffed naturally. Some men like polish, but it's different.

I always thought that gangsters have their nails polished because they wear diamond rings.
Many men who wear rings like polish because it shows the whole hand off more. Sometimes people that work as truckdrivers, people who work in the sanitation department, they come for a manicure.

How often should you have a manicure?
Every two weeks, because if you go too long without a manicure, the nails get out of shape and it's more difficult to make the nails look nice.

How long does it take to do a manicure?
A good manicure takes half an hour. Some people want it to take ten or fifteen minutes; they say, "Just push the cuticle back." There's no such thing as pushing the cuticle back. You have to cut cuticles as far as you can go.

DR. JAMES L. D'ADAMO
Naturopath

Mr. Scavullo: What is your definition of a naturopath?
Dr. D'Adamo: A naturopath is one that treats in a natural way, using nature's medication—food, herbs, vitamins.

Do you have any general nutritional guide that you think is best for most people?
I think that's a mistake that's being made in America. One person writes a book and says everyone should be a vegetarian. And he'll give you five thousand real good reasons why. Then another writes a book and says everyone needs protein. And he'll give you many good answers there. Then you have your fruit nut, your nut nut . . . Adele Davis says if you have a cold, you should take so much vitamin A, so much vitamin C, so much vitamin D. The major mistake that's being made in all these cases is that they're attempting to treat all people alike. And the fact of the matter is that there are no two people that are alike on the face of this earth. No two people have the same fingerprints. No two faces are completely identical, even those of identical twins. No two voices are alike—the police department has voice tapes. No two lip prints are alike. There are so many things that make each person different from the next person. So there's no one answer in treating all man's ailments so far as doing things in a natural way.

How do you know what kind of diet to recommend to people? How do you examine them when they come to you?
I use blood types. There are basically four types: A, O, AB and B. Depending upon the blood type, I will make a patient a vegetarian, a meat-eater, or the best of both kingdoms. For some people all food is good. But one man's food can be another man's poison. So there is no one way of treating people.

The examination basically consists of iridology—the science in which the eye becomes a map of the body. Every time a person eats improperly or does something wrong to his or her body, the eye records this information. It's really not very mystical, it's very simple. From every organ of your body you have a nerve which traverses all the way up to the eye. And every time an organ has been abused, it causes a slight color change within the iris of the eye. Skilled iridologists can see these color changes and put them into words. I can tell you a great deal about your past without your telling me anything. And the past is important because you and I are only a reflection of the past. It's the weaknesses of the past that come together to produce the symptoms of today. Treating a symptom is a very foolish act because you're treating the end product, which can be very far removed from the actual cause. So we have to go into the past, locate the weaknesses, take this information based upon the blood type, and then come up with a menu tailored to your specific needs.

Do you generally advise patients against drinking or smoking or taking drugs?
I don't like to give people so much health that it would isolate them from the rest of the world. I want to put as much health as possible into their body in a natural way, but

keep them in society. But excessive drinking is going to have its effects upon the liver, upon the kidneys, it's going to take a great deal of energy away from the mind; there's no question but that it has its deleterious effects upon the body. And we suggest that people don't drink while they're under treatment for whatever problem, but later on, small quantities of white wine are certainly not going to hurt anyone.

And cigarette smoking?
Cigarette smoking is very harmful to the body.

What about marijuana?
There is not a patient that I examine that I wouldn't be able to tell if he was smoking marijuana. It automatically shows up in the liver. The liver is the great filter of the body. Even if you go to the dentist and get a little Novocaine while he's fixing a tooth, the liver must filter that debris. And the liver, being a constant filter, has no way of getting rid of the debris itself. So the liver must be cleansed. And one way to cleanse it is to cleanse your diet. The first thing we do is change a person's menu to give his body the nutrients or the vitamin supplementation or the proper herbs it needs to cleanse the liver.

Do you recommend that people avoid foods with preservatives and chemicals?
No question about it. That's one of the big problems that we have in America. Beef is all injected with steroids and other chemicals and tenderizers. It's really horrible. Much of the fish in the ocean is being totally destroyed by chemicals. Tuna fish is full of mercury. Swordfish is full of mercury. In Japan it's affecting the central nervous systems of people. Has any of your friends ever caught a tuna and brought it to you? It's interesting to note that the meat it not as white as you see it in the can. It's gray. And then it's bleached with lime. If you were dropped into a lime pit, you would dissolve.

Do you think it's generally better if people can get their vitamins from food rather than through pills?
Some people can do very well without any vitamin supplementation or any vitamin pills; others will need vitamin pills all their lives because the food today no longer has the nutrient value that it should.

The average American consumes something like two hundred and fifty pounds of sugar per year. Sugar is one of the most harmful things. Low blood sugar is a very devastating condition among the American public. Its actual name is hypoglycemia. There is generally a weakness in two systems: the pancreas and the adrenals. These two organ weaknesses come together and produce people who crave starch and sugar. This starch and this sugar play such havoc in the body that they affect them physically and mentally. Of course, many times it's a genetic weakness. But because of the refined foods that we eat today and the nature of those foods, we activate this genetic weakness. Then it manifests itself in the form of low blood sugar, and as we grow older this low blood sugar invariably becomes diabetes. This is something that's spread right across the country.

Do people come to you once and get examined and you tell them what they should do? Do they keep on coming back? What do they come back for?
What I say to a patient is based upon the examination. A residue and a filth are often built up in the colon walls because of years of eating improperly, so some patients may need colonic enemas to cleanse the body. If that is so, then that is done in the office. That would mean a weekly visit or a monthly visit or whatever need be. There are various other types of therapies which could be given on a manipulative basis or a wave basis—many things. What each person needs, he receives. But mainly it's the menu, the diet, the vitamins, the herbs.

What kind of herbs?
All herbs, of a nontoxic nature. Phenobarbitol is an herb, but I would never use it because it is of a drug nature. All those herbs that are nontoxic I most certainly use. An herb is nature's medication. That's what was left here by the Creator for us. It acts in a natural way and in the same fashion that a medication would work. For example, if someone had difficulty with his stomach, he would take some drug to heal his stomach. I may use goldenseal or stinging nettle or camomile or common oat to soothe and calm and heal that stomach. Or I may use a combination of many different herbs put together which would accomplish the same end product but would not cause side effects. If I were to treat a sore throat, it might take me a whole week to get that sore throat better. Whereas if you go to a medical doctor and get a shot of penicillin, tomorrow it's better. But at some time in the future you may develop arthritis from the penicillin. You'll never develop a side effect from the use of the herb. whole endocrine and hormonal system in a woman is of greater perfection that than of a man. No question about that. Their bodies are created more intricately than men's bodies.

Do you find that men who have a lot of pressure, really big tough jobs, have more problems?
Most certainly, because stress, tension, anxiety, fear, worry, held in the mind long enough and strongly enough, definitely manifest themselves in the body as a physical ailment. Actually a patient's job is something we take into deep consideration all the time. We treat a person both ways, mentally and physically. One of the great natural healers, Bach, used to say that disorder in a person's life produces disease. Order is godliness, and godliness is health, so just beginning to regiment yourself into a new way of eating begins to organize the mind. And eating properly gives the body the nutrition it needs. As you give strength to the body you awaken in the morning feeling healthy, vibrant. That energy, that vibrance, is transferred to the mind. Then it's much easier to be positive, to be happy, to be at peace with yourself, when your body is healthy. But regardless of what good mental attitudes you have, if you awaken in the morning and feel ill, if you're not feeling very good, it's so difficult to be positive—even if you practice meditation or whatever. So the physical body does affect the mind.

We are literally and totally being poisoned to death in this country, and people are unaware of what is going on. Look at Red Dye 2—for years people were eating this. God knows the cancer it's caused. It's really a pathetic chain. There isn't a person who has come here that I haven't found something wrong with, because we have all lived and in our livingness we've all developed weaknesses. We've all done things wrongly to our bodies. Or someone else has in the form of drugs. You may be symptomatic-free today, but those weaknesses will produce a condition in your future. So the idea then is to erase the past and treat you prophylactically. The menu that I give the patient is only a menu for a moment. As certain weaknesses are corrected we change the menu until we come up with what I consider to be the most liberal menu giving you the most abundant health. Not producing any illnesses. And I try to be as flexible as possible. When I look at you I don't see people, I see an individual. And when I examine a patient, all I'm doing is becoming subservient to the wishes of your body. Period. What your body tells me it wants, I tell you you should do. No more. I'm not looking down at you, I'm looking up at you. There's a big difference. I'm not playing God in a white jacket. I have never healed a patient in my life. There's only one healer—nature.

DR. MICHAEL HOGAN

Plastic Surgeon

Mr. Scavullo: What percentage of your clientele is male?
Dr. Hogan: About fifteen percent. There has been an increase in the whole field of cosmetic surgery—more women are coming and more men are coming. The most common operation for men is the eyelid operation. And then the face lift. That's virtually where it stops.

Do you work on the body as well as on the face?
Not on men, except men who've had enormous weight losses, particularly in the abdomen when the skin hangs down to the thighs like an apron. But basically there are two main areas that are interesting regarding men and cosmetic surgery—first of all, the type of men that are having it. It's an enormous cross section, it's not just people in the entertainment industry. I have a patient who was an ambassador, I have a patient who is a baseball manager, I have a patient who is a former police sergeant—he retired from the force in his early fifties and had to find other work. So it's not just a specialized group that is having it. And that's true of all cosmetic surgery, which is getting more and more common.

The results of the eyelid operation last about ten years. You start aging right away, but it takes about ten years to get back to where you were before surgery. Then you have to have it done again, but you're not compelled. A lot of people are under the impression that once you get into this kind of surgery you have to keep going with it. You don't. You can stop. You're just always ahead of where you would have been if you hadn't had the surgery. And in ten years probably all you would need is to pick up the skin and not as much surgery as you had the first time, and that would probably take care of you for the rest of your life.

How long does a face lift last?
We believe men's faces look better longer, in general, than women's. One reason is the freshening of the surface of the skin by shaving every day, it stimulates the skin—and this has to do with the beard itself basically.

What about the exercise the face gets with shaving?
I don't believe that the muscles of the face are underexercised in anybody. I think that they're the most exercised muscles in the body because every time you talk you're using them, every time you eat you're using them. What sags is skin, not muscles. But let me stay on the area of blood supply to the face because that's what makes the beard grow. And if you have a healthier blood supply—and we know this is true for men because men have more bleeding during surgery than women—your skin will stay younger just because everything is moving much more rapidly. So, because of the blood supply, because of the shaving every day, men's skin has a tendency to stay younger longer than women's, leaving out all the other factors. Now, some of the general factors in aging are: genetic, which is the most important; your exposure to the sun, which breaks down the elastic tissue in the skin and causes it to lose its tone; weight gain and weight loss, which stretches skin out and it never comes back; cigarette smoking; severe trauma in life of either a physical or a mental nature; or illness, long-term illness will age the face. And then, of course, the effect of gravity.

At what age do you recommend that a man have a face lift?
Age has nothing to do with it. It's a question of whether the condition is present or not. You could put ten men in a room who all have the biological age of forty; some will look twenty-five and some will look fifty-five. Biological age is meaningless in this area. What we're interested in is whether the patient has congenital fat pockets in their eyes. I've operated on people who had congenital fat pockets in their eyes when they were nineteen. My youngest complete face lift was a woman of twenty-seven, my oldest was eighty-six—the point being that age is no contraindication of surgery at all. It has nothing to do with it. But if you need surgery, I feel it is better not to wait until it's too late, when it's really sagging. Do it earlier. If you sag a long time, it's like getting a pleat in your pants. So even if you get rid of the sag, it leaves a line because it's been there so long. When you start to feel you need it, go and see a doctor and get his opinion.

How long do you have to stay in the hospital for a face lift?
Three days. One day before and two days afterward. And you generally get most of the bruising on the neck area, not on the face. You do get swollen on the face and around the jowls. The stitches come out one week and at two weeks, but there's no pain. Doctors always say this but it's true. There's no real pain. If you touch an area that you've been operated on, like the eyes or the face, it'll feel sore the way a bruise feels sore. The awareness you have of it is the same as if you had a bruise on your thigh. But you're not in pain. Men are a little more sensitive to the face-lift operation. I don't know exactly why; maybe we have more pain fibers growing in our beard. That's just speculation, but I find that men are a bit more uncomfortable with the surgery than women—not that they're in pain.

Is plastic surgery very expensive?
The fees vary—from East Coast to West Coast, and they vary within New York City. I can give you a range of fees: eyelid surgery runs between $900 and $2,000; face-lift surgery runs between $1,500 and $4,000 tops. Then you have your hospital costs. Some individual surgeons will charge outrageous fees, which attracts a certain group of people because they feel if he charges more, he must be better.

Do you find most men prefer to keep plastic surgery a secret more than women?
I never tell anybody anything. Ever. If it gets out, then I feel very comfortable knowing that it got out because either the patient wanted it to or there was some inexplicable leak. But I think men are as secretive or as open as women about it. I think men are tougher to get in; they won't take that first step. But once they've taken that first step, they almost all go through with it. And the psychological effect of cosmetic surgery, for a man, just like a woman, can be enormous. A man looks at himself, he feels younger inside than he looks on the outside, he sees it all going one way, and it's depressing because it starts to show his mortality. He has an operation which brings his eyelids or his face into consistency with the rest of the body, which he's worked at very hard to keep in shape, and there's a whole different self-image, a whole different feeling about himself. He's up and ready to go again.

DR. NORMAN OHRENTREICH

Dermatologist

Mr. Scavullo: Let's start with acne. How do you suggest a young man treat that?
Dr. Ohrentreich: Acne is very complicated because it's not only a skin problem, but also an endocrine problem. If one doesn't get acne, one doesn't have hormones of the male type. Even when women get acne, it's caused by male hormones, usually from the adrenal gland, and even sometimes from the ovary. Most people may not be aware of this because they don't sit and look at acne patients for years and years and years, as I have, but in families where acne is

prevalent, it is usually much worse in men than it is in women. The male hormone is the prerequisite for acne. **The castrated male gets practically no acne at all.**

Now, acne is a disease of oil glands. These oil glands have an affinity for the male hormone; they convert this male hormone to a specific chemical that increases the size of the oil glands in the skin. And as each little oil gland begins to grow, its opening, which is very small to begin with, just isn't large enough to let the contents empty. You get plugging in the pore—little blackheads or little whiteheads. Then it becomes a pustule or an inflammation, a little red spot. Then, of course, it can blow up, explode like a Molotov cocktail, and if it gets to be very bad, the explosions can actually go deep enough to destroy the support of the skin and produce an acne-scarring problem. So acne itself is treated both directly as a skin problem, by opening up the pores to fight the infection, and internally, to correct hormonal imbalances if they do exist. Some of these hormonal imbalances can be so severe that if they are not corrected, no matter how much you do locally on the skin, you don't help the patient.

As a rule, we start with the skin, and add internal therapy appropriately. Now, the word "hormone" has to be explained. We don't inject female hormone into males. We wouldn't do anything like that. But you can neutralize some inflammation with anti-inflammation hormones. The word "hormone" covers a very broad category. You'd be dead without hormones. There's male hormone, there's female hormone, there are the sugar hormones, there are the salt hormones that keep the salt in the body in balance. All the word "hormone" means is a chemical made by a gland that gets into the bloodstream. That's a hormone—a chemical that's transmitted. It's a communication system. Hormones tell different parts of the body what to do.

As I said, with acne in young people we usually start with external therapy. What I like for men, in particular, to clean the skin is the Buff Puff, because they don't like to use medication; most men are averse to putting on make-up, lotions and things like that. The Buff Puff is a 3M-Reichert Division product which is a nonmedicated sponge. Most men react favorably to a device. You know they shave—that's a device. And for the average male acne patient we'll recommend special medicated soaps, astringents because they react positively to an after-shave-lotion-type astringent, and Buff Puff sponges to help remove blackheads. If they are really infected, we'll have to use an antibiotic because we don't want scarring. Not only do we want to treat the acne, we want to prevent the sequel. The acne will burn itself out, but you don't want that to be at the expense of the deeper layers of the skin, so that later on you have to do grafting and use silicone and perform dermabrasion—the removal of scars with wire brush, for example. And to go one step further, if a young man is very badly inflamed, remove the blackheads judiciously without traumatizing the skin, drain infections without hurting the patient, inject very inflamed lesions with anti-inflammatory medication, apply topical antibiotics. There's a whole spectrum of treatment. We usually don't resort to hormonal therapy in men. We try to work within the framework of normalcy, assuming that most men, if they have lots of male hormone, want it.

What advice would you give men to take care of their skin so that they would age as best as they can and not need silicone or dermabrasion or surgery?
Two basic bits of advice: epidermabrasion and sun aversion. Minimize exposure to the sun. Tan but don't burn. There's nothing more damaging to skin in relation to aging than sunlight. Now, that doesn't mean you have to be a recluse or You use a conditioner? Fine, use a conditioner. But *don't*

rotisserie style of sunbathing—lying there rolling over and over—or playing sundial, so that when someone looks at your nose he can tell what time it is because you're pointing at the sun all the time. Avoid the mid-hours of the day, from ten to two, eleven to three. Use a sun block or a sun screen, a hat. Tan slowly, because there's nothing more protective against sunlight than pigment. Blacks—though they can tan, and they do, and though they can burn, and they do if they aren't careful—are truly protected against aging. And they're truly protected against skin cancer. It's almost unheard of to see skin cancer or wrinkles on a black. Yet the albino black ages and wrinkles just as badly. As for Caucasians, the lighter their eyes, the lighter their hair, the thinner their skin, the more the sun will damage. Look at men who have been outdoors a lot, like a lifeguard. They may have the most wrinkled, weathered, sailor's or farmer's skin as it's called, a rugged complexion. But look at their buttocks—beautiful young skin.

Let's talk about hair, and baldness. How should a man care for his hair to avoid losing it?
One of the most important things you can do for your hair is shampoo it. It took many years for people to overcome the concept that if you shampooed your hair, you would lose it. You've got to understand that hair is there as a protective layer. That's its main function in animals, too, which is why we wear animal hair on our bodies in the form of wool and cashmere, etc. Human beings lost a lot of the hair on their body through the evolutionary process. The hair we have still has a protective function. It would be very difficult to live without eyebrows. Try it. When you sweat it gets into your eyes. If you went out in the sun without hair on your head, it would be mighty uncomfortable. Take your finger and touch the hairs on the back of your other hand very lightly. Now take that finger and touch very lightly where there's no hair —and you'll see the difference. Hair is an amplifier of sensation. Each hair has a very heavy nerve ending around the base of it.

Now, in nature where you're outdoors with your dog and rain is beating down, his hair gets cleansed and gets purified. You take that same animal, bring him indoors, don't bathe him, he begins to smell, he begins to look awful because the natural environmental cleansing elements are removed. Well, I treat my hair as if I were living outdoors. I rain on it every day. And I have found that frequent shampooing is probably one of the most effective ways of treating dandruff, oil diseases of the scalp, which can produce hair loss. It is not the major cause of hair loss. The major cause of hair loss is the male hormone, and hereditary predisposition in both men and women. But there are contributory factors to hair loss— seborrheic dermatitis severe is one, and other factors in oil which becomes rancid on the surface of the skin in relation to bacteria. So I'm for washing the hair every day. I wash my face every day—I don't see the loss of beard. Has anyone worn off his beard by watering it every day? You wash your body every day; how much hair have you lost on your body?
Do you use shampoo with soap in it?
Soap happens to be not the most elegant way of shampooing hair, because of residue effect. But there are soaps, there are detergents, there are mixtures. We have a half a dozen different shampoos that we use, depending upon the type of scalp—dry scalp, oily scalp, dandruff scalp, psoriasis scalp, eczema scalp, folliculitis scalp, infective scalp. The dermatologist has the advantage of recognizing disorders on the scalp, so he can tailor a shampoo. But there are so many good shampoos on the market. If you find a shampoo that's good for you, use it. Use it frequently. Alternate shampoos. live under a rock. You don't have to look pale. But forget the

overbrush. Groom, comb, brush, blow it dry, style. But don't worry your hair. A hundred strokes a day is bad. Hair does not have to be massaged to grow. I don't know how often you massage your face, but look at the way that beard grows. This rubbing, massaging, manipulation, these hair treatments are nonsense.

When you wash your hair, don't you massage the scalp?
If you shampoo daily, you don't have to. If you shampoo once a week, you have to scrub off the crud, you know. If you wear a shirt one day only, it doesn't take much washing. If you keep a shirt on for a week and wash it, it'll take a lot of scrubbing. But scrubbing your scalp pulls out hair. So that's the second thing after washing frequently: treat your hair gently, moderately.

Length isn't terribly important; wear it short or long—obviously it's easier to groom short hair. But I think a man should use his hair to the best cosmetic advantage. You can color it gently, you can straighten it gently, you can curl it, but remember: every time you do something chemical to your hair, like dyeing, straightening, curling, you are breaking the protein structure. There's no way of bringing that protein structure back. It's like a paper clip: one, two, three, four, five . . . cracks, fractures, split ends, etc. The only thing you can do is cut the hair back. And protein products are for the birds. They just don't work. Protein conditioners are no better than ordinary conditioners. Conditioners are good for the hair because most shampoos do leave a slightly alkaline residue and some people do better if they switch to an acid residue—that's the idea of the old lemon rinse or the old beer rinse. That's what a good conditioner is, and I'm for them. And then, of course, once we get beyond that, I think you've left the beauty parlor, the drugstore, the supermarket where you can buy things. Then you have to go to the dermatologist who specializes in the medical diseases of the scalp, and there are many medical diseases of the scalp that affect the hair, including common hair loss—which today we understand. We know the specific chemical that produces hair loss in men. It's called dihydrotestosterone. We have chemicals that block the formation of this chemical in the scalp. There is an enzyme in the scalp called 5-alphareductase. This enzyme takes the normal testosterone, a male hormone which occurs in men much more than in women, and converts it into dihydrotestosterone. Men have obviously far more male hormones. That's why they show so much more hair loss. But a woman *can* lose hair just as readily.

How do you treat a man whose hair is thinning?
I first check to make sure that there is nothing going on in his system that is abnormal. A lot of that I get by taking a careful history. We take routine blood tests, and there are also some special blood tests that we do that specifically measure those things relating to hair—highly specialized hormone studies. Past that point I make sure that the scalp, the skin itself is healthy. Then, beyond that, if we're left with just common ordinary garden-variety baldness, male-pattern baldness caused by dihydrotestosterone, I apply local medicine in the office and give the patient things to use at home to block as much as possible those chemicals in the scalp that contribute to hair loss. We have very good evidence that this can be done today. In addition, we are working toward medicines to turn on hair growth. We now have specific chemicals that will turn on hair growth on certain parts of the body, like the beard, chest, underarms, pubic area. If a man loses his pubic hair, it could be very embarrassing in a sexual situation. If we have an individual who's got very thick hair on the sides and the back of his head and he's losing hair on the forehead, we'll do transplants. I frequently combine hair transplants with medication, using a little transplant to keep it thick in the thinnest areas, using medication to save hair as best we can. The day will come when we will be able to turn hair on and off anywhere on the body, with safe local medicine. That day is coming.

JOHN WINTERS
Director of Pilate's Exercise Studio

Mr. Scavullo: What age group of men come to the studio?
Mr. Winters: We have all ages. The oldest is eighty-two. He's had several operations, so he does a limited amount of exercise, but he never stops. The youngest male is twelve. They all get the same exercises. The only distinction we make is with men in their twenties; because they're not properly developed in the chest and shoulders, we work on them in that area. But basically the exercises remain the same for all ages. What happens to the male as he exercises is that his shoulders expand and the waistline falls in. If a man continues regularly and doesn't cheat, he will see tremendous differences even in four or six weeks' time.

What about men who, as they get older, start to get stomachs? Can that be controlled by exercise?
It can be controlled to the extent that as you learn to exercise and move your body, you also strengthen your stomach—the muscles hold in your stomach. That's all it amounts to. You see kids running around with their stomachs stuck out, and it's just because they're not using their muscles. We do *not* tell you that you'll lose weight coming to us. You won't. You lose weight by cutting down on your food. Eat half as much as you normally do and immediately you'll start losing.

So if a man exercised, and if he watched his diet, he could keep a good body.
He would certainly have a good body. You'd be amazed at the young men with beautiful bodies who weren't beautiful until they came to us. Then all of a sudden the legs become beautiful, the torso becomes beautiful. I have several men in their fifties who also have marvelous bodies for their age. It's not the body of a twenty-year-old or a thirty-year-old, but it's a good-looking body when you stack it up against people in the street who have never exercised. They can't even bend forward. All of these people are *movable*. It's incredible—a new person comes in who's not exercised, and I say, "Lift your leg." He can't, and once he gets it up, the leg is shaking all around—because of no exercise.

Do you have any weight lifting?
We use weights for injured knees, to build up the muscle that protects the knee, and for injured shoulders, to make them more mobile. But we use only weights for a very short time. We don't go in for the pumping-iron bit. I don't approve of that at all. The minute you stop it, that muscle all turns to fat.

Do you find men's posture improves with your exercises?
Definitely. Because the stomach muscles are tight, the behind muscles are also tight, and that immediately lets you stand up. It's amazing how good the posture becomes in just a short space of time.

Is there anything else you would like to say about your philosophy of exercise?
I feel sorry for people who do not exercise, regardless of the reasons, because I think it's essential to the body. And the rewards are so great for the minimum amount of time that you put into it. In a week you spend three hours exercising your body, and the way you feel after that is a great reward for such a little amount of time spent.

ROBERT ALTMAN
Movie Director

Mr. Scavullo: How did you get into directing films?
Mr. Altman: I started writing during World War II and I painted a little bit and I was kind of a cartoonist in school and I really believe I became a director because I just failed at everything I tried.

What kind of background do you come from?
Upper-middle-class. Catholic. I went to Catholic schools. Occasionally Pauline Kael will refer to Francis Ford Coppola and me as Catholic directors. But Catholicism was never a very strong thing in my life; my mother wasn't a Catholic. I had no problems. I just grew up. It was kind of dull, as a matter of fact.

What's your day like?
When I'm shooting I usually get up very early—five or six—and write. On *Three Women*, for example, I started out with a thirty-page outline, and I shot in sequence, and I waited until the last minute to write each scene.

Do you write alone?
I prefer working with another writer because that's the hard work, I think. Alan Rudolph, the director of *Welcome to L.A.*, wrote for me for a while. When asked "What's it like to write a screenplay with Altman?," he said, "He sees the light and I dig the tunnel." That's what John Considine now does in my apartment every morning when I'm not shooting. He shows up at nine o'clock and sits there at the typewriter, and I get up and I read and then I talk for about twenty minutes. And then each time we cast somebody, we change that role.

Do you take a shower?
I take a shower every morning.

Breakfast?
I don't eat breakfast unless somebody cooks it for me. Considine will occasionally say, "Shall I make some eggs?," and I'll say, "Oh, good."

Do you live alone?
I have a wife and children.

She never makes breakfast for you?
Not unless I ask. But then, she doesn't eat breakfast. I can have it if I want it. But I don't care about food when I'm working. I never leave my office. I eat six or seven sandwiches a day.

Do you need a lot of sleep?
Nope. I'll go to bed at nine or ten when I'm shooting, but I usually get to bed by one or two. When I'm shooting I sleep for twenty minutes during the lunch hour. I can just lie down anywhere and sleep.

Do you have a lot of patience?
When I'm working on a movie, working with people, I have a lot of patience. I have a very short fuse when the picture is finished and the ad doesn't come out right, or they don't send the print—after we've done so much work, I hate when it gets fucked up.

It seems to me that you had a pretty pessimistic point of view about America in *Nashville*.
And I didn't make anything up in *Nashville*. I'm really not interested in America as much as mankind. I don't feel particularly nationalistic. It's what I see; I'm no different from a painter or any artist. I'm not interested in telling people my philosophy, what I think they should do, what I think they should be. That's for philosophers and politicians. I merely want to show what I see through my particular window. That's not to say that I don't have opinions and that those opinions aren't automatically reflected in my work. But I don't investigate them and I don't think about them very much.

Are you worried about the future of mankind?
No, I think it will take care of itself, like everything else. I don't think about it very much.

Does anything depress you?
I never get depressed about work. I'm up pretty high all the time. I have a really high energy level and I'm kind of an optimist actually. But I do get depressed about stupidity and the bureaucracy that goes along with it. I don't know what to do about it. Who doesn't feel that way when you see the news? It almost interests me more to see violent wars take place than apathy, and people just being born and dying of starvation on the streets with no hope. I feel that Africa is going in a stronger direction than India; I think Africa is going to, at least, come to some sort of conclusion.

Revolution is always extreme and I think that it's good for the adrenalin factor if you are revolutionary. But if you're a revolutionary, your life is short-lived, because once the revolution is lost or won there's no place for you. You're like the front line of attack and I think a lot of energy comes through you during that time. I think that there are people who like to do that, who are cut out for it and very good at it.

Looking back, I think that one of the most remarkable revolutions that ever took place on the face of the earth was the black revolution in America. And it was literally bloodless. A few thousand people got killed, but that's nothing compared to the speed with which it happened. And I think that's a very positive thing, politically.

I don't want to say that I like our new President, but I like him better than our old one. I don't want to go to the White House and be a pal, but I think some good things can come out of what he's doing.

Do you like violence in films?
I use violence where I see it. It is the only calculated thing I do in a film. It isn't just "Oh this feels good." It's not organic. Usually it's to wake the audience up—not literally, but to draw their attention. *McCabe and Mrs. Miller*, for example . . . This funny cowboy was looking for a whorehouse, and then suddenly we had him just whacked—killed. He was not a principal, but he was a real innocent, and that was a big shock to the audience. In *The Long Goodbye*, Mark Rydell hits a girl in the face with a Coke bottle. Some people think that's the worst thing they've ever seen on the screen. But it made a point. My opinion of violence in drama or literature or film is that if I'm walking down the hall of a dark building at night, and I know people are looking for me, and somebody is playing spooky organ music, I'm going to get the hell out of there. When real violence takes place, nobody's prepared for it. We could be sitting here having a party and your doorbell could ring and some guy could come up and you could say, "You got the wrong address," and we could laugh at him, and one second later he could have a gun and kill all of us. Usually you're laughing when it happens, because you don't expect it. If you get scared ahead of time, you avoid it. I don't think that violence is planned.

Have you ever experienced violence yourself?
Not really. The most frightened I've been in years was when I was walking by a neighbor's house and two big Airedales got loose and started hitting me from both sides. And I didn't

ROBERT ALTMAN
Movie Director

have anything in my hands. Just a drink.

Do you ever get violent?

I'm going to punch John Simon as soon as my lawyers tell me what it can cost me. I don't care if it costs me a little bit of money, but I don't want to go to jail. He has to be handled in the most basic way, the same way he handles other people. He wrote something about Art Carney in his review of *The Late Show* that I just find despicable. He basically said: Art Carney manages to pull this off pretty good but he always makes me feel dirty. I think that's so uncalled-for from a film critic.

Do you get angry with other critics?

I don't consider Rex Reed a critic, and if he gave me a good review, I would be worried. I've been treated very well by the critics. If it weren't for the critics, I probably wouldn't be sitting here right now.

Is it difficult to make creative movies in Hollywood?

I live in California, I work there, my staff is there, but I am totally outside of Hollywood. I have not been in a major studio for years, except for two days to score a picture. I have my own editing place. I'm self-contained. I live above Malibu and my office is in Westwood, and I never go anywhere else, except, occasionally, to a friend's house. And I don't know a restaurant in Los Angeles. That's not an exaggeration.

Don't you like social life?

Very much. I'm very gregarious. The cocktail hour is a terrific time for me. But I do it in my own office. We never get out until ten, eleven at night. People come by there. And we get more creative work done from six o'clock on than we do all day, because the people that stay are there because they want to stay.

What do you think of actors and actresses?

I adore them. I couldn't work without them, unless I did animation. And I think more comes from their input than from the input of the script or from myself. They're the ones. It's very easy for most artists to hide. They can stay in their room and do their paintings, they don't even have to show up at the gallery. I mean, I can hide. Writers can hide. But the actor stands out there and says, These are my eyes, this is my body, this is me. I think it's very courageous, and I don't care what drives them to do that. They really give more of themselves to their art than any other artists do.

Do you like working with big stars?

If I like the person. The only big star I have worked with is Paul Newman, whom I find terrific. Sometimes you need to use stars in movies. I think I needed a star, a recognizable person, in the part of McCabe because I didn't have to use two reels of film to develop his character. As soon as you see Warren Beatty ride up on a horse, you know he's an important guy. Then I can start to tear him down. If I'd had somebody that was not a star, I'd have had to build the character up to what I wanted it to be, and only then could I tear him down.

Why do you think someone becomes an actress or actor?

I think everybody starts at what he eventually does for the wrong reasons. It's pretty obvious that most actors really want attention—there's a lot of glamour, adulation, wealth, in an acting career. And then they find out that it's a helluva way of life, it's really marvelous. Movies are a terrific sham. I had a special-effects man up in Canada, a guy about fifty years old—Jesus, he had fun. He said, "What better job could I have? I get to blow up bridges, I get to kill people and I don't go to jail for it. I get to make it rain, I get to make it snow." It's like going through your life with a pass to remain a child!

Do you think that applies to directors too?

Sure. If it isn't fun, I promise you I wouldn't be doing it. If it got to where it wasn't fun, nothing would keep me in it, because I don't think that the work is important. I don't think it has any real value, it's very temporary.

What kind of work do you think is important?

I think architecture is important. I think basic physics and sciences have the most value. Writers, artists of all kinds, contribute, but I don't think it's going to make much difference if I do thirty-five more films or if I walk out of here and drop dead.

Do you think about death?

I'm aware of it. I don't think I like it. I'm not afraid of it. I'm not manic about it. But there are a lot of things that I would like to do that I know are going to be fun.

Do you find life more fun as you grow older?

In my mind I'm twenty-two, and I'm fifty-two now. There's nothing I could do at twenty-two, other than run faster, that I can't do now. My eyesight isn't as good; my hearing is better. I'm not frustrated.

What do you do in your free time? Do you watch TV? Go to see other people's films?

I really don't have any free time. When I do have free time I like to be with friends; usually we're talking about a project. I don't see many movies other than the ones I do.

Do you make a lot of money?

I have my own company, and I usually put up the completion guarantee for my films, so I'm on the hook. If I go over budget, it's my money—but that gives me more control. I have the freedom to do what I want to do.

How do you feel about sex in films?

It's certainly a part of life, so it's certainly part of art. My film *Three Women* has to do with sex, sexes and relationships. The only explicit sex scene is John Cromwell making love —he's ninety and she's ninety.

Do you think it's becoming more difficult for men and women to have long-lasting, one-to-one relationships?

I think the whole structure of male/female relationships is changing according to the needs of the society, but I don't think it's changed a great deal. For example, formal weddings are coming back in style. I've seen people, not in the Midwest or in rural areas, but actors and rock stars, people who are freaked out all the time, and they're saying, "Oh, we're gettin' married in three months. Debbie's picked a date." Young actresses come in and say, "I want to get married on either June twenty-sixth or twenty-seventh, I'm waiting to get my numbers straight to see which is the best day. We've already rented the Plaza for the wedding reception." I don't expect it. My son—he's got a ring in his ear—moved away with a girl to Washington State to live in the trees, and then they had a baby and they came down. I found out through his brother that he got married in Washington. And I said, "Gee, Michael, I understand you got married." He said, "Who told you! Dad, don't tell anybody." I said, "Why did you do it?" He said, "It was for Jade"—that's their son's name.

Are you a good father?
I don't know what that means. I didn't beat my children. I have five children from three different marriages. I like them all. The youngest one's eleven, he's adopted. I find that the older I become, the more interested I am in the children. I was much more self-oriented when the kids were younger. My oldest daughter's thirty and her son is three months older than my youngest son, the adopted boy—who's racially mixed, his father was black. My grandson is a gold-headed WASP and they play together, and my grandson calls my son "Uncle Baby."

Do you see your ex-wives?
No. The first one is still living out in Carmel. Our mutual daughter, the thirty-year-old, sees her all the time. And my current wife contacts my second wife because of the two boys by that marriage. They're nineteen and twenty-one. One of them works for me.

Your current wife contacts your second wife?
They talk on the phone. There's no animosity.

Why have you been married three times?
I don't know. I was afraid of the dark and I didn't like to sleep alone.

Are your wives career women?
No. They're just women.

Are they beautiful?
First one was; second was quite un-beautiful. My wife now is very attractive.

How old is your current wife?
Same age as I am.

What does she do?
She deals with our adopted son, and a mutual son, who's seventeen. And she travels with me when she can. But she has no pursuits really.

What do you think of women who work with men?
I've always dealt very easily with women. I have as many women working for me, in responsible jobs, as I do men. I don't segregate. I find that it's difficult not to get at least sexually involved with certain women who are very attractive to me. I may not pursue that involvement, but that always is in the area of possibility and it changes your relationship a little bit. I'm usually lucky or smart enough not to get involved with a woman I'm working with—sometimes after I've worked with them, but not during. I don't think I could face that pillow talk.

How about an affair with an actress with whom you are doing a film?
I've never done it. I had an experience with a girl who was a very, very well-known actress—very serious quick love affair. I think her feeling was that we would become a matched

set and work together, but I could never do a film with her. I think it would be very unfair to the other actors and to the project. It would throw the balance off.

Are you going to continue directing for the rest of your life or is there anything else you'd like to do?
I'm going to try to keep producing a couple of films a year and maybe do some musical stuff on Broadway. In other words, if you asked me what I want to do most, it would be my next film.

Does it interest you at all to work in television?
God knows the medium is powerful and it certainly reaches a lot of people, but in the condition that it's in now, I'm not very interested. I don't think I could make any contribution. It's too controlled, but I think eventually it'll change. Art will creep into it.

Is freedom necessary for art?
Totally. I mean *freedom*; most people want certain strictures and structures and restrictions—but I've got to have total freedom. Television is a "current" medium: it's great for sports, for news. I think it stopped the Vietnam war, because it brought reality of it into your own living room. I think a television series like *M*A*S*H* is abominable. I don't care how well it's done; it's the worst sort of propaganda because it's really saying, every Tuesday night in living rooms all across America, that our enemy is people with slant eyes.

Do you care about clothes?
I wear pretty much the same kind of clothes all the time. I like to be comfortable. I tend to perspire a lot. I'll wear a necktie only if the restaurant's *really* good. I would not go into Régine's, and if I did, it would only be to find out what "evening elegance" is. She has a sign on her door: MEN MUST WEAR TIES AND DARK SUITS; LADIES EVENING ELEGANCE. I like to stand in front and watch evening elegance pass by.

Do you diet?
I try not to get too fat. That's the main thing. Right now I know that I've got to cut back for a few days.

Are you concerned about chemical preservatives in food?
Everybody around me is, so I don't have to be. My wife's very conscious of all that; she's in terrific shape. I don't eat sugar, because I get enough in the alcohol I drink, so I don't have any desire for it. I drink a lot. I like it. It's a habit: I'm sure liquor is a narcotic. I get a feeling about five-thirty when it's time for a drink. I drink a great deal of Scotch in the evening. I can drink continuously with no problem until I get into brandy. If I start on brandy after dinner, it wipes me out for two or three days.

Do you get drunk?
I'm usually counteracting alcohol with grass and vice versa.

Do you smoke cigarettes?
No. I gave it up thirteen years ago. I had asked my doctor for some diet pills. He said to come in for a physical first, and he took a cardiogram. I was smoking, literally, six to seven packages of regular Chesterfields a day. After that cardiogram my doctor just took the cigarette out of my hand and he said, "You'll be dead in two years if you don't stop smoking." I stopped.

ROCKY AOKI
Sportsman, Restaurant Owner, Entrepreneur

Mr. Aoki: I want to know more about everything—I want to steal ideas from everybody—so I can be not only in the restaurant business, but—you see, life is short—I want to do everything. I want a challenge. Everything. Anything. I want to fly from New York to Europe—in a balloon. I've been balloon-flying at least four or five times already. But money helps success; money helps challenge, too. I race boats. I win. Not all the time, but I win. When I lose—too bad. I try again another time.

Mr. Scavullo: Have you done anything outside the restaurant business?
I promoted Muhammad Ali in Japan. But I don't like to be called a promoter. In this country and in Japan, people think a promoter is not a legitimate businessman. Besides, I want to be an all-around businessman, not just a promoter.

Is Rocky your real name?
My Japanese name is Hirocki. I eliminated "H-i." So it's Rocky. It's a strong name. I started out as a wrestler. I came to this country with a Japanese wrestling team for the 1960 Olympic Games. And I wanted a stronger name—any little thing can help to win—so I took the name Rocky. Then I came here to wrestle. I became amateur champion of the U.S. in 1962, '63, '64. I got a cauliflower ear.

Do you smoke?
I don't smoke, I don't drink, and I exercise three times a week, using Nautilus equipment.

What sort of clothes do you like to wear?
I like to wear modern clothes. I don't want any leftovers, I want to follow style.

Can you tell me more about your Benihana chain of restaurants?
Yes, but I don't want to stick to one business, I want to be everything. And in this country it is so easy to become a professional anything. I could be a professional moviemaker within three months to six months because I have access to enough money to learn quickly—to hire a top director, top actors and actresses, for me to become a top producer. I played backgammon and I beat the champion, Jacobi, within two years of my practicing backgammon. I started a restaurant business and I think I am one of the biggest privately held corporations in the restaurant business today in the United States.

Are you married?
Yes. Married, with two kids. I bought a house in Miami, so they moved there. Weekends I go to Miami, where I have my headquarters, and weekdays I stay here in New York. We saved a little money, $1 million, just moving our offices to Miami. And I think the climate is good for my wife and kids.

What kind of women do you like?
I stay away from dating Japanese girls because my wife is Japanese. I like blondes, beautiful blondies. Small, not tall. I'm five foot four; I like girls the same height.

Do you like career women?
No, a woman should be feminine and a woman shouldn't have money. She shouldn't have more money than a man.

That way he can control the woman. I don't want a woman to control me. In Japan we control women. I go out at night by myself, instead of taking my wife anywhere. A woman should stay home and take care of her own things such as raising kids and giving me good food to eat.

Do you think your wife should give you love, too?
You can get love anywhere. Even in Japan. Love is a secondary thing. Of course, you have to have kids. But sex and love are two different things. But you have to like the girl to have sex, don't you?

Do you buy presents for your wife?
Not much. I buy presents for my girl friends. Just watches, reasonable things. I think sex is beautiful; why should I have to pay for it?

Are you afraid of dying?
I'm not afraid. If my time comes, my time comes. I have exactly $5 million in insurance, so I'm not afraid of death. If I die, it's my time.

Are you religious?
No, but I carry a Buddhist medal to save my life from accident, but only from accidents in a car or boat. I used to fly airplanes. But I had an accident, so I don't fly anymore.

Are you worried about getting older and not being able to race or fly?
The reason why I race now is I don't want to rust. I don't want to watch somebody else playing football on television in the living room. I want to participate. And if I participate, I want to win. I challenge to win.

Why are you obsessed with winning?
I have four brothers and we always fought each other. We were wise guys. When I was in high school I even got into street fighting. And I had to win. I wanted to win, I wanted to be tough.

What kind of family do you come from?
My father is a comedian, a song-and-dance man, in Japan. He was quite famous in his time. My mother was his student.

What do you find is beautiful in life?
Sex is a beautiful thing. Working hard, using our heads—these are beautiful things, too. I don't see so many beautiful things in my life. I collect beautiful Japanese antiques for my restaurant and my house. When the American GIs went to Japan after World War II they bought a lot of antiques and shipped everything to the United States. There are no antiques left in Japan. My idea is to buy these antiques in the United States or Europe and return these beautiful things to Japan. That's why I have collected over $1 million worth of antiques. You can see them at any Benihana or in my warehouse in New Jersey.

What kind of car do you have?
I had eight Rolls-Royces. I used to collect them. I had American cars, such as a Pierce-Arrow 1935, and other old cars, too. That was my hobby two years ago. But people change their hobbies. I used to fly airplanes, I don't fly anymore—I used to collect cars, I don't collect cars anymore. I have only four Rolls-Royces now.

ARTHUR ASHE
Tennis Player

Mr. Scavullo: When did you start playing tennis?
Mr. Ashe: I was seven. I lived ten yards from four tennis courts. My father was a park policeman in a then-black playground in Richmond, Virginia, so I was surrounded by sports all my life and it was just osmosis, I guess.

How long was it before you realized you were good at it?
I was always good, relatively speaking, in my own area. I was good in the twelve-year-old's category, and then I was good in the fourteens' and then the sixteens'. But then you find yourself being good, you know, a hundred miles away and then five hundred miles away—it just spreads out.

Does being a professional tennis player require a lot of discipline?
Yes, because it's not a team sport.

What's a day like for you when you're playing?
Everything is oriented around when I play. Play is usually in the afternoon or at night, and I plan my day accordingly, I schedule my meals around when I play. I schedule my practice around when I play.

What time do you get up?
I get up late. I am an afternoon-evening-night person. I'm not a morning person.

How long do you want to continue playing tennis?
I had major bone surgery in my left heel. If it mends sufficiently, I'll play for another three or four years. I was born with an enlarged heel bone in my left foot. Five years ago it started irritating the Achilles tendon, rubbing up against it, and it got so bad that a lot of calcium was deposited and attached itself to the bone, and the bone got bigger and, of course, rubbed even more, which deposited more calcium, which rubbed more, so they had to go ahead and just cut it right off.

Was that frightening to an athlete like you?
No. The timing was unbelievable. I've had an extremely lucky life. I've been in the right place at the right time five or six times in my life. Backtracking, it's easy to say that had I not been in those places at those times, I wouldn't be sitting here. But I got what I wanted two years ago—I was ranked number one in the world. And soon after I got the number-one ranking, the injury got very bad and I had to either quit the game altogether or have the operation. So I had the operation. I had nothing to lose then. I couldn't continue playing the way it was.

Did it get you depressed at all?
No. It proved a blessing in disguise in a way. I've been able to do a lot of things that I had not been able to do for the past ten years because I was playing so much. You see, tennis is not seasonal. It's not like basketball, which stops in May and starts again in September. You play tennis all year round if you want, on and off. When it's winter here, it's summer in South America, South Africa and Australia. And you have an indoor season in the United States, and then you go to Europe until Wimbledon's finished, and then you come back to America until Forest Hills Labor Day weekend, and then you go to the West Coast and then Hawaii. And then there are two circuits in the fall—one in the South Pacific and in Asia and one in Europe. Then back indoors again. So it never stops.

Do you play or practice every day?
God, no. Forget it. Everybody's different, though. Players who are naturally gifted don't have to practice as much. Like Ilie Nastase. He never practices. It doesn't help.

Didn't he recently lose in Madison Square Garden?
Oh, team tennis. I don't give a shit about team tennis.

Do you have good days and bad days?
There are some days when I get up and say, "Jesus, I'm going back to bed, but I have to play"—it's like anything else in life.

When you have a big tennis match, do you usually abstain from sex before? Some athletes do.
I don't think that's right at all. In fact, sex can relieve tension. It all depends on how you have it. Hell, sex can take you five minutes, or if you're really into it, it can take you all night long or all day long. If I make love at nine in the morning, it has absolutely no bearing at all on how I'm going to play at six o'clock that afternoon.

Do you ever take drugs before a tennis game?
No. Tennis players are the cleanest livers in the world. Unbelievable. Some of us smoke grass. And hash.

Do you smoke cigarettes?
No.

Do you drink liquor?
No. Everybody drinks beer, though—the girls as well as the guys. Beer is a part of our diet.

Why?
You lose a lot of water when you play. And beer's nutritious, too; it's got a lot of calories and grains and stuff like that. But you have to watch it—if you drink too much beer, you'll go piss it away and three hours later you'll be thirsty as hell because alcohol does dehydrate you.

Are there any special foods that you eat to give you more energy?
I eat carbohydrates in the morning for breakfast and for lunch, and protein in the afternoon for dinner. But everybody has his own diet.

If you don't play tennis anymore, what are you going to do?
I'm not really sure what I am going to do. I wouldn't have to work anymore for the rest of my life if I didn't want to, but obviously you've got to do something. I don't know what I might do yet. I might go back to Virginia and run for Congress. Politics intrigues me. It always has.

What about acting?
No. I probably will expand the sports-commentating career I have with ABC television, though. That's fun.

Were you ever married?
I just got married to a free-lance photographer. She used to work for NBC. She was a combination photographer and graphic artist for Newscenter 4 every day. But when we got married she started free-lancing.

What kind of women do you like?
Independent women.

Do they have to be beautiful?
It helps, but it's not necessary. I don't like fat women at all. I tend to like women who are built like me—tall and slender.

Do you like smart women?
That's important, perhaps even more important than physical appearance. Physical beauty is skin-deep, believe me.

How do you like being married?
I love it. It's just something I wanted to do anyway. I was

ARTHUR ASHE
Tennis Player

ready to quit fooling around and get down to brass tacks, so to speak. I was looking forward to it.

Is your wife your age or younger?
She's twenty-five, I'm thirty-four.

What do you think of people who are living together and are not married?
I'm very much for live and let live. I think there has to be a certain moral standard or yardstick which keeps society on a track, keeps anarchy from taking over.

Do you cheat on your wife?
I would never cheat on my wife. I really wouldn't. My own moral system is quite strong and I would not cheat on my wife ever.

Do you want to have children at all?
I do. It would be fun.

How do you feel about raising children in this world of violence and drugs and . . .
I don't really look at it that way. It's just that I selfishly want children. I don't feel I have to apologize for it. I just want to perpetuate my bloodline. I'm not ashamed to admit it.

How do you feel about getting older?
I'm learning to live with it because everything's relative. First of all, it's inevitable. It will happen to everybody, so it's a collective concern. Everybody worries about getting old. We're conditioned to associate getting old with an increasing sense of worthlessness. That isn't as it should be, but that's what we're brought up to think. You know, if you're eighteen, you're in the prime of your physical life, you can have ten orgasms a day. When you're forty-five you might have one, three, four or five a week, and your skin starts to wrinkle and you think you look less attractive and you can't run as fast. And men, especially athletes, associate this with masculinity. It takes a while to deal with it. For an athlete dealing with getting old is much tougher, because we have defined our masculinity in terms of our physical prowess. I mean, Arthur Schlesinger probably doesn't wish he was Muhammad Ali. He's got a better brain than Muhammad, and he probably has made a more lasting contribution to society than Ali, but so what?

Is money important to you?
It is. For security and freedom. I like having a lot of money —not because of the feeling that it's all mine. I think I have a pretty well developed altruistic consciousness, so the money doesn't just sit in the bank or under my mattress.

Do you buy luxuries like clothes, cars, jewelry, houses?
No. I'm not materialistic at all. I have a very, very small wardrobe. I own two suits. I wear jeans mostly, but the things I do have are elegant and, I think, tasteful, but I don't have much of anything.

What colors do you wear?
Almost everything I have is blue or brown. I have some black, but that's about it. Blue and brown.

Do you like boxing?
I love boxing. I love watching it. It's the ultimate. It's a very sexy thing. Did you ever see the movie *Women in Love*? Do you remember that nude wrestling scene with Oliver Reed and Alan Bates? Oh shit—I mean, even as a man, a heterosexual, it was about the most sensuous thing I've ever seen on celluloid. It was unbelievable. I thought it was terrific. I want to go back to see it again.

When you vacation, what do you do?
I haven't been on vacation since I've been married, but I usually wind up in East Africa. I love the solitude and the wild animals. I've been over there quite a bit.

What do you think about the phenomenon of *Roots*?
Being black, it's very important to me, because the history of Western civilization was written by white Europeans, and I am defined in terms of white European culture. And I don't really like seeing myself defined in terms of somebody else.

What do you think about the way Western civilization affected Africa?
Technologically, it was just a resounding success. And today civilization is going to overtake everybody, I don't care who you are.

Does that bother you?
It bothers me only in the sense that some people can't keep up with civilization technologically and retain their sense of cultural identity and security. You can have a strong sense of cultural identity and still be damn insecure. The two don't necessarily go together and a lot depends on your history. That's what I think. Japanese-Americans have no insecurities at all. The Japanese culture goes back lots of years and it's a very honorable thing for them. They can look back with pride. But we're brought up with Tarzan and shit like that. So what am I going to say?

There was a conscious effort by historians and anthropologists to delete the positive. Europe, in the seventeenth century, had to find some moral way of justifying the plundering of the African continent as well as the East Indies and those places. And the best they could do was to come up with a Biblical interpretation that the darker races of the world were inherently inferior. And Europeans were supposed to be their masters to civilize these natives. Before that, if a guy was a slave, it had no derogatory connotations at all. If you were a slave in Egypt five thousand years ago, that only meant that you had lost the war. It didn't mean that you were less of a person. Starting in the early 1600s, if you were a slave and you were black, then it had a bad stigma attached to it.

Do you think you'll ever live to see a black President in this country?

No. I was just playing tennis with my friend Andy Young, and we were talking about that. Not President. I think Vice President is a real possibility—one heartbeat away. That's very close.

Why do you think not President?

For the same reason it would be very difficult for a black man to be president of General Motors. You would have to deny the black community's idea of blackness so much that you would become another person. And I don't think the black community these days would allow somebody to get that high without a firm sense of group identity. And the stronger your group identity, the less powerful you are to white Americans right now. This will change. It will take a couple of generations—this black-awareness bit—to subside. It's now the rage for us to be as big and bad and bold as possible—to be an uppity nigger, as they used to say in the South.

Do you have any religion that you were brought up with or that you practice?

I am a religious person but not conventionally so. I believe there is a higher being, but I've been exposed to so many different kinds of religions that the Judeo-Christian ethic is not enough. It's too limiting, it's too narrow—and worse, its practitioners don't practice what they preach. It just doesn't make objective sense to me at all. Look, it all depends on where you were born. I was only a Christian because I was born in the United States. If I had been born in China, I would probably have been Buddhist or Taoist or something.

Do you think that traveling all over the world has opened or expanded your mind?

A lot. The entire world is provincial, though. I mean, the average person anywhere in the world is quite provincial—his world ends at the corner.

Can you name some people that you admire or respect very much?

My father. He didn't have much, but he practiced what he preached, which was extraordinary. And Karl Marx—he was quite a thinker. I tend to admire people who go against the grain of the time, who point out flaws which are so damn obvious that nobody else really wants to face them.

Do you have any fears?

I have fears. I was brought up with a healthy respect for authority as the primary reason that society seems to work better—the nation seems to progress when there are some agreed-upon rules and everybody adheres to them by and large. But there is that devilish streak in everybody that

wants to break out and be an anarchist, once a week. And I like doing that, but my fear is that since I have been able to do what I did in the system, that if I buck the system too much, the system would take away what I have. The papers would call me a bastard or I wouldn't be invited to parties or I'd be ostracized. You pay a price for what you have. And the price is usually some degree of conformity. And if you really are a freethinker and you want to just follow your own conscience, then you have to pay that price.

What kind of things really bother you and get you upset?

The arms race bothers me. I think the world has its priorities in the wrong place. I think the most pressing problem in the world is overpopulation. Too many people. But nobody else seems to think so. You know, that goes back to a man/energy ratio right now. If there weren't so many people, then there wouldn't be such a great demand for oil.

How do you think we should control overpopulation?

Through education and economic incentive. But we're bucking strong religious beliefs.

What about abortion?

I have no strong feelings one way or another about abortion. I think that's up to the woman. But obviously not all sex is for procreation. Hell, you just happen to get it on one night, you forget that it's that time of the month, so you get pregnant, and if you don't really want it, why have it? But population is a problem not only of numbers but also of distribution. New York City is an exciting place for me because I don't have to get up in the morning and ride a subway to work, but it's a hellish place to live. I think it should have more parks and fewer people. I think some streets should be barred to cars, but you can't change all that.

Do you have any fear of dying?

Not at all. I think I've come to grips with that. If the doctor told me tomorrow that I only had one year to live, I honestly don't think I'd be that upset about it because I've already lived tons of lifetimes more than the average person. I've just about seen and done everything. I think I represent just one thread, literally a thread, of life that is passing through this world. As Gibran says, "Your children are not yours, they're of you." They pass through you on the way to wherever. But more important to me is that I have the opportunity to pass on to somebody else whatever it is in me that has me living and breathing and thinking. That's what seems to be the driving force of evolution. The survival of the species. I see nothing else, really. I hope to one day pass my life forces on to my children. And they pass it on down and down and down. That's really all that matters. But dying, you've got to die.

BILLY BALDWIN
Interior Decorator

Mr. Scavullo: When did you start decorating?
Mr. Baldwin: I started working when I went back to Baltimore, where I was born, from Princeton. I'm seventy-three years old and I was born on the thirtieth of May—Decoration Day in the South—in 1903. All my life I really wanted to be an architect, but I wasn't able to become one because I didn't graduate from Princeton—I didn't study hard enough. So the next best thing to designing houses was decorating the insides of houses. After I'd been back from Princeton about two years I got a job with a decorating firm in Baltimore. Then I came to New York in 1935 and really got serious. I worked with Ruby Ross Wood. I was with her until the war, then I was in the Army, and then I came back in 1945 and stayed with her until she died in 1950. And then I was on my own.

Did you get all of your experience in America or did you have to go to Europe for some?
I got all my experience every place I went. I constantly went to museums. And I was very lucky because my family went to Europe every summer. But I never, ever went to a decorating school, and I'm sorry I didn't, in a way. I think people should, because like a pianist, you have to know the scales, you have to know what you're doing. I think it's very important to have a fundamental education in architecture and decoration because then you know the rules, and when you know them the whole point is to break them. But it's a very good idea to know what you're breaking.

As a man, what were your feelings about becoming a decorator?
Since the day I was born I've never had the slightest idea of being gay. It just seemed perfectly normal. In fact, so many people that I know say "How terrible" when they realize that they are gay—I want to burst into tears when I hear that. And I grew up in Baltimore, which was a very conventional city in one sense, but also almost amoral. It was the most exciting place socially, in the twenties and thirties, and everybody wanted to come there because they had a very good time. Still, it certainly was very unconventional for me to become a decorator.

When I first came from Princeton I went into my father's insurance business. I wanted to shoot myself, it was so boring, I loathed it. Then I tried to be a reporter because I always liked to write. But the real thing that was always there in my head and heart was pretty decorating, I suppose, actually more than architecture. I didn't even realize it. So I was very unhappy in the newspaper world and one day I said to my mother, "I just can't stand it. I really want to be a decorator." Well, we had a rather pretty house and my mother had very good taste and she had a decorator, an older man, absolutely straight, with whom she worked for years decorating the house. I was always allowed to sit there and pick out some colors, so she said, "Maybe you can get a job, for nothing even, with this man who's always done the house." She said, "Of course, your father is going to absolutely die. He will never forgive you. But I think it's more important for you to be happy because you're not going to be successful unless you are doing something you like." So my mother told my father. He said, "I feel as though I never want to see him again as long as I live, but I'll just have to swallow it and do the best I can." We didn't like each other

very much anyway, so it wasn't that terrible. But I don't remember any of my friends or my friends' fathers or mothers ever calling me a sissy. I think that they minded that I was *selling*, more than *what* I was selling. They might have adjusted better if I'd been a tailor; but a dressmaker would have been out of the door. I was just able to stay in.

Did you drive yourself a lot, push your career?
I did after I left Baltimore, which was *the* city of absolute pleasure. Baltimore was *to die*, simply wonderful. But I awakened one day at the age of thirty-three and I thought, "This has got to stop. I've got to get out of here, or I'll become a fat pig full of mint juleps. And I'll be miserable." I knew that I had to do something serious to fulfill my desire for decorating. So I got out. And my whole life changed entirely. I stopped playing bridge, I stopped going to an awful lot of parties; then I got involved in parties again because all the clients make you go out with them. But—and this is not a boast—nobody's ever worked harder than I have for forty years. Because my work went on until midnight and on weekends. In decorating there are no hours.

Are you still working a lot?
I don't do a goddamned thing for anybody. I closed my business in 1973. I absolutely will not do a lampshade for even my best clients. When you quit, you quit; you can't make exceptions.

Are you writing another book?
No, because I certainly can't write any more about decorating. I've said everything I possibly can on that subject in my first book, *Billy Baldwin on Decorating*, which was more or less a textbook for students. I'm very glad to say it's run into three editions and now they're publishing it for $8.95, so students can afford it. My second book, *Billy Baldwin Remembers*, was much more about the social side of decorating, which is fifty percent of it anyway.

Is there any difference between an interior decorator and an interior designer?
Michael Greer, if you please, was the first person to call himself a designer so people wouldn't think that he was gay. Designer is supposed to make a man of you. It's perfect crap. But there were extremely well worded definitions of the two terms in *Architectural Digest*, in an interview with David Hicks. He mentioned that he had been influenced by certain people, and he said, "Billy Baldwin as decorator, not designer." He feels that if you're a decorator—and I've always said that I am—you interpret the taste of your clients. My whole wish is to do rooms that are as personal as possible, that do not have the evidence of a decorator dictating taste to the person who's going to sit on the sofa or live in the house. A designer, according to Hicks, is a person who disregards entirely and utterly the taste of his subject. For instance, I did that huge salon for Kenneth, the famous hairdresser. I think I was a designer there because I was not working for any one person but a million women. That was a straight tour de force design: the first time pattern on pattern was done on a big scale. So I think there is a difference. Decorating is a very personal thing that you do with an individual. Designing is more like commercial work.

Do you think interior decorators or designers are important to society today?
If used properly. If a man or a woman or a couple wish to

BILLY BALDWIN
Interior Decorator

have a room done in a house, I think that they can save a great deal of money if they go to an intelligent decorator. First of all they should investigate the decorator by seeing work that he's done. They should know his financial status; they don't want to get in a mess if he fails. He can, however, save them a great deal of money because he can avoid mistakes. In addition to that, no layman can possibly know the sources. I don't care how much you read *House and Garden*—you don't honestly know. And the great thing a decorator can do is to produce something that isn't in *House and Garden*, an unknown rather than a stereotype. I think of decorating as a service; there's a terrible lot of legwork. I'm talking about a serious job; I'm not talking about these damn little people who have no establishment, no artists, no education, nothing. The woods are full of them, you can't stop them. And a lot of them operate on a ten-percent commission. I never did. I bought it wholesale and sold it retail. Always.

Were you the most expensive decorator?

I was not *the* most expensive decorator, but there weren't very many who were more expensive. There was a perfectly good reason for that, which I have never been ashamed to state: I know that the quality of my workmanship was as good as could possibly be. That means that experts were working very carefully and for hours for colossal wages. And I wasn't interested in cheap materials. I don't think there's any economy in something that is going to wear out in a year, because the labor to replace is very high. On the other hand, if there was a budget, I stuck to it. My bills were simply copies of my estimates.

What's the lowest price that you ever worked for?

I've done a perfectly attractive room in my day for $10,000. A damn good room.

Do you think art is important in decorating?

Very much so. If the people love art. I'm not very stuck on people who say, "See my Cézanne." I like people who love the picture and don't care whether it's a $500,000 picture or a $500 picture. I think it's awfully nice if you go to somebody's house and you feel that they love everything in it. I love people who really save up to get a very good picture. But I think that art is like gravy—just as I think that it's very nice to have flowers, but who can afford flowers today?

How do you feel about people asking you to do rooms with nothing on the walls?

If they want nothing on the walls, for God's sake, don't make them put something on the walls. I know my own taste is getting less and less and less interested in color. My eye wants practically nothing. On the other hand, when I helped Diana and Reed Vreeland with their apartment, believe me, I didn't want Diana to take out a single little box. Because that's so much her. I would shoot myself in that apartment. I live in one room. Everything is so difficult today, so expensive, that the thing to do is *simplify*. I only need a bed and a good reading lamp. But I would never say to a client, "You can't have a picture." It's castrating. And it also is uninteresting, because I love going from house to house and remembering each person as associated with the room he or she lives in.

What do you think about modern buildings?

I think modern architecture has to do with the simplification

of everything. I think most people want to live in attractive offices. I'm profoundly interested in everything modern. One of the reasons that I quit was that not enough people thought I was interested. I love contemporary architecture and decoration. I think, however, so much of it is the same that it really has become period decoration even while it's alive. It has become a formula.

Do you have a lot of money?

I've hardly any money at all because you can't make money in the decorating business today. With taxes and salaries it's impossible. The last two years we couldn't even make the mark-up that we should have because the wholesale prices were so high that nobody could pay them. Now I have, thank God, a pension fund from my office, which is very small, and social security, and that is all. I am able to have an apartment on Sixty-first Street, and a shack on Nantucket, and I really can't imagine anything more.

Do you think that you're spoiled?

In some ways very much so; in some ways not. I think my values are pretty good. I really pity most rich people, and I don't want to see very many of them. I think they're boring. My old boss, Ruby Wood, said to me, "Now, Billy Baldwin, you're coming here from that nice town and you're going to have a hard time because New York is very tough. But don't forget one thing: you're going to see an awful lot of rich people. You get as much of their money as you can. That's all they're worth—money—and we're lucky because we're going to get some of it." And I think that's true.

Do you miss going to the office and working?

No, and I always was at my office before anybody, and stayed later. But I decided to quit for several reasons. First of all, I think to be a has-been is the most pathetic thing in the world. I don't think it's very attractive to see *Applause* and have people come out of the theater and say, "My God, she kicks well for her age." Many people stay on because they want the money. I do not want any more money. I never have had very much. I never have owned a car and I never have lived extravagantly; I've lived well.

Also I got awfully tired because the people got far less interesting and far more difficult to work for. And the cost of labor, thanks to the unions, was absolutely killing us. As a matter of fact, on the last estimate I sent out I wrote: "Don't do this, it's too expensive." That wasn't any fun. And then I think that everybody has his day. I know that my taste is not, for instance, as suitable for today as Arthur Smith's, who was my young partner.

What is your day like now?

My day now is entirely different because I don't get up until half past eight. I used to get up at seven. I go to the museums very often. I write a terrible lot of letters to people; I have a big correspondence. I look for a pair of shoes. I have lunch with people, which I never used to do before. I sometimes go to the movies. It's actually difficult to describe my day because it's so fantastic how quickly the time goes. Really it does. I'm not lonely. I never have had to be with somebody all of the time. I love to read a great deal.

Do you watch much television?

I don't own one. I'm not anti-TV. I never seem to have the time to look at it. I'll either go out with somebody in the evening, or I read. I have a little radio so that I can hear if

Manhattan's been bombed.

Are you a very healthy person?
I have a little emphysema; I smoke a little bit. But I've never smoked even a pack a day.

Were you always conscious of health?
Never. Never taken one single bit of exercise in my life, except the Charleston. An aspirin is the height of any medication. I've never taken a sleeping pill, except in the hospital, when I had to. I don't think I drink to any excess, but I certainly do drink. I've never dieted and I've kept the same weight almost exactly as I did when I was at Princeton, which is now 112. And I've had a very good time and never thought about anything sensible.

How do you take care of yourself? Do you take a shower or a bath? Who cuts your hair?
I despise showers. They're not at all sexy. The most wonderful thing in the world is to get in a boiling, scalding bathtub and stay there. And I have a barber called Tommy who runs something called the Napoleon—no, the Bonaparte. I've had him for years and I really love him.

Do you have a manicurist?
I do it myself at home. I can't bear to have a woman hold my hand that long. I am one-thousand-percent homosexual.

How do you take care of your skin?
After I shave I put on After Tan. I do it every single day of my life because I think that it softens my skin. Most after-shaves are so tart. I don't use a toothbrush; I use an enormous amount of mouthwash and a prodder, and I rinse and gargle violently.

Who is your tailor?
I used to have a tailor; I can't afford one. I do have a perfectly wonderful maid who comes to me twice a week and who's old and loves me. But I have a very hard time getting clothes because I am so short, and shoes—I'm size 5D! This suit came from De Noyer. Every now and then they call me and say, "Billy, come in because we've got a mistake in sizes; a couple of suits are too small." But the price!

I don't dress up any more. I used to have a dress up every single day of my life. When I was decorating I had to be dressed exactly like my clients, who were all dressed up. So another thing that I love about not being active in the decorating business is that I can wear a turtleneck and jeans.

What do you think about plastic surgery for men?
It's probably a very good idea; I'm not against it. But I'm not going to do it. It's too late. I don't think it's sissy and I think it's awfully nice if people admit to having it done. What I hate is a phony. And a closet queen, I think, should be locked in the closet and starved to death. On the other hand, I don't see that there's any reason why you should go out to dinner with a woman and say, "I had a fine time screwing last night," and mention the boy's name. I don't think you have to do that. But I think that dishonesty and lack of guts is also unnecessary—what's the point?

Do you worry about age?
I don't worry about getting old and I'm not one particle afraid of death. I'm afraid of *life* to this extent: I don't see any reason why I should live much more than a couple of years because I can't imagine anything more terrible than being infirm or invalid or bedridden or dependent upon other people. I think that would be hell. I've been lucky in my life;

I've been awfully healthy. I don't think about myself very often. If you're a serious decorator, you really have to lead, to a great extent, a very selfless life.

Have you ever been in love?
Violently, deeply, twice. That's really not bad for seventy-three years, is it? I've never been sexually promiscuous at all because that didn't interest me.

Are you as sexual now as you were?
Much less so. Only because it's too complicated for me now. I don't mean the act. But it's exactly like retiring, I don't think it's very becoming for a man of seventy-three to behave sexually the way a man of thirty-three, forty-three or fifty-three does. I don't like the idea of a dirty old man, and I don't expect to have people interested in me that way.

You think you should retire from sex?
It depends upon the public whether I retire sexually.

But you're so bright and alive.
That hasn't anything to do with sex. You don't go to bed and laugh, do you? I think nothing is better than to be able to laugh afterwards, it adds an attractive extra quality, but I don't think you should start out in hysterics.

What do you think is positive about getting older?
As you grow older, you should become more mature, more tolerant. Unfortunately, a great many people become less tolerant. But I think one of the privileges of getting older is that your life should have made it possible for you to demand a great deal less, expect much less, give much more and also to be less critical.

What has affected you most between the twenties and the seventies, as far as the way you felt about life?
The war was certainly the greatest change in my life. I was brought up very fortunately; my family was not rich, but it certainly wasn't poor either. And I had a very restricted life. I didn't meet anybody except sons and daughters of people like my family. Then I was drafted into the United States Army. The night before I left, a very attractive woman decorator gave a dinner party for me at the Pavillon. The next night I was up to my ass in KP with a lot of Italians and black guys at Fort Dix. When I first went into my barracks somebody said, "You look like Shirley Temple." That was rather horrid. The Army, however, did me a lot of good; it equipped me for life.

Does your small size bother you at all?
The best thing I ever did in my life was a job for Cole Porter, who was just about my height. I'll never forget something he said: "You know, sonny, we're lucky; we were never pretty but we were cute." Sometimes I'd like to be able to see a little more without getting up on points. One of my greatest friends since childhood was Pauline Rothschild, and she was six foot two. We used to do the Charleston a lot together, and I remember very well one time when my lack of height was brought to my attention because somebody said, "Go on, now, stick your nose in her navel and have a good time." Then I did feel slightly short.

Are you attracted to taller people, shorter people or people your own height?
I have enormously catholic taste in everything. I've never been *overcome* by anyone shorter. Not even Truman Capote. He is actually half an inch shorter than I am. But, listen, I've had a perfectly marvelous time, don't worry about that.

GATO BARBIERI
Latin American Jazz Musician

Mr. Barbieri: A lot of people will say, "Your new record is different, it's not like your last." I say, "Yes, it's different, but it's always me." I think that the most important thing for a musician is not to lose his integrity, because on the way to becoming famous you play a lot of banal music. When I play I don't think. Even if it's my tune, I don't know the notes I'm playing. I feel the music.

I know a lot of musicians, they know *nothing*, but they are fantastic! They play everything! There are musicians who know everything and some others who are in between, but they are no good. Never in between!

I also feel this way about women, like my wife, Michele. We are together, we participate, she helps me. If I am down, Michele knows she has to support me. I am very emotional, and with Michele I have more balance.

Mr. Scavullo: Do you think that black musicians are more accomplished than white musicians in the nineteen-seventies?
The problem is that white musicians want to follow the black musicians, and I think they are making a mistake. I don't play like American black musicians. I *feel* how they play the music. But I don't play the saxophone in the American style. You know, when I was young I played the dance halls—I played tangos, boleros, mambos. So when I play now, I play like a Latin musician. I feel my roots. I scream, I sing, I participate all the time. But, for instance, I don't speak like the black musicians. All the white musicians, they immediately want to speak like the blacks—they go, "Hey, man!"

I am Gato, I come from a Latin country. I am like this. In fact, everyone thinks I smoke marijuana. I don't. Latin people are more daydreamy.

What do you do to relax?
Well, we go to the islands, and we swim, but we're not very disciplined about exercise and things like that. In the first place, we're people that live by night, so it's not till that hour that we start to come alive. If everything happened at night it would be much better. I have a lot of ideas in the night. Incredible! Michele writes them down, and we try to do them the next day. Sometimes they work out, sometimes they don't. But in the middle of the night we have wonderful ideas. For instance, I can't sleep very well in Rio. So one day I got up at five-thirty—Michele was fast asleep—I looked out the window and I saw the sun go up. So I thought, Sunshine!, and I went to the beach. There were a lot of people doing exercise in front of the sea. It was beautiful. Now here, I get up at eight o'clock, and I don't know what to do. I would like to go out, but where? I hate New York—and the weather—though it's okay for a few months. The people are faster. In South America it is slower, more relaxed. It is like a Valium, no?

I know you wrote the music for *Last Tango in Paris*. How did you like the movie?
I loved the movie. And the proof that the music is beautiful is that I listen to it as if somebody else wrote it.

I would like to say something about the television. A lot of Americans say television is made for stupid people. I say, it depends. The television is like *cinémathèque*. In no other country can you see these films. For instance, yesterday we saw *Bringing Up Baby*, with Katharine Hepburn and Cary Grant. So beautiful.

I very much like to look at basketball because when I was young I played football—South American football, so I like to see basketball . . . and I like music. Sometimes I put on music to make me feel happy. Though sometimes music bothers me.

Where are you from?
I was born in Rosario, three hundred kilometers from Buenos Aires.

What did you think of Evita Perón?
In the beginning she was an actress. But, you know, in Argentina the situation is incredible, so I don't want to talk about it.

What do you think of strong women in general?
They have to be very romantic, but at the same time they have to be strong. I am romantic, but I don't want to be boss. I think the argument of the feminists is right.

What kind of women do you like?
Well, Michele is something special. I like the older style. Marlene Dietrich. I like Gladys Knight. I like Greta Garbo, and I like my mother. She explained life to me like a man. She gave me the money to go to a prostitute. I didn't ask my father, I asked my mother, and she understood.

Latin American men are incredible. *Very* incredible. My father was like a sheriff in our house, a very good man, but *macho*, you know. And he was not the only one, every man was like that. He only became *no machismo* when he had a heart attack, and he understood that he was not this strong man, and that he needed my mother. My mother became strong, because he needed her, but in the beginning my father was . . . wow! If you go to South America, it is still the same. They use the woman like an object. She cooks, and does everything.

What kind of men do you admire?
I identify with creativity, so I would have to say I admire Bernardo Bertolucci, and Pasolini, because they are poetic. I like Karim Abdul-Jabbar, the basketball player. Or Marlon Brando, or Henry Fonda. I like Muhammad Ali, for instance. He's very intelligent. I love Malcolm X, I read his book. I think they killed him because he was so intelligent. I like Robert Redford, but he is not very special. He is beautiful. Montgomery Clift was very special. Bogey. Pelé. *Very* special. And Marvin Gaye is super.

I'd like to know something about your clothes.
Well, Michele teaches me. She has very good eyes. I am very neurotic in boutiques. I like Saint Laurent.

Do you have fears?
Flying. Playing. Each concert is for me like the first. But when I go out there, it's okay!

ALAN BATES

English Actor

Mr. Scavullo: Do you think it's important for an actor to be attractive?
Mr. Bates: Yes, I do, really. I think so much of movie history is concerned with people being good-looking that you tend to be conditioned to think that they should be. It's an advantage because it's more adaptable. But I don't think it's necessary.

Did you go to acting school in England?
Yes, at the Royal Academy of Dramatic Arts, which is nothing like the Actors Studio. It's much more traditional and concerned absolutely with techniques—some of them good and some of them not so good—how to speak, how to move, how to dance—never how to think.

At what age did you start training?
Seventeen. I knew since I was about twelve that I wanted to be an actor. I latched on to that and just stayed with it, and I didn't really care about anything else. I mean, I wasn't academic at all.

Really?
Yes. I always wanted to get into learning, but not before my late twenties did I ever really like the idea of actually studying.

What caused you to like acting?
I've tried to analyze it a few times, but I've never been able to. I had a huge resistance to acting or speaking in public at grammar school. I would panic and withdraw from it. Then I suddenly reversed; I just jumped and couldn't wait to do it.

Do you think it's possible for an actor to be good on stage and also in movies?
I've been lucky because I've managed to do both. I started films when I was young enough not to be entrenched in the theater. And in the theater I started in mostly modern naturalistic works, although I have done classical work. So before I was thirty I had a pretty good experience at both film and theater, and for me they contributed to each other. Films teach you to trust your personality and who you are, because what they photograph is you. In theater you can always hide from yourself. You're playing another character in a much more overdone way—and you also hide behind your make-up.

Which do you prefer? Movies or theater?
Theater. But the results are so different. In the theater, once the curtain goes up, it's yours. Nobody can do anything about it except you. You're in charge of it and that's thrilling. That's the reward of it. I enjoy films for a totally different reason—the indulgence of acting for one person. And I love the total reality of acting on location, in particular, because you forget the crew and the whole setup of the film—that becomes like a suitcase, it's just there with you.

What do you think when you see yourself on the screen?
I don't know what I think of myself. Sometimes I think it's awful and sometimes I think it's terrific. I think I'm fairly objective. And I almost always look at the rushes. The only shock I've ever had was in the beginning, when I first saw myself on screen—so huge. It was a terrific shock. And then, for some reason that shock wilted entirely and I could judge it, change it, learn from it.

Is the director more important on film or on stage?
He's more important on film, I think. Because he controls what happens afterwards as well. And it's much more of his personal vision. Of course, he's important in the theater, but

the writer and then, finally, the actor takes over.

Do you ever have fights with people when you work?
Not in an overt physical way, but I certainly fight or resist or occasionally don't speak.

Where were you born?
In Derbyshire, England. I still have a place there because it's a very beautiful part of the world.

Do you travel a lot?
I do. Films took me away a lot. To begin with, *Zorba the Greek* was made in Crete and *The Fixer* in Hungary, so I really developed a terrific taste for traveling. I love to travel.

When you travel what does your wife do?
They all come with me usually. This time they didn't.

Do you have children?
Yes. Twin boys.

How old are they?
Six and a half.

Is it hard being a father and an actor?
It's hard, but it's terrific. I like it. This is the first time I've been away, and that's hard. I've been away for short periods of time, but I've never been a long way away for a long time. That's something you just have to get used to.

Are you concerned about your two sons growing up and taking drugs?
I don't think about that yet. It does cross my mind, but they are already a couple of other people. I don't believe in the idea that you can actually make children emulate you or conform to a set of rules. How can you? They're other people. In another five years they're going to turn around and tell me what they think. So all you can really do is try and provide an atmosphere in which they can develop fully and find out who they are and what they want to do without feeling dictated to—and yet at the same time somehow try and provide something that they can relate to, not necessarily an authority but a sort of relationship, so that they don't feel lost or panicked. But it's natural for a child to rebel and to turn around and say, "This is me and I don't care what you think." We've all done that. Whether your parents are rich or poor or drunk or marvelous, you'll find some way to establish your own identity and it's bound to include a form of rebellion, isn't it? So you can't really worry about those things because they're going to happen. You just have to watch, watch and watch. Guide. Influence.

Do you live in the country or in the city?
City, but it's country-oriented. I think the simpler life is better, especially for children. And the danger of being an actor and traveling about is that the children automatically lead a semisophisticated life. I think the best thing you can do for children is to keep them out of it and ordinary as far as you can.

How long have you been married?
Seven years.

Were you ever married before?
No. Not officially, anyway.

What kind of women do you like?
I don't know. I just like people.

Do they have to be beautiful?
No.

Any type of body in particular?
No.

Fat?

ALAN BATES
English Actor

Fat is lovely.
You don't like skinny?
No.
Do you have a problem with your weight at all?
Being an actor, I'm always conscious of it. The best thing for the camera is to be slightly underweight, which I can never quite manage to be.
Do you take care of your health?
Oh yes. I have a naturopath. I have an orthodox doctor as well, but I believe in the natural concept of living. One can't stick to it, unfortunately, all the way through. I move around so much and lead a city life, a pressured life. But I think if you have a knowledge of a natural regime, you can usually find some way of keeping a part of it in your curriculum. And I believe in it medically because my naturopath has actually found a way to cure one or two things that I've had from time to time—just through eating habits. I think an awful lot of things can be controlled by what you eat.
How do you feel about getting older?
I don't really feel any different from when I was seventeen. And as long as that doesn't get completely self-deceiving, I think it's good.
Do you have a fear of dying at all?
Sometimes. I mean, I really don't want to die until I've lived a very long time. And then, sometimes I think, If it happens, it happens. But I like life.
Why don't you like flying?
I really don't know. I flew a lot for a long time and then I suddenly realized that I was not enjoying it and that I was, in fact, in a state of tension, so I stopped flying for ten years. I flew over here for the first time in ten years. And it wasn't too bad, but I don't like it. I've done anything—anything—to avoid it. I've been on extraordinary trains and boats and cars, and stayed overnight in extraordinary places when I couldn't get connections. By God, I enjoyed that. It's a terrific experience.
What do you think of progress and technology, tearing down old buildings to put up big new ones?
I think it's horrible. It seems to be wild and uncontrolled. We really have to stop and reconsider the way we live and what we need and what are luxuries. We've lost a very basic, simple concept of living. People say, "What about progress? Isn't that retrogressive?" But when we reach the edge of a precipice, what is progressive about going over it?
Do you find it difficult to live in England because of the taxes and the economy?
It depends on how much you earn and what you want. If you want to make money and keep your money, it is very difficult. If you want to make a million, then don't live there. But if you just want to make money to live by, then you can live there.
Is money a concern?
Not really. I've been guided in fairly conventional ways by lawyers and accountants to do this and to do that, and to save this and to put that into this account, and to form this and to form that. But I don't work for money. Money doesn't make me take a job.
Are you very picky about what you do?
Yes, I am. I can do a film for fun, but I prefer to do a play or a film or a television program because I like it, because I want to do it. I don't like doing it just because it's good money.
Who are some of your favorite actors?
Gérard Philipe, Mastroianni, Mason, as movie actors. They seem to have a fantastic ability to act in front of cameras. Jean-Louis Trintignant.
They're all Europeans.
Spencer Tracy was a great American movie actor. I think there's a difference. I think the Europeans are much freer. I think American actors—not always, by any means, but often—are obeying an image rather than really freeing up. Some of the new people, however, Pacino, De Niro, Hoffman, do have that freedom. They really care much less about what the image seems to be. I just wish they all did a lot more theater, too.
You do television?
I haven't done any for years. There's just something in that medium which is less satisfying—you do it and then the next day it's gone. I did two plays on TV by Simon Grey and one by Harold Pinter in the last eighteen months and I really enjoyed them. And I'm going to do a Thomas Hardy adaptation now.
How many films have you done?
About fifteen.
Do you have any favorites?
Women in Love.
The wrestling scene in *Women in Love* was amazing.
It is an amazing scene. It's a great expression of physical closeness that is not necessarily sexual. Sometimes there is a need to actually fuse with someone that you feel for, but it doesn't have to be a sexual thing. Sensual, yes. Physical, yes. There's a difference.
Was that a difficult scene to do?
It was technically difficult. That's why it was choreographed. And of course it's very charged emotionally. And it was also the first time two men have ever taken their clothes off on screen. So we had quite a lot to deal with. But it's from such a great book and it's such a terrific conception of friendship that I thought it was exciting to do.

PETER BEARD
Photographer and Author

Mr. Scavullo: What do you like to do?
Mr. Beard: I like to look. I like to cruise through life looking. It's a funny world. Everybody is doing something and everybody is looking at everybody doing something. So we not only have the thing that's being done but we also have millions of little eyeballs observing what's being done. There's something very unrealistic about it all, because a lot of what's being done seems to be being done bearing in mind the eyeballs—that's the trouble.

Why are you so nervous being photographed? You're a photographer.
Being in this studio is like being in *Black Orpheus*. This is really like being on the moon. The sixties was love, the seventies is cement. I actually feel like Prometheus at the very edge of plaster of Paris: the scenery is supposed to imitate the world in a Kubrick film, and the thing that goes through my mind is, Will there be another scene after this one?

Do you feel like an animal caged in the studio?
I'll tell you something. I think things have gone so far that we can't remember what it's like to be an animal.

I saw a movie on cable TV in which you slice open an animal's stomach and stand there while hundreds of vultures eat its guts. What is the point of that scene?
That scene, to me, is exactly the kind of thing that takes place in this studio. It's about the last animals of nature. It's vultures who were preoccupied with getting something to eat so they didn't think about what was actually going on, like there might be something wrong with the light, like some idiot like myself would be running in and disturbing their greedy feast. They were shoving all this stuff in their faces and eating it, but they'd been eating too much for too long. The image is a little bit like what Leonardo da Vinci, in the fifteenth century, described as the future of human beings. He said that human beings were so greedy that they were going to eat whole parts of the world, and that after they died they'd want to go to heaven because of their religion, but their stomachs would be so full that gravity wouldn't allow them to rise. I'm doing a book now about twenty thousand elephants dying of thirst. The photographs of them taken from an airplane look very much like me in this studio. They're lying down on the floor and they want a drink.

Why do you follow Mick Jagger around so much?
To me, that's a really good question. At the very edge of the world in this incredibly precarious universe, there are very few people or things that ring true, that encompass or incorporate all the ingredients of our time. And Mick is one of the very few people. Andy Warhol is one of them; Francis Bacon is another. They seem to be aware of, they seem to be products of, they seem to be echoes, they seem to be in demand, they seem to be beyond anything you could say about them—in other words, however bad their photograph might appear in the worst issue of *People* magazine that could ever be imagined, it would still be great. And that is the genius of Andy Warhol and that is the horror of Francis Bacon and that is the paranoia and the fantasy of the Rolling Stones emergency: at the very end of the earth, the last sign of human life blowing in the wind on Mars will be a little tattered final issue of *People* magazine with Mick Jagger on the cover or Andy Warhol or Francis Bacon. How do you get

beyond the infinite joke? How do you get beyond infinite emptiness? How do you get beyond infinite silliness?

But why do you constantly photograph Mick Jagger in particular?
In the same way that Artaud ricocheted around the forties, Mick Jagger is meaningfully ricocheting around the seventies. But as the seventies are more demanding, as the velocity is much greater, as we know much more, as the perspective is higher and the space less, Mick's is a more monstrous accomplishment. And I don't mean monstrous in a bad way, mind you. When I think of monstrousness I think of Picasso in terms of artistic accomplishment, Mick Jagger in terms of multidimensional artistry.

What about your photograph of a box filled with human limbs bit off by an alligator?
I didn't think of that in terms of shock value. It was a biological phenomenon, the first time in recorded history that anybody has been documented coming out of the stomach of a crocodile. In a sense it's very much like the picture of Nixon and Frost. I feel like they've come out of the existential stomach of a crocodile. And have been photographed in color by *Time* magazine next to Farrah Fawcett-Majors and the Stones and Margaret Trudeau. It's like a monster age and there's no escape. It reminds me of Sartre's *No Exit*. It's a joke, but the trouble is human beings are laughing at themselves laughing at themselves laughing at themselves laughing. We are a gigantic multidimensional entity which is a trap for our own monstrousness. We are an enormous trap into which we are going to catch ourselves.

Are you pessimistic about the future of the world?
Words like pessimism don't mean anything, because the layers of artificiality have gone so far. We are living in a time when an animal that represents millions of years of evolution can still be seen, just barely, because we're about to obliterate it. And we know what it's like to go out in the wilderness, to experience life amongst elephants, lions, New Yorkers, Montaukers and Canadians because we can travel. We can go to Toronto where sixteen zillion tons of cement have been poured over the surface of the earth, so that you never see anything except gray cement. That's my only memory of Toronto: looking out of a hotel window, hearing the air conditioner, all the cement, gray sky and a lot of dirty snow. We have very cold winters now.

But you have your summers in Montauk.
Oh, you want to speak to the salamander. We're pretending that the sun is going to come back this summer and cast its beneficial rays on us. During the winters now I think, Is the sun actually going to come up in the summer and pour ultraviolet onto our skin, so that we look healthy? Are we going to try and pretend that we're natural, healthy animals, actively part of nature's scheme, playing in the fields of the Lord, frolicking on the beach as the tar and the dead porpoises and the oil spills come washing in. It's very interesting to me that everybody is sitting around watching this pollution wash up all around us, slowly overcoming us, slowly suffocating us; and they're watching it and they're trying to pump color into those pictures, because when all that stuff comes over us it's going to take all the color out of us.

Is the situation any better in Africa?

PETER BEARD
Photographer and Author

We could be sitting in Africa right now. That's the truth. And that's frightening.

Do you feel sad about Africa now?

My tendency is not to believe in any words like "sad," "anxious," "worry"—I think we've experienced those words years ago and now we know much more than those words.

Even in Africa?

I honestly believe that Africa's exactly in the same condition as we are, because of the nature of man. He has this incredibly aggressive and greedy craving, this curious desire to be everywhere and have everything all at the same time, at once —he's insatiable. In no way will there ever be such a thing as enough for man. We want a video tape right here now of Idi Amin killing a hundred thousand Christians so that we can see it. There are probably technicians stringing wires under the Atlantic Ocean at this moment so that we can electronically observe these people, who we have forced to catch up to us overnight, in their backward stage of cannibalism, treating each other the way we used to treat each other three hundred or four hundred years ago. We can see it all now, we've got the equipment to record everything. I have a picture of myself in 1966 standing on the Pahooha Bridge in Uganda, and within just a handful of years, over that exact railing, roughly, seventy to a hundred thousand human bodies have been dumped. It's very weird.

What makes you move around so much?

I think it's part of the trap. When I move it isn't me moving, it's this enormous thing which is undulating and shaking, so that, beyond my actual awareness, I'm moving. I'm part of humanity, which, like it or not, is involved in a kind of a climactic crescendo—it's the last photograph, it's a desperate urge to record everything that's happening, because we're going through the final stage. One of the things that I'm doing now is reprinting a pathetic little innocent African adventure, in all of its naïveté, that I wrote about twenty years ago, called *The End of the Game*. The end of game hunting, let's say. The end of the big game, let's say. What it actually means is the end of the biggest game that there is, played by the biggest animal that there is, who has reached his position at the peak of the evolutionary spiral mountain, through a very curious process, in that bigness is what got him there. If you look at the hippo or the horse you'll find that they originally were very small. But by tracing fossil series, you'll find that they became more successful as they became bigger. The bigger, the more successful, and the bigger, the more successful, and the bigger, the more successful. And, finally, here we all are, we're really big now. Our bigness is in numbers, density, the size of our brain, and the size of our population. We're huge, we're number one. But the incredible irony is that enormity is a built-in ingredient of our own demise. What got us to the top is actually the thing that's going to finish us off.

You think we are at the end?

There's definitely going to be a future. The future I see is like Zeno's arrow: every year the arrow goes halfway to the target and it never reaches the target but it keeps going halfway. I'm in no way excited about the future. I'm fairly convinced that the present, this exact moment, is the unique point in all human history where the number one species is turning a curve. Suddenly this enormously complex process, about which Darwin had quite a lot to say, has turned a corner and things are no longer getting better. Evolution always gave us the feeling that we were improving and that there was such a thing as progress. I think we are now experiencing those years when the human race is looking at itself turning the corner.

What about space travel?

It's an absolutely necessary delusion. It's a blind hope. We have to hope that there is something out there.

Do you have any religious feeling?

Absolutely no religious feelings, thoughts, affiliations, sentiments.

What about dying?

I'm convinced that dying is one of the major absolutes we're all going to participate in. I think there are a million kinds of dying. What the human species is going through right now in evolution is a very curious kind of dying. We have removed, layer by layer, connection after connection with our origins, with our—what's that awful word?—roots! "Roots" is a nauseating joke, like "ecology," "environment," "nature," "natural"; these words become laughingstocks. "Haywire" is the most natural word I can think of right now. It reminds me of Gatsby standing out there on the edge of Long Island looking across the Sound at that green light, as if he were trying to look into the past, into some remote connection with something green. Green is so far gone in my mind now. Green is grass, green is gone, hay is the next thing, hay is no longer green and the next thing is wire, wire is not even organic and haywire is a really good term.

Do you have any desire to have children?

None. Well, I shouldn't say that categorically because there could be very selfish reasons for having children, like wanting to see some tragic little version of myself rummaging around in the cement playgrounds so I can look down on this little image of my own ego and say, "There's more to me than me"—that little glob of protoplasm that occasionally says "da-da," that's me, you know. That little guy with cement dust under his fingernails, that came out of me. Think of the poor little fucker. You know, at some point in our farcical history, most human beings thought that animals only saw in black-and-white. That's the way I see the future shaping up: if I had a child it might not see in color. Because everything would be gray. The weather would be gray, the clouds would mix in with the sky, the sea, the cement, the pollution, and the kid probably wouldn't be able to recognize green. We're in the cement age, the age of grayness. You know, the photographic process almost looks like cement, doesn't it? It *looks like cement.*

Do you ever think about suicide?

I think anybody with an IQ over a hundred thinks about it every day. I think suicide is the various forms of death of a species that is clearly in the slow but remorseless process of annihilating itself due to its own enormity. What else is suicide but that? Don't you think that you're part of a lava flow?

But if you take a bottle of sleeping pills, you choose to die?

I personally have a sort of curiosity that makes me realize that life is the only thing we've got, so we might as well clean our cement fingernails and hang on to it.

Are you worried about getting older?
Every day I look in the mirror and I watch myself get one day older, one little lava flow nearer.

Did the knowledge you have about the world come to you as you got older?
I never thought of it as knowledge. I think the destruction of innocence is what we all experience. In many ways we grow like the earth has grown. We evolve away from the Garden of Eden, paradise, all the myths of innocence and eternal spring.

How long have you been keeping diaries?
Since 1952.

What was your favorite year?
I don't believe in things like "favorite years." I guess the best moments are when I'm outside and actively deluded in the wilderness. I have to be honest enough to admit that happiness is a delusion; it's being involved in something that is interesting enough to delude me into thinking that it's more important than something else.

What do you think about money?
It's the golden vegetable, isn't it? But you can't eat gold, can you?

Marriage?
It's an institution that allowed a lot of children to think they were born in wedlock. I've been married. It was an interesting participation in a social scheme and I certainly enjoyed it.

What kind of woman turns you on?
What was it that old John Keats said? You know, there are so many things in the world now that in many senses we're suffocating, so it's more economical to repeat what somebody else has said. And, as Keats said, "Beauty is truth and truth is beauty. That's all you know and all you need to know." That's what I think. When I see somebody really beautiful, somebody who has a certain amount of truth for those moments that I'm looking at that thing—of course, it's all words.

What about love?
What do you think love could mean in Manhattan, where people are so removed from any kind of biological connection to whatever love might have meant once.

Why do you keep snakes in Montauk?
They interest me. In *Heart of Darkness*, Joseph Conrad described the Congo River as a massive snake whose tail was stuck in the jungle and whose head came out into the sea. And actually that river was, of course, very much like life itself. But snakes seem to deeply disturb people. People have thrown paint remover into my snake pit, rocks, cigarette butts—it's incredible. Way out there in Montauk they have found that snake pit and have coughed up their archetypal resistance and thrown it down in there.

Do you like the ocean?
Yeah. I like to fish but I never do. I'd fish for a thousand hours. I was brought up fishing.

Where were you brought up?
In a lot of boats.

Do you like the mountains?
I love to ski. I like exercise. I like delusion.

What do you do on a vacation?
I like to go thousands of miles away from everybody, out on some stretch of the northern frontier. I like to wake up in the morning and hear a few birds and the old sidewinder slithering by—I don't care what it is as long as it gives my nervous system a sense of rest.

Do you like to be alone?
Correct. There's very little time anymore to be alone. It doesn't come very often.

Are you into TV?
I always have the TV on. It saturates one's whole being. I like to have it on because I hate to miss anything. I don't usually have the sound on.

Who are your heroes?
I had heroes, but I don't anymore. I like athletes. I like people who perform under monstrously tense circumstances and come out alive. I'm not sure that bullfighting isn't one of the greatest arts, actually. It's a sad, cruel, paradoxical, terrible truth that we've grown way beyond. But it has heightened moments, dense moments, and great bullfighters performing during those moments give us great artistic insights. Because they're up against the biggest thing there is, of course, which is mutilation or annihilation. They're putting their money where their mouth is; they're not just gambling with words. I think chess is probably a great sport. I think you stand to lose an enormous amount when you lose a chess match, because chess is the master game.

What do you think of a very physical discipline like body-building?
I understand it perfectly. Life is a game, it just depends which game you choose to play. You can choose to play the best game of chess, or to be the most perfect physical specimen, or to climb the highest mountain by the most difficult route. Life is simply a game in which you pursue whatever field you choose.

There are people who don't choose, workers who are forced to do things they don't like for their whole life.
I once went to the St. Louis Meat Packing Company and I know just what you're saying. The workers get up at six o'clock in the morning to execute livestock. The packaging of meat products is an amazing thing. It's necessary and frightening.

Do you eat meat?
Very little. Not because of any moral beliefs, I'm just too lazy to chew. I prefer seafood. I don't know what to think about vegetarianism. There's probably some good in it, but there's also a great deal of affectation and ludicrousness in all these absurd diets. Because, after all, we're all going the same route. Whether we eat a few hamburgers or not, we're going to live sixty, seventy, eighty, even ninety years, and that's it.

Wouldn't you rather live them in good health and vigor?
Health is the most important thing there is. That's why I joined the Euthanasia Society. It's a society that has taken steps toward guaranteeing the right to expire with dignity instead of going the vegetable route with tubes and all that. To me life is so quick. I expect to be gone tomorrow. I believe in here today, gone tomorrow. I think it's our duty to really get as much out of life in the meantime. And with a heavy accent on pleasure. I don't believe in this suffering business at all. No way.

GEORGE BENSON
Jazz Musician

Mr. Benson: My biggest fear is missing phone calls when I'm away. Even though I have an answering service, I can't afford to let all the calls go by, because the answering service doesn't realize the importance of calls. They only answer and say you're not in. I get calls from all over the world—Japan, Europe, Los Angeles, Seattle, Washington, Chicago—from students who want to learn how to play the guitar to my relatives who think I'm a billionaire and have some scheme of beating me out of my fortune. But a lot of times it's legit things like photography sessions, radio interviews, interviews with the major publications, or one of the guys in the band calling me about music or a song that he's heard or he's writing.

Mr. Scavullo: What time do all these phone calls start?
They start at about five o'clock in the morning and they stop at about five-thirty, twenty-four and a half hours later.

Do you talk to just anyone that calls you up?
I don't like to be too far removed from the public, man. You lose the pulse of the people, you know.

Where do you get your inspiration from?
I like people. I watch their response to different types of environments. It's amazing to me what goes on in discotheques. The music is usually so crappy, it has no meaning, just boom, bam, boom, bam, bam. That's what a musician hears. And even though we can dissect a song and find musical things in it that no one else can, basically the songs are designed for dancing and so the interest is not always too great for me. There are a few artists now whose records are played in discotheques that are interesting; some of them are very interesting but most of them are just a repeat of the last song. It amazes me how people can get so much enjoyment out of the same thing over and over again.

Do you think there should be something new in music?
Well, everything can stand improvement. I think the people should be getting a lot more quality music than they're getting. More important, the industry isn't geared up for quality music. It's always geared up for whatever's selling, and as a matter of fact they help to shape what is going to be selling tomorrow. Just like the fashion industry. If they say the mini-skirt is in this year, that's what you're going to get. Music is the same way. They decide that disco music is what they're going to put their billions in back of and they're going to program their radio stations and use that as a format, and that's what we're going to be eating for the next year or until they change, right? They make the decisions and unfortunately we have to abide by them and conform to them to some degree, if not totally, because if you don't, you're out in the cold.

How long does it take you to do an album?
It depends. The last album, *Breezin'*, took a little longer than the one before—three days of sessions which lasted six hours each day, so we recorded it in eighteen hours.

What I think is amazing about the new music is that the guitar almost sounds as if it's talking.
I do think of my guitar as a second voice. I try to make my guitar phrase as if I was speaking. A lot of people are calling that a gimmick now, but it's strictly not a gimmick, it's very hard to accomplish. When I practice I can hum anything that I play. I've always wanted to do that and record it, but the other producer I had would always tell me, "No, that won't work." I finally got a chance to do it with Warner Brothers,

on *Breezin'*—in the song "Masquerade" I duel with the guitar and it was a smash, which I always knew it would be. But the thing is, I had been doing that for years and years so my guitar was actually doing what my voice gave it. Now, one can't do what the other can. My fingers are a lot faster than my voice can phrase it, but they know exactly the same thing. The same brain controls them both.

Haven't you invented an instrument?
I designed two guitars for a company called *Eyes and Ears*. That was another dream that I had for twenty years. When I was a kid I'd press my face against a music-store window and dream about having enough money to buy a certain instrument that my mind would be fixed on. I'd go by every day and look at these instruments that I couldn't possibly afford. And years ago I had imagined what my dream guitar would be like. Even though I've had many associations with musical-instrument companies that came to me and asked me for ideas, they would always embellish my idea until it came out another instrument altogether. It was never what I had planned. So recently I got a chance to do my own thing with a company. They worked with me for five months putting it together. They told me what was possible and they let me make the decisions. So we came out with an instrument that was mine. And we took all the standard bugs out of the guitar because the guitar today is required to do things it wasn't twenty-five years ago. You've got a lot of kids out there who are playing music that didn't exist then.

Do you think that the more successful you are with your music the more freedom you gain?
Of course. When you're generating capital, everybody wants to be in on it. Everybody wants to pick your brain. Nobody lets you breathe a little bit. I just want to have a part in it. I want to have a name before I collect it all. I'm the one who's going to catch the rear-beating all of my life if something goes wrong—they're going to blame it on me. They're not going to blame it on the producer or the record company or the side men, just whoever's name is on that album. That's who gets the beating—me.

How many albums have you made?
On my own I have about fifteen albums, which rounds out to almost an album a year since I came to New York. It seems like a lot, but when you spread it over a period of years from 1963 to now it isn't really.

But this one, *Breezin'*, was the biggest hit?
That was the album that made the difference in my career. It changed the complexion of my career and it made people in the industry think of me as a major artist. Before, they knew that I had some talent but they didn't think of me when they thought of capital. But now every time they think of money they think of a certain group of people and someday in that group you'll find my name popular.

What do you think of money? How do you feel about it?
Money's very important. I feel a person should be rewarded when he's doing good things, especially if he's spent his life doing it and especially if he's doing something that makes people's lives better. I don't think that a person should become famous and then live like a pauper unless he desires it that way. Now, a lot of people just can't stand fame. Some people run, they're hermits. You know they could invent the atomic bomb and then—what's his name—Einstein, he had nothing to say. He was just his own man and he didn't need

GEORGE BENSON
Jazz Musician

money and fame. Some countries support the people in the arts, so they never think of money because they don't have to. In this country you have to because the rent man is going to make sure that you don't forget that lease, whenever the rent comes due. So we're forced into thinking that way, and if we don't, we end up working in post offices or on welfare instead of being a credit to the state or to the people. Man, I know great musicians who are walking the streets. I know some great artists, a lot greater than the ones that we hear on the air. You'll never hear them.

Do you try to help them?
I try to help them. Some of them surface. A lot of it has to do with your way of thinking, too. You have to want to be a part of it. Some people don't want to be a part of the system. They've tried it, it's too boring.

You had a mother who was home and took care of you?
Yeah, and we needed that, man, you know we really needed that. In New York especially—it's a nutty town. You can hire a baby-sitter and they're liable to throw your kids out the window. I mean, you see that on the news and you say, man, that could be me.

What do you think about all the violence and crime in our country?
I grew up in that kind of environment in Pittsburgh, so I can really appreciate how terrible it can be. But it starts from way up on the roster. The people we have in charge ain't no good, so they keep letting the other things happen. There's no excuse for dope in this country at all. The Japanese did away with it overnight and we could too. But too many higher-ups in government are benefiting by it. That's the only answer, because why wouldn't they pass the laws that would do away with it when they know for sure it can be done away with. In Japan they don't have one junkie anywhere because he knows he'd be in the penitentiary for the rest of his life.

And the same thing with guns. Look at England. You can walk the streets at all hours of the night and feel safe in England. There are no guns there. In this country a man could walk in the street with a machine gun in his hand and it's legal. Now, isn't that terrible. People are scared in this country. As soon as you start getting some revenue together here comes a mob of some sort that takes you over. And you can't go nowhere. No one can help you. You feel helpless. There are a lot of great things about America as opposed to other countries. This country is full of wealth, of all sorts, but we're not really getting the full benefit of it. Unfortunately, the people do not benefit from it as much as the ones who have money, the crooks. You know, when you see these kinds of things happening in front of your eyes, you see a man commit a murder and then he walks the street the next day, you can't feel safe. You're scared to death.

Do you raise your sons to be strong?
I try to give them the hands-off attitude: Don't mess with nobody 'cause you never know how a person is going to react. You might knock a man down but you can't knock no

bull down, and a knife will kill anybody—I don't care if you're three hundred pounds or fifty pounds, that knife will cut or slash and you can die. I mean, if you win a battle don't mean you won the war. That's the attitude I try to give them. But I try to get them into being able to defend themselves because you never know when somebody's going to go nuts out there. So just knowing how to get out of the way and knowing how to put your guard up might save your life.

Do you bring up your children with any religious training?
I'm a Bible student myself, even though winning that Grammy has taken a lot away from my study time—it might be a Satan-oriented scheme. See, we never know in this system because we don't run it. Satan runs it himself. He picks who he wants to be successful, he gives it to who he wants to. He could be part of my career.

You don't think that God gives success to people?
Everything that is good comes from the Creator. This is my thinking and my learning. You see, the whole thing is brought about by His knowledge. He's the Creator. Satan isn't the creator. He's the father of the first lie. And this system is built up on governments which are run by people who are nonrighteous, they're not completely clean. When a man gets into higher office the people who put him there are usually atrocious—known criminals that took part in the election and put him where they wanted him. I mean, if the labor unions go against a man, you can bet it's over for him.

These are all things that we know exist. We can't ignore them. We can't say for sure that it happens that way, but it's very strange that we have all these peace-oriented organizations that never work. The only explanation for that is there's some element that's keeping us from peace. We are intelligent people. We know what war can do, but you think they're trying to avoid it? I mean, they do anything they can possibly do but it all comes down to that confrontation thing. To me that's Satan. He's at the base of all of that. If you know anything about Scriptures you know that he's tried every righteous man that ever existed.

Do you think divorce is wrong or right?
Well, the Scriptures say that the only reason for divorce is when the man finds his wife unfaithful. That's the only time. Not because he suddenly got tired of her. I get tired of my kids but that doesn't mean you kick them out in the street.

Was your first wife unfaithful to you?
Yeah. But, you know, kids in this system are taught to be so disoriented—that do-your-own-thing idea hurt a lot of people. You do what's right, that's what I say. Hey, man, there is so much to enjoy about life. The thing that really takes me out is seeing people getting bored to death. Man, we got how many countries? Hundreds of countries. All of them have their own way of preparing food and they all have different varieties. How many of us can truthfully say that we tasted or tested at least one tenth of the amount of cuisines of the different countries around the world? There's not many of us that can make that claim. Here in New York we have about

two hundred different ethnic cuisines, but we basically eat the same foods every day. When my wife goes to the store she talks about fish, beef and pork. But there isn't any more pork coming this way no more, because it contains trichinosis.

Are you concerned about what's in foods, preservatives and chemicals?
We can't be more than what we eat. We came out of the ground. Food comes out of the ground. We take it in our systems. That's us. If you eat poison, you are a poisoned man. If you eat vegetables, you are a vegetable man—you're a man whose body is made out of things that come from vegetables. You know it's as simple as that as far as I'm concerned. I think of the body as a complex chemical factory that could take care of itself, but it needs the basic raw ingredients which come out of the ground where we came from in the first place. Now all we need is to find the right ingredients for what the body needs.

I think that basically there are people that could tell us a lot more than we know about our bodies—but they don't. They let us live on what is popular. They know that pork is killing us. How come those people don't stop it? They know that cigarettes kill us. How come they don't take them off the market? Now, isn't that terrible. That is a crime. Our lives are priceless, man. All the gold in the world can't replace one of us. So why are we dying by the millions over something that the government has the power to flush like that? That's the crime. It's like the Vietnam war. I mean, it could have been all over but the man prolonged the war so that it could be advantageous to his next election. He prolonged it a few months longer so that when he did chop it off, people would think of him as a great man, he did a great thing. That's terrible, man. You know, even if it only caused the death of one more man, it's terrible, because he did it for his own selfish reason. I don't want to point to a particular individual but their life styles speak for themselves, man.

How do you feel about getting older? Does it bother you?
Yeah, because I feel there's no reason for it. I know why we get old. I believe what the Scriptures tell me about our life and why we die. But theoretically we're not supposed to age like we do. It's a crime to see our mothers and fathers and people we love crumble up and die right in front of our eyes. We watch them die, man. We see them take all that garbage in their systems and we try to tell them, but they're so oriented into something they learned years ago, there's nothing you can do. So you have to slowly watch them die right in front of your face. And then when they get old, to show you how crazy the system is, we discard them like we do old clothes. We get them out of the way. Isn't it terrible, it's as if we're not going to get old ourselves. We are really shallow-minded, man.

Does that worry you?
Sure, because I know I'm going to get old.

How do you deal with it?
By talking about it to people who are interested. I have that

hope that it won't be that way in the future. That's the thing that makes life bearable—otherwise I'd probably be in some military group somewhere trying to blow up something because it's really very frustrating. I see why young people go nuts. I shouldn't say "go nuts," but they do what they believe will change the system. And they blow up buildings and trains or kidnap. They do it because they think that's the way. The system is so frustrating—you can't beat the system. I mean, they own it. They've got the armies. They keep saying it's our system. But it's not our system. If they decide to charge ninety-nine percent tax, there's nothing we can do about it.

What do you think about dying?
I believe what it tells me in the Scriptures about what happens at death. My physical body isn't ready to die, of course. I think that even Christ the man cried out about that just before they came to arrest him because he didn't want to go through that physical ordeal, but his knowledge of why he was here gave him the strength that he needed to go through that. I understand there's nothing we can do about it except to make sure that you're on good terms with the Creator because He has the power to undo everything and to re-do. Death is nothing to the Creator. It's just like us with an automobile that breaks down. If it's worth saving, we save it. If it isn't, we junk it and start anew.

To change the subject, are you interested in clothes at all?
I like clothes. I like neatness because it says that a person has order about him. When I see a person whose clothes are irregular or funny, I know he isn't really together. He's unpredictable. And I don't down him for that, it just helps me understand more about him. But a lot of the world is disoriented, so it's no big thing. Some people just don't care about clothes. Rich people have learned not to worry about things like that because they're really not that important. Truthfully, it's not that important. It just tells us something about the person's life style. I know a lot of very wealthy people who don't dress well at all. They're so busy doing things that they don't have time for that.

What makes you very happy?
When I'm doing what I'm supposed to be doing. If I'm playing for people and they're really getting off on what I'm doing, I'm happy, man. I feel I did what I came to do. Or watching my kids grow. Seeing them not have to go through the things I did. Because I had it very rough, you know. I like to look at art, some of the things that are man-made that came out of our heads. It shows you what we can do. That makes me happy to see. It gives me a glimpse of what the future is going to be like and it makes me think of a world where we didn't have all this crazy stuff going on. We could turn this world into a paradise, man. It could be fantastic. And not one that just has "Paradise" written on it. This country has "Paradise" written on it, but when you look at the streets, brother, we're walking on the rubble, we're walking on dirt.

JULIAN BOND
Georgia State Senator

Mr. Scavullo: How did you get started in politics?
Mr. Bond: I was interested from my late teens, but I didn't become a candidate until I was twenty-five. I worked in other people's campaigns. I was more interested in the mechanical part of it: How do I make you vote for someone? How do I convince you, and once I've convinced you, how do I make you vote on election day? I was much more interested in that than running myself. And then I ran myself and it's like narcotics; you become sure that you're the guy God has chosen to represent these people, and you have to do it over and over again. I don't really think so, but people in public life do believe that God has chosen them—or some mystical force—it's divine right. It's very much like being in the entertainment world; people are always telling you how great you are.

What kind of background do you come from?
My father was a college teacher and administrator, and eventually president of a place called Fort Riley State College, and then he went from there to Lincoln University in Pennsylvania, and was there until '57; then he went back to Atlanta.

Are you optimistic about the future of America?
Some days I am and some days I'm not.

In the morning, are you happy to get up and go into the day?
Oh, yes. That's my day, that's not America's day.

What is a typical day like?
It depends. I travel an enormous amount. I earn a living making speeches; Georgia legislators only get $7,000 a year. We only work forty days a year. So I spend about a hundred days a year traveling. A typical traveling day means waking up in a Holiday Inn someplace and eating breakfast by myself, and then catching a plane to go to someplace else to make a connection to go to someplace else and then coming to my final destination, where I am met by students. They say, in sequence, "How was your trip, how was your trip, how was your trip . . ." And they take me to another Holiday Inn. I check in, I go to dinner with them—it's usually two political-science students, the campus queen, the head of the Black Students' Association, and maybe a faculty adviser. Then we have a press conference, then I make a speech, then I answer questions, then we have a reception, then it's back to the Holiday Inn.

If I'm home, I get up and go to my office. People come in with complaints and I'm like a feudal lord and say, "Never mind, my son, I will take care of this," and they usually go away happy.

What do you think is happening in civil rights today?
We're in limbo. There used to be a very vibrant Southern-based movement, which was carried on by relatively strong civil rights organizations—the Student Non-Violent Co-ordinating Committee, the Congress of Racial Equality, the NAACP, the Southern Christian Leadership Conference; with the exception of the NAACP, all of those groups have just faded away. And so there's no institutionalized civil rights movement anymore. It's largely an individual movement. Some people in Buffalo, for example, may decide they don't like the way the school system treats black children and they begin a movement which may last two weeks or several months or several years, but it's an individual thing. But you don't have mass protest anymore, and it's much harder to figure out where it's going. It's like treading water, to keep from going under.

Do you think part of that is because many of the goals of the civil rights movement have been attained?
The surface goals have—the right to sit in the front of the bus, to sit downstairs at movie theaters, to have access to public accommodations, to register and vote. Those things have been accomplished. Now it's a much harder job to make those accomplishments real. For example, we just lost a very important congressional election in Atlanta, Tuesday, only because black voters did not turn out. They don't turn out primarily because like other people they tend to be lazy, but also because they have a history of knowing they couldn't vote, and have only been voting for a relatively short time, ten years. And they're not organized as well as they ought to be. You ought to be able to, with a few phone calls, put into motion a mechanism that eventually seeps down to every block so that every house gets a knock on the door: "Don't forget to vote tomorrow." There's a tremendous mopping-up operation to be done.

Do you think there should be more black people in positions of power?
Yes, but what's happened is that we have almost reached the limit of blacks elected by blacks. What we haven't been able to do, with a couple of exceptions, is to get blacks elected by whites. Ninety-nine out of every hundred black elected officials are elected by blacks. I represent a constituency that's eighty percent black. What we've not been able to do on a large-scale basis is convince white voters that they could vote for a black candidate. It's very difficult to do. The fear is that all the white city or state workers will be fired and they'll hire ignorant, unqualified blacks. And it hasn't happened anyplace so far, like Newark or Los Angeles, which have black mayors.

Do you think there's ever a possibility of a black becoming President of this country?
It would not be inconceivable for Andrew Young to be Vice-President four or eight years from now. Suppose Walter Mondale stays Vice-President for eight years and then decides to run for President. He's not an old man, he's in his forties, I guess, so he'll be fifty-something when he runs for President with Andy Young as his Vice-President. This is after Young has spent four years as UN Ambassador, four years as Secretary of State, he's learned how to control his utterances, and he becomes like Moynihan, a revered and respected figure. He's Vice-President for four years, that's twelve years from now. Andy would be fifty-two. So it's not unlikely that he could be President.

Do you feel better getting older?
I feel much more comfortable with myself. At the same time I have the feeling that I'm getting younger, and this is difficult to explain, I feel less mature. I don't mean that I'm silly, but I feel much freer and less rigid now, at thirty-seven, than I did when I was thirty-five or thirty-two or thirty. I am a very formal person, and I feel less formal now than I ever have. I'm just much looser. And as I get older I'm learning that you don't always have to be as nice as I once thought you had to be. I once thought you had to be nice to everyone. And you don't have to do that. You can say

JULIAN BOND
Georgia State Senator

"Fuck off" if you want to.

Do you have ambitions for higher office?
I have ambitions, but I don't have any opportunity. I had a chance to run for Young's seat, but I don't want to be in the U.S. House of Representatives with four hundred and thirty-five people—it's an enormous pond filled with little fish. I'd love to be a U.S. senator. I'd have a six-year term. As it is now, I'm running for re-election every two years, and I never stop. As soon as I win one election I'm working on the next one. And being in politics is attractive in some ways and unattractive in others. I'm constantly having to be nice to people that I would not ordinarily be nice to, people I wouldn't have in my home. But, you know, Georgia is a very conservative place; they would never elect me.

What would you do if you switched careers?
I have no idea. Maybe I'll be an entertainer.

What do you like to do in your free time, if you have any?
I have a lot of free time. As I said, I work forty days a year as a senator and a hundred days as a speaker; that means I have two hundred and twenty days a year to do nothing.

And what do you do?
Well, I have five children. I try to spend some time with them. I read a lot, listen to music.

What kind of music?
Two kinds: regular popular music, whatever's on the radio; as well as late-fifties jazz, Charlie Parker, early Miles Davis, early Dizzy Gillespie, Chet Baker—boy, he's got a voice like an angel. I used to try to sing.

Does your wife work?
She takes care of the children. She would say that she is a working woman.

What do you think about women's lib?
I'm all for that. I want them to have whatever it is they want. I want people to have whatever it is they feel they're entitled to.

Could you see yourself married to a career woman?
If I weren't married, I'm not sure I could really see myself married at all. But I think so. I think it depends on the person and the circumstance. But I wouldn't at all mind, if circumstances were changed, if she had a job, even to the point where she became the breadwinner—it would be fine with me. I wouldn't mind staying home. I don't think I'd like keeping house. It does seem to me to be drudge-work.

What kind of women are you attracted to?
Live ones. No, that was facetiously said. Attractive ones, and I don't mean just physically, but personally, too. Because I think you can be physically not really unattractive, but not attractive, and personally very, very attractive. I don't want to mention any examples because they'll say, "My God, I thought I was attractive." But I like attractive people, or people who attract you to them, bright people—I don't mean happy, silly people. "Attractive" is too broad a word to describe what I mean; I just like people who are pleasant to be with.

Does it make a difference to you whether a woman is black or white?
No.

Do you believe in love?
Oh, yeah. I used to fall in love every day.

Do you think that love and sex are the same thing?
They can be, but they are not.

Is sex very important to you?
Oh, yeah. I like to think I'm a very sensual person. *Cosmopolitan* chose me as one of the thirty sexiest men in the world. I wonder who told them, though. I thought it sort of odd, really, because who knows who the world's thirty most anything are? It was nice, but it doesn't mean anything. Just because I've got thousands of copies reprinted, scattered around, it doesn't mean anything.

Do you think about what you eat?
More and more I do. I'm very, very slowly becoming a vegetarian. And not for any religious reasons or anything; it's just that meat becomes unattractive to me as a food, as something to put inside me—you know, the idea that this thing used to be alive. I still eat meat. But I normally would eat meat for breakfast, lunch and dinner—bacon in the morning, a hamburger for lunch, and a piece of red, bloody meat at dinnertime.

Do you smoke?
Like a furnace. Two packs a day. I know it's bad. I can't run up stairs like I used to; I couldn't run around this block, I would drop. But I like it so much.

What about drinking?
I drink, not to excess. But I like a little drink.

What do you think of the drug problem today?
There's a serious problem. In Atlanta, until ten years ago, you literally did not have to lock your doors. You could leave packages on the seat of your car with the windows down and the door unlocked. But you can't do that now, and the rise in that kind of street crime is attributable largely to drugs. Not to mention the people who are all zonked out on the street.

You think that there's any remedy?
I don't know. I would be against legalizing or having prescription heroin, the way they do in England. The addict population is so much larger here, it would just frighten me to have it so readily available. But I don't think stronger laws serve any purpose. New York's law, for example, is a vicious law: you get caught in the street with some cocaine, you're in jail for life—that's frightening.

Is money important to you?
It is, but not so much for having things as for having time and freedom. I have a large income, but I don't buy a lot of stuff with it. I just want to be able to be selective about when I work, for example. And I want my children to have whatever they want—within limits. I don't say, "Here, kids, take this and buy what you want."

Are you worried about things like pornography?
No, because these children will grow up very differently than I did. My parents were progressive at the time, but my children are being raised so that they can see whatever they wish—within some limits. I mean, I'm not going to let my seven-year-old daughter thumb through copies of *Hustler*, but there will come a time, I hope, when she'll be able to see that and she'll be able to make up her mind herself. I hope that I am making them into the kind of persons who would be able to say, "I can look at this or not"; "It's my own choice"; "I don't have to get heavily involved in it." For

another example, they know much more about drugs than I ever did when I was their age, because their school has a fairly extensive and realistic drug-education program. When I was young we were told that marijuana would make hair grow on your palms, and that if you smoked two joints, you would be mainlining heroin the next day. Now, that obviously is not true, but that's what we were told and we believed it. But my children know better than that, they know what heroin is, they know what marijuana is, they know what amphetamines are—the older ones, anyway—and they have a much better sense of what's good and what's bad in that vein than I ever did.

Do your children watch TV much?
Too much. I have to chase them away. Pull out the plug.

What do you like to watch on TV?
I like to watch things that I can watch while reading, like talk shows. A lot of the watching I do is at night. If I speak in Wichita, Kansas, and am through at ten-thirty and back in the room at eleven, there's only the Johnny Carson show. I watch that avidly. I've been to places where they're playing last week's *Tonight* show. It's either that or Future Farmers of America report on crop failures.

Have you traveled out of the country much?
Not much. I've been to England for three weeks, to France for three days, to Cuba for a week, to West Africa for two weeks, to East Africa for about three weeks and to southern Africa twice.

Did you feel an immediate rapport with the Africans?
I wanted to, but they're very quick to tell you that so far as they're concerned, black Americans are Americans first and black second. I was in Guinea, in West Africa, and a guy came to me on the street and said, "What tribe do you belong to? Are you Fulu, a Susu, a Malinke?" I said, "We don't belong to tribes in America." He said, "You look to me like a Wabenzi." I said, "What is that?" He said, "Well, *wa* means 'tribe of,' and *benzi* is short for Mercedes-Benz." He said I belonged to the tribe of Mercedes-Benz. The average guy there thinks that all Americans are rich.

Does the idea of studying your roots fascinate you?
My father's already done that for us. He traced us back to someplace in West Africa. He didn't have names and details, he didn't put words in people's mouths—"Hello, how you doing?"—like Alex Haley did. But he had already done that. My father was an amateur genealogist. I'm glad it was done. I don't think I'd be a very different person if it hadn't been done. But I think it's important as a general proposition to be able to do that. So many people, both white and black, go back two generations and it's gone; they have no idea.

Do you have any fears?
I occasionally get frightened of automobiles, particularly if I'm not driving. I'm never worried about the other guy; I'm worried about me sitting in the passenger seat. I think I'm going to be killed in a car. And I worry about being embarrassed, in some way, but those are the only fears I have.

Do you have any fear about dying?
Only in an automobile. I don't think I'm willing to die before my time. I don't know what my time is, maybe sixty, seventy years. I don't want to be feeble. My father had a stroke and

was in a semicoma for six months. I don't think he knew where he was or who he was or who we were. I don't want that to happen to me.

Is there something that really bothers you that you would like to see corrected, made different?
In the larger world: the tremendous unemployment rate among black young men; the black-white income gap, which is getting wider rather than getting closer together; these kinds of societal problems bother me a great deal. More and more I think they're almost outside my ability to correct them. At best I may make a tremendously minute dent in them. At one time I thought that just a few of us could get together and settle these things. But they're so much larger than any of us, and require forces for their solution that are much larger than any of us.

Do you think that people are getting very lazy today? Maybe that's why civil rights is not as important.
Well, they're lazy, they're much more self-centered . . . In not altogether a selfish way, but you think of the latter part of the sixties, particularly when young people had this tremendous interest in Eastern religion (which is looking inward, not looking outward), in certain kinds of drugs (contemplative rather than energizing), in an experience which was personal just to you—the whole, you know, all these mind-expanding schemes, EST, all these sorts of things which generally are personal, they're not to make you save the world. They're to make you save yourself. And when people begin to think of themselves in this selfish way—and I don't mean that in a bad sense—but when they think that way they don't think about other people. They are laid back. They say, "Well, if I'm all right, then never mind about how the others are." And that's had a serious effect on the civil rights movement.

Do you like the idea of revolution?
I like the idea of revolution; I'm not sure I'd like the fact of revolution. The idea is very appealing because the inequities in this society are so glaring that you must think that only a radical revolution could set them right. There is more mobility in America. You can be born poor here and become a millionaire, which you can't do in most societies. But the odds against your becoming a millionaire are so great as to be discouraging. I'm not a millionaire, and I doubt if I ever will be.

Who are some people you admire today?
I admire hundreds of people, but most of them for singular reasons. I admire James Baldwin. I like words, and people who put words together well. I admire Ray Charles. I *admired* Lyndon Johnson, not for what he did, I just admired the man. I thought he had a tremendously clever mind and an ability to work with people, to get from them what he wanted without hitting them or twisting their arms. He was a masterful worker of men.

So far, all men.
I don't want to be a chauvinist. Let's balance this: three women of different religions and races. I admire Barbara Walters. Not that I think she's the best newsperson ever, but she gets so much criticism and she just goes on. I admire that. I like someone who says, "To hell with you, I'm going to go ahead and do it."

WILLIAM F. BUCKLEY JR.

Political Columnist, Author and TV Commentator

Mr. Scavullo: What do you think about the way Americans use the English language?
Mr. Buckley: A lot of Americans know a lot of words they don't ever use. In England, more usually, people use their vocabulary. In America they will recognize a word but they won't use it. Another thing I've found which is interesting is that Spanish-speaking people hardly ever make a grammatical mistake. They're almost incapable of doing it. For instance, semiliterates 'n Mexico would never fail to use the subjunctive when it's called for, whereas in America, grammatical standards don't seen to make much impression during the learning peroid. Twenty years ago it was widely assumed that with the spread of television there would be a standardization of American English, that people would all use Walter Cronkite standards. That hasn't happened. It must mean that Americans are less good as imitators than foreigners. Foreigners are much more natural polyglots than Americans, and it's because they imitate. If you imitate, even if you are illiterate, the grammatical constructions that you grew up with, then you don't make a mistake—like "He gave it to he and I"—if you've never heard anybody say that mistake. But in America, although you'd never hear Walter Cronkite saying that, let alone Edwin Newman, nevertheless people are capable of saying that. It strikes me as interesting on several grounds, one of them being that Americans are very musical. And you usually think of music as being associated with a good ear. But Americans don't seem to have a very good grammatic propensity; whether that's cultural or genetic, I don't know. It must be cultural.

Does that bother you?
I think it's an abuse of the language. Inflections are developed as a result of requirements of language for tonality: it takes more inflections to communicate finely tuned thought. And to wade through life without any recognition of this amounts to a cultural abdication. If you can't handle inflection, you can't handle the uses of the language. You can handle it instrumentally—"Give me a hamburger"—but you can't specify subtle thought. When Knox translated the Old Testament in 1947, he remarked that the scholars surrounding King James in the seventeenth century had taken thirteen different Greek words and subsumed them under the single word "righteous." In the course of doing so, they set back ethical distinctions by almost two millennia—i.e., distinctions that had been carefully thought out sixteen hundred years before were lost. And since those distinctions covered real distinctions, it required from the seventeenth century on to rediscover them, except insofar as they survived in the works of Plato and Aristotle, and so forth. But they were all joined together in the Bible, and in that sense it was a problem.

Did you start reading at a particularly young age?
No. I'm aware that if you start reading young you develop, above all, your capacity to memorize. I don't have a very highly developed capacity to memorize.

Do you like President Carter's accent?
It doesn't offend me. My mother's from the South, my father's from the South. Carter was on my program in January of '73, and about a year ago I was lecturing at the University of Georgia, in Athens. My host was an associate professor who had been Carter's press chief at that time, and he said that he gave a party for the junior members of Carter's staff to watch him on my program, to see how he did. When Carter started to speak someone kicked the set; they thought something was wrong with it. What had happened was that Carter had changed his accent. He had been working, like Eliza Doolittle, to change, to de-regionalize, his accent. He used to sound like his brother Billy, and then he sprang his new accent on that show, which was his first national television appearance. And that's the voice that we know: clearly Southern, but not rednecked, which is apparently the way he used to sound.

Do you like to debate?
I sometimes take satisfaction from having debated, sometimes not. I don't just look for a debate. I think if I were on a desert island I probably would never debate. I mostly debate because in the course of doing so, I elicit information I need, feel out a situation I want to probe. Or I do it for pay.

Does it pay well?
Sure it does, if you're on the lecture circuit, and you're a hot property. Personal appearances mean so much in America; Americans are so theatrical—it's show biz. Universities pay as much for an evening's speech as they'd pay a professor for half a year's work. But that's up to them.

What's your day like? You have a column to write, a TV show to prepare . . .
Well, for instance, yesterday morning I wrote a column, and a book review for the *New York Times*. Then I started on a reply to an editor from Des Moines who alleges that I have a conflict of interests. And then I finished a four-minute television rebuttal to Ken Galbraith's series on economics, which will be taped tomorrow. And last week I finished my novel, and tomorrow I'm lecturing at Yale. That kind of stuff. I wrote a book about it once, called *Cruising Speed*.

Do you think television is more important today than print?
No. I think it has wider instant impact but I still think the people who make the fundamental decisions in society are the people who read books.

Do you go out much at night?
Not too often. My wife and I live a couple of months a year in Switzerland—that's probably the most orderly time we spend, and we go out maybe two or three times a week.

But she often goes out without you in New York.
Yes. Because I'm often on the road.

You work so much, how do you find time to be with your wife?
Spending time with someone is largely a matter of proximity. It's not all that often that a husband and wife get up at eight o'clock in the morning and talk to each other until eight o'clock at night. Most men spend five days working and two days at home, during which they might go out and play tennis with their wife—they're not talking to their wife very much during that—or they might play music or read or watch television. So that the notion that a social relationship is based on a continuous dialogue is totally schematic. It's based on proximity. And I probably spend more time close to my wife than most people because I have a very independent life. I work largely on my own and at home.

Is there any special kind of woman that you like?
Just feminine.

Not aggressive or strong?

WILLIAM F. BUCKLEY JR.
Political Columnist, Author and TV Commentator

Some feminine women are very aggressive. An obvious example would be Katharine Hepburn.

What do you think about beauty?
Beauty is one of the sources, but not the only source, of sensual pleasure. If you look at a beautiful piece of art, you admire not only the craftsmanship—that's really a derivative intellectual end—but you derive sensual pleasure as one does from a beautiful woman. Schopenhauer said that a sixteen-year-old girl is a smash triumph of nature.

What are your feelings about getting old?
I'm all for it. If I could take a pill that would make me twenty years younger, I'd throw it out the window. It seems to me that it is built-in to an understanding of life, that there is a beginning, a middle and an end. And to want to start it all again is like wanting to see *Parsifal* again, when you've finally reached the last act, even though you enjoyed the whole thing hugely. I suppose ideally you would age, but visually you wouldn't change. That would mean a lot, especially to women. I regret biological deterioration. I haven't experienced it yet, fortunately, but I can anticipate it. When my knees get creaky as the result of walking around the block, I will regret that part of the aging process. But I won't regret the fact that I am approaching death.

Does your mind get sharper as you get older?
No, but you know more. The mind doesn't necessarily get sharper, but you make up for it later on by a strategic capacity to dispose of your faculties. That's why sixty-five-year-old lawyers, though they may be slower, are worth four or five times what twenty-five-year-old lawyers are, because there is a capacity there for concision which is extremely useful. Now, artistically, you sometimes get to the point where you are in fact suffering from a mild arteriosclerosis. That's when you start to make mistakes. And the trick is to know when your quality as a writer or artist is diminishing. Then quit.

Then what would you do?
Something else concerning which I don't feel a professional sense of responsibility. Artur Rubinstein, for example, now that he's over the top as a pianist, will only play unknown works, works that he's never played before, because then there's an implicit compact between him and his listeners that he's experimenting.

Do you want to live to a very old age?
I want to live until I naturally give out, and, preferably, not much beyond the time that my family and friends die.

Do you have any children?
I have one son.

Are you a strong father? Do you give your son directions?
I outwitted him until he was about fourteen. Then his sense of cunning made us pretty much equals. But I never let him doubt what I thought was the right thing to do. Or let him doubt that this was not just an obligation to me, but that, on an objective basis, there is a right and wrong. It's not easy to ascertain what's right and wrong; but that has to be the implicit commitment of trying to decide what to do.

Do you think marriage is right, not only for yourself, but for your son? In other words, do you think it's a good system?
I think it's a divine institution. I can't imagine a defensible society that isn't centrally monogamous. I think marriage is

the nuclear unit of society.

Do you think that homosexuality is bad for society?
I think it is. It's *contra naturum*; it is a deviation from that which is natural. I believe the social policy toward homosexuality ought to be totally permissive without being totally indulgent. It's one thing to say to a homosexual, Do as you like and I'm not going to stand in your way. It is another to suggest that society is so constructed as to permit a homosexual the range of satisfactions that are available in other circumstances. And I think that the tendency is in that direction; the tendency is not to say that we want rights for homosexuals, which I think they should have; it's to say, There is no such thing as abnormality. This is in effect the *Playboy* line.

What about pornography?
I believe that the community has the right to censure pornography, that there are legitimate matters for corporate social concern.

What about freedom of the press?
Nothing is clearer, I think, than the fact that you can't have an indefinite extension of more than one freedom. Because if you indefinitely extend two freedoms, they're going to run into each other. How do you have absolute freedom of the press plus absolute right of a fair trial? The two are incompatible. They hit each other. How can you have the absolute right under the Fifth Amendment not to testify against yourself, and the absolute right under the Sixth Amendment to compel testimony? The answer is that these things tend to run into each other. Oliver Wendell Holmes used a very nice image. He said that everybody agrees that you own the space above the roof of your own house. But the fanatic extends that principle on into a shaft of light that reaches from his house into the Milky Way so that no child can fly a kite over the area. That's a fanatical extension of a right. The notion that the First Amendment was about the rights of *Hustler* magazine is a caricature. And to the extent that you strengthen that notion, you weaken the First Amendment, you don't strengthen it.

What do you think about the increasing use of drugs in our society?
It's suicidal. I'm using a metaphor: it's suicidal in the sense that it is a way of preventing you from experiencing life. And since life stays with you and the drug does not, all that does is give you a very brief escapist alternative to life. The one absolutely predictable thing is that people who take drugs will be unhappy. And the tragedy of it is that they take drugs in order to be happy and their happiness is so fleeting. It takes a certain amount of wisdom to recognize the strategic disability of taking drugs. I'm talking about heavy addiction, I'm not talking about social use.

Do you think that the government should restrict the availability of drugs?
The government ought never try to get into the business of making people happy. The only excuse the government has for interfering at all is that the taking of drugs is empirically provable, I think, to be contagious. That is, people who mainline, for instance, want to share the experience. In fact, economic enterprise requires them to sustain their habit by a

synthetic income which is mostly made by persuading other people to buy the stuff. The argument that there wouldn't be that economic enterprise if drugs were freely available on the market does not cope with the psychological appetite that people have for sharing their own vices. And to say nothing of the fact that it does not cope with the innocent-victim problem; the notion that you are the sole victim of drug taking is something that can only be made in an entirely selfish society. Most people who take drugs are depriving other people of something—a family of an income; children of a mother's companionship—so I think it is a social problem and the intervention of the state is justified. On this matter, incidentally, I take a highly empirical position: if it is proved that the intervention of the state did not solve the problem but created a whole series of other social problems, then I would simply yield. That's one of the reasons why I'm in favor of decriminalizing marijuana.

Have you tried marijuana?
I only tried it twice. The first time it didn't do anything for me at all. The second time it made me terribly sleepy. I gather different people react slightly differently. I was with two friends and they found everything that was said hilariously funny. "Good morning"—laugh, laugh, laugh, laugh, laugh. "How are you"—laugh, laugh, laugh, laugh.

Do you smoke cigarettes?
Used to. I think it's safe to say that there are two classes of people who smoke cigarettes: for one of them it's highly toxic; for the other, not so. My wife smokes and it doesn't bother her at all. In my case I gave it up when I was about twenty-seven, because I would have to get up in the morning and gargle and have to clear my throat all day long.

Do you watch your diet?
I watch my diet. I try to exercise. I hate it but I do it. I exercise on one of those stationary bicycles, which are a terrible bore. So I bicycle about three miles every morning while talking on the phone. It's only about the last half mile that they realize something's going on. But then I usually try to let them talk. Then at night I do some sit-ups.

Are you involved in any other sports?
Skiing. I do a little tennis. I sail. I've done a lot of sports in my life. When I was young I rode horseback every day for two or three hours.

Do you watch TV?
I don't watch it much, but I've got a new gadget which allows you to record. That intrigues me. I find myself watching the news much more often so that I can have the fun of recording it. I'll tire of that novelty.

Do you enjoy watching yourself on TV?
I've watched myself four times in ten years. It makes me sick that I didn't say it differently, whatever it was.

Are you concerned about your appearance, your clothes?
My wife buys my clothes. But it isn't a mannerism, because there's no reason in the world why men shouldn't pay attention to their appearance. I do to the extent that I don't like fat ties—that's just my old reactionary self—so I have thin ties. I could still find little ghetto people who had thin ties up until a few years ago, but they ran out. So I had some made: I bought a lifetime supply in ten minutes.

What do you do to relax?
Play the harpsichord or read.

Do you ever take tranquilizers?
Sleeping pills occasionally.

What about vitamins?
I occasionally take one or two. I don't use them systematically, which I probably should. I received a marvelous letter from a woman saying that I could do without glasses if I took vitamin B-something.

Did it work?
No, I wear contact lenses. I didn't need glasses until I was about forty, and I really felt constrained by them.

Are you interested in having power?
No, I'm interested in influencing.

You wouldn't like to hold a powerful office?
I wouldn't mind being President, but senator or governor absolutely not. I'd have much less influence than I do now. I am published in three hundred and sixty-five papers three times a week. My show, *Firing Line*, appears on two hundred television stations each week. And I'm not saying anything that's in any sense self-serving. But, after all, if you have one vote out of one hundred, that isn't as much influence as being able to say what you have on your mind to millions of people three times a week. If I ran for Congress and was elected, I'd lose all that. And to get up in the Senate, as a conservative, as a Republican, in the minority, as I would be, and give a speech every three weeks listened to by three other senators, plus the clerk, is hardly influence.

Do you think a strong leader is necessary?
Yes, strong in the sense of affirmative, emphatic—yes, strong as opposed to ambiguous. The leader who is strong is somebody whose principles are either articulated or implicit and who does not doubt those. I'd hate to have a leader who is ambiguous.

Are you religious?
I'm a Roman Catholic, a *practicing* Roman Catholic. I sent my son to Catholic school and he still is a Catholic. I think that anybody who is a Christian and believes in Christianity is irresponsible not to attempt to pass that along as the most important part of his heritage.

Do you think that the Church's ban on birth control has caused people to drift from the Church?
I think that's true. That doesn't mean that I'm against the stand on birth control. I mean that I internally assent on the question of abortion. I am dissuaded from abortion by the Church. I am not dissuaded on the matter of birth control. But, in a sense, I find that I most admire a religion when it is standing athwart history, rather than piggybacking on it. Because it is uniquely a function of the Church to say no when everyone else is saying yes. They're supposed to have a divine insight.

Do you miss the Latin mass at all?
Very much. I think going to mass nowadays is, in most places, an aesthetic ordeal.

Do you go to mass every Sunday?
Yes.

Confession every Saturday?
I'm not that sinful!

SEAN BYRNES

Fashion Editor and Photo Editor

Mr. Scavullo: How did you get interested in fashion?
Mr. Byrnes: Since I was very young I always liked attractive people. In fact, people thought I was snobby. I always liked beautiful people—even girl friends I had when I was fifteen or sixteen were very beautiful blondes with blue eyes, beautiful bodies, tall, and very smart. As I got older my taste expanded to include brunettes, redheads, etc.

I would like to know about changes that you've felt and seen in your own life and the life around you during the past five years, since you were eighteen.
I've changed from a little boy to a young man—from a little boy who didn't know much about professional beauty, clothes, style, business, all of which I learned by working during the past five years, styling many covers, interviewing people for *Interview* magazine, editing photographs and film, working with you. But it was not an easy period.

Do you find that there's too much you can do, that you don't focus in on one thing?
Everyone says that you should specialize, which is maybe true, but I find that I enjoy doing a lot of different things. I don't have any particular need or want to just become a photographer or just an editor or just any one thing. If I could have the freedom to do all of the things that I'm doing now for the rest of my life, I would love it. I would get quite bored doing the same thing my whole life.

What would be an ideal workweek for you?
A good week's work to me would be interviewing two interesting people every day, styling five beautiful covers—making them look beautiful, different, special. After work I enjoy calling up all my friends, saying hello to them, going out to dinner, maybe to a movie or a play or the ballet, just having a nice time. And also, of course, going to a discotheque maybe twice a week and dancing and having fun. And summer weekends I like to go away and rest.

What do you like about discotheques?
I like the energy and escape. It's hard to talk and it puts people into a whole different mood. You have the lights and dig the music and dance, and somehow it makes people looser and it's a completely different world, it's nighttime.

Is music very important in your life?
I love music.

Do you like television?
Yes. I get up and put it on and watch the news, whoever's on the *Today* show. Then I'll take a shower and shave. It's a slow process. I'm not a fast waker-upper. I don't really wake until two hours into the morning, and then I start getting snappy and turned on. But I really do like television. I like all of those old black-and-white movies. And I like sports on television.

Do you go to a lot of fashion shows?
I don't go to that many anymore simply because they don't interest me that much. Only certain shows interest me because I don't think that this is the most creative moment in fashion. I think it's at a slight standstill. This year's collections looked like last year's collections, etc., etc., etc. There's no big changes for most designers. I think there should be some change, some new ideas, some statement made.

Who do you think are the most exciting people in the world today?
Racing-car drivers fascinate me. I think they're incredible, extremely daring. And I always think what a shame that all the most attractive bachelors in the world are dying in racing cars—all these poor girls are losing such beauties. It's such a crazy thing to race at so many miles an hour. But, still, I admire the way they play with their lives, their dangerous living.

Would you like to play with your life?
No. I do love fast cars. By the way, I also admire scientists very much.

What women do you think are exciting or interesting?
I think Martha Graham is exciting. And there are lots of actresses that I love but I don't want to just mention any one. I love beautiful women. I happen to like Bianca Jagger a lot. I suppose I admire most women who have a position in life, that make a statement, that do something with their lives, and no matter what people say, they just push forward. I like a woman who can take a stand. I don't like little birds like in Ibsen's *A Doll's House*.

What things depress you about life?
Violence, murder, fighting. Prejudice is depressing and I find I have to fight that within myself. When I'm nasty to people —that depresses me.

What are your fears?
I fear ever having to live in the suburbs. That really frightens me. I would rather be dead. Another fear is that I'm just going to be the same all the time, that I won't grow. I always like to think I'm growing every day, or every other day, and if not, I get slightly frightened and think I'm stagnating.

What do you do if you feel you're stagnating?
I try to work harder, to get new interests.

Do you have any fear about getting older?
No. I guess I would have said yes about a year ago, but like I said, I went through changes. In fact, in a way I look forward to it because I like the idea of my face changing. I don't mind a few lines. I wouldn't be happy if my hair fell out or my face fell or I gained two hundred pounds. I wouldn't want to look like an old monkey. I'd rather be dead. But the whole development process taking place naturally doesn't frighten me at all.

Do you have a fear of dying?
Sometimes I wish I was dead, but, of course, most of the time I don't wish that, so it usually means nothing to me. If I'm seriously thinking about it, I don't think I'd care to die. I do get frightened on airplanes. And I don't like to think of myself decaying in the ground with all the maggots chewing at me.

How do you feel about the world today, the pollution, food problems, the whole way that the planet's going? Does that worry you?
It worries me when I see Africa being forced into Western civilization—natives having to wear clothes. Pollution, carbon monoxide in the air, the dirty habits of people, that all concerns me, but on the whole I still feel pretty good about the world. Progress doesn't drive me crazy. I think if people care more about themselves and more about their environment, then it could only stand to get better and not worse. And I like living on this earth. I don't want to be anywhere else. I also like living in New York. I like the city. I like to see people on the street. I like the energy that's flowing around. I like to be able to walk around midtown, downtown, uptown or just go out and grab a taxi. I like to be

SEAN BYRNES
Fashion Editor and Photo Editor

able to go into a thousand shops in one day looking at clothes and talking to people. New York is always a very turned-on city.

You seem to have a fascination for clothes, not only for yourself to wear but just clothes in general. Why?
I like to see inventive ideas, I like colors, I like to see how people express themselves in clothes. It's always interesting. I'm not quite sure why. But clothes can change you in a way. They can make you feel good or bad or dull or bright.

What do you think about the way American men dress?
I think that American men have a long way to go in their way of dressing. They're still uptight and forced into traditional dress. On the other hand, they're forced into polyester and all those machine-washable things. And they're not really that interested in their looks. Certain men dress okay—they wear Levi's and Levi's shirts, not purple polyester polka dots. I think Levi Strauss is the best designer for men in America.

And in Europe?
Yves Saint Laurent is the best in the whole world. He has created a whole casual way for men to dress and still look very elegant. You can put on a silk shirt with no collar with just a pair of black pants and a nice belt and go anywhere. It's very futuristic in a way. That men still have to wear black tie is a shame, since women can wear little sexy T-shirts or see-through blouses with their nipples showing or skirts cut up to their ass.

Do you think it's important for a man to be sexy?
I like men's clothing to look sexy.

Is sex very important to you?
Maybe in my head it is, but physically—no.

What about make-up for men?
I don't think I'd like to see men wearing make-up other than in the theater. I think most men are attractive without make-up, so I don't see why they need it. And if they do wear it, it's probably just to look healthy, so why don't they just become healthy naturally and not have to wear make-up?

Do you exercise to keep healthy?
I walk a lot, but I never exercise. It doesn't keep my interest. I just can't do a hundred push ups, I'm not that interested in my body. I just keep thin. I don't eat too much. If there was some machine that I could sit in that would do exercises for me while loud music was playing in my ears and I could dream of something else, it would be fine. But the physical work involved to improve your body doesn't interest me. Certain sports, like water-skiing or riding horses, are fun and they build you naturally. I never go to doctors unless I'm dying. I haven't had a checkup in five years.

Do you read books?
I used to read tons when I was in school. And now, I must say, I'm very lazy. I don't read very much anymore. I read magazines and newspapers.

What magazines do you like?
I like a lot of European magazines. Even though I can't read them, I like them—I like looking at them. But when I think of magazines it's hard to say which I really like. *Newsweek* and *Time* sometimes. I don't see *National Geographic* that much, but whenever I do I always think it's great. I think we need a few new magazines.

Who are your favorite contemporary artists?
I like Francis Bacon, David Hockney and Giacometti sculpture.

Do you think photography is art?
I'm never quite sure what art is. But I think that certain photography is art. Irving Penn's "Street Material" show at the Metropolitan probably hits the highest level of serious art for photography in my opinion. But, as I said, I'm not quite sure what art is.

To change the subject, what kind of relationships do you need in your life? I mean, do you have friends, do you have family?
I love to have friends. I need them. I like my family but sometimes we just don't hit it off too well. I repect them but they don't understand me. They invite me to dinner and when I arrive they've finished dinner. But I love them, and to put up with children is such a task. And they put up with me, God knows, so what could I say?

Do you think it's more difficult for parents to bring up children today?
Yes. I think it's very hard because children now are so smart. At ten years of age they know so much, maybe not educationally, but as far as what's happening on the street, you know, slang, sex, drugs, violence. They know it all. And it's not easy for children. I feel bad for a lot of parents today because it's a tough thing to raise children today.

Do you think that young people are more into drugs than they were in the sixties?
I think they're more into a certain kind of drug in the seventies than they were in the sixties. Then it was hallucinogenics. Now it seems to me people either want to be up or down and that's it.

Do you think that's destructive?
No, as long as people don't do it habitually, as long as it's not something that they depend on all their lives, then it's fine. But if you can't exist without it, then I would say you have a problem.

Do you have any idea what's going to happen in the eighties?
I think there's going to be a lot of creative people popping up. They're popping up now, but they're going to be in full force in the eighties. I have a feeling there's going to be a lot going on. I think people are going to be more daring, more outrageous, more open, more free—freer than we've ever been. So I think there's going to be a lot of good things in every field, and hopefully there won't be any wars.

Are you interested in politics?
I was, but no longer. I can't relate to politicians. I never quite understand what they're saying. They always beat around the bush so much. None of them come right out and make a statement. I'm a very open person. I state what's on my mind, and I find they don't. They're always giving us a bunch of innuendos. So how could I say I like politics? But I loved Martin Luther King. He spoke very bluntly and openly about how he felt. And President Kennedy—who's also dead. Unfortunately, when you say what's on your mind you get shot.

Do you have a philosophy of life or a religion?
I do believe in God and I do have a philosophy. I don't like to hurt people and I try to remain open and to learn and to give. And to be myself. My philosophy of life is: Just be yourself.

DR. WILLIAM CAHAN
Surgeon and Cancer Researcher

Dr. Cahan: The question I'm asked most often is, "Are we getting anywhere in cancer, Doctor?" And one of the most glaring examples of where we're getting in cancer research is an awareness of the environment. We swim in a sea of carcinogens—cancer-causing agents—from the very obvious ones like sunlight and cigarettes to subtle ones like exhausts and industrial ones like asbestos and polyvinyl chloride, and so forth. These are established as cancer-forming agents now without much question. We feel that eighty or ninety percent of cancers are preventable, which means that if we can ever solve the riddle of the environment, we've got a lot of cancer being prevented. However, we have to account for another group of possible carcinogens and other cancers they may cause. Diet, for example, is under scrutiny in an effort to determine whether or not it is causing cancer of the colon, which is one of the most predominant cancers other than skin cancer in America at the present time. We think that in most instances there is unquestionably a diet-connected factor. When you talk about cancer-forming agents you always have to take into account the substrata of somebody's susceptibility. In other words, Is this genetic? Perhaps if you inherited certain chromosomes from a father, grandfather, uncle, and you are exposed to the cancer-forming agents, you could be the unfortunate one. I could eat the same diet as somebody else all through my life and never get it, but somebody else might. So we have lots of riddles of susceptibility, plus the riddles of cancer-forming agents. One interesting point which I think is riveting: natives of Japan rarely get colon cancer. If and when they move to America, the adult Japanese will begin to get colon cancer more frequently, and the kids get it at the same rate as American children as they grow up—suggesting that as they pick up American diet they indeed pick up American cancer.

Mr. Scavullo: Does it get you down sometimes to be working in caner researh?

No. I have a basically optimistic personality. And secondly, what I have learned is to convert the unhappiness that one automatically feels into action. In other words, I go from the concern to, What can we do about it? Instead of wringing my hands, I do something with them. Plus, I have a good, healthy, happy home life at the present time with a peace of mind that makes me feel that I can continue working and not be destroyed by it.

Do you work every day?

Every day, including weekends. Let me tell you what work is for me. I'm a surgeon. I'm a teacher. I'm a professor of surgery at the Cornell Medical School. And I'm a researcher at Memorial Sloan-Kettering Cancer Center. I have a practice in which I treat mostly lung and breast cancer. And the research is my lifeblood because it is what I've done all my life. So on weekends I'm either doing research or writing about it for the medical journals. I frequently wake up at two or three in the morning and write. Fortunately, I need very little sleep—four hours, maybe five at the most.

Do you rest during the day?

If I've done a long operation, I'll take a fifteen-minute snooze.

Do you ever take off?

I take off three or four weeks in the summertime, and occasionally one week in the wintertime, but none otherwise. You get a sense of dedication about this work. Two very close friends with advanced cancer recently came in to see me. And I felt totally helpless and frustrated, and that renews my interest in trying to solve this problem as quickly as I can. Now, of course, there are thousands of people working on it; I'm not the only one.

Do you think you will ever retire?

Thank God, my hospital is understanding. We become eligible for retirement at sixty-five, but we're allowed to keep operating until seventy. I'm sixty-three, so I have to start thinking about it. I hate to, but I do. I had a mentor who was dragged screaming out of the operating room at age eighty-four. I don't think I'm going to get to that point, but I'll probably stay on until seventy, if I survive that long. At that time I may do lots and lots of writing about nonmedical things, which I can't seem to get in at the present time.

Do you have any cases where you keep people alive, vegetating, prolonging their life?

I think that none of my colleagues and I like to prolong hopeless problems. And we don't prolong them—in the sense that we don't give them blood transfusions and we don't give them vitamins if they're going into an inevitable disaster. We keep them comfortable, which is different, and we don't, of course, give them the one charge that sends them on their way. That is, unfortunately, illegal. On the other hand, some people have made remarkable comebacks. Granted, it's not too frequent, but it's the kind of thing that keeps you trying up until near the last, if not to the very last. You give it the go and sometimes miraculous things do happen. We don't know everything there is to know about cancer; some things do happen unpredictably. But, by and large, most people die in comfort and that is very important. With the new drugs for pain, the new ways of handling sedation and so forth, most people, die, we think, with reasonable dignity.

Do you think people should have the right to decide to die if they want?

I certainly do, and some of my patients have done just that.

Are your terminal patients frightened of death?

Most of them want to live, but they're not frightened of death. Absolute disbelief is the first reaction to the knowledge that they have hopelessly advanced cancer. The second reaction is anger: Why did it happen to me? And the third is philosophic resignation. Although most people have the opportunity to do themselves in, it's a very, very rare experience. We must have thousands of cases of cancer at the hospital, and I don't think we've had any suicides in the last four or five years. There's always that hope and possibility that something is going to change for the better.

But we now have a very good concept of what is important to the patient who is knowledgable about his own inevitable death—and that is to keep the door of communication open. Patients in the past have felt isolated by their imminent death. People were afraid to talk about it. Patients had many fears, many things to solve. And the family, the physician, kept this barrier between them and the patients. And now we encourage them to talk and it's made a great big difference in their whole psychic approach, because dying can be just as fascinating as living. It's an extraordinary experience. I know

DR. WILLIAM CAHAN
Surgeon and Cancer Researcher

that's a very macabre statement, but it's true. I had a patient who was a famous adventure woman, she used to shoot animals. And when I told her about her problem because she insisted on knowing, she said, "Dying, now this is going to be a fascinating experience." And it was. That's the way she took it. It's a very sophisticated attitude. She made it that way. She talked about it, she wrote about her reactions, she did everything.

Years ago, there was a stigma to having cancer in your family, like tuberculosis or syphilis even. We used to do a great deal of white-lying, particularly to the older folks and often at the insistence of the children or the wife or the husband. In this day and age, we don't believe too much in that. We may not tell every fact and many people say, "I don't want to know what you don't tell me." But we have much healthier relationships between patient and doctor by telling the truth. It becomes particularly important if you're instituting chemical treatment. You've got to justify the use of medicine if its going to make somebody quite sick and make their hair fall out. You can't give that for just no good reason. So the majority of contemporary patients are well aware of their problem and we no longer are as gingerly or tentative about diagnosing it. And it works better. They are more cooperative. They trust you more if you level with them from the beginning. But we just don't walk in with hob-nailed boots on.

Can you see cancer?
You can frequently see it. You can feel it. For example, the lung itself is a spongy organ and in it will be an area which is hard, and if you cut in, you'll find it's grayish white and firm.

Have you ever performed an operation on video tape?
Oh, quite a few. There are some movies of operations I devised. By the way, I like to think that the present operation for lung cancer is one that I developed. I initiated quite a few others, particularly cryosurgery, which is the use of extreme cold produced by liquid nitrogen to destroy diseased tissue. It has also been applied to cancers of the skin and bone as well as many other non-malignant abnormalities. I worked on this project with Dr. Cooper, a neurosurgeon, who was using it for Parkinsonism in the brain. I designed new instruments and applied cryosurgery to the rest of the body. Some of the tapes of these and other operations have been circulated throughout the profession.

How do people react to being scarred by operations?
It depends on where the scar is. Right across the front of your face is different from on your belly. Most people take it philosophically. They usually say, "I don't care about the scar so long as the cancer is gone." The breast operation is a perfect case in point. We try to be as cosmetic as possible, but you have to have a scar. I think most surgeons are quite mindful of a woman's desire to keep as much breast tissue as she can; it's difficult to reconcile cosmetics with survival.

What about your attraction to bodies? Since you operate, what is your feeling about the human body?
I think that's a very valid question. There are two feelings which are divided by a razor's edge: the aesthetic and the scientific. And it's quite possible to go from one to the other quite rapidly. There is nobody who glories more in a beautiful object, whether it be the body or a photograph or anything

that's beautiful, than I. I have a great love of beauty. And knowing all the Latin names that construct a beautiful body doesn't destroy its sense of beauty for me in the least. On the other hand, when a problem comes up where Latin names are indicated anatomically, I can make the transition in a flash. There is a compartmentalizing of my attitudes on this at all times, and one does not intrude upon the other at all.

Do you discuss your problems in medicine with your wife, Grace Mirabella?
Rarely.

Does she discuss her work as editor of *Vogue* with you?
Frequently. As you may have noticed, there is a fair amount of medicine in *Vogue* these days. May I tell you an anecdote about this? When Grace and I first began going with each other she used to smoke two or three packs a day. Well, it didn't take long for me to discuss this matter with her. And the next time I saw her she wasn't smoking and I said, "What happened?" And she said, "I've quit smoking." I asked, "Why?" And she said, "Because it made you feel uncomfortable." I think if a girl thought that was worth considering, she would be great as a wife. She stopped on a dime, didn't gain any weight, any of those things your're supposed to do.

Would you advise most women to marry doctors?
I wouldn't advise any woman on whom she should marry. Physicians are not, shall we say, always the easiest company. We do have a fair amount of ego. And it makes a difference *when* you marry the doctor. Many marriages are made at the medical-school level only to flounder later on because the doctor suddenly gets a new position in life and the girl he used to think was absolutely indispensable suddenly hasn't grown with him and so it stops there.

Do you ever have fights with your wife because of the fact that you work so much and she wants more of you?
Zero that that transmission. We have—and really, I say this with all honesty—total respect for each other's profession. We're both extremely hard-working, amiable, and there's great professionalism in both of us, so there's absolutely zero conflict.

Who takes care of the house?
We manage beautifully. We have a housekeeper, a lovely litle girl. And we have other girls that come in during the week; it seems to run very well without much problem.

You were married before?
Twice.

Did you marry too young, would you say?
No, I don't think so. I was twenty-seven, an intern. And the second time I was thirty-six. I was married nine years, twenty years, and now three.

Do you think your marriage with Grace is a happy one because she is a strong independent working woman?
I think it's happy for many reasons. I think the greatest one is our mutual respect, which is really total. I am more mature, although I don't know if age always grants maturity. We both have a challenging life at all times. She's trying to do better with her magazine, I'm trying to do better with my research. We lace it with many other mutual interest. We both play tennis, she plays a beautiful game of tennis. We're interested in music and the arts and the theater

and things which make a three-dimensional life. And what is even more important is mutual trust. Peace of mind is the greatest thing in the world. And I see nothing to disturb that—that I can control.

What things really upset you?
I'm very frequently disturbed by a lack of sensitivity or compassion. That's something which I can't tolerate in anybody, my colleagues included. And ignoring reality disturbs me. I'm particularly hyper on the subject of cigarettes and lung cancer. I've told everybody that I'm invited to the best of houses—once, because I usually get on this goddamn subject fast. But here is a preventable disease of the most destructive type staring you in the face. It is a little like going around during a smallpox epidemic and nobody's taking a shot against it. And we have an epidemic of lung cancer in our midst. The women's rate is going up like crazy, the men's rate is already high. And to think it's a preventable disease.

Do you think that "spree" drugs can cause cancer? Cocaine? Marijuana?
There's been no proof of it yet. I use the word "yet" because remember how long it took us to get on to cigarettes. Marijuana is a thing that burns, and anything that burns that you inhale is carcinogenic. But, on the other hand, no one smokes two packs of marijuana a day. I don't think cocaine has any carcinogenic properties.

How about being in an environment of smoke—like, say, spending a lot of time at smoky parties.
The inhaling of other people's cigarette smoke certainly does not help. But, you know, you apparently may have to eat tons of saccharin, let's say, to get cancer. The idea is not to eliminate just one carcinogen but to recognize that we have this sea of carcinogens which can work with each other to produce a cancer. It is saccharin *plus* meat with the saturated fats *plus* smoking *plus* alcohol—who knows what subtle combinations make for the final cancer? Alcohol associated *with* tobacco, for example, is now recognized as bad news. We believe cancer of the esophagus or the larynx is tobacco-alcohol-related; there's no question that alcohol in large quantities with tobacco will cause more cancers. We now know that alcohol disturbs the cellular enzyme system, which may make it more susceptible to the cancer-forming agent that's nearby. We see that in animals now.

What kind of diet do you keep?
I don't drink any hard liquor at all: no martinis, no whisky. I drink wine occasionally with dinner. And my diet is simple. It's got bulk in it in the breakfast food. You know, bulk is a good feature for a diet. It's the craziest breakfast in the world. Grace and I have eaten the same breakfast for three years: grapefruit, natural Quaker Oats cereal with skim milk and a cup of Brim with sugar. I never used saccharin because I never liked it. And every day for the past ten years I've had a chicken-salad sandwich and a glass of ginger ale for lunch. And dinner is *the* meal. We have meat twice a week, but it's lean. Of course, we eat out a lot.

Do you take any vitamin supplements?
No. Somebody once said the greatest source of vitamins in New York City is in the sewers. Everybody in New York takes so many vitamins and they can only be absorbed so much, so they pass out of them and into the sewers. It's loaded with vitamins down there.

What about tranquilizers and sleeping pills?
I think you ought to get off all pills that you possibly can at all times. Any medicine should be treating an existing problem, usually of an acute form. Knowing medicines, as I do, the best thing you could do is to avoid them as much as possible and take them only when absolutely needed. The most prevalent disease in America today other than the common cold is not cancer or heart disease, it's iatroegenic disease—disease caused by the treatment of disease. The treatment is frequently worse than the disease.

How often do you get a checkup?
Usually twice a year. And then time will go by and I'll suddenly say, "My God, it's a year!" I don't think I've had one for a year, but I'm glad you mentioned it because I think I'll go and get myself my usual chest x-ray and electrocardiogram.

Do you think it's dangerous to be x-rayed?
X-rays are only bad when they're used incorrectly. You have to balance the radiation exposure against the revelation that you're going to make about a problem. If you have a question about an ulcer, it's much better to get the ulcer understood than it is not to have the x-ray. Actually, x-ray machines are now marvelously guarded against overexposure.

Do you exercise a lot?
A lot. Mostly tennis and plenty of that. I used to be an athlete in college, and then when I went into internship I never had five seconds to myself, so I got used to living without exercise. About ten or twelve years ago I began noticing that after very long operations—which, incidentally, would take from six to seven hours, some maybe longer—I would really drag for a couple of days. And I knew it was lack of exercise. Now the operations no longer faze me. I feel much better. Everything is better. Exercise is an absolute, important ingredient in a busy surgeon's life. Everybody should mix it in somewhere.

How do you have fun?
Just living. I think that I give the impression that I enjoy every minute of it.

Do you watch TV or go to movies?
Oh, sure. Love sports, love theater, love to go to museums. I love music. I've written music. My father was a painter, an etcher, so I got a few of those chromosomes. I love people, by the way. I really do enjoy socializing, this so-called going out, because I find I bounce ideas off people. Most of the conversations at these parties, which are usually considered to be unrewarding, I find most rewarding. I can usually get down to basics with people.

At what age did you decide to become a doctor?
About fifteen. My grandmother died in my arms and it was a very harrowing experience, and I felt helpless. I had remembered the Boy Scout things to do, but none of them seemed to work. I had a lurking interest in scientific things before that, but this crisis really did activate the idea that I never wanted to feel that helpless on a medical basis with people I care that much about ever again. And I'm glad to say that in five or six instances I have saved the lives of people I've been close to: my two sons, my mother, my father have all had something which could have killed them which I treated in time. So in a way it has all paid off.

PATRICE CALMETTES
French Photographer

Mr. Scavullo: I've seen lots of photographs of you going to costume parties in Paris. In one I think you were with a leopard?
Mr. Calmettes: A baby lion. That was at the Oriental Ball given by Baron Alexis de Rede. The night before I went to a restaurant and there were some people who used to carry that poor baby lion and take a Polaroid and sell you the Polaroid. I took that lion in my arms; I wanted to buy it. And they said, "No, no, no, we make a living out of taking that poor lion out." So I said, "Tomorrow I go to a party and I would like to rent it from you if you like." But the lion was not at all ready to go to parties and see so many flashes and so many people. The first thing it did when I arrived at the party was to pee all over my costume. I was covered, completely wet, and the photographers start to flash, flash, flash, flash. And each time there was a flash the lion grabbed its two claws on my costume. And it got torn. It was disastrous. I was left with the pee and no clothes.

Do you like the simplicity of American style?
I like fashion, but I think that clothes are not very important. It's how you wear them. The person makes the clothes. It's just a certain mood and everything, but it's not the clothes themselves.

What about a man wearing a diamond bracelet like you do?
I think diamonds and jewelry look much better on men than women.

Does it make you feel better if you have a diamond bracelet on?
You know, there are a lot of people who go to parties, who just go out and don't make an effort. They don't want to dress up. I like the idea of dressing up and having fun and I get into those clothes like I get into a pair of jeans.

Do you think the way you dress is romantic?
I like mystery more than romance. It's very difficult nowadays to be romantic, or even to look romantic. Life is much different now, it's not the same speed as the past. Maybe romance now has a different value.

What kind of women do you like?
I like very strong women, women with a lot of character, intelligent women. I like the kind of women who could turn any man on.

What do you think about women's lib?
They are a bunch of very dry, bitchy women, lesbians. I don't think they are clever at all.

What kind of work do you do?
I've done a lot of photographs, mostly fashion. And I worked at public relations for Zandra Rhodes in Paris and Brazil and Gstaad; I took her clothing everywhere. I was a promoter of clothes. And two years ago I produced a musical in Paris that I discovered in South America. It ran for eight months.

Do you get bored very easily?
I never get bored, but I love to travel, and I don't like doing the same thing all the time. I like to go from one place to another, to change my head, because it clears up everything when I travel. I forget my problems. Of course, traveling is not really changing, it just gives me the idea of changing. At the end it's the same thing: it's always a projection of myself everywhere I go. But even the idea is very nice, the illusion that I am free. I'm too young to find a place to stay, I'm only twenty-six years old.

Do you get better as you get older?
I get better, but I have to get really strong. When you are young, life is much easier; when you get older, it's more difficult. You become more difficult for yourself. I don't care about what other people think, but for myself I want to be better and better. I think the only respect is the respect you have for yourself.

Do you drink?
No, and it's a big handicap for me because I'm French and I'm supposed to know about wine. Every time I go to dinner in America, I'm asked to choose the wine and I just pick any wine and say, "This is the best!"

You never drink?
I never have any drink or cigarettes or drugs.

Do you exercise?
No. The only sport I like is riding, but I don't consider it a real sport. I love to ride and I love to walk. I used to play golf and tennis, but I gave them up. I just liked the surroundings, the idea of a club. I would love it if I could go just to meet a lot of people and not play tennis or golf.

What do you think of make-up for men?
The only thing I like is kohl around the eyes. I don't think it's really make-up because it's been used in the Arab countries and India forever. I think it makes the eyes very beautiful; it gives a certain light to the eyes, and strength. But I don't think any man needs make-up.

But all the make-up companies have a feeling now that men are going to be wearing make-up.
People will do anything to make money. It's nothing new that a man wears make-up or even dresses like a woman, it always existed, but now people want to commercialize everything. And everything now is homosexual, that's a fact. Everything you touch is homosexual: your clothes, your sheets, your perfume, the dress of your woman. I think the whole world is directed by homosexuals and you can't do anything about it.

Is there anything that makes you happy more than anything else?
No, there isn't one special thing.

What makes you unhappy?
Everybody's unhappy.

52

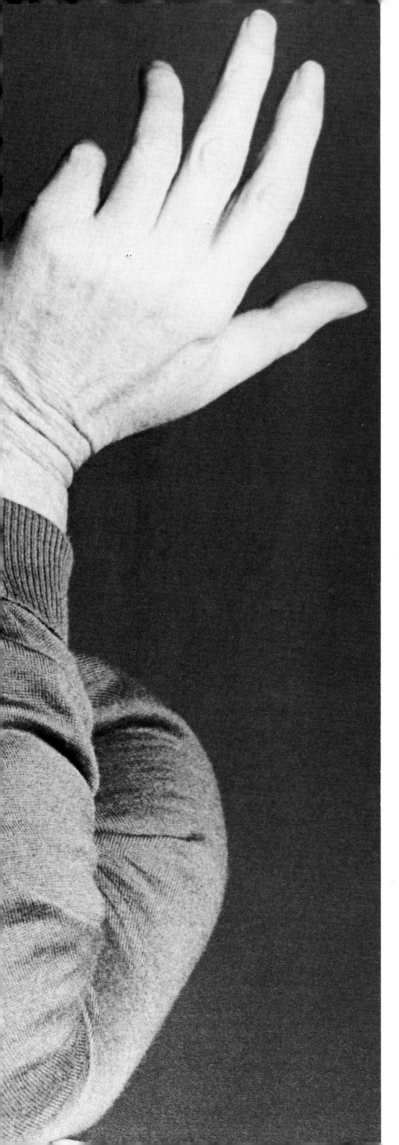

TRUMAN CAPOTE
Writer

Mr. Scavullo: Why did you go to Switzerland for a cure?
Mr. Capote: Because I have a house in Switzerland. As a
matter of fact, I've had a house in Switzerland since 1958.
And I stay there every winter for at least two months. And
there is an Italian doctor called Dr. Foletti there that I like
very much. And he said, "You're here, why don't you just do
this?" And I did it. It consisted of taking a lot of vitamins
and losing weight. But I had actually lost half of the weight
before I ever began doing the thing. And I did a lot of
exercise, walking, skiing. And the end result is that I now
look about the way I did ten years ago. During those ten
years, for one reason or another, there was so much pressure
on me—finishing *In Cold Blood*, starting *Answered Prayers*,
all kinds of other things—that I just sort of lost sight of
myself. And then suddenly I thought, Gosh, this is ridiculous,
you know. I just decided to go back to looking the way I did
originally . . . and I have. Don't you think?

Did you feel unhealthy when you decided to do it?
No. Well, I used to drink much too much wine, and I stopped
doing that altogether.

Did you drink a lot because you were unhappy?
No. It was just a habit. Just a pure and simple habit. I didn't
drink all that much. There was one period of about a year,
maybe even two years, that I drank too much: when I was
doing a lecture tour, something I never would do again. It
was so exhausting because I was doing a two-hour program
five nights a week, back and forth across the country. And I
was simply, utterly, totally exhausted. I used to get on the
airplane and have a drink, another drink, just to bring up my
energy level. Because on those tours you never eat properly;
they really exploit you terribly. I don't care how much money
they pay, it's not worth it. I never would do it again. Under
any circumstances.

Do you smoke?
Not really. Sometimes I smoke one or two cigarettes. I used
to smoke a lot. About fifteen years ago. It's very curious.
Most people have a terribly difficult time giving up smoking.
I just gave it up from one day to the next. Without even
thinking about it, I stopped smoking. The thing I had to
learn, really, was to write without smoking. Because when I
was writing I always was smoking.

What are you doing now, Truman?
Well, I'm just too good for my own good. I'm trying to work
up some naughtiness. I'm far too virtuous.

What about your writing?
I'm writing my book, *Answered Prayers*, and I keep changing,
alternating, switching, adding and taking out. Everybody
keeps saying when am I going to publish it. It happens to be
my book. It's not *their* book. You know, people take on
these extraordinary proprietary attitudes, they get mad
because they want to read . . . well, *no*. It's *my* book. I've
spent my entire life to reach the technical ability to be able to
write that book. And I'm a great technician, if I don't mind
saying so myself. I am. The technical equipment required to
do this particular book is very, very special. And it's taken
me thirty-eight years, since I was twelve years old, to reach
the point that I am actually technically able to do this and I
am doing it, and it's my book and I don't care when it's

TRUMAN CAPOTE
Writer

finished or when it's published. I'm not going to publish it until I think I can't do another thing more to it. I've written one of the chapters seven times. I only changed twenty-eight words the last three times, but I did it.

Are you afraid of people that you might upset with this book?
No, I couldn't care less. And that's a lot of bullshit. Most of the people who go around saying that they are this or that person in the book aren't the person in the book at all. *At all.* It's really hilarious.

Do you like gossip?
I don't consider my book gossip at all. But then, all conversation is gossip. Every novel that you've ever read is nothing but gossip, but it depends on what level of artistry it's done on.

Do you have a regular pattern of writing?
I write four hours a day and that's it. I never write more and I never write less. Usually I write during the period from about five o'clock in the morning until ten, with an hour off between juggling around and getting ready to do it.

When do you sleep?
I usually go to sleep by eleven. I don't go out too much. And I don't watch television. And I don't go to the films just to see a thing. I'm not remotely interested in films for professional reasons. I read a great deal, about five books a week. And I do read certain books that I really wouldn't read if I wasn't a writer. I read them because I've read the reviews and I just want to see what a book's really like.

What do you think of critics?
I don't know any critics. I know a lot of reviewers. To be a really good critic you have to be capable of achieving the same thing that you are criticizing—and there ain't too many of those people around. There ain't nobody. I think the *New York Review of Books* is a big joke, the most boring, stupid thing—and they think they are critics. But if a critic is creative on a somewhat equal basis, then I'm interested in their opinion. I've been very interested in almost all of the writers who have been writing about my book. They have read the chapters published in *Esquire* and they really are very excited about it—because it *is* completely different. And that's one of the things that really excites them, that I have the actual nerve to do this, aside from the technical skill and ability—it's a kind of a moral breakthrough. But my comments mean absolutely nothing unless you've read the whole book. The whole book is quite something. It stands you on your head. But—oh, wow, to actually do this is a form of suicide. And it's also exactly the opposite. I mean, what the hell have I been doing all this time? I've been gathering this material! I was not exactly the kind of fool who just spent my time with those idiotic people. I had a purpose.

Do you think there are any good writers around today?
There's a lot of talent around. Bill Styron is very talented. Norman Mailer. I don't like his novels. They're not novels. I don't know what they are. But I think he's a very good essayist. He could be an absolutely terrific literary critic. He's got a very, very shrewd insight about other writers.

Did you want to be famous when you were a kid?
I didn't think about it in those terms. I started writing when I was twelve because I wanted to write. I don't know why. It just happened. It was like I came down with scarlet fever or

something. One day I just started writing. I can remember the exact day. I had this terrific compulsion to write a story and I did. Then I got a typewriter and learned to type, and I've been writing ever since. And I never thought about it in terms of fame, because I was just thinking about what I was doing—I was writing stories. And finally when I was sixteen I sent two stories to two very good magazines, and they both were bought. And then I sent a story to *The New Yorker* and they bought it. And I sent them another story and they bought that. And they sent me a letter asking me if I would be interested in working on the staff. That was in the heyday of *The New Yorker*, it was the best magazine in the world. So I said sure, why not? But they didn't know anything about me at all. I was living in New Orleans then. So I came to New York and they were very surprised at how young I was. I only looked about eleven or twelve years old; I was very small and very slim. There was a lot of discussion about child labor, it was embarrassing—a little boy working on "Talk of the Town"—but they resolved it. And I wound up working there almost three years. Then I figured I'd learned everything I could possibly learn from them about publishing, so I went back to New Orleans and wrote my first book, *Other Voices, Other Rooms.* It was a great success. And *then* I was famous.

What do you think are the good magazines now?
There aren't any. I don't know a single magazine published anywhere that I consider a good magazine. I have a feeling that *Esquire* could be a good magazine if they got a lot of money and four or five top people working there. I think they could turn that magazine around and make it a good magazine because they have access to a lot of good writers. *The New Yorker* is down the drain. It's so dull and it's getting duller and duller, and the person who's becoming the new editor when William Shawn leaves is even worse than he is. Not that he's bad. He's an excellent editor, but he's keeping a museum going.

What kind of people do you like?
I like most everybody. I don't have any problem. I don't even dislike Gore Vidal despite the fact that Vidal dislikes me intensely. He really hates me, with an all-consuming something. He really ought to go to a psychiatrist about it.

Whom do you admire?
Well, I admire people for different reasons. Some people I admire because I think they are very gifted. Some people I admire for their kind of disciplinarian qualities or their generosity toward other people. I don't like selfish people. I run into an awful lot of people who are paranoid. It seems to be the prevalent illness, especially among semi-failures. They may not be semi-failures in actuality, but in their own mind they are and that's what makes them more or less paranoid.

Do you believe in love?
Yes. I have a good reason to, but I ain't going to tell you.

Do you think that sex and love go together?
I think they go together for a while, I don't think they go together all the time. I think that it starts that way, and then it turns around and becomes something else. Luckily, it becomes something else that is better. Unluckily, it becomes nothing. My own question about loves is: Is it more difficult to love somebody or to have somebody love you? It's never actually equal. You may love somebody more than they love

you, or they may love you more, but it never is actually balanced. I think it's harder to have somebody love you more than you love them. Because you have to work at it so much harder to keep some balance, without hurting them.

Does the fact that you are small bother you?
I've always found it an advantage, especially when I was a child because then nobody would pick on me. They wouldn't pick on me, anyway, because I had the fastest tongue in the South.

Do you like people who are your size or do you like tall people?
I never had an affair with anybody who was over five feet eight inches—that's as tall as they can be. But I don't mind people being very, very tall. I have lots of very tall friends.

The way you speak is so unusual and special . . .
Isn't that nice? I mean, it's really nice not to sound like Cary Grant.

What do you think about getting older?
I don't even think about it. I have a marvelous doctor, probably the world's greatest geriatrics expert, whom I see often. And he says that I'm the only person he knows that actually gets younger every year.

Do you fear death?
That's the one thing I definitely do not fear. A lot of people can't even make a will because they cannot face the fact, but it doesn't bother me. If I walked out of here, went downstairs and dropped dead on the sidewalk, it wouldn't bother me. I would prefer that it be quick. I've been in an automobile accident and nobody can understand how I survived. The whole car was demolished. I had a lot of cuts and this and that, but I wasn't killed.

Do you have any fears?
Every now and then I get what analysts call "floating angst." That's the technical term for it and it's not fear of any specific thing, like taking an airplane, but just a general floating anxiety: you expect something disastrous is going to happen but you don't know what it is. I guess everybody has that now and then, don't you?

Do you have a lot of money?
The other day I was offered double the highest amount ever paid for the paperback rights of a book, which was $1.5 million—so that's about $3 million. I turned it down—not because I expect I'll get more; I just didn't want to be under obligation. All I can tell you is that I'm not living in penury and you don't have to worry about me.

Do you like acting? I saw you in *Murder by Death*.
No, it was boring. I thought it was going to be a lark, fun, but I was mistaken. I didn't like the movie, and I didn't like me in it, and making it was a big drag. I would never ever dream of doing anything like that again, although I was offered a very good part the other day—but I turned it down.

Would you like to be a film director?
No. I've written a lot of film scripts, but I am totally a prose writer—that is the beginning and the end of it. I have all the technical equipment to do that. And there is pressure in back of it. If there is no pressure, then there is no art. A work of art is always the result of tremendous pressure combined with total technique. If you are able to handle the pressure, the volcano, then you get something. The only script I ever wrote that I really enjoyed doing was *Beat the Devil*. And there was a certain pressure in back of me doing that script. Of course, I also enjoyed writing the adaptation of my story *A Christmas Memory*.

What do you think about beautiful women?
I put them in two different categories: professional and nonprofessional. Professional beautiful women don't interest me—I mean, as an aesthetic thing. Nonprofessional beautiful women do interest me. I'm always interested in what motivates them. Because it's a helluva lot of hard work; there's nothing harder than to be sixty years old and to be beautiful, like Babe Paley. That is true dedication. But professional women—one understands precisely why they are beautiful, so it's not psychologically interesting. The leading character in *Answered Prayers* is the best study, at least that I have ever read, of a nonprofessional beauty and what motivates her.

Are you ever mean to anyone?
No, I'm always very kind, very considerate and very generous.

Have you ever been beaten up?
Never. People are too afraid of me.

You've interviewed a lot of violent criminals?
Oh, yeah, but they all loved me. They love me for one simple reason: I understand them and I don't make them feel self-conscious, and within half an hour they feel completely loose and free with me and I know everything that's going on in their heads. Because I know all of that world so well. I spent five and a half years researching *In Cold Blood*. That's more than any college professor who's teaching criminology. I mean, I virtually lived with violence and murder psychologically for all those years. And I interviewed about two hundred and fifty multiple murderers. You should read my mail. Every day I get at least five letters from multiple murderers who are friends of mine.

Do you like them better than most people?
No, but I don't dislike them. And that's the whole secret of why I get on with them. When most people meet somebody like that for the first time, they think, Ugh, this man is a murderer, he's murdered three people. They don't see them as real people with all the little tiny problems that are driving them out of their minds, they don't see them as somebody with "floating angst."

What do you think of the death penalty?
It's ridiculous. Absurd. I think it's gone and they're not going to get it back. They think they are, but they won't.

How do you think we should deal with murderers?
Well, there are several that I know quite well that should never be let out of prison. There's one boy I know who's murdered four people. He's very bright. But he tells me, "If they let me out of here, I know something will happen and I will kill somebody." I interviewed Charlie Manson four times. That's somebody who should never have been let out of prison in the first place. He's really homicidal to the nth degree.

But what is the value of keeping someone in prison for life?
They don't use these people the way they should be used—for research, as medical subjects. They just throw them in there and let them vegetate. These people are living gold mines of psychological information. I think I'm the only person who has really researched them.

LEO CASTELLI
Art Dealer

Mr. Scavullo: How long have you been in the art business?
Mr. Castelli: Forever. I started in Paris, actually, back in '39.
I had a marvelous gallery. There was one room after another
with beautiful velvet wall coverings, facing the garden of the
Ritz Hotel. I started out with a friend of mine, Eduard
Drouin, who designed Art Deco furniture—we didn't know it
was Art Deco at the time. Then war broke out and there was
the German blitzkrieg, so I had to go somewhere else, and
the place I got to was America. For a while I was considered
an enemy alien, being an Italian citizen, after all. So I chose
to become an American, and therefore I got inducted into the
Army. Which I did very gladly—one felt that one had to do
something about Hitler. After the war I went back to Paris
and I found Drouin operating there. For a while I worked for
him in New York. I liked it much better here. I found it
much more interesting. Nothing was going on in Europe
after the war, but here very interesting things were beginning
in the Abstract Expressionist school. But it took quite a
while before I got up the means and the courage to open a
gallery, and a very modest one on the fourth floor at 4 East
Seventy-seventh Street, where I also lived. That was in
'57–'58—it's the twentieth anniversary of the gallery, but
almost the fortieth of my activities in the art world.

Did you study art?
I was born in Trieste and went to school there. I had a
substantial course in art history, which stopped at 1850;
Impressionists were *not* included. That was all of my art
education. I was interested in literature then. In Trieste there
was no art conservatory, no museum. There weren't many
books on contemporary art to be found—anywhere in Italy,
for that matter. But I read what I could. One book that was
very influential for me was Clive Bell's—he was one of the
Bloomsbury group—*Since Cézanne*. That was the first serious
art book I read and it got me on the track of art.

Do you represent the masters of the sixties?
I started out with Jasper Johns and Bob Rauschenberg. And
then the Pop artists: Lichtenstein, Warhol, Oldenburg,
Rosenquist. Pre-Pop, Pop and also Minimal Art are areas I
would say that I dominate. A few years before I opened my
gallery, in '57, I had gotten sick and tired of what was going
on in the Abstract Expressionist field. There were great
masters there, De Kooning, Kline, Rothko, Newman, but all
the ones that followed them were just terrible. I was looking
for something new to handle. And the something new that
happened was Rauschenberg and Johns. And Cy Twombly,
don't forget him.

What's happening in art now?
Andy Warhol is still happening and Jasper Johns is still
happening and Robert Rauschenberg is still happening. Oh
God, there is so much. Until around '68, everything seemed
to be pretty clear and developing along certain understandable
lines. Then a new group of people came up—for lack of a
better definition, they are called Conceptual—and everything
went haywire. Artists have gone in a thousand and one new
directions. The whole thing is very interesting but one doesn't
see anybody emerging who is really major. Some very good
people have come up among the younger artists, like Bruce
Nauman, Joseph Kossuth; also people that I have not had
any contact with but who are very good, like Sol LeWitt,
Carl Andre, Bryce Marden. Probably the most important
artist since the great Minimalists like Morris or Flavin or

Judd is not a painter, but a sculptor, Richard Serra. He is
probably the greatest artist that has come up as a figure, as a
personality.

Who do you think is most responsible for setting taste in art?
Critics or dealers or patrons? Or artists themselves?
A combination of all of those. If, for instance, I heartily
believe that something is great, my opinion, at least to begin
with, is not sufficient. It takes a while for me to convince
other people—some critics, some museum curators.

Is owning an art gallery a moneymaking business?
I have two now, Seventy-seventh Street, and a very large one
in SoHo. It's always a difficult, uphill business because I
spend a fantastic amount of money to run them on a very
lavish and generous scale. For instance, for each show—and
the shows change every four Saturdays—I repaint the gallery
completely. Everything is always pristine. And I have quite a
number of people working for me. There are archives that
are kept. Every work of every artist that I've shown is
photographed, and all the articles that appear on an artist are
stashed away, so that when museums or students need to
know something about an artist they find all this material,
and they are welcome. It's like a museum enterprise. When I
do a show, I never think whether something will sell or not.
As a matter of fact, I frankly never expect anything to sell.
But, somehow or other, they do sell.

New York has very few great collectors now. So you have
to rely on a tremendous spread across the country: museums,
art dealers, in California and St. Louis and Minneapolis,
wherever they are—in Europe, too. It's widespread, but that
makes it possible to survive. And it's always a hand-to-mouth
operation. In the beginning it was a question of a few
thousand dollars. Now it's a question of a few hundred
thousand dollars. But the trouble is still there. I still don't
know from one month to the other how I will get all that
money together to pay the artists, to pay my personnel, to
pay for advertising and all those things that you have to
spend money on if you run a gallery.

When you sell a painting, especially if it's a painting you've
had in your home, do you miss it?
I rarely sell paintings that I have in my home, but there are
many, many paintings that I do sell because they are there
for that purpose. In one sense I'm pleased, and then I'm very
sad, too. It depends on to whom they go. If it is somebody
that I don't particularly care for, then it's particularly
annoying. If it goes to a good friend or to a museum where I
can see it again, really keep in touch with it, it's less painful
—it remains in the family.

What kind of an apartment do you live in?
My apartment is in a Fifth Avenue high-rise building. It's
relatively small but has a very beautiful view of the Park that
makes it seem larger. The furniture is half antique and half
modern. There is a table by Roy Lichtenstein. I have some
Tiffany things around, Art Deco things, a long beautiful
Shaker table in cherry wood, some chairs that go back to
Charles X of France—it's a mixture of things that I bought
here and there. There is absolutely no lighting. The paintings
are all in the dark.

How old are you?
Very old. I'm ancient.

How do you take care of yourself? You look like such a
healthy man.

LEO CASTELLI
Art Dealer

I am incredibly enthusiastic about life. I'm very active. I love what I do, not only what I do in the gallery but what I do in my private life. It's very exciting and it keeps me alive and in good shape. Also, I exercise every morning a little bit, and I'm careful about eating. I don't eat too much. No special diet, but I'm careful. I weigh myself every day and if I go beyond a certain weight, then I cut down. I drink. I do everything, but not too much of it.

What about your clothes?
Clothes are difficult to find because unfortunately they don't have them in my size, but I do buy Turbull and Asser at Bonwit Teller's.

Did you ever have any feeling about being small?
Oh God, yes, especially when I was much younger. Therefore I indulged in sports. I wanted to be, if small, strong. It's obviously played an important role in my life.

Do you find that you have less fun or more fun as you get older?
I have more fun. I get much more out of life, out of people, than I used to. And also I feel more sure of myself. I feel less and less inhibited as I go along. It's not only age but experience. I had quite a few problems when I was young. I was very shy. I was shy when I began the gallery. But when you see so many people you get to know so many people— from all walks of life—so I began to be more self-assured.

How many times have you been married?
Just twice. But I've had many other relationships. My first marriage was to Illeana Sonnabend, the famous art dealer, who has remained my great friend after a cooling-off period when we divorced. More recently I was married to Twoiny and we have a boy who is thirteen years old. My daughter from the previous marriage has three children, and she will be forty-two this year. Just imagine, my age, more or less— that's the age I feel!

Do you see your grandchildren often?
I don't see them at all. They live in Washington, D.C., and I have no real contact with them. I am much too busy. But I'm very involved with my son, who is around and is young and is very charming. I love him. He is my child and grandchild.

What kind of women do you like?
I fall in love with women who are pretty tough and difficult. But my greatest pleasure comes from women who are really feminine. For some idiotic reason, everyone seems to fall in love with those rejecting women. Fortunately, there are other ones who are not like that.

Why do you think that until recently so few women became artists?
Well, there is Georgia O'Keefe, there's Louise Nevelson, who's a big personality, and there are all kinds of good young women coming up. But women have a different type of life cycle. Very few decide to lead a life similar to that which men lead. They have to tend to various other things. They usually want to have children; they, generally speaking, are dependent. In spite of the women's-lib movement, I know quite a few very independent women who still are women.

They remain what they are, and thank God for that.

What's your typical day like?
I get up at seven o'clock because the dog comes and wakes me up. I walk the dog for half an hour in the park. Then I spend one hour on breakfast and reading the papers. I pick up my mustard-colored station wagon and drive down to SoHo. I drive myself. I pick up my secretary, Susan, on the way, and we drive down the East River Drive talking *rigidly* about business. And then things begin at the gallery. All those luncheons. I drive uptown about six-thirty to avoid the worst traffic and I'm home at seven. I stay home pretty often at night because one wants to spend some time with the child and one is also tired. It's a long day.

I wish you would tell me how old you are.
Well, let me say, without saying how old I am, that I was born in 1907. Now you can figure it out.

How many hours of sleep do you need?
I'm very pleased with seven hours, but I can do with six.

Do you watch television?
Just skiing, tennis and the President. I used to play tennis, but I don't anymore. It's too much, too complicated. I am going skiing in Aspen.

Do you see a doctor regularly?
I have a very good doctor, just a simple general practitioner. You can phone him in the middle of the night if you have a stomach ache, and he comes. He is one of those very reliable persons you can always count on. I don't take vitamins. I never take tranquilizers. Never. I don't wait to be sick to go to the doctor. If I feel there is something wrong—God knows, maybe dry skin—just go and find out what it is. If he thinks he really doesn't know what it is, then he sends me to a specialist. Last year I had an operation. I had a very slow pulse, perhaps due to sports, or perhaps it was just congenital, and in certain situations I would faint. Just to explain what it is: you have in your heart a couple of little batteries to keep the heart from stopping. Mine were very weak, and what they had to do was put in a battery—it's called a pacemaker. After a period of adjustment I started feeling much better than I ever did and resumed doing exactly what I did before. At first it seemed a bit odd and I would feel its presence. Now I don't feel it at all. It's as if it did not exist. I am apt to be less tired now than I used to be. The pulse was really getting slower and slower. So it had to be done. I tried to avoid it actually. I was annoyed about ruining my anatomy. After all, you have a slight bulge on the chest. Not much, but it's visible and that sort of annoyed me. I hope that I will see the year 2000. That is my great ambition. Even from a wheelchair.

Did you ever have any emotional problems about getting older?
I had all sorts of emotional problems, always connected with women, naturally, but I never had any feeling that I was getting old. Never.

How's your sex life?
That will not be discussed—I'm a married man. Not in front of this machine.

CRAIG CLAIBORNE

New York Times Food Editor

Mr. Claiborne: I have had a parade of chefs going through my house for this past week or two to be interviewed. They are an awful lot of work—a lot of fun, too, but they do dirty an enormous amount of dishes. The other day I interviewed a marvelous guy named Alain Chapel, who is the owner and chef of one of the greatest restaurants in the world—it's near Lyons. One of his famous dishes is Poulet Bressan Farcien Vessie—chicken stuffed inside a pig's bladder. He tried to smuggle pigs' bladders into this country. And, of course, customs took them away from him. So he got excited about doing another one of his great specialities: calf's ear stuffed with sweetbreads. He ordered calves' ears and they sent him cows' ears—they weighed eighty pounds apiece! He finally made a dish I love. It's a marvelous mousse with chicken livers, foie gras and a lobster in cream sauce on top. It's got ten egg yolks and five whole eggs, one pound of chicken livers. It floats. It floats. It absolutely floats.

Mr. Scavullo: Do you ever feel that you never want to see food again?

No, no, no. Over dessert we were talking about what we were going to make next.

Do you eat a different meal every day?

I rarely eat the same thing twice except some basic foods. I love spaghetti and meatballs, I love chili con carne, I love hot dogs with sauerkraut. And when I'm alone, which I am frequently—I live alone, I'm a bachelor—I'd be out of my mind to make something like Gâteau de Foie Gras for myself.

Do you have any special recipes that are American instead of French?

Of course. I grew up on soul food. I had never tasted a French dish in my life until 1949 on the *Ile de France.* I flipped. I knew I'd finally discovered it. It was a small filet in a white-wine sauce, and in all my life I'd never tasted anything like it. I love fried chicken. My mother was famous up and down the Mississippi for her spaghetti. And I still make my mother's spaghetti, which is not Italian, it is very American—cheddar cheese and meatballs and chicken—and, God Almighty, it is sensational. If I serve this to Frenchmen or anybody, they flip for it. It's good. It's got cream, it's got tomato sauce. I love black-eyed peas, I love chitlins, I love collard greens, turnip greens.

Is there any particular food that you hate?

I hate grape jelly. Can't stand maraschino cherries. I don't really like peanut butter, except in Indonesian and Malaysian dishes. I hate pretzels. I hate marshmallows. There are a lot of things I do not choose to eat.

Do you think that gourmet French food is healthy?

Good food is good food. I am convinced that if you do everything in moderation, you'll have no problem. You might as well eat and enjoy yourself. Americans are obsessed with the idea of becoming terribly slender and remaining terribly young all their days. So they have an enormous fear that if you eat cream it's going to kill you. There's almost nothing that's not going to kill you if you eat it. Clams give you hepatitis; oysters give you hepatitis. Anything smoked gives you cancer; charcoal-grilled steaks give you cancer. Salt gives you hardening of the arteries. Sugar makes you fat—ages you, too. Butter and cream give you heart failure, cardiac arrest. You can't do anything. I've even read that too much

sleep will give you heart trouble. The only thing I've never heard anybody say anything bad about is sex.

Has your doctor ever told you that the food you eat is wrong?
My doctor says, "Whatever you're doing, you're doing the right thing." I get more letters from leading nutritionists in America saying that I'm absolutely right. They agree that people are getting so neurotic in America about eating. And it's so sad.

Do you worry about chemicals in food?
Not really; life is much too short. And I insist on enjoying myself and not being plagued with all these things that plague everyone else. I don't feel guilty about sex. I don't feel guilty about what I eat. I don't feel guilty about what I put in my mouth, pardon the expression. I have no apologies.

How many meals a day do you have?
Three. But everything in moderation. What I eat at lunch or dinner is related to how much I had for breakfast. I don't like coffee, so I combine clam broth, tomato juice, Worcestershire sauce, Tabasco sauce, salt and pepper and heat it up. And I am convinced that the greatest thing to eat in the world is grapefruit; it's the absolute secret to a long life. I'm a grapefruit freak. I take the whole grapefruit, peel it with a knife, section it, get rid of the pulp, season it with a little salt—salt brings out the flavor nice and sweet. It's not true for everybody, but I think that each individual body craves something different. People have weird cravings. I love anything with vinegar. I drink vinegar. My body needs vinegar. It never gives me indigestion. I drink it every morning of my life. I hunger for it. I have this uneasy feeling that I need something, and I go in and drink vinegar and I feel fine. I eat a lot of pickles, and I drink pickle juice. And sauerkraut juice. It's fantastic.

I also like to vary my eating around international foods. At lunch today, for example, I went to a Japanese sushi bar. I had six pieces of sushi because I know that there are so few calories in this. Tonight I may go to a French restaurant where I know I'll eat rich sausage because breakfast and lunch were light. And I know that, so I eat what I want to.

What about drinking?
Too much. That's my problem. Again, I'm out to have fun. But I have too much fun with my drinking sometimes. My tolerance for alcohol is very low. Consequently, if I have four or five drinks before dinner, it will put me into a small stupor. I don't like to go beyond that, because then I feel bad the next morning. But I love drinking.

Where are you from?
Mississippi. I was born in poverty in a rural area. My father was a lot older than my mother and he lost everything the year I was born during the Depression. So I grew up with my mother in a boarding house. When the other kids were out playing football I was helping my mother with the cooking. That was a blight on my soul as far as the entire town was concerned. Then I went to premedical school because my mother convinced me I wanted to be a doctor. Every time I saw blood I fainted, and every time I smelled formaldehyde I fainted. Then I went to Missouri University and got a degree in journalism. Then I spent a lot of time in the Navy—I was in World War II—all that long episode. Had a ball; I just loved it. After the war I went to Chicago, which I loved—it was a wild, fun, marvelous city. It was my first big city— there are lots of funny restrictions in small towns—and my first time away from the family, so Chicago was marvelous for two years. Then it started to close in on me and became like a very tiny town. You know that feeling? Every time you walk down the street you see somebody you know. Scares you to death.

I had a roommate, and I was very involved in my job. I was with the Kennedy family—they didn't know it—but I was working in the promotion department of the Merchandise Mart, which is owned by the Kennedy family. Jean Kennedy sat at a desk next to me. Everybody kept saying, "You should get next to her, she's terribly rich." But I didn't know who she was, not that I'd be so inclined. My immediate boss was a man named Bob Johnson, just above him was Sargent Shriver. I loved Sargent—he was a knockout to look at. But it was closing in on me, that town. But I didn't have the guts to just pack up and tell my friends that I was going to New York.

Happily, the Korean War came along. So for the first time in my life I decided to do something and not tell anybody; I didn't tell my roommate, I didn't tell the Merchandise Mart people; I didn't tell anybody. I wrote a letter to the Navy and I said: "For patriotic reasons, I'd like to be called back into the service."

One night I went home and looked in the box and there was this big brown envelope. I went upstairs to my friend and I said, "My God, this envelope is from the Navy Department. What if they call me back? I better have a martini." I couldn't wait to open that envelope and find out where I was going, but I had one martini, I had two, I had three, and I finally opened it up and it said: "From the Bureau of Naval Personnel to Craig Claiborne: You will report to USS DE352, wherever she may be." It turned out she was in Hawaii.

I went back into the Navy. I sat on an island in the Pacific for a year and a half. Having an absolute ball. I had nothing to do except sit in the sun. I took along a Bible, the complete works of Shakespeare and a long-playing record player, one of the first, back in those days. And I bought all of the Puccini and Verdi long-playing records I could possibly afford. And I had a lot of time to think. I was thirty-three years old. Now, I had heard about a marvelous cooking school in Europe called the Professional School of the Swiss Hotelkeepers' Association. I wrote and applied for admission, and when I got out of the Navy, I went to the Swiss school.

This is the greatest school in all the world. I just loved it. I'd been so unbelievably insecure all my life. I was scared to walk across the street. Scared to death of life. But for the first time I knew what it was all about. All of a sudden I had everything I wanted. I had no money, but I really found myself in that cooking school. And I loathed, I hated educators. To this day I can't cross a campus without becoming terribly depressed. If I go to Yale, I die. Even the thought of going to New Haven kills me.

Did you feel embarrassment about wanting to be a cook, considering the fact that in the United States a man shouldn't be cooking?
It was worse in those days than it is now. But it never entered my mind. In the first place, it's not like that in Europe. In the second place, I didn't go to this school thinking I'd become a cook. I wanted as great a foundation as possible in cooking because I always wanted to write about cooking. I like to write and I like to cook. I wanted to combine the two things. I had no intention of becoming a chef. Anybody who wants to be a chef has to be slightly mad. It's killing, absolutely killing. So I took six months of an intensive cooking course, and six months of an intensive banquet service course. Some guy in school said to me, "What do you want to do when you get out of here?" I said, "I want to be food editor of the *New York Times*." It was one of those colossal things you joke about.

What interests you other than food?
I'm afraid it's sex. But when I'm in Europe I'm terribly celibate. God. They don't wash. Not in the right place. Let's see, what else obsesses me? I'm obsessed with music. When I

get up in the morning, the first thing that goes on is my stereo. As a matter of fact, I spend endless quantities of money on records. I'm so easily satiated.

Do you watch TV at all?
I am a closet TV watcher. I have a set which I keep in my bedroom, and if anybody's assassinated, or has a great stately European wedding, I will bring it out.

Do you get depressed often?
Nope. I got that whipped. I have seen and gone through so much shit in my life that there's nothing I have not endured, and I refuse to go through any more. And there is no circumstance that I know I cannot surmount. I have literally lived through so much pain, so much agony—you know, cooking I got to be the big-town sissy, all those *macho* types trying to get at me. I finally caught on to them. And I'm in sort of a euphoric state, now that I've got the system beat.

Do you have any philosophy or religion?
I believe in everything in moderation. I believe in being happy. I believe in being nice to other people, unless they're violent. Then I believe in kicking them in the teeth. But do it in such a way that they can't get back at you.

Do you care about getting older?
I don't get older. I'm just sitting here not aging, that's all. I am aware of inevitabilities. I see them. I've got it all worked out. I can't express it, but I know what's going to happen. And I'm rather taken with older people. I like people who have suffered enough to make them human. Not been spoiled. I just like nice people, that's all.

Do you like rich people?
I love rich people. I love what they eat. I like what they wear, I like the cologne they sport, I like the cars they drive, I like the places they go for vacation.

Do you like clothes?
I never owned a suit that fit me until I was about thirty-five years old. If I had one great goal in life, it was to be able to go to a tailor. And I've arrived at that point in life. I go to Dunhill Tailors. And it is an absolute joy and delight to stand before a mirror and say, "Thank God, fifty years later, I've got a jacket that fits."

Are you optimistic about New York?
I don't care. You see, I have a lust for life. It's the only way to live. I do not worry about anything on this earth over which I have no control. And I will do anything on this earth to correct something over which I have control if it will give pleasure to my friends or me.

MERCE CUNNINGHAM
Modern Dancer, Choreographer and Director

Mr. Scavullo: Do you have a classical dance background?
Mr. Cunningham: Very slight. I don't think it's necessary.
I have dancers in my company who studied dance with me,
others have a classical background. I think now most dancers
study all kinds of things. It depends on where your interest
lies. And, of course, there's so much more dance training all
over the country than there used to be. And a lot of it's better
than it used to be.

Who influenced your dancing?
Originally Mrs. Barrett, who taught me tap dancing. Her
energy was astounding to me. I was about ten years old, and
this amazing lady did all these marvelous tap dances. I was
so impressed that I'm sure she was an original influence and
has remained so because of the kind of image I have of this
woman. And then, obviously, Martha Graham. I studied with
her before I went on my own in New York. But I suspect I
probably always liked dancing. I can't tell you why, but I
always did. And so when that became what I did, I found I
just continued. It sounds so simple that way. It isn't simple at
all. It's just long hard work.

Do you like to break the rules in dance?
As far as I'm concerned, if there are rules, then one must
look for a way to see around them. Of course, there are
limits to that. After all, you only have two legs—you can't get
around that. When you're doing a step it's not the same thing
as a dog might do, because the dog does it with four legs and
that makes a difference, but that you accept. It's human. But
given that, it seems to me that anything is possible and that
there aren't really rules. I never thought of dance as rules,
but rather, humans are given this kind of a mechanism to
move with, and you move around on that. And the ways of
moving are very limited but the variety within those limits is
endless.

**Do you feel your dance has any content other than the
expression of the body in movement, in the dance itself?**
I think it's about dancing; it's about dancing in different
ways. It does not reflect something else, but it's like a story
or a mood or an expression. I prefer that an individual
spectator in the audience would look at it and decide for
himself what he felt this was. That sometimes is confusing
for them, but they have to make a decision.

**Do you think that you've helped inspire people to be
interested in dance more than they have?**
I think there's more of an interest in dancing, but it's not
necessarily because of me or other people—it's because of all
of us, perhaps, who have been working in dancing. But I think
it's also due to the fact that everybody has looked at television
so much over the last twenty years, and it's changed the
way we look at things. I don't mean dancing on television—
that hasn't been that interesting. But just the fact that people
look: with TV they got used to looking and then they began
to see that they can look at dancing and not have to worry
about it and not think that there was something they weren't
seeing. Two generations of young people have grown up who
have spent their time looking at pictures on television. And
many of them made their own continuity. They could go
from one channel to another on it. They made their own kind
of visual thing. And I think that's contributed to the art of
dancing. Another reason is that dancing is international. You
don't have to know a language, as you do if you were going

to see a play from France or in France.

**At what age would you like to get a student to develop into
a good modern dancer?**
I don't have a school, I have a studio which is primarily for
my company and we do hold regular classes. But if I had a
school, I would like to have it organized for the young, like
ten years old to start. It's not that you can't start later;
Americans have, although now I think probably that the
majority of dancers start much younger than we used to here
in the States.

How tall are you?
I'm about six feet.

Do you think it's good to be tall as a dancer?
It's probably better to be short, because I think that if you're
not the way you are, you're better off. But I have a feeling
that for certain kinds of dancing a compact body is better.
On the other hand, a lot of my dancers are tall, long.

**Do you feel that after thirty or so the body starts to change,
that it loses its shape, tautness, tenseness, the close-to-the-bone
feeling?**
I know that that's a general idea about the body, regardless
of whether it's dancing or something else. But I'm not sure
that need be true. I don't mean you can maintain it forever,
obviously, but that you can maintain some kind of elasticity
longer than that I'm quite sure. I think it probably depends
on personal chemistry, as well as the way you work. One of
the things that always interests me in dancing is the fact that
I thought that if it needed to change, it could change. That is,
I could continue to do it and do what I could do while I was
doing it, rather than think I had to do what I used to do.

What's your day like as a dancer?
If we're on tour, I get up ahead of my company and go to the
theater and work myself for at least an hour. Then I give my
company a class and then we rehearse from anywhere from
two to three hours. Then we rest a little while and we give a
show in the evening. And that goes on every day. Here in
New York, it's much the same thing. I work in the morning
myself, then there is a class, then there is a rehearsal, then
there is often another class if we're not performing.

Do you take care of your own health in any particular way?
I used to smoke long ago, but I gave it up because it seemed
such a bother. I never did very much drinking. I went to a
nutritionist, Dr. Alan Pressman, about two years ago. I'd
always been involved in nutrition but not so seriously as this.
And he gave me a nutrition diet which I've mostly followed.
It's a little difficult when you're out on tour to get out to the
supermarket and get celery and all those things. But I more
or less like what he put me on, so it's not a problem. He gave
me a lot of possibilities and I just picked one because I
generally have the tendency to get the simplest possible thing.
For breakfast it's granola and a grapefruit. Then two or three
hours later I have a banana. For lunch some lettuce and
some juice and some cheese. And then two or three hours
later an avocado, and then, around five or six o'clock, some
fruit and some sunflower seeds, and then around eight
o'clock or whenever, dinner. And dinner is not terribly
restricted: he said vegetables, which I like, so it's no problem,
and some salad and some kind of fish. Mostly it's a question
of not having stimulants. I can have herb tea, which I'm not
very fond of.

JEAN-LOUIS DAVID
French Hairdresser

Mr. Scavullo: You recently opened your first salon at Bendel's. How do you like New York?
Mr. David: I love the life here. And I love the possibilities for the future here, because in Europe we don't know about our future. I have fantastic success in Europe. I have ten beauty shops in Paris and Milan, you know, but the political direction there is anti-capitalist. So we don't know what will happen tomorrow. America is the one place in the world where we are sure of the future.

How long have you been doing hair?
Twenty-five years. I started when I was very young, about sixteen years old. My parents were hairdressers and my grandparents were hairdressers. And very good hairdressers. So for me to be a hairdresser is very easy. It's normal, it's natural. It's not a job for me. It's my life.

Do you think being a hairdresser is a masculine trade?
It's certainly a feminine business. But all men have a certain feminine part.

Are you married?
Two times.

Were they models?
My first wife was not a model, but she's a very beautiful woman, the most beautiful woman I know. She is the manager of a very important designer in Paris. My second wife, Danielle, was a model but she's not working now. She used to work with me, she was in charge of engineering all my organizations and my school.

Do you think it's good for the husband and wife to work together?
It's not good. If your wife is without personality, she always accepts what you say, but if your wife has a personality and she's always working with you, she cannot be herself. It's better if she has her own life, her own work, the possibility to be what she wants to be and do what she wants to do. And it's better for family life because after work you have a real meeting, she has something to say to you about what she was doing during the day. Since I stopped working with Danielle it's really better. We are very close, we both love fashion, we have the same outlook of life.

What's your favorite type of a woman?
A woman who is free. Not because she has a social position but because she's really herself and loves to be an attractive woman. I didn't say "sexy," I said "attractive." That's my type of woman. And it's the type of client we have in our beauty shops. And age is not important. Sure, I prefer young girls because it's easier for me to make them attractive. But I think that for a woman to be attractive she must want to be attractive. That is most important. It is more of an intellectual way to give beauty—and I love beauty. But I hate beauty or fashion that is just for the Establishment. When beauty's limited to select people, to the chic, it is nothing. I think that beauty is inside of people, it is—I don't want to say it's natural, because natural is not beautiful, but between very natural and very chic is something real. And for me the most important thing is something real. A real beauty doesn't need fashion. She is always beautiful and I am attracted by real beauty, sure. But at the same time, beauty is my business, so I'm really impressed by a woman who is not beautiful, but with make-up, hairdo, clothes, how she walks and how she speaks, she becomes the most beautiful woman in the world.

All the movie stars we have loved are like this—in the beginning they were not beautiful and one day they became fantastic.

Do you think that beauty takes a lot of work?
A lot of work, but this is not really natural, it's not real. And perhaps it's better that a woman doesn't work so much to be beautiful, but really enjoys herself. I think the future of beauty is more psychological than in the way make-up or hair is done. We are working now to understand psychologically from where beauty comes and why people attract other people. This is certainly the future, new way, for fashion, for beauty, for hairdressers. You know, people who enjoy what they are become more beautiful because they accept themselves. Most people don't accept what they are. They say, "Oh, my nose is too long, my head is too large." And I think that in the future the most important thing will be to give to girls, or men, the possibility to be sure of what they are, and then they will look more beautiful, be more attractive and enjoy life more. You know, if we are good in the beauty business, as hairdressers, it's because we understand the woman and we don't work from fashion, we work from the *feeling* of the woman—and that is why we have success.

What about the feminist movement?
I am not racist and I don't understand why women want to be. You know, if the woman belongs to this kind of movement it's because she feels in a low place in society. I don't understand this, because I give woman the same place as man. I cannot understand this type of revolution, because there is no revolution to make. We accept women working in business. I think they are equals. I think that a man is stronger than a girl, but in muscles, not in brains. So for me this movement is not important, because it doesn't need to be, *for me*. This is very personal and I know that in society there is a problem because we live in modern times with an education from the nineteenth century—we are all people from the last century.

Do you like power?
I have power, a lot of power. I think that it is very important to have power to run a company. You must fight to have power and to keep your power. In Europe there is a socialist revolution. Then who keeps the power in the company? Is it the social organization or the capital investors or the manager? But that is in business. Power is very important in business and even more important in a creative business. I don't like power in my private life. I don't want power over my kids, over my mother.

Are you working for money's sake or are you working for the beauty of the world?
I don't work for other people, I work for myself, for my own satisfaction. I don't think I work for money. I don't need a lot of money. Some money, yes. I like luxury in life and a very easy life. I like my apartment, I like my Bentley, I like my Rolls-Royce, sure. But I don't work for those things. I work for myself because I think it's very important to prove to yourself that you are good, that perhaps you are the best. There is competition in my life, and I think competition is very important for a man, especially in my business, because it makes you try to do something new in fashion. What is fashion? Fashion is change, movement.

JEAN-LOUIS DAVID
French Hairdresser

Can you describe your day?
I am top manager and I have a lot of companies and I need to be relaxed. I need to enjoy myself, to feel perfectly well, to have time to do sports. The most important thing for my business and for my private life is that I feel good. I also need to have very good relations with the people running my business. And if I work too much, I am always nervous, I give people a very hard time. My business is doing better than ever because I am more relaxed. I don't work as much, I am very far from the problems. Therefore my outlook on the problems is better. That is why I need a lot of vacation time. I need to be really free. I need to walk in the street to see how people look, what they want. I need to have time to have lunch with my kids, to dance with my daughter, water-ski with my son. And if my wife wants to go to a movie with me in the afternoon, I must have the possibility to go to the movie. This is really a European idea of a manager. It is completely different in the States. In the States, a business-man thinks if he is not at the office, somebody will take his place. In Europe a good manager is always suntanned. In a good organization the manager doesn't have to be in the factory. And he has time to relax and get new ideas, to dream. In Europe we have more opportunities to dream, but I love to work in the States because you give reality to a dream. But I don't want to become completely American, all business, you know. Don't think that I don't work hard. I work very hard, but I protect myself. And I think that in fashion and beauty, in businesses that are *for* people, we must love people. Business is business but you must love people. If you don't love people there is nothing.

Do you have any plans to do anything else besides running your salons?
I like photography. It's a fantastic hobby for me. I'd like to do a movie. I do photos for my company because I need a lot of photos of girls and I cannot pay a very good photographer. So I do it myself and I think it's better.

Do you ever get depressed or unhappy?
There were bad moments in my life. It was hard to turn forty years old. Thirty was not a problem for me. I was working a lot and I was not thinking about my life. But when I turned forty I went to Maxim's with a lot of friends for my birthday and I said, "I'm forty years old now and it's finished. I cannot be attractive, I cannot give something, I'm an old man." Now I've decided to be a *dirty* old man. It's easier for me now because I understand some things about getting older, which is harder for Europeans than Americans. In the States you have a different feeling about life; there is always possibility. In Europe, old people are old people; old people are very sad. In the States, old people are really incredible; they are alive and going strong. Now I understand that if you feel young, you are young. I feel younger than before.

Do you get wiser as you get older?
I think I was always very intelligent.

Do you ever think about death?
I know one day something will happen, but I don't think about it. And I think it is normal.

Are you concerned about your health?
When I was forty I stopped smoking. I was smoking three packs a day. At that dinner at Maxim's I said, "Look, this is the last cigarette." And that was the last cigarette. And I really feel better. I do a little gymnastics; I like to exercise. I'm very good at water-skiing, always in competition with my son. And I love massages.

Who cuts your hair?
I am so expensive a hairdresser, I don't make enough money to pay myself. No, I cut it myself because I don't like to be sitting at the hairdresser's. For most people it's nice because when you are in a beauty shop you are relaxed, but for me it is impossible. I have my scissors in the bureau and I cut my own hair—one side is shorter than the other.

What do you think about men's hair styles today?
We cut men's hair with a technique that is for women, but that is nothing new. We cut a little shorter now than during the hippie movement when all men's hair was longer. That was something important. Now there is nothing important. If you prefer short hair, you have short hair. If you prefer long hair, you have long hair. Fashion has become very free. The new fashion is to not have fashion.

Do you think that men will start wearing make-up?
I think there is a way, and why not? But it's absolutely not like the traditional concept of make-up for women. The feminine products try to transform the face. I think men's products should make you good-looking, but not transform you. It's possible now to give men a good tan and perhaps a little cheek shadow. But it must be really simple. No eyeliner. But I think that it's very important for the future to accept the idea of make-up for men because it's a problem that we don't accept this idea. Why can't we accept it? Because we have education from the last century.

Do you wear any cologne?
Monsieur Chanel.

Do you like to wear jewelry?
No. But I love to give jewels. It's always fantastic for a man to make a gift of jewels to a woman.

What type of clothes do you wear?
Yves Saint Laurent. I go into the Saint Laurent boutique once a year and say, "I want this and that, that, that, that." They make a big bag, I pay and it's finished. And I love to go to flea markets and American Army-Navy shops. Then I mix everything. I think it's fantastic that men now have the possibility to be different. Before, you were a hippie or you were traditional. I love to change, to be completely different from day to day. Perhaps I'm good at fashion because I don't like to always be the same. I always like to be new.

What do you dislike?
Anyone not intelligent. I love intelligent people, clever people, and in that sense I know that I am not really a good person because I don't accept people who are not clever.

What was the worst time in your life besides hitting forty?
The best time is always—I hope—tomorrow.

Do you have any plans for retirement?
Yes. At one hundred I want to go to Hawaii.

MORTON DOWNEY
Retired Singer

Mr. Downey: I just came from my doctor—Dr. Antonucci. He's supposed to be the number-one internist in America. He's seventy-two years old now, and he's been my doctor for about thirty years. He's the doctor for IBM; he's the doctor for the Mellons; he goes to Paris once a month for the Duchess of Windsor. He took care of the Duke.

Mr. Scavullo: How often do you have a checkup?
Twice a year.

Are you ever sick?
Thank God, not much. I've been very tired, though; I'm on some pills for high blood pressure that eliminate the potassium in your system. And potassium is important because if you go below a certain level you're so goddamn tired you don't know what to do. All you have to do to correct it is eat bananas or apricots.

Is your weight a problem?
It has been a problem ever since I started making money.

Did you make a lot of money from singing?
I made big money singing. But you can have a tremendously high income and wind up at the end of the year with damn little because of taxes, so I started looking for other things to get into. And I got into real estate here in New York. And I had a good guy steering me—Joe Kennedy. And I went into other things, stocks. So I did all right, thank God.

When did you start singing?
Before you were born! I started in 1925 with Paul Whiteman, then I went with Ziegfeld, and I went into night clubs and vaudeville and all that sort of thing. And I went over to England to work; the first time I sang on the radio was on the BBC. And I got so damn much mail. I thought, Jeez, this is for me, because you get a hell of an audience right away, you know? So when I came back I made a deal to go on CBS, on what they call a house show: no sponsor. And I opened in a night club in the Delmonico Hotel. And I was there three weeks when I got a sponsor: Camel cigarettes. And I went on radio for Camel, stayed a couple of years. And then I had a spell for about three or four years when it was rough. I couldn't get a radio show. And one night a guy came into the club and he wanted me to make a test show for Coca-Cola. I said, "Sounds good"—because it started with a *c* and the only other successful show I had was Camels. I thought, Jeez, if I get another one of those . . . Well, I got a year's contract, and I stayed with Coca-Cola for thirty years.

Do you drink Coca-Cola?
Sure. Too much.

Do you like being retired?
Oh, sure, I have enough things to keep me busy all the time. I catch up on a lot of reading, number one. I just got back from Mexico. I was down there ten days and I read twelve books. God, when I get interested in a book I can't put it down; I don't do much sleeping a lot of times.

Do you exercise?
Why the hell should I exercise, would you tell me?

Do you play tennis?

No, I'm Catholic. When I was a kid the only ones who played tennis were Protestants. We used to hide behind a hedge and throw rocks at them. I never went in for sports. I wish I had. I probably wouldn't have weight and high-blood-pressure problems.

Do you feel a difference from being young to being older?
No. I never had enough education to be smart enough to worry about getting old. It never bothered me; I worked all the time, all my life.

Do you have a fear of dying?
No, I'm not worrying about that.

Are you married?
I am now. I was married three times. My first wife was Barbara Bennett, Joan's and Constance's sister. We were divorced. I had four kids by her. Then I married Peggy. She died. We were married ten years. And then, after Peggy had been dead about four years, I met a gal, Anne van Gerbig, who I knew down in Florida. I met her again, and I wound up marrying her. She's a decorator. She works like hell at it, which is stupid because she shouldn't be doing it. But she does awfully well in it.

How did you feel about divorcing your first wife?
My wife divorced me. She got stuck on some guy.

What kind of women do you like?
I like ladies.

Who are some of your favorite beauties?
I've known a lot of them. I think Garbo was a sensational face. Hedy Lamarr was a great face. I saw Lauren Hutton yesterday on a television show. Jeez, she's got a nice personality. She seems like a nice kid.

Are there any men that you admire in the world today?
I think that Bob Woodruff, who controls Coca-Cola, is one of the most individualistic and fantastic men in the world. He's over eighty now, and he made that company. He took this goddamn drink and made it the most famous trademark this world has ever known. Not only in the USA, but all over the world. Another guy I like is Sinatra, who gets a lousy press. He's really one of the most remarkable guys I've ever known in my life. He's so damn honest. I know people he's helped and, Chrissake, he never mentions it. Sure he gets a kick out of doing it, otherwise he wouldn't be doing it. But he's more interested in people who are honorable and honest, who are having hard luck or something, than any guy I ever knew. Anywhere. And he's intelligent about the way he does things, whether handling money or anything else.

Do you have any kind of religion or philosophy?
I'm Catholic, but I believe that no matter what the hell religion anyone has, they're entitled to it. I've never known a religion that teaches people to be thieves and bastards. I think they all want you to get on better with your fellow-man. It's like manners: manners were invented so people would get on better with each other. My philosophy is to get on with people and let them believe what they want. And just leave me alone and I'll believe what I want.

ROBERT EVANS
Movie Producer

Mr. Scavullo: Where did you grow up?
Mr. Evans: I grew up on the West Side of New York—
Eighty-third Street, 110 Riverside Drive. In fact, Bobby
Rafaelson lived in the house, Babe Ruth lived in the house. I
led a very unorthodox life, I didn't play with other kids. I
was always working on radio shows like *Henry Aldrich, Right
to Happiness, Young Widow Brown*, I did a soap, I did a
show called *Let's Pretend* on Saturday mornings. I started
around eleven, twelve years old. And worked in almost three
hundred radio shows, and then started in television. I played
the young Earl of Essex when NBC first did live television
shows. Then I was all the way down in Palm Beach with my
mother and father when my lung collapsed and I was
incapacitated down there. I was a kid, I was just exhausted.
And I wanted to live there and take it easy while my lung
opened up again, so I got a disc jockey show down there. I
became the youngest disc jockey in the country, seventeen.
And then I came back to New York, knocked around, had a
tough time getting work. My brother had started in business
and I went into business with him—Evan-Picone, made
ladies' pants.

What kind of an education did you have?
My education is very limited. I went to high school. I was a
good student, as a matter of fact, because I got good marks,
but I never went because I was always on radio shows. And I
graduated and never went to college. Because I was working
as an actor. I made a damn good living as a kid as an actor.
Radio really paid a lot of money for that time.

But when I came back from Florida, I had a very tough
time getting work, so I decided to give up being an actor. I
really had no interest in staying as an actor because I learned
something as I made the rounds seeing these guys at fifty and
sixty years old filling out audition blanks at the Equity
library theaters, at NBC and CBS, at all the advertising
agencies that used to book all the radio shows. And I really
didn't think I was that good, that I wouldn't be filling out
audition blanks when I was fifty or sixty. See, actors are in a
strange field: either you're very much in demand or you've
got to look for work. There's no in between. You're looking
or looked-for. And I'd always be looking. And that's why I
went in with my brother and I was out on a business trip to
Los Angeles. I remember it was the day Eisenhower was
running in 1956, and I wanted to get back to vote but it was
ninety-degree weather. I didn't want to leave the pool, so I
said, "Fuck voting, I'll stay." And that day Norma Shearer
approached me and asked me if I was an actor. I said, "No, I
was an actor." She said, "I have been noticing you around
the pool here, and it has nothing to do with your looks,
because your looks are different, but watching you on the
telephone"—I had a telephone connected right at the cabana
—"you remind me so much of my deceased husband, Irving
Thalberg, that I would like you to play him in the picture
they're making at Universal called *Man of a Thousand Faces*
starring Lon Chaney. I allowed them to use Irving's name
and character on the condition that I would approve the
actor who plays Irving. And all of these young actors they
send up look like young actors, they don't look like they
could ever run a studio. And watching you, you just remind
me so much of Irving when he was younger. Would you
consider it?" I said, "I'll have to call my brother."

I was sent out to test with Jimmy Cagney for the part, and
they resented the fact that she interfered. I didn't think I was
going to get the part. I was packing to leave at five o'clock in
the afternoon when Cagney called me and said, "Kid, you're
in the role. You got the part. I want you." And Norma was
very happy I played the role, and under Norma's influence, I
wouldn't sign a contract—at that time the studios wanted
commitments. I said, "No way, business is the only thing I'm
ever going to do."

And when I came back to New York in February, a friend
of mine had arranged a blind date for me but I fell asleep
with my clothes on. Twelve o'clock at night the phone rings:
"Bob, we're waiting for you." "Can't get down; I'll see you
tomorrow." He says, "I've been sitting here for an hour, for
Christ's sake, I have two girls here and it's not right." So I go
to El Morocco and I meet this girl and I dance with her once
or twice and the captain comes over to me: "Mr. Evans, Mr.
Zanuck would like to talk to you. Over in the corner there."
The captain led me over to Zanuck. He was smoking a big
cigar. He said, "Are you an actor, kid?" I said, "It's a long
story," and I tell him the story of what happened to me.
"How'd you like to star opposite Ava Gardner? For the last
year and a half I've been looking around the world for
someone to play the bullfighter in *The Sun Also Rises*. My
wife and I watched you dancing on the floor and you remind
us of all the bullfighters rolled into one. I've tested at least
fifty bullfighters for this part. The bullfighters that look like
bullfighters can't speak English, and the ones that can speak
English don't look like bullfighters. I can't cast this part, and
I know you're right for it, and I want to use you in it."

I couldn't believe it. I was signed to do the picture with a
long commitment to do films for Zanuck, that's the only way
he would sign me. I went down to the location—I tell you
this story for a reason, it's the great key to my life—and
nobody wanted me in the picture. Ava Gardner was going
with Walter Chiari and wanted him to have the part. Mel
Ferrer, who had played a bullfighter, thought I was totally
wrong. Tyrone Power, who had also played a bullfighter—in
Blood and Sand—thought I was totally wrong; Errol Flynn
liked me, we got along great. He didn't care. The director,
Henry King, was concerned. Even Ernest Hemingway thought
I was wrong. He resented the fact that a bullfighter wasn't
playing the part.

We were shooting at a place called Morelia, in Mexico.
Zanuck was in London. I was down there for two months
rehearsing in the bullring every day with a bullfighter called
Alfredo Real. The only reason he would work with me was
that he had been hit in the groin and he couldn't work that
season. I lost fifteen pounds. I knew I was going to get
thrown off the picture, because I knew everyone didn't want
me in the picture. We had dinner every night, I would sit
alone, no one would invite me, the word gets around—it's a
very uncomfortable feeling. And the director wired Zanuck:
"Everyone in the cast thinks Evans is wrong for the picture. I
beg you to recast part to save the picture." And Zanuck flew
over from London to Morelia, Mexico. The director came
and told me, "Report into the bullring in one hour, Mr.
my suit of lights, my legs were shaking. I knew I was going to
get thrown out. And I walked from one end of the bullring to
the other and Zanuck's sitting up there with the whole cast.
And he says, "Okay, kid, do some passes, do some
veronicas"

Zanuck's in the ring. And put on your suit of lights." I put on —made me go through the whole thing. Then he picks up the megaphone and he says, "The kid stays in this picture. And anyone who doesn't like it can leave." Cut. From that night on I was treated marvelously, everyone accepted me, everything was fine.

I did the picture and I think I did proud by him. Because I got the big reviews, my picture was in *Time*, the whole thing. But it taught me what a producer is. He saw something and he wanted it. It so happened it was me, but it could've been anybody. He had the balls to say, "The kid stays in the picture. Anyone who doesn't like it can leave." I never thought it would affect me in later life but it certainly did. Because I've done that many, many, many times. If I hadn't lived through it and seen it and had it happen to me, I would never have had the balls to do it. On *Love Story*, for example, the director didn't want Ryan O'Neal, and I did. He said, "I won't make the picture with Ryan O'Neal. He's going to ruin the picture." I said, "I'll take that chance." I didn't even know Ryan O'Neal. And he wasn't fashionable then, he couldn't get a job at that time. And the director insisted, "I won't make the picture with him." I said, "That's up to you. I want Ryan O'Neal." And he backed away and eventually came back to me and said, "Okay, if you insist."

How did you become a producer?

We sold our business to Revlon, and part of the deal was that I had to stay full-time in the business. I had made several pictures, but it was a very unique opportunity monetarily. So I went back to the clothing business and I gave up my acting contract. I had made *The Best of Everything, The Fiend Who Walks the West, The Sun Also Rises, Man of a Thousand Faces*, and I was signed to do *The Chapman Report* and *The Longest Day* that year. But my career wasn't going that great as a film actor. I was fashionable for about a year and a half, and then my talent caught up to me. I just wasn't that good as a film actor. I wasn't loose enough. It's tough to look at yourself in the mirror and say, "Hey, you're not that good." I'm not saying that I wouldn't have liked to be a big star, or to be admired. Sure I would. But I didn't have it in me, and at least I knew it. And I had to work for Revlon.

So I hired a person to work for me from *Publishers Weekly* by the name of George Wieser—I knew the only way I could get a foot in the door as a producer was to have a property to make into a movie because they wouldn't want to buy me—an A-minus actor in the clothing business—I couldn't have more working against me to be a producer. So I hired this George Wieser and the first thing he got hold of was *Valley of the Dolls*, Jackie Susann's first book. I read it and said, "This would make a hell of a picture." I wrote to Twentieth Century-Fox and they read it and they bought it for themselves. I was aced out. Then George brought me a book by a new writer named Roderick Thorpe, called *The Detective*. The book became a number-one best seller and I owned it. So in order to make the picture they had to buy me. They didn't want me, but they had to buy me. They would have paid me $300,000 to sell my original $5,000 option. But I wouldn't have sold it for a million. Not that I couldn't use the money, but it was my opportunity to get my foot in the door. So I made a deal with Fox and moved out to Los Angeles—I knew I had to be on the scene; I insisted upon

offices at the studio. And within four months I put together six or eight different pictures. I don't want to sound boastful, I'm just giving you the actual history of what happened.

How many movies have you produced?

I was head of production at Paramount for nine years, and I personally was responsible for and oversaw many big hits and big flops. Among the big hits, we can date back to *The Odd Couple* and *Romeo and Juliet* up through *Rosemary's Baby, Love Story* and *The Godfather*. And it was very exciting because I put together pictures that the company owned a bigger percentage of than any of our competitors. For example, on *The Godfather*, Paramount owned 84 percent. And although it wasn't as big as *Jaws*, Paramount made more money from *The Godfather* than Universal made from *Jaws* because they gave away over 50 percent. *The Godfather* was a house-produced picture. We developed the book. It was given to me as a thirty-page treatment about the Mafia and I kept on throwing $2,500 at a time to Mario Puzo over a two-year period to develop the book. So we owned it for nothing. And the highest paid actor in the picture got $35,000, including Brando. And the picture grossed over $400 million around the world.

Love Story was a different situation. We made it into a book after it was a screenplay. That's the first time it's ever been done—we had the script and I insisted upon a book being written. We brought it to Harper & Row and said make a book of it. I said, "I'll give you twenty-five thousand dollars for advertising if you print twenty-five thousand copies." They only wanted to print six thousand copies, and I knew with six thousand copies the book would never take off. So they printed twenty-five thousand copies and both the picture and the book took off—it was a phenomenon. It was the only time in motion picture history where a picture premiered *and* the book was number one on the best-seller list, hardcover and softcover. And I suppose I gained a rather tyrannical reputation for being a stickler about detail. I've always been very involved in nuance, and not many people spend time in nuance. I was a lousy executive: I was a bad financier, I was a bad budget man, I was a bad employer. But what I did, I think I did well. And I never looked at myself as a brilliant executive, but as a moviemaker.

But now you're an independent producer for Paramount.

Right. I had seven more years on my contract. I said, "I don't want to stay this way." When we made *The Godfather*, as a bonus they gave me the right to make five pictures, one a year. My first picture was *Chinatown*, which was very successful both from the critical and financial points of view. And everybody just resented it terribly because they felt I was paying too much attention to my own picture, not to other people's pictures. So I had a choice to make then: either give up my position as head of the company and just make pictures, or give up my contract to make pictures and go back into the company with a very advantageous deal. And I gave up my deal with the company. I just wanted to make pictures—with my own name on them. As head of production for Paramount I was responsible for fifteen pictures a year. I was involved to a point that I had no personal life at all. My priorities were all screwed up. And I didn't want to continue that way. I was gaining nothing from it except a divorce and a bad back.

How many marriages have you had?

I'm on my fourth marriage. My first marriage lasted a few minutes—I mean, a few months. I don't call it a marriage. My second marriage to Camilla Sparv, a beautiful girl, lasted a year and a half because I was always so involved in my work. I didn't give any time to her. So we got divorced and I married Ali MacGraw. That lasted three years, and again I was so totally preoccupied; I was always working. I was working seven days a week.

Why did you get married?
I think I basically am a romantic. Two weeks before I met Phyllis George, my current wife, I told my sister there was no chance of my ever marrying again. I said, "I don't care. I've got everything going for me, a marvelous home, help, a son, I have everything." Two weeks later I called my sister and I said, "Alice, I'm getting married." She said, "What?" I had her in total shock. Because until I met Phyllis I was very happy at being a bachelor. I don't mind being alone. I like spending time alone.

What do you think about women becoming stronger and going out to work, the whole women's-lib idea?
It doesn't bother me. I understand women's lib. I don't believe in it to its extreme. On the other hand, I don't want my old lady in the kitchen, I want her to be interesting, informed, and I'd rather have her in the bedroom than the kitchen, or in the drawing room enticing me, keeping me interested. I don't need someone to cook me a meal. I get very bored with ladies quickly. If a girl can turn me on headwise, it's the best turn on I can have.

Does a woman have to be beautiful for you?
No, and I mean that. She has to be interesting. I get bored with beauty very easily.

Do you get jealous of your women?
That's my big problem, I don't get jealous. I wish to hell I could. The only time I get jealous is when I'm left. Up until that time I am totally not jealous because—I hate to say it, but it's true—I have such an ego that I'm not jealous. I go to a party with a girl and she talks to whomever she wishes, dances with whomever she wishes—I'm never jealous. But I've been left several times in my life and then I'm miserable. And women love jealousy—don't tell me they don't, it's not true, they love it. It makes them feel wanted. So that's a big fault I have in my personality, I have no jealousy. And I have no right not to have it because I have lost enough women by not having it. And still I haven't learned. I'm forty-six, I've been on my own since I'm fifteen, and I really haven't learned. That's thirty-one years. Shit. In thirty-one years I've been married cumulatively five years. So that means for twenty-six years I've been out there.

Is sex very necessary for you?
Yes. But I've never had a chance to be very horny in my life. I've never been away someplace for three months alone.

Do you care about your looks and your clothes?
No. I'm one of the few guys who doesn't blow-dry his hair. I get dressed in five minutes. I spend no time putting myself together.

Do you go to a tailor for your clothes?
I don't even do that anymore, because I don't wear suits anymore. I have very specific things that I wear, I know exactly what I want. I don't go to stores, I have everything brought to me. I get claustrophobia in stores. I just wear certain colors: black or beige or white—and that's all.

Sweaters and slacks and a jacket. I never wear a tie. Not even when I address the board of directors. No one is going to change me. I want to be what I am.

Do you exercise?
I've never done it in my life. I play tennis and I swim. I'm so bad at exercise that I have a guy come over to my house to stretch me because of my bad back, and half the time I pay him to leave me alone. I hate exercise.

Do you care about what you eat?
No. I don't watch my diet. I'll most probably die at an early age because I eat everything.

Do you drink?
I'm not a big drinker, and I don't smoke.

Have you ever been attracted to another man?
No. A lot of men have been attracted to me. I'm not a very butch-looking type guy, so a lot of guys have looked at me since I was a kid. I have had a lot of problems with it, a lot especially when I was acting. But I was attracted to girls at a very early age. I started very, very young with ladies, and nothing else ever interested me.

Is there a difference between working with actors and actresses?
Lot of differences. Men are basically easier to get along with than women. Men are generally less neurotic, more relaxed. The women are far more ambitious. I think when a girl works in a role she's more dedicated to it than a man. It means more to her, it's her whole life. A guy can do a role and be involved in a lot of other things, but a woman puts her whole soul into her work. So men generally are just easier to deal with. But I think part of the excitement of an actor is his or her neuroses. If a girl is too nice and too simple, she's usually boring on the screen. I don't know why. But think of the actresses who have been really important stars—Marilyn Monroe, Elizabeth Taylor—most of it is their mystery, their unknown neuroses. You see, a guy has a lot of props. A guy can fight, run, jump, drive cars, shoot; a woman doesn't have those props. It's much easier to write a man than a woman. A woman must have layers and textures of mystery.

Would you like to bring glamour back to the movies?
Very much. I'm a big believer in glamour. The habit of going to the movies is really over. However, the desire to see a movie is bigger than ever, and to get people to go to see a movie you've got to give them something they don't see, something that will take their head away from their life for a couple of hours. That's why glamour is very important.

Do you sleep a lot?
I'm a lousy sleeper. I need pills to sleep. I can fall asleep but I can't stay asleep. I'm up at three-thirty in the morning.

Does it sometimes drive you crazy to work with all the people you do?
Yes, but that's what a producer is—you have to satisfy people. It takes time. I've grown up with these people. I've lived with them, and I have it in myself, so I see the frailties in others and have compassion for it and work with it. I'll take all kinds of shit, workwise. On a personal level, I give a great amount of loyalty and if I don't get it, if I'm really double-crossed, I don't forgive. I'm not that way on anything to do with money or work, but on personal things I'm very naïve. I have a strange code. I'm a giver. And when I'm taken, really taken, obviously taken—it's happened to me—*that's it*. I just wipe someone off the slate.

Mr. Scavullo: What are you doing now?

Mr. Felker: My job now is to think up my future. I'm trying to separate the way I think from the way I've thought for the last fifteen or twenty years, and I'm trying to do it quickly and emotionally because I don't want to waste that much time. I want to try to come up with the magazine of the eighties if I can. All right, if it's not *the* magazine, it's some publication, or some way of communicating. I think that *New York* magazine was the magazine of the sixties and seventies. Maybe it wasn't the only one, but we were in the forefront. Our format—which is to focus very tightly on one community and examine what makes it work and how best to be useful to the reader of that particular community—has become widely used all over the United States and the rest of the world. I don't think that standard format is going to change, though I think we have experienced a big change in America. As we have passed Watergate, Vietnam, the recession, there has been a change in focus in what American people think and what they want. The old cliché says that people are always the same, but they work out their sameness in different ways at different times. Now is a period for optimism in America—we no longer have the anti-hero that was so popular in the sixties and the early seventies. It doesn't relate to what's going on anymore. This is a time for the creation of new illusions, new heroes in America—people are ready to believe in something again. This is what I am trying to find. I am looking for what people are going to believe in; I want to talk about that, because I think that's the most exciting thing going on in America today. Jimmy Carter, for example, is a man out of nowhere—no political machine, no money—who positioned himself as a little man fighting against the Establishment. And he became President. He's one of the new American heroes. And we see it in movies, in television shows, and things that work and things that don't work. This is a time when cynicism is going to become less viable. The Nixon Administration shattered all of our illusions about the presidency, and we also suffered a very savage economic inflation-recession. And people learned their lessons: not to believe in politicians, not to believe blindly that whatever our country did was right, no matter; they learned to question the goals of the country. They have learned to question everything, and yet, in spite of that new realism, there is a longing for something to believe in. It's the natural optimism of the American people. They are going to find something to believe in, find new illusions. People need these. And I feel that way personally, so I am not discouraged by what's going on in America.

Do you think there are any great magazines today?

I'm not sure that there can be any great magazines at this point. One of the most interesting publications in its own way is *Rolling Stone*: it's unique and daring and a reflection of a very interesting individual editor. But it's hard to tell, when you're in the middle of something, whether it is really great or not. I think that magazines certainly should be better than they are. We too often settle for just being professional, instead of striving to be great, to do the best that we possibly can. I think we can become too reliant on formulas because we know too much about marketing.

Is it refreshing to be able to change your job in middle age?

No question about that. It's a very good thing to be able, in effect, to wipe the slate clean and start over again. I hadn't planned it that way, but I find that it's extremely exhilarating. It's pretty scary too.

Is money very important to you?

Yes. Money is important to the degree that it gives me freedom enough to do what I feel is important. But it's not important just to accumulate money and to know that it's there. I think it's destructive to inherit a great deal of money. I think it's very bad for society because people who inherit focus totally on preserving what they have instead of being creative and positive in what they're doing.

How did you start out in journalism?

My parents were both journalists and I somehow never thought about being anything but a journalist since I was a little boy, and I put out little newspapers for the block that I was living on in Webster Groves, Missouri. I would sell them up and down the street. It always fascinated me. This is an age of journalism; maybe it's better to say it's the journalistic age, where the role of the journalist, or those in communications in general, has become increasingly important. This is because people don't own organizations anymore; a man doesn't own a newspaper by himself anymore. He is an editor, elected by a board of directors or a publisher elected by a board of directors, which is elected by stockholders. This is an age of managers, in private industry, in business, or in politics—people are elected but there aren't any hereditary kings or dukes. And as a result people only become managers or win political office, get into positions that they do in modern life, because of their reputations. And people in the press have been given great power because they are the arbiters of reputation; they create reputations and destroy them. Thus people's jobs, to a greater extent than ever before in history, depend on the press. So this is a very exciting period.

Also, it's a period marked by the shrinking of the world; people need to know what's going on all over the world in order just to survive. The world has become far more dangerous with the creation of the atomic bomb, and political tensions can literally destroy us all. We have to know about these things in order to head them off. We have to know about threats, not only the atomic bomb, but others such as environmental threats or cancer-producing modern products. So communications is literally now a life-and-death matter. I think that's where the action is. And that's why I want to be a journalist. Let's face it, if you are not a great creative artist, who is creating things for immortality, the only option that you have, if you want to be alive in the fullest extent, is to have an impact on the time that you live in. And you can do that best now, I think, through journalism.

Do you think that in order to survive we have to know every last detail of every murder?

No, I absolutely don't. I think that is a perversion of the function of the press. But, unfortunately, in order to have a free press, you have to allow people to violate it with impunity—despite the fact that it violates our sense of community standards and even human privacy. Sure, it has gone far too far, and is going to go even further. And what worries me, as a journalist, is that we in journalism will not exercise enough self-discipline at some point and that the community—by that I mean the nation in general—will begin to take some of our freedoms away from us because we have gone too far. Because of that, it becomes more and

more important for us to be more accurate and fair and not merely instruments of individuals who are just grinding their own axes. I think that accuracy and fairness have to become increasingly important as the press becomes increasingly more powerful.

This can only be done if the press and the public, particularly the most responsible aspects of the public, constantly examine the press and demand accuracy and fairness. And as a matter of fact, in the free American system it can be done by the public boycotting that aspect of the press that degrades the rest of the press, that part of the communications world that engages in violence for violence' sake or pornography (despite the fact that it's hard to define it in the Supreme Court), in order to sell magazines or newspapers or hike the ratings on television shows. People who feel that something is pornographic, without indulging in legal censorship, should simply not buy those publications— personally and economically boycott them. We could then avoid governmental censorship. Once *that* takes place, there won't be any free society whatsoever and we will very rapidly have a dictatorship.

It would be very hard to recover from such a dictatorship, too, because of the modern means of control. Between the use of computers and the fact that people don't have individual power much anymore, as I was discussing earlier, by having hereditary positions or by owning things, we have all become part of the system now. Power does not reside in individuals. It resides in the system, whether it's corporate or governmental—and it's increasingly governmental. Without a free press to check the system itself, we could lose our privileges and our freedoms very quickly. Because there has also been a decline in other institutions that did provide other checks: the family; the church, although there is some evidence that the church is coming back, particularly fundamental Christian; decline in the respect for institutions in general. After a while you begin to wonder how much there is between the system—whether it's governmental or corporate, sometimes it's hard to tell where one ends and another starts—and dictatorship, except for the press and its ability to mobilize public opinion against encroachments of freedom. That's awfully abstract, but I find it is, in and of itself, a worthy lifetime fight. Because everything is a lifetime struggle. You never really totally achieve your goals.

What do you think about New York City today?
I think New York is poised at a crossroads: it can become the great postindustrial city of the future or, if the proper leadership is not provided and the proper policies are not followed, it can slide back into just an unhappy morass of misery without any hope for its citizens. A postindustrial city is one in which the economy is not basically supported by a manufacturing, the way New York City has been for many years. New York City is strategically located halfway between Europe and the rest of the United States, and with its great port and the infrastructure of office buildings, subways, docks and great airports, and the cultural tradition, we have what is necessary to make New York the great imperial world city, under the proper leadership. New York City is the world capital now for finance, for the legal profession, for communications, for marketing, for the creation of taste, which can only be done when you have a critical mass of tastemakers acting on each other in a competitive way that

keeps them sharp and always advancing. Tastemakers can be great artists, great novelists, or someone who creates great advertising or great fashion.

Do you see any great leaders around New York?
We have a paradox here in that New York is, in a way, the best example of a working democracy in the United States because we have so many different pressure groups, ethnic groups, economic groups that make themselves heard and get their share of the pie and their share of the action in terms of political power. This is a marvelous thing on one level; on another level these groups cancel each other out, and as a result leadership becomes very difficult except in a period of crisis. Then, when you face absolute disaster, the groups can pull themselves together for a short period of time, and something happens. The question is, Can this great working democracy of ours really provide a consensus or will it paralyze itself by conflicting views? All of these are questions I can't answer, but I think we're going to begin to see the answers within the next decade.

Do you travel a lot out of New York? Do you have a country home to get away?
I travel quite a bit to other parts of the country, particularly to the West Coast, and I go to Europe quite often. And, yes, I go out to the Hamptons. But the Hamptons are just a summer camp for adults. It doesn't have much intellectual influence on the city. It's just more of the same.

You don't enjoy going to real country?
I love it. But I am a journalist and I like to go where things are happening. I am constantly seduced by pure action.

What do you do when you want to rest yourself?
I'll just go away someplace, any place where it's hard to get a telephone call through, and stay there for ten days or two weeks.

What's your day like?
I wake up shortly before seven and I read for two or three hours; then I begin to take telephone calls. If I don't have a breakfast appointment, I'll begin having appointments about ten-thirty. It's a rather flexible day because I usually work until eight o'clock at night. I think it's a hangover from working on a morning newspaper, where you didn't come in to work until ten or eleven o'clock and you always spent the morning really going over the day's newspapers fairly thoroughly—the New York morning papers plus the Washington *Post* and whatever magazines came out that day.

Do you care what you eat?
I've begun to be very concerned about things that I eat. I try to avoid junk foods and to have foods that are fresher, more natural. I try to stay away as much as possible from red meat because, as much as I love it, it's perfectly apparent that it is not all that good for one.

Do you smoke at all?
No, I've never smoked. I got sick smoking cigarettes when I was seven years old and never could stand it again.

What about liquor?
Well, I don't owe myself any drinks; I'm not against it. But I don't do much drinking because I really don't like to be handicapped the next morning by being fuzzy.

Do you have any interest in clothes?
I do. But I'm very traditional about that. I've had my suits made at the same tailor since the early fifties, my shoes made by the same shoemaker and my shirts by the same shirtmaker

80

—all in London. And I haven't changed where I've gotten anything except sportswear since the early fifties. It's kind of ludicrous, but I did a story on London in 1954 and I got to know these places. I may not go back for a year to a year and a half, and by the time I get enough fittings, my weight will go up and down—it can be a ludicrous process, but since I've been going through it for so long it doesn't make any difference.

Does getting older worry you? Dying?
There are many things that I want to accomplish and I don't want to run out of time. I would like to start another great magazine. Maybe I would like to start a newspaper. At some point I want to write a book. But I'm not ready to do that yet because I feel it should be useful to people, not just a self-indulgent way to talk about my great and glorious career. True art should be instructive, even if it's just to tell you what the truth is. And I'm not sure that I know what the truth is at this point. I know what I think is accurate, but the real meaning of something keeps changing in my mind as I think about it.

What do you think about women in the world today?
All the energy is coming from women. This trend will continue as women become more important economically and politically. More and more women have to work because of inflation, but work is not really new for women; what is new for women is the chance to be leaders. This is an egalitarian age, and women want to be equal with men, they are *demanding* it. And when you get any group that is making demands and thrusting forward the way they are, that creates excitement. At some point the role of men will need to be reanalyzed because to a large degree the role of men has been altered significantly and, perhaps, permanently by the emergence of women in leadership positions. Men are confused, because men have not really been culturally conditioned to know how to react to the woman as aggressor and the woman as leader. And it causes severe psychological damage, confusion and acrimony. Men have to come to grips with that—to work out a new philosophy that is simultaneously aware both of men's natural biological strengths and nature and of women's new position in the world. And I don't think that we really have worked that out yet. The question really is, Will there be a backlash which will wipe out a number of these women's gains? I personally think that would be very damaging for men because, as captors of captives, we will live with severely dangerous illusions that can kill us.

Do you personally feel comfortable in the company of women who are in leadership?
I find them the most fascinating people in the society. Endlessly fascinating. Very sexy. In fact, I think they're the sexiest. I think that women who are simply sex objects are increasingly less sexy.

Are you married?
I've been married twice; I hope I can get married again. But no more. Just one more time. I've never had any children, though I love them. I'd love to have children. I think about it a lot.

What happened with your marriages?
The first one was just the wrong time; I got married too young. The second time our careers took us in different directions. We were married for seven years. She was an

actress and she was away all the time making movies. You really don't have a marriage if you're not together. After a while the bonds of marriage become eroded and then there isn't a marriage anymore.

I assume you don't like being alone very much.
I don't mind it. I'm not alone very much, but I can be alone for long periods of time, and I have been. Sometimes when you're absolutely busiest you are totally isolated because you don't have any really deep human contact. You just have formal contact, and then you might as well be alone.

What about beauty in women?
Beauty is very important, but beauty is so transitory. In human terms, people change, and your own concepts of beauty change. In the end the most important thing is the spirit of the person. That begins to dominate your vision. Someone who can be just ordinary or plain or routine in her looks becomes radiant in your vision. Or, someone who may be very beautiful to others can become very detestable, and you begin to see that visually. At least I do. I'm a very visual person. I tend to get meaning from the way things look. I believe very much in interpretation through my eyes.

What was your feeling about Marilyn Monroe?
She was very vulnerable but increasingly terrifying to look at as the world and she combined in destroying herself. She, for some reason, didn't know enough to put herself in another path. She really became a parody of femininity and sexuality. At the same time there was this increasing awareness of her vulnerability, of the pathetic aspect of her life. Even before she died it was almost too painful to look at her. I remember seeing Marilyn Monroe in *Some Like It Hot*, the last really good movie she was in, and she was just crossing that line into becoming a painful parody with a pathetic quality showing through, still being very kind of exuberantly exciting as a woman. You saw the transition in that movie. It was really terrifying to see what was happening to her become more and more apparent.

In person or on the screen?
On the screen. Her public image was what she was. You don't have to know anybody to get some meaning out of his life. I think that what politicians, for example, or public people, in general, are in private is meaningless. It's what they are in public that counts—because those are the actions that have significance for the rest of us. We can be fascinated by their personal life, but it really doesn't mean anything if somebody is a monster publicly and is good to his wife and kiddies privately. Richard Nixon may have the love of his daughters, but he was destroying certain fundamental things about the United States.

What are your feelings about gossip?
I think that gossip is part of human exchange. It's not only what people want to know, but what they need to know in order to get along in the world. It simply depends on how you define gossip. I'm not horrified by gossip; I think that we just have to know what we're doing and we shouldn't gossip just to be vicious.

Do you have dislikes?
I dislike sham and hypocrisy. I hate disloyalty. I hate dishonesty. I hate treachery in people.

What qualities do you like?
I like people who are open and honest and creative, and who make great contributions to the world around them.

MILOS FORMAN
Movie Director

Mr. Scavullo: First of all, you're from Czechoslovakia, right?
Mr. Forman: That's correct.
What is film directing like in Czechoslovakia?
Actual film directing is the same all over the world, but how you get to it and whom you deal with before you are making your film, that's where the differences are. And you can't really generalize about these things because, for example, the freedom one has to make a film depends entirely on the people who are in power to decide which film is going to be made. And if these people are open-minded, liberal and intelligent, then everything's possible. As it is very often in countries like Czechoslovakia, people are replaced and the next day there is somebody who is narrow-minded, silly, stupid, and then nothing is possible. So that's a frustration. Otherwise, the good thing about that system is that since they don't give a damn about commercial success because the Communist government considers film as a part of an ideological weapon, propaganda, they don't ask that films make money. But, of course, they are imposing their own ideas and ideology on what the film should be about and what kind of message it should have. And as I said, in the hands of intelligent and liberal people that can be very creative, and in the hands of narrow-minded people it can be totally destructive.
Did you study directing in Czechoslovakia?
No, I studied writing. I started as a screen writer. But like every screen writer, I wanted to finally direct my film myself.
What films did you direct in Czechoslovakia?
I didn't do many films. I did *Les Pires, Loves of a Blonde, Fireman's Ball* and *Competition.*
Do you prefer American democracy to Communism?
I have learned one thing—politicians all over the world are using us naïve people for their own purposes. I didn't participate in this game in Czechoslovakia and I don't want to participate in it any place in the world.
Do you miss your country?
Sure, I miss my country because I spent thirty-five years there. I can't just dismiss that many years. I spent my childhood there, I have my friends there, I have my children there.
Were you married?
I was married twice there.
Are you divorced now?
No, I am separated from my second wife but we are very good friends.
Do you see your wife or your children?
They were allowed to visit me once for the first time since I left Czechoslovakia in 1969, for ten days. And that's about it.
Do you go back and forth to Czechoslovakia?
I don't go because I don't have guarantees that I would be able to come back here without problems.
How did you get out?
It was rather easy—I had a contract with Paramount, so I came more or less officially or legally. And when I finished my business according to the contract, I didn't go back.
What do you think of the film industry in America?
I think the American film industry is the healthiest, the most versatile, the best—absolutely the best.
Which was your first American film?
It was called *Taking Off.*

MILOS FORMAN
Movie Director

When you direct a film, do you have to believe in what the film is saying?
Yes. That's why I make so few films because I am too lazy to spend a year or two of my time on something I don't believe in, something that is just a source of bread.

What do you think about fantasy in films and glamour and things that are not real?
Every once in a while I love to see such a film. It all comes in waves for the audience, too. Suddenly they want to see something very real. And then suddenly they want to see total fantasy and dreams. Then they want to see blood and violence.

Do you find a big difference in working with American actors?
I think American actors are the best. I guess it's the pressure under which they are all the time. In Europe, even in France and Italy, if an actor establishes a certain level, it's that way forever. Once you become a star in the theater or films in Europe, you're like a national monument. Untouchable. Here the actors know very well that today they are up and tomorrow they can be down. Suddenly their salary can drop a thousand percent, from one film to another. But this does something positive to their egos, I think.

What qualities do you look for in a female actress?
That she fits the part and that she is believable. I want to believe the person—on the screen, I mean.

What kind of women do you like in real life?
Well, that's the problem. We always run after our own dreamlike women and we are always choosing the worst. My first wife was an actress, and when I divorced I said never again. My second wife is an actress, of course, and when we separated I said never again will I get involved with an actress. But I love them. I admire actors and actresses. I just admire them for what they are because I can't be an actor. I envy them. Anyway, I had another love affair with an actress and then another one . . . I am like the moth to the flame.

Why are you attracted to actresses?
They are different from other women. They're more paranoid than women in other professions because theirs is so insecure and so fragile. They are always waiting to be asked. It's very funny—on one hand they are idols and on the other they are slaves to people who decide whether to hire them or not. And then they may end up in the hands of a director who is not right for them. And all this contributes to this strange—not paranoia—schizophrenia.

Do you ever feel like staying away from the movie business and actors and actresses?
No. It's a great business.

Is there any kind of physical looks that turn you on about a woman?
I don't know. When I look back at the four women I have been in love with, they're very different. I found them very beautiful, all four of them. But that's very personal.

Are they aggressive women?
When they are getting what they want they are very agreeable, very nice and very passive. When they are not getting what they want—my God, they are very, very aggressive and ruthless.

Can you work with an actress you're in love with?
I never did that—though I met both my wives through work. I brought my first wife into a film which I wrote. I didn't direct it, I wrote it. And I found my second wife for my very first film. We worked together then, but never after. I can't do that, I guess, because for me working with an actress is like a flirt. And it's somehow very phony and awkward to flirt with your own wife—she knows you so well.

Can you describe a typical day in your life?
Normally I have problems falling asleep, so my day starts at around two o'clock in the morning when I'm desperately trying to fall asleep because I know that I have to be up at eight or nine o'clock in the morning. I hate sleeping pills, so I won't ever take them. Alcohol is not bad but you have a hangover in the morning, so that doesn't help either. If I'm lucky, I fall asleep in time and I wake up in a good mood and I can go through the whole day very easily.

Well, what do you do during the day?
I work. I have meetings. I work on the screenplay, I have costume sessions—a lot of things.

Where do you live most of the time?
Since I've been in America I've lived in New York for about four years and then on the West Coast for about two years, and then I moved to Lake Tahoe, Nevada, where I'm planning to buy some land. I have an apartment there but I'm planning to build something nice there and make my base there. Because, first, I like to ski very much and, second, I was practically born and spent every summer at a resort area in Czechoslovakia which was a lake in the woods. And Lake Tahoe reminds me of that period of my life so strongly that I feel very much at home there.

Do you like any sports other than skiing?
Tennis. But I don't really like tennis because I like things that I can do well. I don't ski all that well, but one skis alone.

Do you like solitude?
No, I like competition. In skiing you compete with the

mountain. I discovered that I like golf very much, but alone, competing against the course, because I hate to have to find somebody who's as bad or good as me so that we can both enjoy it. I hate to play tennis with guys who play much weaker than I do. And I feel sorry for a pro, despite the money I am paying him, because he has to be bored to death pretending how wonderful I am.

How do you feel about getting older?

If I work on it, I can talk myself into believing that it doesn't bother me, but I don't like it. Because physical stamina is somehow leaving me and that bothers me. I'm sure it bothers everybody. I used to go two or three days without sleeping fifteen years ago and still work. I can't do that anymore. I could run in a marathon fifteen years ago. Now from time to time I run in Central Park and after twenty minutes I'm exhausted.

Has sex decreased as you get older?

That's somehow better. I don't use my lungs as much as I did before—you know what I mean—but sex is getting better, which probably means that sex has more to do with the head than with the body itself. What do I know? It's always funny to answer these questions. When I finished *One Flew Over the Cuckoo's Nest*, for example, you wouldn't believe how many people called me and asked for medical advice about their lunatic relatives. I became an expert on lunacy.

Did you ever have any mental problems yourself? Depression?

I had a very bad nervous depression about six or seven years ago. But I wasn't hospitalized.

Did you see a doctor?

It was a funny situation because it was when I first came to New York with a friend of mine, Ivan Passer, who's a director too. We shared a small house in the Village. And I refused to go to a psychiatrist, so Ivan went for me and talked to the doctor as if my problem were his problem. I didn't know it. He would tell me what I should do and what I should take. Then I later found out that once a week he was going to a psychiatrist. But it just lasted a few months and slowly passed.

Do you take care of your health or do you worry about what you eat?

I'm sort of a hypochondriac. When I feel a little pain I go to a doctor right away, and from time to time they find something, so I must eat this and this and this. Well, that's fine for the dinner the same day, but the next day I return to my old habits. Food is something I really like so much that if I weren't able to eat what I like I'd be ready to quit.

Do you ever think about death?

Yes. Death is something very stimulating because you have to constantly fight a fear of death. And that brings out positive energy in you because basically until a certain age you behave as if you were immortal. Then suddenly one day—it can happen overnight—you realize that death can happen at any moment. You start to think. Without death there wouldn't be philosophy in man's history. Even the little tiny philosophy that each of us is developing in our minds is programmed by our thoughts about death.

Do you think there's life after death?

I would love to believe it. Unfortunately, I don't.

Are you religious at all?

I'm not religious. I believe there are things which are beyond our understanding and our knowledge, but a white-bearded god is not my preoccupation.

What do you like to do that makes you happy besides work?

It's a funny thing that happiness very often comes to you when you are not expecting or looking for it. In school you are taught that accomplishment will bring you happiness. It's not true. It gives you a certain satisfaction, a certain pride. It brings you money, but that's not a synonym for happiness. Happiness is very often a matter of surprise.

Is money important to you?

I prefer not to have money and to do whatever I want to do. On the other hand, I am very, very happy now to have a substantial amount of money coming in because that gives me a great feeling of freedom. Freedom without money is very abstract.

Do you think that films are getting better or worse?

Definitely not worse. But I don't think that that's the question—whether films are getting better or worse. They are under the pressure of television. Film, generally, is getting rid of the so-called B movies because you have them on television. It's very interesting to look at what kinds of films were the biggest box office in the last few years. They are all somehow socially and philosophically conscious movies. *The Godfather, Dog Day Afternoon, Annie Hall*. Even *Jaws* is a film that is not about just a shark. Even *Jaws* has a social consciousness in it. You have this little town, and the mayor and business trying to corrupt the situation. And you see that many films that are designed to please the audience fail terribly. So finally you know that the audience that goes to films is not a stupid audience.

Do you ever want to produce your own film?

Not really, because I don't have the necessary knowledge of the business side. I would not feel comfortable doing that. So I appreciate a good producer.

HENRY GELDZAHLER

Curator of Twentieth-Century Art,
Metropolitan Museum of Art, New York

Mr. Geldzahler: Being photographed is a performance, and the fact that it's a photograph means it's going to last longer than most other performances. So you get excited about it. I did a minute ad for Channel 13 once, and I froze. My friend Chris said it looked like a Channel 2 "editorial reply." I didn't move. On television you've got to bob around, or you look dead. I should have known better, since I spent a long time working with Andy Warhol. His first films were made in my apartment on Eighty-fourth Street in 1962. He rented an 8mm camera and said, "What shall we do?" I said, "I'll smoke a cigar, put it out, and then brush my teeth." And that's what we did.

I started smoking cigars in Athens, in August 1957. When I graduated from Yale my father said, "What do you want?" I said, "A trip to Israel, Turkey and Greece." At the end of the trip I had some money left over, so I had a good meal and wanted to finish with something special. I found a cigar that cost ninety cents, an Upman from Cuba. It traveled from Cuba to Athens to go up in smoke. I liked it, and it's been downhill ever since. I smoke five or six a day. Is that a lot? The nicotine hit from them lasts two or three hours. I don't inhale, but neither did Sigmund Freud, and he got cancer of the jaw. They told him he could live an extra five years if he stopped smoking, and he said, "Thank you very much," and went on smoking. He died at eighty-something, but he had a big piece of his jaw cut out. On the other hand, Churchill smoked cigars all his life and died of senility at age ninety-two.

Mr. Scavullo: Do you smoke a cigar first thing in the morning?
No, I have breakfast first. I'll smoke another one after lunch, another in the late afternoon, and then I take a nap. After dinner—from about nine till two in the morning—is when I really start going. What saves me is that you can't get Cuban cigars in America. They're much stronger, much purer, and if you smoke five or six of those a day you're really wrecked. When I go to Europe I feel like smoking them two at a time to make up for the fact that you can't get them here. David Hockney sends them to me as a posing fee. Posing for you, Francesco, is very different from posing for David. After seven hours he'll say, "You moved," and you think, Oh no, I moved! But I'm alive, that's why I did it. The worst, though, is when you've sat still for seven hours and you hear—*bang!* —"That's terrible!" You feel like *you're* terrible; you failed him as a model, you didn't inspire him that day. It's very tiring, but David is a great cigar smoker like myself and gives me poses I can smoke in.

When did you meet David Hockney?
I met David at Andy's studio in '63. Andy was entertaining David, and I brought Dennis Hopper over to meet them.

You were close to Frank Stella during the same period. It seems that the artists you've chosen to be friends with have a certain passivity.
That's interesting. I never really thought of it as passivity. They're not very comfortable in the world, and in a certain way I can make it easier for them. Anyway, I don't think that I've *chosen* them; it just sort of happened. I met Frank—and *pow!* I met Andy—and *pow!* I'm fascinated by art, but I have absolutely no interest in creating bad art myself. The way I think of it, there are artists to whom I'm very close, and can talk to, and to whose art I can contribute. For

instance, I'm proud of having given Andy the ideas for the Disaster paintings and the Flower paintings. I said to David about five years ago, "You're never going to understand yourself until you do a portrait of your parents. Not only understand how you feel about your parents, but how you think they feel about each other; because in order to make a composition with them in it, you have to invent a relationship between them." He resisted and resisted, but he's been working on it and he's almost finished now. It's been one of the most painful things he's ever done.

What is your background?
I was born in Belgium. All my great-grandparents came from Poland, and stopped in Belgium and Holland on the way to America. They're all in the diamond business. We came over in 1940, on one of the last Dutch ships to leave before the occupation. The English Channel was already mined. I grew up in New York and went to public schools, including one of the heaviest junior high schools in the city, Joan of Arc at Ninety-second and Amsterdam. Then I started going to private schools: to Horace Mann up in Riverdale, to Yale, the Sorbonne, and then Harvard. It seemed very natural to me to get into the art world; in fact, it all just happened. I'd been hanging around museums since I was fourteen. I went to see a Gorky show at the Whitney Museum in 1950, when I was fifteen. And I came home and threw up, then slept for eighteen hours. I was completely knocked out, and that's when I first realized that art could be that moving or upsetting. I went back two days later and the same thing happened. When I was seventeen I came home and said I wanted to be a curator.

When I was nineteen, a sophomore at Yale, I wrote a letter to the Metropolitan Museum saying I was going to be in New York for the summer with my parents, could I volunteer? My parents said, "Don't be crazy, you can't volunteer because no one will respect you, you've got to get a job." I said I didn't want a job, I wanted to work at the Met to see what it was all about. The Met wrote back to Yale asking: "Is this Geldzahler guy any good?" I guess they said yes, so I went there for the summer. I got to know three or four of the curators, and one of them, James Rorimer, became director that year. I wrote a letter congratulating him, and then forgot about it.

I finished Yale and went to Paris, then went to Harvard and taught while I was working on my Ph.D. During my third year Mr. Rorimer came up to Boston for a meeting of the Fogg Museum board of overseers. He invited me to breakfast at the Ritz at nine one morning, and at quarter to one we were still there talking, so I knew something was up. He said, "Would you like to leave Harvard and come to work at the Met?" I said no, I wanted to work at the Whitney. He turned gray with rage and asked why, so I said, "Because I'm interested in contemporary art and you aren't." There was a silence. I said, "Very nice chatting with you," and left. About a month later I got a letter from him saying come to see me in New York, we'll talk. I went. He asked, "Would you be willing to work here at five thousand a year?" I called my father and asked if he'd pay my rent for two years, and he agreed. I was in the middle of psychoanalysis and also teaching. I'd passed my generals but hadn't yet started my Ph.D. thesis, and both my psychiatrist and my professor said, "Don't do that! If you don't finish your analysis you won't be

HENRY GELDZAHLER
Curator of Twentieth-Century Art,
Metropolitan Museum of Art, New York

happy, and if you don't finish your Ph.D., you'll never get a good job." I said, "Fuck that. This *is* a good job." Then, the only time in my life, I asked the *I Ching* what to do—should I go to the Metropolitan Museum or should I stay at Harvard to finish my analysis and Ph.D.? I cast the sticks—a friend had a set—and they said: Go South. Rapid advancement will follow.

So what could I do? I left Harvard and came down here, got an apartment, and within a month I'd met Frank Stella and Andy Warhol and Jasper Johns and Claes Oldenburg; I was in Claes's happenings immediately and met Marcel Duchamp and Salvador Dali through that. There I was at the Met, hideously underpaid, but on the other hand, they really were paying for me to continue my education, which in this case was meeting all the artists, one after the other. It was a magic moment. George Kubler, who's a Yale professor, wrote a book called *The Shape of Time*. In it he talks about entrances. For instance, if Raphael had entered ten years later, he wouldn't have been who he is, because his genius was to balance the classical moment exactly. My happy entrance was in July 1960, just when the Pop artists were making Pop art in their studios but didn't know each other. I introduced Rauschenberg to Warhol, I introduced Lichtenstein to Rosenquist. They didn't even know about each other. Frank Stella was just painting stripes, but nobody knew about them. He hadn't had a one-man show yet.

So as I went around, I was able to make these connections between people. I didn't have fixed ideas about art being this or that; instead, I had a strong background in art history and could relate whatever I was seeing to traditional art. So it was curious—I was associated with the avant garde, but my training was so classical that nothing really freaked me out. As it says in the Old Testament, there's nothing new under the sun. For instance, happenings—theater by artists—sounds really mad. Why should an artist spend so much time making something that disappears? But it makes sense if you realize that when an archduke had won a battle, Dürer and Rubens would make papier-mâché triumphal arches that would dissolve three days later in the rain.

In 1965 there was an article in *Life*—ten pages about me and the younger artists—and it ended with a picture of me floating in a swimming pool, smoking a cigar on a rubber raft being pulled by Barbara Rose. Three trustees called the director of the museum and demanded my head. They said, "How can you have a curator who floats around in a pool like that?" It seemed ridiculous to me—I was totally clothed in a bathrobe, smoking an expensive cigar—what was the matter? In my seventeen years at the Met, I've been saved twice from trustees by directors of the museum.

Have you ever gone back to analysis?
I've gone back once or twice to therapy when I've been in a really bad situation—to untie a knot. But I've never gone really deep down. Therapy helps you solve a problem in your life today, whereas analysis tries to make you understand

what the basic character formation is so that you can work on that. One of the things I liked about analysis was that it was so expensive. It was an act of aggression against my father in that respect, I think. Extremely healthy!

I was in analysis three years, four times a week. I was getting my Ph.D., teaching—I was twenty-three, my students were twenty-one and a half—it was mad. I got up at seven in the morning, went to analysis, then prepared for my classes, worked on my thesis. I was also doing LSD and peyote and all that kind of thing—it was Harvard in '58, '59, which was just like every place else a few years later. I also ran a coffee shop, and somehow accumulated $500 from it, which I lent to friends who opened a second coffee shop, where Joan Baez sang for the first time. She was seventeen. Now when I look back at it, I can't believe that it was possible to do all that, to work on all those levels at the same time.

How do you feel when you get up now?
Great, until four in the afternoon, then I crash till about six-thirty, and then I have a second day that goes on until two in the morning or so. I bounce out of bed like a piece of toast, at eight or eight-thirty. Chris is very slow in the morning, and in that respect we are totally incompatible; he has a different rhythm. When I first wake up I go on about my dreams—which often deal with easily understood things like childhood, family, the politics of the museum—and I feel like I'm babbling because there's almost no response from the other side of the breakfast table.

I think staying in bed in the morning is painful. It's like hiding, like escaping. You just have to jump right up. If you stay in bed an extra ten minutes, there's no reason to get up at all, and then you might as well just check into the mental hospital. In my twenties I used to stay in bed on Saturdays and Sundays till twelve, one or even two. When I think back on it, I was miserable. It's much better to wake up and make up an activity, and imitate happiness or normalcy.

It's like Pascal said in the seventeenth century about the Church: if you say your prayers every day, even by rote, there will come a time when they will mean something to you. I think the same thing is true of everyday activity: you don't give in to whatever it is that makes you want to give up. For instance, there are days when I hate the museum desperately. I just make myself go in for an hour or two, and by then I remember what it is I'm doing and why, and I get back into it. I think the way down is to give in to a whim, like staying in bed or not going to work.

Other than work, what do you do to have fun?
I read. People think I'm out on the town all the time, or at restaurants or parties. The truth is, that is what I did in the sixties. Now I try to choose what I call fulcrum events: the three or so per month that you'd definitely go to even if you went to all the others. I usually leave places a bit early. I found out a couple of years ago that if you leave early, everyone who's there thinks you have some place better to go. Well, the place is home to finish a book! That's better! I stay up reading till two, and if I can't sleep, I sometimes get

up at five in the morning and read for a couple of hours, then go back to sleep.

Do you ever paint?

No, I hate bad painting. I could never get through whatever it was—clumsiness, lack of incentive—to get to the next stage of painting. I could never get through it because the evidence of what I was doing was so offensive.

Do you write much?

Yes. I suppose my greatest professional weakness is that I can write endlessly, on order. But if nobody wants anything for a while, if there's no show coming up at the Met, I don't write spontaneously. It's like being in school. I can meet any assignment, but I don't generate writing on my own. Norman Mailer told me in the fifties—we shared a place in Province-town for a couple of summers—that I should be taking notes because I was going to have a very interesting life. I never did anything like that. I do remember the interesting things, but that's not the same as keeping a diary. The problem with doing that is getting involved with triviality. I think that time orders things rather nicely, and if I wanted to sit down five years from now to write a book about the sixties, I would remember what was worth remembering.

Are you rich?

Not at all. I don't have any money except what I earn; that's pretty good, but I run through it every year. Whatever I accumulate is in the form of art. I have the luxury of not feeling insecure, since I've rarely made less money in a year than the previous one.

I have a house on Ninth Street, a nice house, and rent a place in Southampton year-round, $250-a-month, so I can go out for the weekends, and I manage to get to Europe two or three times a year. I'd love to have more money, but I have a feeling I could expand or contract to whatever was available. No matter how much was running through my hands, it wouldn't be quite enough, but just about. If I had more, I'd just buy more art. I'm interested in supporting artists, younger and older, for whom the world isn't quite ready. Artists like Edward Avedesian, Michael Hurson, Richard Hennessey, Christopher Wilmarth and Stephen Buckley. The thing that's nice about all these people is that they follow their own paths, they're not members of a movement, they don't make works in series, where each one looks exactly the same as the others. And their art has nothing to do with SoHo.

Are you interested in clothes?

Clothes interest me, like Nudie shirts and Borsalino hats. I wear only bow ties—David Hockney taught me how to tie a bow tie about three years ago, and I got so excited I've never looked back.

Are there any men you admire, public figures other than artists, movie stars?

No, I feel kind of sorry for movie stars. I go out to Hollywood for a month every year, and it's not a very admirable situation. I mean, I get along with them, but they're really a little lost. Warren Beatty, Robert Redford, Dustin Hoffman, Dennis Hopper—the ones that I know are always a little

vacillating, out of focus—they want a role. I admire writers: Truman Capote; Gore Vidal when he's being bitchy and accurate.

How do you like the Museum of Modern Art?

I love it dearly, because it's where I got turned on, and where I learned everything I know about quality in modern art. I'm a little sad that they didn't understand the way things were going about ten years ago. I suggested, I think eight or ten years ago, that the Fifty-third Street plant was getting so crowded that they were playing three-dimensional chess on a two-dimensional board. They were trying to continue as the center of the contemporary art world, at the same time that they were expanding their collections of Picasso, Brancusi, Matisse, and they couldn't continue to do both those things in the one place. I suggested that they rent a building in SoHo in which they could do all of their contemporary shows, and use the West Fifty-third building as if it were the Frick —to display art of a period which is over, the modern period. To expect a small museum to be able to document the modern period, and also be responsible for what's going on today in the post-modern period is physically impossible. Nobody at the Modern wanted to do that, and I think they've suffered from their decision.

I don't think it's an insoluble problem; I suspect that in time the Met and the Modern will come to some kind of agreement. The Met is missing so much great twentieth-century art: we don't have a Mondrian, we don't have a cubist Picasso or Braque, we don't have a big Brancusi. And if I wanted to go out and fill ten holes in the collection, it would cost $30 million. Those pictures are down at the Modern, and it seems mad to have two museums which should be sister institutions competing in the same city. After all, it's not Ford versus Chrysler.

I did a show in 1969 called "New York Painting and Sculpture." We took down all the paintings in the museum, all the Cézannes and Raphaels and Rembrandts, and put up Rauschenberg and Warhol and Poons. When the show was announced in the *New York Times*, I got a phone call from the director of the Museum of Modern Art. His voice was breaking. He said, "All we've got is eighty years, you've got five thousand, so why do you have to—" I said, "Come on, they're not *your* eighty years, they belong to everybody." I didn't understand that attitude, because whatever's going on today belongs to all of us. I had the opposite problem within the museum: there are trustees who are in their seventies, and who love eighteenth-century art. I've tried to explain to them: "Look, you've lived your entire life in the twentieth century. Isn't it time you come to terms with its art?"

I seem avant-garde in the museum, and conservative outside the museum. It's a tightrope. I'm the interpreter to the trustees of what the avant garde is doing, and while I don't want to lose my constituency among the artists and the receptive public, I can't go too fast. At the same time, of course, I insist on being myself, which can be a little . . . hair-raising.

VICTOR GOTBAUM

President of New York State and
City Municipal Workers' Union

Mr. Gotbaum: My background is international labor affairs;
I have my master's from Columbia in that. I did a stint in
Turkey on labor education. It was an accident that I got the
job. The accident was Senator Joseph McCarthy. Most of the
other people who applied for the job had better qualifications
than I did, but the security restrictions were so tight they
were knocked out and I wound up going to Turkey as a labor
education specialist. I then decided that one of my real errors
of omission was labor-union work, and I thought I would just
take off, go into the labor movement, get a more solid,
practical background, then apply it to international labor
affairs. My side jump was twenty-two years ago, and I've
stayed in the labor movement and never gone back to what
was really my chosen profession, international labor affairs. I
started as assistant director of education for the Meat Cutters
for a few years; then I moved to my present work—state and
county municipal employees—in Chicago. I tangled with
Mayor Richard Joseph Daley and always came in second.
We had a palace revolution in the union. Jerry Wurf led the
revolution; I was one of the soldiers in it. We deposed the
then national president thirteen years ago. Jerry moved up to
the presidency. I came into New York, and was subsequently
elected to take over the New York area. Nationally we have
around 650,000 members; locally 100,000. We're the largest
piece of the action. Public-service unions are relatively young
within the labor movement, and they're more progressive,
more active.

**Mr. Scavullo: Do you think that firemen and policemen
should be able to unionize and go on strike?**
I would classify a policeman as a workingman. And I believe
any workingman should be able to unionize to protect his
rights. For police and fire I think you should have the *right* to
strike; I think you should *not*. See, I regard the right to
withhold labor as almost God-given. If you use your hands
and you work, use your mind and you work, you should have
the right to withhold labor. I believe so strongly in that right
to strike.

**Do people resent you for being so strong about pushing
the union?**
I think in the profession that I'm in, they resent it, yeah. It's
a peculiar aspect of American democracy: in spite of the fact
that we elect those that govern us, we really resent
government in America. It's part of the tradition, almost a
myth in a way. And then, you resent public service, you
resent the public employee. So it's only natural that there
should be very strong resentment against a union that
solidifies that group and gives them strength. On a personal
level, I'll say with all modesty, when people know me they
rarely resent me. I believe, and I think it's accurate, that I get
along with people. I enjoy people, have a good nose for
them. If I don't enjoy them, I'll have nothing to do with
them. I'll just build a wall.

Who was the most helpful mayor to you?
I'd say Lindsay was, to the union—that is, he helped the
unions through fostering professional labor-management
relations. People talk about his giving away fantastic
contracts. That was nonsense; it just wasn't true. But he did
help foster excellent, excellent labor relations—and that
helped. The unions became more professional, and collective
bargaining because more professional.
 I don't know if the unions are running New York City. I

VICTOR GOTBAUM
President of New York State and
City Municipal Workers' Union

don't know what there is to run. In fact, we have almost less power now. You have this rather pathetic paradox: despite our fiscal involvement and our saving the city, in a sense, from going bankrupt, it's put some very severe limitations on us. That is, we almost have to become conservative to save our investment. But we would have had to become conservative anyway, because a city, a municipality, is no different from an industry or a trade. When the situation is depressed, when you have a linear recession, you can't expect too much or get too much out of the community. The situation is having an inhibiting factor upon us.

But I love New York and I almost have to be optimistic about it.

I was born in New York. Left in 1950. Returned at the end of '64. I may leave it temporarily, but I'll never leave it.

The less of old New York they tear down, the happier I am. In fact, one of the things that made me survive when I came back to New York was New York itself. My wife remained in Chicago; Jerry Wurf was in Washington; I really had nobody to pull me along. I think what kept my spirits up was this city: going to the Lower East Side, eating a late meal at Ratner's, walking on the promenade in Brooklyn, just going down Third Avenue.

I can't conceive of the city going down. It's too great, too magnificent to go under. And I believe we won't. I think there's enough toughness and resiliency and variation to keep us afloat. We'll survive and make our contribution.

But still, I'm very much the pragmatist. I guess that's what makes me a good trade unionist. I don't try to kid myself. There are obviously some individual emotional involvements, but basically I'm quite practical. Workers are practical people. They don't have any intellectual nuances. They don't kid themselves. I use the terribly erudite statement: workers never bullshit themselves.

I love my work. I love New York. I get right up in the morning; I like the day. I like the job. I love the people I work with.

I usually start my day between nine and ten and finish about ten or eleven. A lot of the stuff is in the evening. Food is business-social. When jobs are being cut, the deputy mayor drops off to have breakfast with me; maybe some other trade unionist joins me for dinner. I usually plan one luxury meal, be it business or not, just to relax, sometime during the day.

I'm separated from my wife and I'm very comfortable, very happy. In these last years, despite the crisis, I've learned more and more how to relax. There used to be a time when I came from Chicago to New York when it was an impossible situation. I took over from a guy who was quite ill, and I came into this terribly complex, vulgar, magnificent city, and tried to figure out how the hell to make it. I would get up at six-thirty, seven in the morning, and not stop work till midnight. It was almost impossible to relax. Even if I went away from it, you know, I just couldn't relax. After a few years of this I finally discovered that I could do it, that I personally would survive. Then I began to relax, to feel a lot better. I do get depressed—not about the job or city per se—but about the situation. We have some real tough

difficulties here. I'm representing a membership which, if you take their spouses and families, is as large as the city of Rochester. So if workers are laid off, this is very upsetting—when a man is deprived of the ability to work, I get depressed.

Did your separation make you unhappy?
I guess after thirty years of marriage it has to. But for the same reasons that it's a large break to make, it's a break that you make because you feel it's necessary. I felt that I was really living in two worlds and not enjoying it. I'd rather not talk about it, not because it depresses me, but because I'm in transition from a wife who's terribly sensitive about it.

Now I almost do nothing alone. I'm living with another woman now. I love her very much. I don't like being alone. I want to be with her.

What is your future wife like? Is she much younger?
She's not much younger. She's thirty-nine. But she looks very young. She embarrasses the hell outta me. I feel in good shape, so I honestly don't think about age. I enjoy life; I really enjoy my new life with her, and I am adjusting to it. The transition in terms of a separation is done. It's almost a sense of relief. We have an apartment in Brooklyn Heights now. Such a nice feeling. I used to feel schizoid living in the suburbs and working here—and guilty. And now I just feel great. I feel so good about both living and working in New York. So I just feel young.

Do you exercise?
I love tennis. I keep my weight at 195 and I play tennis every day. I love walking in the city. So I keep in fairly good shape. I love wine. But I don't smoke.

Do you take the subways?
On occasion. The union affords me lots of luxuries.

Does that seeem to be a contradiction to you at all, to be representing workingmen and having luxuries which they don't have?
No, because they have a luxury I don't have—I mean that—and that is that they put in an eight-hour day, a five-day week, while I generally put in a six-, seven-day week, and a minimum of a ten-hour day. You almost need the luxuries to survive. I don't apologize for them. If I get mashed in the subway and I had to take that kind of time out, it would be terribly burdensome. I don't feel corrupted for one reason: I work at my trade, and I represent the workers morning, noon and night. So the fact that there's a car and an individual to drive me around, and the fact that I can go to a good restaurant for a meeting—I don't feel corrupted by this at all.

Do you think about food a lot?
Not especially—the woman I live with is very much aware, aware of health and cholesterol and stuff of that nature. She's an excellent cook. I want to stay around 195 pounds, that's usually it. So I look at food that way. If I have a big heavy meal for lunch, I make sure I don't eat much at night.

Do you care about clothes?
No, I don't—as you can probably tell. But the woman I'm going to marry, she does. She's converted me from a slob to a medium slob.

Did you have idols when you were a young kid?

I was never really a young kid; that was my problem. I started to work at the age of twelve and a half. Almost full time. So I wasn't the typical young kid. I was putting in fifty hours a week as a dishwasher, soda jerk, making tomato sandwiches, ham and egg, short-order cook in a luncheonette. We were on relief. My mother was born here, my father was from Russia. My mother's background is Russian-Jewish also. But I started to work at such a young age that I didn't have time to idolize. As I grew a little older I began to realize the importance of FDR and he became an idol.

Do you have children?
Four. Starting in order of seniority, as a good trade unionist: the oldest is twenty-five and he's now getting out of Harvard Law and is a student at the Kennedy School of Public Affairs. The next is twenty-two, at Brandeis. The third is Noah, who was just accepted into Amherst, but he's diddling with the thought of maybe going to Dartmouth. He's the politician in the family. My three sons will all graduate law school, but I suspect number one will be the lawyer. Then, the only handsome member of my family is my daughter, who's thirteen, the baby. The rest of us are pretty ugly.

Do you look in the mirror a lot?
No, I don't have to look. I never do. I'm not modest or immodest. I just don't think about it really, I guess because of the working and the nonsocial life as a kid, just growing up and working and doing . . . I'm clean, you know. I'm very fastidious about washing and bathing, but I am a slob when it comes to clothes and looks. I don't use after-shave or cologne. I won't take a razor cut. I distract the hell out of my barber, who keeps begging me to do something with my hair. I say, "Yeah, shove it up your ass." I don't have time for it. I never did and I still don't.

Do you like women who spend a lot of time on their physical looks?
Oh, I go out of my mind. My wife had some faults but that was the one thing that I couldn't accuse her of. And the new woman I'm going to marry and whom I love very much, there's just something clean and good-looking about her, but she prides herself on being able to get dressed and ready ten minutes before I do.

What do you think of women's lib and women becoming powerful today?
Well, they haven't become powerful. I think what we're facing now is a transition period. The women's-lib movement has made its impact in terms of what I call raising our consciousness. I know that as a labor leader who does hiring I've become more conscious of it. And I've been watching my language. But I think that in terms of their goals one can't say they've reached any fruition at this point.

What about someone like Barbara Walters?
I'm bothered by anybody making a million a year. The assumption is that Miss Walters is as good as any other person, but males or females don't deserve a million a year as far as I'm concerned. This to me is an almost incomprehensible figure and I know I'm dealing in finances in terms of billions, but there almost has to be a distorted value about one person making that much money. I have friends who might be characterized as millionaires. And I must say it

pleases me when they talk about money in terms of concern. I've noticed two or three friends of mine, millionaires, who are concerned about money. They never throw it around. Or display it. And I think, whether I realize it or not, it probably was a conscious choice on my part. I don't think that if I was approached by somebody who had money and flaunted it, I would choose him as a friend. I like to live well, I admit that. *But* I always want money to have meaning to me.

Do you go to movies or watch TV?
I don't go to movies as often as I'd like because of the schedule. But I just love a good film. And TV is almost an escape for me. I get home at eleven at night, I'm very tired, so I just flip on the news, sometimes I won't even hear it. But I like TV. I love specials. I love sports. I could even watch my *mother* play football.

Why did you name your third son Noah?
My wife liked Biblical names. I only had a say in my number-two son's name. And people are always surprised: they say Noah, Joshua, Rachel and *Irving*? How'd you get this? My number-two son was born four months after my brother, whom I loved very much, died, so I wanted to name my son after him.

Did you ever go to a psychiatrist?
Yeah. During this transition. I've gone twice in my life. Once after the Army, adjusting to civilian life, and now, adjusting to the breakup. I think it does help. Very much so. Now, I know there's supposed to be a cult of self-analysis. I don't believe that anyone can really analyze himself or herself. We sometimes need someone to analyze us objectively. I just really needed somebody to talk to. I went for about a year.

Do you ever have problems sleeping?
Oh God, no, I just pass right out. When I sleep I can really sleep. I can sleep almost anywhere at any time.

Are you religious at all?
I call myself a cultural Jew. I have a strong, strong cultural bias. I was brought up in the Jewish ghetto of Brooklyn. I feel very comfortable and secure about it. I'm emotional about it: I was part of the troops that liberated Buchenwald. In fact, my fiancée wants to convert if I'd let her. I really want to get married by a rabbi, just for the symbol of it. So crazy me. I just have to go to the synagogue, I just have that need. We'll probably spend the summer on vacation in Israel. But I'm not really religious. I don't think about God. I don't believe in Him; I don't disbelieve in God. I don't carry that around as excess baggage. As a deity, there's a deity. Those who need Him, I hope they have a good time with it.

My favorite saying is: If I die tomorrow morning, it'll probably be with a smile on my face because I've done so much that I've enjoyed.

I'd like to retire early. I'd like to go into a second career before I'm sixty. If I give you the exact age, they'll all start salivating. Let's just say under sixty. I'd like to go back into international labor affairs and finish up my second career in that area.

You should try to develop a union for photographers.
You couldn't do it. I imagine they're individualistic bastards who would be impossible to organize. To me, photography is an art form. I don't think you can organize art.

GARY GRAFFMAN
Concert Pianist

Mr. Scavullo: At what age did you start playing piano?
Mr. Graffman: My father was a violin teacher, so I grew up with music. I started with the violin when I was three, but that didn't take. I began piano when I was four. All pianists start very young. You have to, because it's a physical thing; also, at an early age your fingers can learn to do certain things they are not born to do. Swimmers do the same—great swimmers are thrown in before they can move, practically. And I was very musical. I was interested in it very much. Three or four months after I started at the piano I was way ahead of where most people would be in that time. But my father showed some intelligence about the whole thing knowing that because you play better than other eight-year-old kids doesn't mean you're going to spend your life giving concerts. He made sure that I had a normal education and a normal childhood. I used to go out on the streets with kids who lived in the neighborhood—the Upper West Side—and play stickball. But, in addition, I practiced piano two or three hours a day.

How much do you play now?
All the time. Ten months a year I'm on the go, giving concerts all around the world.

Do you ever take a vacation?
Sometimes within a tour. I had a Japanese tour, for example, and my wife and I went two weeks earlier to Nepal and Afghanistan because those were two of the very few countries that I had never been to and am very interested in.

Do you always travel with your wife?
Yes.

Do you have children?
No, that's why she's able to.

Would you like to have children?
Yes and no. Our whole lives for the last twenty years would have been very different if we had. I would perhaps have played fewer concerts and taught instead of being in one place. My wife certainly could not have traveled with me practically at all. I am not unhappy with the way things worked out.

How long have you been married?
We got married in December '52. She worked for Columbia Music Management before we were married and for the first few years of our marriage. She paints, not professionally, but very well. She goes to the Art Students League, which is next door to our apartment in New York, when she has time. She has studied music, so she's a good critic of my work. And she's my secretary, she does all my correspondence. I say this half as a joke, but it's true: she types very well, she uses he English language very well, and she writes good letters.

Do you still feel romantic toward your wife after twenty-five years?
How does one define that word? I guess so.

Not many marriages last twenty-five years.

I know, these days especially. We do have a very large apartment. Nevertheless, we are in it together. I spend much of the day at the piano. I'm learning a new repertoire all the time, as well as reviewing what has to be played in concert in the next couple of weeks. And she is coming and going, shopping, going to museums. In the evening, we're with friends.

When you wake up in the morning, do you feel good?
About me, my life, yes, but not the world. I'm doing what I want to do—not many people are. I love music very much, I enjoy playing the piano, I work at it very hard.

Have you ever been so depressed that you couldn't play the piano?
No. But I've been depressed, who hasn't? But it never lasted long enough for me to speak to a doctor about it.

When you are depressed, do you find that music helps?
Yes, Artur Rubinstein said that if you sit at the piano a certain amount of hours a day and give a lot of concerts, you get rid of the frustrations, the things that are troubling you, without ever especially thinking about it. Reading also helps—anything that gets my mind on something in which I'm very interested, like Oriental art. Taking walks is another thing that's good if I'm annoyed or depressed. That's the only exercise I get—serious walks to Chinatown and back.

Do you watch your diet?
I try not to get above a certain weight. But when I'm on tour, two hundred and fifty days a year at least, I have to eat something before the concert and I am always hungry after the concert, so I have four meals a day. And I don't have much control over what I eat when I am staying at a Holiday Inn or dining at somebody's house and having to be polite. So I always eat too much when I am on tour. I certainly would not be considered a health nut in any way.

Are you concerned about getting older?
My father died at age eighty-five, and the day he died he had a student. He was a little frail during the last few months, but two days before he died I played at Carnegie Hall and we went to a party afterwards and he had wine, and he was kissing all his friends. He never gave his health much thought, except where smoking was concerned. I don't smoke now, not because of what's been written about it, but because it never gave me any pleasure at all. I like wine, so I drink wine. I like to have one or two vodkas before dinner. I don't drink the day of a concert, because it's hard enough to control the situation when you walk out on a stage without alcohol.

What do you think about when you walk out on stage?
The piano is so important: I almost never walk out on stage not having worked on the piano that afternoon. Maybe, because of some airplane mess, I'll arrive just before the concert. In that case I'll make them put the curtain down for ten minutes until I try the piano.

MICK JAGGER

Rock Star

Mr. Scavullo: What's your sign, Mick?
Mr. Jagger: I was born July 26 at six-thirty in the morning. That makes me a Leo.

What beauty products do you use, if any?
I really quite mix them up a bit, which I know is not right. I use a lot of Elizabeth Arden for painting my face and once a month I use a face mask. I use any kind of skin toner I get hold of without alcohol. But I don't use any make-up at all except when I go on stage.

What about perfume?
I like Chanel's Cuir de Russie, and then I have some special ones I bought in Tangiers. And I can't remember the names because they're all in Arabic. There is this perfume shop in Tangiers which has all the old French perfumes which you can't get anymore. I hate Christian Dior perfumes on women and I wouldn't ever think of it for myself. If a girl comes to meet me wearing Diorissimo, that is the end, forget it.

Where do you put your perfume?
On my ass, behind my ears and on my wrists. Sometimes on my groin. But I very rarely wear perfume.

What is your beauty secret?
It's an old Egyptian trick and I'm not going to repeat it to you.

What are your first thoughts on awakening in the morning?
Mmm . . . sex or orange juice.

Do you like making phone calls?
Not as much as Warren Beatty but quite a lot.

How do you like to spend your evenings?
In the company of young ladies.

What makes you feel great?
Falling in love.

What do you think about sizes?
Sizes of what? Shoes? I'm a size 10 shoe. I wish I was one inch taller.

Discuss your preferences in clothing, including underwear.
I wear underwear sometimes, but if I don't wear underwear I feel sexier than if I do. But I have to wear underwear sometimes like if I'm going on horses or doing any kind of sport. I like silk underwear. On top, especially, it's very nice.

What kind of women are you attracted to?
Well, there's my daughter. She's very attractive. But, no particular type. I'm attracted to all kinds and colors and sizes. I don't care. I don't insist that women be white or black or red or blue or yellow. I don't particularly like redheads.

Name some women you find sexy.
My wife, of course. I don't want to name any more otherwise I'm going to be in trouble. I'm not going to name Jackie Onassis.

Name some women you respect.

I like Lina Wertmuller. I respect her. And the Queen, of course. That's about all.

Has the women's movement made a difference to you?
Not really, because we've always had girl singers, and we've always respected them. And I love working with girls, singing with girls, doing harmonies with girls. In music there has been very little sexual friction.

What would be your reaction to having a woman as your boss?
I can't even consider having a boss. I can't imagine it being a woman or a man.

What qualities do you seek in your male friends?
Butchness. No, a sense of fun, kindness, understanding, intelligence. A strength of character. I suppose loyalty, but I don't demand it. It's nice to have. I have an affinity with men that I can't put into words, especially men I work with. I love working with men. Most of my men friends are people I work with. When I say work I mean have a dialogue in some way with a man. I do something with them that's creative.

Is there a particular food you like?
I like so many different kinds of foods. I pride myself on being a very untypical Englishman. Most Englishmen won't eat anything except lamb chops and boiled potatoes and boiled vegetables. But I like every kind of food.

Do you watch your weight?
I don't diet at all except I stop drinking for some parts of the year because otherwise I might put on weight.

Do you worry about your health?
I just haven't ever gotten sick enough to worry. After those famous last words I'll drop dead before I get to say another thing.

Do you have any fear of death?
Yes. Death is a bit of a problem. It's such an unknown thing. And I wouldn't like to lose the use of my legs, have my legs chopped off or something. I'd hate that. If death were very painful and slow, it would be pretty scary. I think death could be the end or it could be an adventure or it could be a really scary roller-coaster ride. But you have to study death and know what you're doing, but I haven't done any study.

Has God or religion been important in your formation?
Spirituality is important in everybody's life.

Is it essential that your work be a source of money or power?
No. It's not essential that it be a source of money or power. I'm very lucky because I don't consider my work a job. I don't want a job. I never wanted one.

How are you affected by money and power?
I think as you get older you can see the emptiness of it all. That is, of course, if you had money. Power is nothing. But if I never had any money to buy a glass of beer, I'd be striving for it.

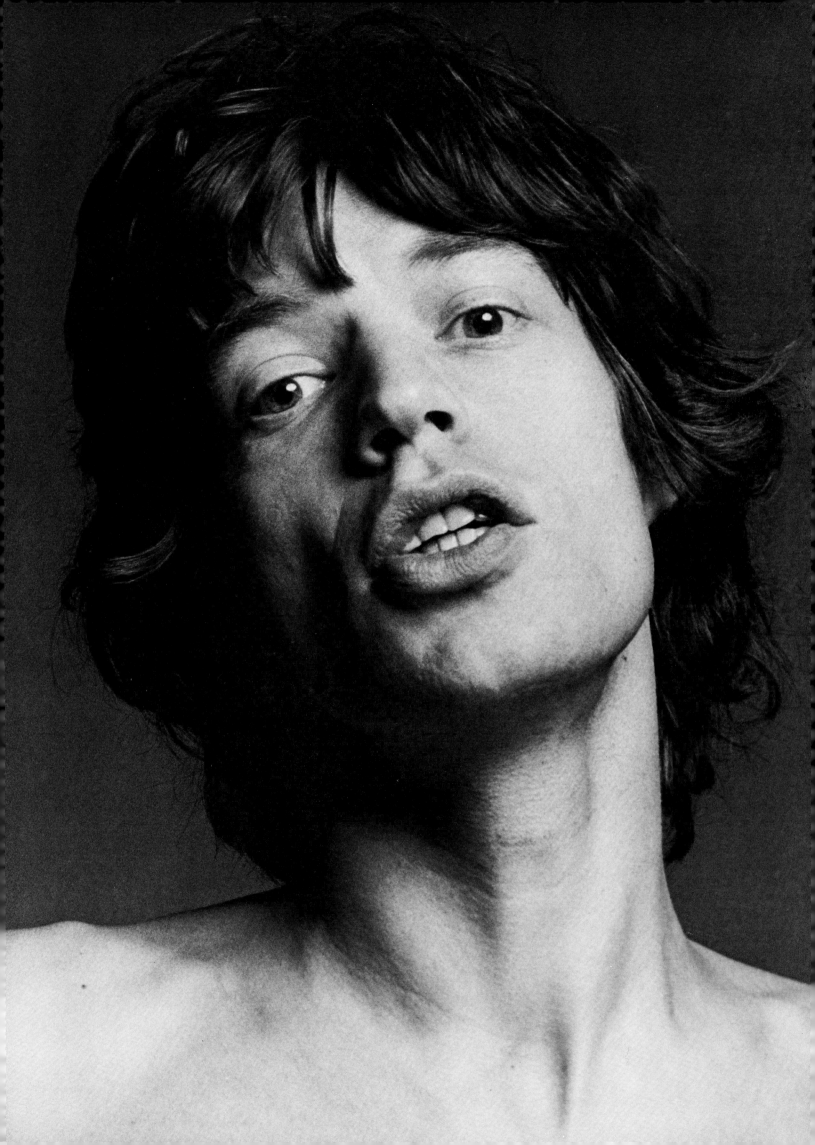

BRUCE JENNER

1976 Olympic Decathlon Champion

Mr. Scavullo: How does it feel to be a superstar athlete?
Mr. Jenner: It's surprising, but I don't feel any different now than before. The thing that's amazing is how people perceive me now, how people look at me. All of a sudden anything I may say has great credibility—especially in the United States, where they love to go with winners. People put stars or celebrities up on pedestals—I think they need to look up to somebody. At times it's hard to cope with because, hey, I've got good points and bad points just like anybody else. I'm a normal person. It just so happens that I was able to accomplish something in my life that very few people are able to do.

How did it feel the moment you won?
It was funny. I had a picture that was taken of me crossing the finish line at the 1972 Olympic Games. I had it blown up and I had a quote of Roger Bannister's that I really, really liked superimposed over the picture. And I thought, When I cross the finish line, in 1976, I want to have a picture of that last stride—because I knew it was going to be the end of my career. I would never do it again. But when I crossed the finish line I put my hands up in the air, I opened my mouth, I contorted my face and came stumbling across the line, and as I was slowing down I thought, You missed it. Here was the shot I always wanted to have, just like in '72, striding across the old finish line, and I missed it. So actually at the moment I won, that's what went through my mind. Then later it came out on the cover of *Sports Illustrated* and I thought it was great because it showed a lot of enthusiasm, so much intensity—like a giant orgasm. But the really tough part was about fifteen minutes after the Games were over at the victory ceremonies. The stands were still pretty full and it was late at night and all of us were a little tired. There were two steps to the top of the victory platform. I looked at those two steps and I got really choked up because I started thinking that I would never do this again. I knew I was retiring, I knew I was getting out of it. For the rest of my life I'll always look back on the twelve years that I was in track and field as one of the best times of my life. I was very sad to see it all go, to realize that those were the last two steps of my career. I had made it, I had fulfilled everything that I wanted to do, I had my gold medal, I had the world record and all the points I wanted to score, everything I wanted to do. And it seemed like I had succeeded, I made it, and that was it.

Since then I've been doing sportscasting work for ABC, and a lot of public speaking. I'm in the process of signing a contract with a major firm—I'll be going some promotion work and acting as a spokesman for their company. I enjoy that. The Olympic Games opened a lot of doors for me, for which I feel very, very fortunate. And they made my life a lot more fun. I know that I'm not the type of guy that likes a nine-to-five job, who gets his hourly wage so he can bring the money home. I enjoy doing things that are enjoyable and I hope that I can get paid for doing things that are enjoyable because, basically, you've got to eat. I am not really a highly money-motivated person. I don't want to make ten million dollars or anything like that.

The thing I enjoy most, though, is racing motorcycles. Motorbikes. I get up in the mountains in Malibu where I've got some tracks set up. Kawasaki's given me a couple of bikes and I've got a guy helping me out, so maybe by next year I'll be getting into some motorcross races, over hill and dale, you know.

Did you have to discipline yourself to get the strength and endurance to participate in these sports?
It came very easily for me since I was doing it because I *enjoyed* it—not because I felt like I *had* to go out there and do it. It was fun. I would train six, seven hours a day, every day, all year round, because I enjoyed it and I knew I had just so much time to be able to accomplish something. I knew there was some sort of finality to it because I said that I was not going to compete anymore after the '76 Olympic Games. I had to do it by then.

When you were training for the Olympics, how did you survive financially?
I had it pretty much made. I sold insurance for about two years. My wife was a stewardess for United Airlines, so she kept the steady money coming in. I would throw in a few bucks here and there. We had a small apartment, a nice litle car, we could get around, and everything seemed to be all right. But training was number one; making money was second. In fact, I completely quit everything six months before the Games. I made sure I had all the bills paid until the Games were over, and then I did nothing but get up in the morning and eat, sleep and train. I put all my eggs in that basket and just went totally after it. I didn't even have a coach. I would do it all myself, just me and my dog Bertha, a golden Labrador. She was the coach. She was great. Every morning she would jump up on the bed and stand over me, breathing that hot doggy breath down on top of me till I got up, so I would go out and run around the track.

Was your family very sports-oriented?
Yeah. Our whole family was a bunch of jocks. I was the only one that really went off and pursued it, but my sister and my dad really enjoyed it. We used to do competitive water-skiing in tournaments, my dad in the senior events, me in the boys' division, my sister in the girls' division.

You and a sister, is that it?
I had a brother who was killed about six months ago in a car accident. He was eighteen. And then I have a younger sister who's eleven. So we have them all spread out.

That must have been pretty hard when your brother died.
It really was. I was home at the time. He asked for the keys to the car, to go and get gas, and never made it back. He was killed about seven minutes after he left the house.

How do you deal with something like that?
I usually deal with depression within myself. In my brother's case, it was very difficult. I didn't like all the burial procedures, didn't like the wake; couldn't stand it. I went for fifteen minutes because I felt I owed it to my family. But I didn't like my brother being laid out there in a casket at all. I would just as soon remember him as he went out the door. He was happy, he was excited, he was leaving for California that afternoon—the first time he was going out of the house really—he was going to live with my wife and me.

Do you have any fear of death?
I have some fear of death because I am the type of person that's always in control of myself, what I'm doing and everything around me, but in that situation—death—you aren't. You don't know what's going to happen. I don't worry about flying off my bike and getting myself killed, that just

BRUCE JENNER
1976 Olympic Decathlon Champion

gets my adrenalin going. I used to water-ski and water-ski-jump competitively. I enjoy that little sense of danger. But while I was competing in the decathlon, especially between 1972 and 1976, I would not do anything to hurt myself. I wouldn't walk up and down stairs fast. Once the Games were over, if I got a banged-up leg, it didn't matter; we could fix it. I'm hardly afraid of anything. I have a great respect for a lot of things that I approach with caution, but I have a pretty good sense of myself physically, so I could handle, let's say, sky-diving with a little bit of work. I would start from the beginning and learn how to do it. I'm not the type of guy to just go running off giant cliffs, figuring I'll survive.

What kind of foods do you eat?
Meat and poatoes. During training I couldn't eat ice cream, cake, all that good stuff. A good Big Mac once in a while never hurt. I'm not a very big eater even during training. I would eat two regular meals a day—a good-sized breakfast, a good-sized dinner—and maybe a very little lunch. Now I find myself eating even less. I eat only when I'm hungry, but I'd rather be doing other things than sitting down at a table eating. I don't smoke, though I think drinking in moderation isn't bad. I don't go out all the time on binges. I have my beer once in a while and I enjoy a good party once in a while, to sort of let myself go.

They say that athletes are not supposed to have any sex before they perform . . .
The only time sex has bothered me is when I do it *during* the competition. During the 1,500 meters there's no sex whatsoever. That's the only time it'll slow me down. Before and after, fine, don't worry about it.

Do you take vitamins?
I'm heavily into vitamins. While I was training I would take an average of sixty pills a day. I'd take handfuls of C, B and A, potassium, magnesium, four times during each day. I don't know if it helped my performance all that much, but when I woke up in the morning I know I felt better. And I felt like I could train harder. I don't know if it was helping my strength that much, but I felt a little bit more alert.

How about sleep?
Lots of it. I used to sleep till I woke up, between eight and nine hours a night.

What is your favorite kind of a male body?
Wrestlers. They're very lean, more wiry than bulky because they have to control their weight so much. I think Arnold Schwarzenegger is in tremendous shape, but his body doesn't seem to me to be that functional. And to me, a really good body is functional. A wrestler is very versatile, he has tremendous flexibility. Not an ounce of fat on the guy. Swimmers may be a little more streamlined, but they just don't develop into real hard types. I consider a wrestler's body more aggressive than a swimmer's.

Do you consider yourself an aggressive person?
No, I'm a fun-loving person. I was very intense when I competed; I didn't let anything slip by me. Maybe that was just a way to get those feelings out. But when I would walk off the track I would be a completely different person, very easygoing. I dislike pushy people. People that are always in there, pushing, do this, do that. Sign this autograph. They don't even say please. Fat people, people that are out of shape also turn me off.

What do you do at night?
I watch a little TV with my wife. We very rarely go to the movies because I'm out so much and on the road, I'd rather stay home. I play pool with my wife, just take it easy, do relaxing things. Twelve is the latest I'll stay up. I'm not the type to go out to bars and fool around or go to night clubs and dance all night.

Do you enjoy music?
I love it, particularly if it has a really fast, good beat and is good to dance to. Before I compete I enjoy listening to music, since it seems to be in the same tone of what I'm trying to do. I'm trying to get very intense, to get my adrenalin up, to concentrate very much on what I'm doing. And music a lot of times will just help that along.

What kind of girls do you like?
The ones on the cover of *Cosmo*. But I also like women who have minds of their own, who are not just following their husbands around or looking for men to take care of them. I like a woman who can be independent, who doesn't make me feel like I have to carry her, in the sense that I have to make the money and I have to do this and that. My wife's very good about that. She's very strong. I always felt that she could always survive on her own if anything happened to me.

Does she still work?
She's just finishing a book about how she's become stronger and more independent because of living with a champion, living with a person who is so motivated to do things. She's done such a good job of it. She actually has more say than anybody else on what I do. I trust her opinion more than the agents whom we have working for us, because they're trying to make a commission. We take their suggestions and we put them in our own little heads, the two of us, and we come up with what we think we should do. The two of us control everything that we do.

Do women make passes at you?
They may make some subtle ones, but I think the fact that everybody knows I'm married discourages a lot of women. There have been some, however, who have come right out and said something. But they're mostly groupies. The younger girls. No older woman with any class at all would ever do anything like that. But all that giggling and screaming doesn't turn me on at all.

How do you feel about the trend toward politicalization of the Olympics?
In Montreal, when the Canadians would not let Taiwan compete in the Games because they were not the actual China, all the shoes the Canadian team wore were made in Taiwan. I think that sums the whole thing up. It's just a bunch of politics. It's all very unfortunate because it lessens the whole impact of the Games. They're supposed to be one person against the next; they never started out as one country against the next country. In fact, when I was out there competing, I was really competing for myself. We have, by far, the best country in the world: you're proud to wear the "U.S.A." on your chest. It's an honor. But I was really competing for myself because I was the one who did all the hard work.

I really am not a political person. I've never enjoyed politics because it seems like nobody's ever right. Nobody's ever a winner.

PHILIP JOHNSON
Architect

Mr. Scavullo: Where did you get those glasses that you're wearing?

Mr. Johnson: Le Corbusier, the architect, wore the same kind.

What kind of design in people do you like?

I like them thin and blond. I'm not very original.

Do you think there's such a thing as universal taste?

Fashion magazines wouldn't be so successful if there weren't. You know, you wouldn't pay a million dollars to a model. I like the cleft-tooth girl—what's her name?

Lauren Hutton.

But when she puts her fake tooth in I don't like it. A little imperfection of that kind is the most important thing. Lips that aren't symmetrical. That's why make-up is so bad right now. It's a mask.

Do you ever wear make-up?

Never have. They used to make you up for television. They don't anymore.

Do you believe in face-lifting?

No. I wouldn't want that Chinese look. The most beautiful woman in the world is Georgia O'Keefe. Age makes no difference.

Do you think about aging?

I just turned seventy, so life is just beginning. You see, I don't have to make it anymore. Poor young people are still striving, working their asses off. But I don't bother with all that because I'm not going anywhere. I mean, I did or I didn't by now. And now I enjoy the fruits of my life. Of course, I never worked so hard, but that's what I enjoy doing. I don't like vacations, never take a day off.

Have you set an age for retiring?

I have to beat Frank Lloyd Wright—he was still working at eighty-nine. Corbusier was working when he died. We don't retire in our business, that's why I picked it.

How do you take care of yourself?

I don't believe in taking care of myself.

Do you watch your diet?

No, I lie down and have another drink.

Do you smoke?

I never tried it.

Do you get regular checkups by a doctor?

No, I never check up. That's a mistake. A doctor once told me to never, never do that. When I feel a pain, I go to a doctor. I had a heart operation that saved my life. I didn't have any pain, but I had to go to a doctor because I was getting exhausted just from walking. I thought, That can't be right. I had open-heart surgery, a by-pass operation. I'm younger now than I have been for twenty years. It's the greatest thing, everyone should have one.

What is a by-pass operation?

Well, the artery that brings the blood into the heart gets clogged up because of the tension of modern life or some such thing, so you take a piece of artery from your leg and put it there, by-pass there, so the blood gets into your heart and you're all right. It's the thought of opening up yourself that's horrible. They take a saw and cut through the bone.

Is there a scar?

Oh yes. A delicious scar.

How tall are you?

I used to be five foot ten, but I shrunk. I stand up, all right, but each little vertebra collapses on the one below it. It's marvelous. I'm five-eight now.

What about your hair?

It went.

Does that bother you?

It used to, when I was thirty and the stuff was coming out by the handful. And I'm a hair fetishist, I love hair. I tried to stop it—the works, Francis Fox, doctors. I never had a transplant because they didn't have that then. But if you don't have it, you don't have it.

Do you still haxe sex?

Of course. Much less. It does go down.

When does it go down?

After orgasm. No, I was in my sixties when my sexual drive slowed down, but I'm sure it was the heart business coming on, because since then I've been more active. If I hadn't had that problem, I don't think I would have slowed down, although I think everyone does somewhat. You think you don't, but you become a dirty old man and your imagination gets better than it ever was because you can imagine more things. Sex is mostly in your imagination, anyway. That's the greatest pleasure. You don't have to *do* it. You don't have to have someone there whom you have to talk to afterwards. It's much more fun to look back to all the delightful positions you've enjoyed.

Do you believe in love?

Yes, but it has nothing to do with sex.

Do you exercise? You're very trim.

No. It's just an accident.

Do you care about clothes?

I like clothes, but not enough to do anything about it. If you have money, it's nice to go and have some more suits made at Wetherall and then look fine for a couple of days.

Have you made a lot of money?

I inherited it. I must confess that that's the best way. And I was lucky in my work besides.

When did you decide to become an architect?

When I was very old, thirty-six, forty.

What did you do until then?

I wandered around, I farmed, I learned languages, I did nothing for a while. And I thought that was awfully silly. But I always wanted to design. I designed a few things, watches, women's clothes, and I was lousy. I'm a better architect.

Was inheriting money bad for you?

It was bad for me, but I've lived long enough to outlive it.

How much do you get paid to design a building?

Well, I don't get the money, the office does, and sometimes it divides up nicely and sometimes it doesn't. Sometimes it costs more to design a building than you get paid.

Someone told me that you won't design a house for less than $1 million.

I'm doing a house for myself now that's only a thousand square feet, it's costing $100,000.

In Connecticut?

Yes, in the same place as my other houses. I can't help it. I'm my own best client, obviously. I won't do this for anybody else, it would cost too much. I don't really know why I'm building this new house, but my place is getting rather big, too sprawled out. I might give it all away, and live in this new, small house. Because you can't get servants anymore; I don't want them, anyway. But it's hard to take care of it all. There are four units: the glass house, the underground gallery, the sculpture gallery and the guesthouse. And all

PHILIP JOHNSON
Architect

the grounds. I spend half my weekends trying to do something with all that.

You like people with imperfection in their beauty—what about in your architecture? You seem to favor perfection.

I used to. This new house is very peculiar, it doesn't look like a modern house at all. It's skinny, all curves and circles. You have to introduce some quirks, or architecture doesn't go on. Perfection like the Parthenon doesn't interest me. I like odd little doors and things. Architecture's changing very rapidly right now. The old Mies van der Rohe–Seagram Building days are over. There are more brooks and slopes and curves that we can introduce to make buildings more interesting. In New York there isn't any building of that kind except the new hotel at the United Nations. That's a good building.

What are the buildings you like best that you have designed?

Well, the most famous one is the Penzor Building in Houston. And then the IDS Center in Minneapolis. Ones you'd note here in New York are my own house where I live and the Brooks Library at NYU, the State Theater at Lincoln Center, Museum of Modern Art.

What do you think of New York City architecturally?

The cityscape, not the architecture, is fantastic—these straight lines that go from river to river. The sunset over the Hudson seen from the East Side is a great experience you can't get in any other city. Central Park you can't get in any other city. Wall Street you can't get in any other city—little Trinity Church against the big skyscrapers.

Are you optimistic about the future of New York City?

No. Actually I'm optimistic that it's going to die. But that's not a good or bad thing. It is good or bad when people die at ninety? Things change. Cities are no longer valid, because we live in an automobile culture until, perhaps, Mr. Carter comes along and says "No!" Our culture is suburban, or Los Angelesian, if you will. Houston is a perfect example. But New York doesn't fit that pattern. I love Houston. In architecture you want to be where the action is and the action is in Houston. It's more exciting there. Here it's all built; I don't have any work in New York at all.

Why do you live here?

I'm stuck here. No, I like it. I'm used to it.

Are you from New York?

No, Cleveland. *That's* why I live in New York.

Do you like to travel?

Not anymore. I traveled too much. The way to get over traveling is to travel too much.

To you, what are the seven wonders of the world?

Two cities I think, Fatehpur-Sikri in India and Teotihuacan in Mexico, are the two most important physical excitements in the world. Fatehpur-Sikri is right next to Taj Mahal, but nobody ever goes there because they want to visit that stupid

building. And ten miles away is this incredible deserted city. It's all red sandstone, temples and courtyards and mosques, sitting on a high hill. And Teotihuacan is a pyramid city just north of Mexico City. I love it. It's been deserted since the tenth century. I love pyramids.

Could you design one?

I wouldn't want to. It's not one of the interesting things to design today. They can be re-created, but nobody wants to— we can go to the moon instead. Right now I'm picking a flower pattern for my walls. I'm through with white. Things change. Today's passion is prints.

Are you designing your own?

Well, I don't like Vincent Fourcarde's. But what do I like? I've always decided on a white background, which we all do. I've never done anything else in my life. But it was high time to make something dazzle there. Even a good painting on that white wall was no longer satisfying. Now I have a problem with all the pictures I have—what will they look like against a print?

What do you think of decorators?

I don't know many. I think it's a splendid profession and I don't see the difference between it and architecture. Paul Rudolf, for example, is an architect who does very decorative kind of work. Decorators can perfectly well do architecture, and the two should overlap.

Are there any women architects today?

Not yet. Good architects take about ten years to nurture and get started, so of course there will be some after that time. But the trouble is that like any minority, when women start getting into a field, people say they can't do it, they're dumb. And *that* makes them dumb, to be told that. And it isn't true. But it's going to take ten years because they have to go to school and they have to have a sense of pride; they have to get rid of the inferiority complexes. Right now the women architects who are grown-up—that is, in practice— are so full of resentment that it hurts their work.

What do you think about young people today?

They're terrific. In New York, especially, there's a great group of young architects—just delightful. The next generation of architects will probably be great. I like younger people; they have more intelligence, more drive. Too many older people give up before they're dead. They're either dying or senile. And architects are only good when they're young and ambitious. I don't see any of my contemporaries.

What was the biggest mistake you ever made in your life?

God knows. There are too many to count. I guess, going into politics, in the first place, because I was terrible at it. Going into business, in the second place, because I'm lousy at it.

When did you go into politics?

In 1932, when I was a kid. I didn't think that it was fair that in the middle of the Depressison so many people had money while so many other people were hungry. It didn't add up. And I didn't like Communism or Fascism or any of that. So I thought I'd go down to Louisiana to see what Huey Long, who was a populist, was up to. But it didn't work out.

You lived in Germany under Hitler?
I was there the same time Chris Isherwood was there; and his book, *I Am a Camera*, is the perfect description of life during that period.

I read about you in Shirer's *Berlin Diaries*.
Well, he doesn't have it quite right, but he had an ax to grind.

What was it like to be in Germany then?
It was fascinating because the rallies were so exciting. There's been nothing like them since, and I wonder if there ever was anything like them. I mean, a million people on a field all saying the same thing is very impressive. Plus Albert Speer's lights. It was incredible, just overwhelming.

What do you think of dictators?
They're not good. Democracy may not be the best system in the world, but it sure as hell is better than the alternatives. We all dream, of course, of getting a pope, a Napoleon to come and say "Build!"—there isn't any.

Do you have any feelings about violence?
I like to watch it—in movies. I mean, people say, "Oh, how awful to have violence in movies." Well, what else? But, you know, I can't kill an animal.

Can you kill a fly?
Yes, when they work me up. Can't you?

Do you have any fears?
My God, that's all I've got—I'm a bundle of fears.

Do you have more as you get older, or less?
Less, because it's all downhill. If I should fall off off the top of a building or drown, it wouldn't really make much difference.

Does death scare you?
No, because I once crashed in an airplane and just before we crashed in the trees there was nothing but a very delightful calm. I don't know what it was—adrenalin?

Was everybody calm on the plane?
Yes. There were six of us in a one-engine plane. We crashed in Westchester. Hit a tree and spun around. Everybody was hurt but me. I walked away. Since then it doesn't seem to make much difference.

Would you like to live to ninety?
Again, I have to beat Frank Lloyd Wright. Look, the old life force still goes on. I thought that when I got to be seventy I'd have more sense, but not at all. I just want to beat them all.

Have you ever thought of suicide?
Yes, semi-seriously. But how do we know? We've all had the experience, haven't we? We don't know how serious we are, or we'd be dead. Obviously I wasn't too serious. And even if you think you are, what if somebody catches you just in time, *were you really?* But you can turn the gas on, it hisses nicely and then you say, All I have to do is put my head in there.

Do you ever get depressed?
Oh, heavens, who doesn't? I just wait for it to pass. I wake up in the middle of the night and I'm no good—I can't design anything and I'll be taken away in the morning by the sheriff for those awful mistakes I've made. The same thing happens to everybody, doesn't it? How could you ever think you ever were any good anyway? Whoever told you? All the mistakes which you do make in life come crowding in. Around four in the morning.

Do you take tranquilizers?
No, I take sleeping pills—Seconal, man's best friend.

Do you take vitamins?
I don't take vitamins. I never noticed the difference when I did. I used to take a whole handful of them and it didn't do anything.

Do you drink coffee?
All day long. It puts me to sleep.

It puts you to sleep in the morning?
When I wake up, nothing could put me to sleep. Sleeping pills couldn't put me to sleep.

What time do you go to bed?
Ten o'clock. I try to sleep till six or seven.

What do you like to do in the evenings? Watch TV?
I don't have a TV. I stay home, read, play parcheesi. You know, it's totally relaxing. I've always been like that. Always went to bed early. Even in my thirties, unless I was catting around.

What do you like to do for fun?
I like to go designing. I go out to Connecticut on weekends and I design things.

Do you like the country?
Yes, but New Canaan is hardly the country; it's getting less so, at least.

Is that where you would eventually like to end up living?
I'm already living. I'm not *eventually* anything. I'm where I want to be. *You* are looking forward. I don't have to because I'm doing exactly what I want to do. I have a house in town, a house in the country.

What's going to be new for you?
I'm going to go to Big Sur for a couple of weeks a year. I'm building a little inn there. It's the ideal place.

What kind of watch is that you're wearing?
It's my grandfather's. It was given to him for fifty years of faithful service. To what? To some goddamn company, I don't know. My watch is broken.

BILL KORNELL
Cowboy

Mr. Scavullo: What does it mean to be a cowboy today?
Mr. Kornell: I'm regarded as a cowboy in the rodeo-cowboy sense of the word. We're professional cowboys. We're not like the old-time ranch cowboys who still drive cattle and ride horses a lot.

Do you think that cowboys are a strange breed in America today?
In a way we are. We're different than a lot of other people. It seems like we have more fun and do more things than a lot of people because we don't get too worried about what tomorrow brings. It's like the old saying: chickens today and feathers tomorrow; one day you got lots of money, the next day you're flat broke. So you get to where nothing seems to really bother you. You just go and do the best you can in the rodeo.

Do you think it's very *macho* to be a cowboy?
I never really looked at it that way myself. It was something I've been all my life. I grew up being a cowboy. I wanted to be a bull rider since I can remember. I started riding bulls professionally when I was sixteen years old.

What makes you want to ride a bull?
Some people think it's lack of sense. It's just something that I've always wanted to do. There's a challenge there. I like things that are challenging. I don't like the everyday bit where you just get up and go do the same thing every day. Rodeo is a definite challenge. You have to do everything right. Or you get thrown off. The better cowboys don't get hurt all that much but you do get broken legs, pulled muscles, you get hoofed, you get run over—if you do it long enough you definitely get hoofed.

Is there an age where you have to stop riding bulls?
There's an average age of around thirty-five. And there's some people that go longer than that, some people don't make it that long. Depends on if a guy keeps himself in pretty good shape, takes care of himself, because it's mostly reflex action.

How old are you?
Thirty-three.

How do you keep yourself in good shape?
I exercise myself. I don't smoke. I do drink. I watch pretty carefully what I eat. I'll eat a good meal in the afternoon, and then maybe I'll eat a salad around suppertime if I've got time. In the summertime I generally only eat once a day. I eat quite a bit of meat, quite a bit of eggs. If I'm figuring on going a long time without eating, I'll eat some flapjacks. They stay with you better than anything else—two or three pancakes in the morning and you're good for the rest of the day.

About how many hours do you sleep a day?
In the summertime I'll get by on four to five hours' sleep. In the wintertime I'll average probably seven or eight hours.

Do you have checkups by a doctor?
I do because I'm also a licensed pilot and I have to get a medical checkup each year. But for the rodeo you don't have to.

What is your background?
I'm from Idaho now. I've lived in quite a few different places. I was born in Oregon, and my folks moved to California when I was pretty small.

What kind of folks did you have?
Father was a writer, Mother was just a housewife. I should say my father was my stepfather. I didn't know my father. I never did have much in common with my parents. I've always been around horses. My grandparents ran a cattle ranch. I used to go and stay with them in the summertime. Then I lived in Arizona a few years, finished my school in Arizona. I moved to Texas when I was about eighteen years old. I started rodeo when I was sixteen. Professionally. I did it earlier than that, but I got my membership in the professional association when I was sixteen years old. That was in 1960.

Can you make a lot of money in the rodeo?
You don't make a lot of money. You make enough money to not be too dependent on anybody. You get what we call a hot streak and a cold streak. When you're hot, seems like everything goes right and you win a lot of money. Then you get cold, you don't draw the type bulls that you need, they'll throw you off here and there, and things just don't go as good as they could. If you're good and you stay with it, you make a darn good living. And you can pretty well do what you want to do. If you want to take off for a while, think you can afford it, you can. A lot of times I'll just take off by myself and go up to the mountains for a little while.

Do you ever get lonely?
Not much anymore. When I first got divorced I was pretty lonely for a while. It wore off.

How long were you married?
Twelve years.

Do you have children?
Two.

Do you see your children?
Once in a while. I'd like to be able to see them more, but I'm so darn busy.

What kind of women do you like?
Ones that are fun to be with. It's hard to describe. After you been with one for a little while, you either like her or you don't like her. If I'm with a woman and I don't like her, I don't enjoy myself, I don't go out with her again. Cowboys really appreciate going out and having a lot of fun. They enjoy it and they don't expect a permanent relationship or something like that. We don't stay in one place very long. So it's hard to get into some of those long-term relationships.

Do women have to be beautiful?
They've got to be fairly decent-looking or I won't go out with them. I don't want to go out with just anybody that happens to be in the bar. I'm thoroughly choosy. Probably choosier than a lot of other cowboys are.

Do you have a lot of sex?
Yeah. I like as much as possible. It's just something that I really enjoy doing. I like to lay there and hug and kiss and caress and do things right. I don't like to just jump on and jump off and wave my hand, say "Thanks, I'll see ya." What I do I do good; I like to take my time with sex as well as my rodeo.

How many times do you have sex in a week?
It depends on the week. In the wintertime probably six, seven, eight times a week. Depends on who I'm with. If I'm in a town and I get a nice girl, I'll stay with that girl the whole time. Wintertime I spend a lot of time in the same places, whereas in the summertime we're in a different town every day. So I don't really have time for much sex in the summertime. Flying like I do—fly an airplane for another cowboy—we'll be up at daylight and I'll fly all day long. Lot

BILL KORNELL
Cowboy

of times I won't even go out at night in the summertime. I go to a night-time rodeo and by the time the rodeo's over it's midnight, and I got to get up at four, five o'clock the next morning. In the summertime I might do two or three reefers at night rather than have sex.

Cowboys spend a lot of time together in rodeos, without women.

That's correct. When I'm in the rodeo itself, I want to take a girl to the rodeo, visit with her a little bit, buy her a cup of coffee, give her a ticket, kick her in the butt and let her go sit down, because I want to get away from her for a little while. I go over and BS with the other guys, see what happened that day while I'm shacked up with somebody because I missed all the local gossip and I want to check everything out.

Do you talk about your sexual experiences with the other cowboys?

Some of them do. I say very little about mine. Far as I'm concerned, who I'm with and what I do is nobody's business but mine.

Are there girls who are like community property?

Yeah, there are quite a few of those around. I don't have much to do with any of them because I'm not really into that sort of thing. But there are quite a few girls around that'll maybe go to bed with three or four cowboys at the same time, and there are quite a few of them that'll go out with one guy for a while and then go out with somebody else for a while. That's not too bad; I'm not too much on taking those girls out myself.

Do they ever get a girl in the stables with them?

There's quite a few guys that'll do that; quite a little of that does happen. I just don't care for it myself that much.

Do they ever have a gang bang of several cowboys on one girl?

Oh, yeah. If everybody consents to it. Nobody forces a girl to do anything she don't want to do. If she don't want to do something, they'll find another one. Because there's lots of girls around. But as far as the gang-bang type of thing, I don't enjoy it. It's not my bag as far as sex goes. I hardly do it at all.

But have you?

In the past I have. One time at Wichita Falls, Texas, there was probably ten or twelve people went to bed with the same girl, all in a row. You stand in a line, bullshit, wait your turn. Jump on, jump off, leave, next guy bales in there. That one was a pretty darn nice-looking girl. She really was. She was clean. When each guy got done she'd jump up and run to the bathroom, clean up, wait for the next one to come.

Is there any homosexuality among cowboys?

No, cowboys don't want anything to do with that. They absolutely hate those kind of people. And it's funny, you know, that cowboys stay together all the time in the same room, we share double beds together all the time, and nobody does anything like that at all. And if one of that type of

people comes into a bar, if he behaves himself and don't get into any trouble, cowboys won't bother him much. They might make some remarks to try to get him to leave, see. They spot those type people pretty easily. If he ever touches one of them, he's right over the barn door, they're going to beat him plumb silly.

What about lesbians?

I've never been to bed with one, as far as I know. So I don't know a thing about it, other than what I've read. But anybody that doesn't really want to go to bed with a cowboy is not going to hang around the rodeo at all. They don't have to go to bed with everybody, but they're going to have to go to bed with somebody sooner or later. Cowboys are pretty free-wheeling. If they like a girl, they'll dance with her, buy her drinks and everything. But if they ever get down on a girl for any particular reason, doesn't make any difference what it is, then they're done with her, period. There's a girl down in Texas who was giving that pussy away pretty freely. And she did some things that cowboys didn't like. Mainly she went cussing one of the cowboys and cussing one of the girls that he was out with; she thought that she should be out with him instead of this other girl. And the cowboys got really down on her. They won't have anything to do with her at all now.

Do you ever strike a woman?

No, there's no reason for that. I get everything pretty well cut-and-dried before I leave the bar, you know. Never have any hassles, any problems. Even if they do go to the room and they don't want to go to bed with me, that's fine, just show them where the door is and tell them, "Hit the road." It's not that big a deal. Guy could get about all the sex he wanted if he just gets out and smiles and tries a little bit.

What do you think of women's lib?

I've been out with a few women-libbers and it wasn't bad at all. But I've been out with some other dingbats; they need a boot stuck in their ass, far as I could tell. Some of them are just way too far out as far as I'm concerned. If they want to go out and work, that's great with me, but you can carry everything too far.

Do you fight a lot?

Not among cowboys. There's quite a bit of fighting goes on, but it's not among ourselves. Most of the time we'll be in a bar, enjoying ourselves, and somebody'll come in and start agitating the situation and making trouble. Cowboys are not too bad about backing down from any situation they get into, but they'll darn sure swat a guy.

Do you have a gun?

I have quite a few guns and a few rifles that I use strictly for hunting. I carry a .357 Magnum in my pickup in case someone tries to do something that I don't want them to do. I've reached for it a couple times, but I've never had to pull it out. I'm dead set against any kind of gun-control program. I just don't feel they work. People are always going to get guns. If they want you dead, they're going to kill you. And I just don't feel that the government should be running our lives, telling us what we can own and what we can't own.

What do you think about the death penalty?

I'm a firm believer in it. I feel it would deter some people. If they knew when they went out and did a certain crime that they were going to face the death penalty, a lot of people would think twice about doing it. The way it is now, it's like getting your hand slapped. They've pretty well got the policemen's hands tied—they can't do much anymore.

Are you religious at all?

I haven't been to church in years. I believe that what is going to happen has already been pre-programmed for each individual. And when your time is up, your time is up. I've been in some scary situations and come out without a scratch, like flying airplanes where it's just as easy to kill myself as not. And I've been in a few situations in the arena where it'd have been pretty easy to get hurt real bad or possibly killed. And I came out in pretty darn good shape. So I just believe that your destiny's already planned when you are born.

Nothing frightens you?

Not very much, no. You can't be frightened or scared of the bulls, and still be able to ride. You've got to have a certain amount of respect for them. But if you get on scared, thinking that you're going to get hurt, then you can't concentrate. And you've got to really concentrate and do things right.

Do you think about getting old?

At times, but I try not to think about it. I think I'm in real good physical shape for my age, and I take real good care of myself, and I'm riding as good now as I have in years. So I don't really worry about it. I'm a good bush pilot, so when I can't rodeo, I can get a job in the north some place, flying. A guy can always work if he wants a job. It may not be what you want to do, but I've always been able to get a job and make ends meet.

What about death?

Everybody's got to die sooner or later. I'm having so much fun I'd just as soon put it off for another thirty or forty years at least. I'm having more fun now than I've had in ten years.

Because rodeos are getting more popular?

Yup, they're definitely getting more popular. More people come to them all the time, and the people that come to them know more about what's going on. I don't know just exactly what the attendance is, but I do know it's pretty close to baseball and football now. It's definitely big business. Prize money's up to over $6 million now.

Do you like luxuries?

I like nice things, but not really luxuries. I don't wear fancy clothes, but I like to look nice and I like to be clean. On the road I like to stay in better places; I call that a luxury.

What do you travel with?

I've got one small suitcase and one bag for my rodeo equipment, my rope and my spurs, bells, chaps. In the suitcase I carry two extra pair of pants besides the one that I'm wearing, about six shirts, two or three pair of socks, that's it.

What about underwear?

I don't even wear underwear.

Where do you buy your clothes?

I work for the Wrangler Corporation. I'm on their advertising staff. So I get all my shirts and pants furnished for me. I also advertise for the Tony Lama Boot Company and I get all my boots free. These boots here run about $300. They're ostrich. They're real tough, durable—a real good boot.

Who cuts your hair?

An Indian barber in Dallas, Texas, does it most of the time. I like to keep it looking nice. That's why I generally go to this barber in Dallas. He's a good friend of mine, and he's really a super barber, he knows what he's doing.

How tall are you?

I'm five-ten. My hat makes me taller; got a high crown on this hat.

Do people look at you in New York?

Yeah, I get lots of people staring when I walk down the street wearing a cowboy hat. They don't know what to think really. The way of life is different. I don't think I could ever live here. Too many people, not enough sunlight as far as I'm concerned. Half of the rodeos I go to are in big towns, so I'm pretty well used to big towns, but I definitely would never want to live in a big town. The town that I call home has only twenty-five hundred people. It's a hundred and sixty miles from the next biggest town, with no trains, no airlines, one bus three times a week.

Do you ever look at television or go to movies?

I go to the movies once in a while, not very often. I watch a little bit of television in the wintertime. Summertime I generally don't watch any at all. I like to watch football games in the fall. I really enjoy football.

Do you read magazines, newspapers, books?

I read books. I don't read a lot of magazines, but I glance at the headlines in the newspaper. I mainly listen to the radio to keep up on what's happening in the world.

Are you very political?

No.

Do you vote?

I vote every year. I believe a person should vote. You can't just sit back and let the other guy do everything. That's one of the things that's probably wrong with the way things are going now, everybody just sits back and hopes somebody else is going to do it. You can't do that in the rodeo, because nobody will do anything for you in rodeo. Friends help you all they can, but when it comes right down to it, it's strictly what you can do. And people that are raised that way are a pretty damn independent bunch of folks.

KRIS KRISTOFFERSON
Singer, Songwriter, Actor

Mr. Scavullo: How did you begin singing?
Mr. Kristofferson: I always liked to sing. Not sure I can remember singing when I was raking out the corral, you know, in Texas. First thing I wanted to be was a boxer. That was at the age of eight or so. That's kind of in the league with cowboy and fireman. But I wanted to be Rocky Graziano. Then I wanted to be a writer. All through high school and college, I was a creative-writing major. I wrote short stories and stuff. Did very well in college—in fact, won a Rhodes scholarship. At one point, back in the fifties, I started to get into the music business but it wasn't the right time. So I joined the Army, and then I started writing songs again, in '65 in Nashville. About five years later I got asked to perform at the Troubadour in Los Angeles. And we went over real well and just stayed on the road ever since. So I sort of backed into performing and out of performing, and then the movie offers came. We were *hot*, you know.

What's more important to you, your music or your acting?
I feel kind of like a little kid and people say, "What are you going to be when you grow up?" I didn't know that you had to be one thing. I'd hate to have to limit it. I can have a lot of fun acting now. And it's working. I get satisfaction out of it. But the writing is something that's always in the back of my mind, it's always going. Not always as fast as I would like, but I'm always writing. I'll probably write until I die.

Write songs or stories?
Both. I'll probably write songs all the time because they just come out of my emotions. I hope I'm always that open. And I'm thinking in terms of longer stuff. I have a little project now, but I don't know whether it's a novel or screenplay. I'm going deeper into the thing. I'm really excited about writing something long for the first time in a long time. It's different from a song. That doesn't mean it's good. I was excited about my last novel, too, and I never got that published.

Do you ever get tired of touring, being on the road?
I was on the road about five years. And I was getting real weary. I didn't even know I was tired. Fortunately I was forced into a period of inactivity when they postponed starting *Semi-Tough*, because it was too late to schedule me on the road. So I ended up sitting around and got a little rest. And I think it was good to see where I was going. Anyway, we had a lot more fun after the break, had a better idea of what to do. Got so I used to live day to day on the road. I'd be eight months at a time just getting ready for that show that night, and the band would end up not having enough development musically because everybody was doing it— almost the same way we started out doing it, when I had to tell everybody what to do—and so everything was limited to how limited my imagination was back then when I told them.

How is your life now? You told me you've given up drinking. Do you have more energy?
I got a lot more energy. I feel twenty years younger. There are a lot of fringe benefits to giving up liquor—less calorie intake and less getting in trouble. Every time I got in trouble I was drunk. But I think the worst thing about it was the effect of the chemical on my brain and nervous system. I thought I just always got depressed, I didn't know that it had anything to do with whiskey. But I think whiskey had a lot to do with it, because I haven't been depressed since I gave it up. You know, those black things, where you think there isn't

any sense in getting up in the morning. When I got to that point I figured I was doing something drastically wrong. Then I was lucky enough to see *A Star Is Born*. I watched the whole story, and the first time it was kind of rough. It was amazing.

And you just quit drinking, cold turkey?
Yeah. I didn't make a conscious decision; it was just the logical thing to do at that time. And I don't look back. But I never even considered quitting until I quit.

Do you smoke?
I did. I smoked four packs a day, but I quit that about three years ago. A member of the band had to, so we made a deal—if he didn't smoke, I wouldn't smoke. The doctor told me, "His throat's rotten like an old tubercular patient and if he keeps smoking he'll die." So I made this deal with him. And it's easier that way, because you're not just doing it yourself.

Do you exercise?
Yeah. I run, and I work on the bags. I feel a lot better for it. I've been exercising more than I have before. I got a rowing machine and I got—it's embarrassing—one of those huge Advent TVs and I set that up in front of the rowing machine. So I watch TV and just row.

What do you do to relax? Watch TV or go out to clubs or . . . ?
Don't go out much at all. See, everything that I've done in the last years has been influenced by the road. You get a road mentality. If you're out working for a month and you've got two days off, you come home, lock the doors and crash. And don't answer the phone. Because you've got two days to do nothing but enjoy creature comfort and then get back out on the road. It sounds like a shitty life. I got a Jacuzzi now. That's a great thing.

At what age did you get married?
The first time I got married I was twenty-four. And I married Rita Coolidge about three years ago, so I was about thirty-seven.

Why did you get divorced the first time?
It was difficult. She was an old high school sweetheart, and I hadn't seen her for a long time, and she knew me as one thing, as a Rhodes scholar, and then I was an Army officer. My next assignment was to teach English at West Point, which was a fairly respectable position, and to pass that up to become a janitor who wants to be a songwriter . . . it was hard for her to like anything about the music business because it represented everything that was taking me out of the house. And for me it was the thing that was bringing me back to life after the Army. And it was very selfish of me, but there's a point in your career or your development as an artist when you have to be selfish. You can't have a permanent relationship, because it will hold you back. You have to be free to go do it when the opportunity comes, and not worry about whether you might injure somebody else's feelings. It's just the selfish part of your life. It sounds worse than it is. It just means that you have to pay attention to your work more than anything else.

How many children do you have?
I got three. One from Rita, two from the other.

Do you like being married?
I must or I wouldn't be. I haven't done a whole lot of things

KRIS KRISTOFFERSON
Singer, Songwriter, Actor

that I didn't like very long. I was talking with Rita the other day about it. If you're involved in a career, there are definite disadvantages to being married. But there are also advantages. You got a home base. You got some security somewhere.

Is it difficult with both of you having fairly successful careers?
The more success both of you have, the better it is. For a while it was very easy because we would perform together every time we performed—that was a piece of cake. Then I started doing movies, which she didn't want to do. I think she's looking forward to getting back to working together.

How do you satisfy your sexual drives on the road?
I've had Rita with me usually, since '72. I think that's about all I should say.

Is sex very important to you? Some performers or athletes don't have sex before they go on . . .
It's not part of my pre-game ritual, but it's very important to me in my life.

. . . a lot of people have an idea that sexual frustration leads to creativity.
I think that's bullshit. A lot of people have an idea that starvation does, too, and I think that's bullcrap. All it does is make it harder to be creative. You got to go out and get another job. That's oversimplification, because success, or *making it* as we know it, can be as limiting to your creativity as failure. You just have to learn to deal with both of them. With success I have to learn to deal with a lack of time and privacy. Before, all I had was time, and I had to deal with a lack of tension. Now I got too much tension and not enough time. But I don't worry about it, as I did before when there would be dry spells of not writing. I feel more creative now.

What kind of women attract you?
I don't know how I can limit it. I see different things in different people. I just like people, and half the people are women. I'm attracted to the same things I'm attracted to in a man: honesty, intelligence, and then whatever it is I just like about a person's mood, or the way somebody looks today.

What about women becoming stronger in the world today?
That's all for the better as far as I'm concerned. No, I think the best thing that ever happened to somebody, especially somebody that's a little shy, like me, is that there's more equality. Takes the load off the guy having to make the first move all the time. I mean, if I had to think about all the people that I ever talked into making love with me, I could probably limit it to one or two or three in my whole life, you know. It's usually something I fall into. It just seems to me, in anything, the closer you are to having two equals, the more interesting it is. It's like a tennis match—not that I'm comparing a relationship between people with a tennis match.

Do you care much about clothes and appearance?
I care a little; I can't care too much, since everything I've got came out of the movies—I don't own any clothes that I didn't get out of wardrobe. But fortunately it's not necessary to wear a lot of different clothes. And God knows if I bought as many as Rita did, there wouldn't be room for us in the house.

How do you feel about getting older?
I don't feel as bad about it as I did about ten years ago.

Probably because of the way things turned out. It was almost like working out with 16-ounce gloves and then getting to go down to 8-ounce gloves, you see. I'm in better shape than I was in the Army. And feeling better.

Do you ever think about dying?
I think you think about dying more as you get older. When I was younger I didn't mind dying. I'd like to live for a long time now and be creative for a long time. I'd like to see my kids grow up.

What kind of father are you? Are you very strong with your kids?
I don't know how good a father I am. I mean, when you break up a marriage, that's not being the best father in the world. My kids love me, and that's more to my wife's credit than mine—for not badmouthing me while I was gone. But I feel like I'm a good father, because I have the love of the kids. I'm better now than I was because I'm not scrambling to find out who the hell I am, or to make a living, so I can take them with me on the road and on my times off.

Do you worry about the permissiveness in our society, pornography, drugs, in connection with your kids?
Life worries me in connection with the kids, but I think my kids are a lot smarter than I was at their age, for openers. I'm not worried about them. They seem to deal with things so well. I used to worry that a broken home would cause damage, but I look at the kids and they're beautiful and I see that they just came out okay on their own, anyway. I have to say that Rita does all the work and I get to enjoy the show. I get more into my kids as I've grown older. It seems funny to even say "older," because I think I'm younger now.

It's unusual that you've become such a star so late in your life.
I was thirty-four when I did my first film and I was that old when I first performed on stage in front of people for money. So it all happened pretty fast. The advantage of it is that you handle it better when you're older. I was pretty dumb when I was twenty-two; I even changed my name to Kris Carson once, that's how dumb I was. I was thinking of Freddie Prinze when he died. Part of the reason was because he was twenty-two. When you're twenty-two you still don't know whether you're tough enough to survive. You haven't hit the bottom and found out that it isn't the end of the world like you think it is. When you're shaky, and you're young, you got nothing to compare it with. If I'm down and out, I know that I've worked ever since sixteen at construction jobs. So I know I'm not going to starve to death. I can do something I don't like to do for nine months. And a lot of young people haven't done that. The disadvantage of being older is that you don't feel like doing a lot of crazy things you would have done that might be advantageous to you. I don't know if they are or not. I'm just so goddamn lucky to get up here right now and be accepted on my own terms.

You're not a temperamental actor, are you?
I can lose my temper. It's easier not to when I'm not drinking. But I don't want to paint a false picture of sainthood here, because I just about cleaned out the crew on my last film. No, really, I get along with the people on the job.

Did you ever take drugs?

I don't do any hard drugs. I smoke grass. When I was working on the road, I'd take anything that was offered to me. Not to excess. I was never a speed freak or a coke head. My main problem was the juice. There's something about doing coke two days in a row that's very unpleasant. So I doubt that I'd get into that, but I'm not going to guarantee anything. I think the whole society is into drugs. But as far as the drug culture that they used to talk about, it's not as heavy as it was back ten years ago. Then everything in life revolved around it. And there were a lot of deaths. I don't hear about as many people on smack.

Do you think the government laws on drugs are right?
I think marijuana should be decriminalized. Everybody I know does. I think it's amazing how far human civilization has come lately. In the four million years that man's been on the planet, it's only been a century that he traveled faster than a horse. It's only been since the turn of this century that they had cars, and then about ten years later the airplanes, then jets for World War II, then satellites and things on Mars. All of this is like a nuclear reaction, going faster at the end. Technologically it's amazing. You don't realize it until you see somebody like Rita's grandmother, who is ninety-six or ninety-nine. And at age ninety-four she's flying out from Tennessee—the first time she'd ever been on a plane. She was born when Billy the Kid was alive, traveling in covered wagons. The change during her life compared to the whole length of time man's been on the planet is very remarkable. If it were all an hour, it'd be like a minute that man was making other things to travel in, and maybe a second that he did the kinds of travel that he has now. And then I got to thinking, my God, if back in the fifties there were politicians advocating the easing of marijuana laws, you would have thought the world was coming to an end. People who smoked marijuana were dope fiends back in those days. When the first one's free, the rest of them hook you for life. Remember that film, *The Cruel and the Crazy*, where a whole high school went berserk from one joint. Look at the difference today. I mean, like co-educational dorms. Christ, they wouldn't let you have a girl in the room with the door closed when I was going to college. I think it's for the better. But what is interesting is how fast the changes are coming. What're we going to take for granted twenty years from now that we are completely flustered by today?

It seems like you went through some kind of dramatic change in thinking, to go from a very straight career in the Army to wanting to be a songwriter.
I went through a change, yeah. It was a realization that if I stayed in this straight world, it was going to be a death sentence to me, because if you're doing anything that you're not suited to do, you're going to be miserable. And I can play the game—I didn't have a bad career in the Army—but I just wasn't suited for it. I was the general's pilot and it was fun to fly, but I hated to wear a uniform, hated to get up on time, hated to have someone telling me what to do.

You like freedom.
Yeah, but I don't think any more so than anybody else. Everybody would like to be free. But it's so easy to say that I chose this course and that I went out and got it through

perseverance and all that crap. There's a lot of luck in it.

Do you like seeing yourself on the screen?
I'm fairly objective about it. I've liked it when I was good and I've been embarrassed when I wasn't. Like in *The Sailor Who Fell from Grace with the Sea*, I was bothered because of the look on my face, the make-up was almost like a mask. It was not the make-up man's fault, this is what we told him to do. But it gave me an odd expression that I couldn't ever forget. And anything that gets between you and an honest interpretation of the work is a failure, I think.

When you make a film, do you go see the rushes?
When I can. Because being as new as I am I feel like I'm learning all the time. It's like watching the game films in football.

Did you study acting?
No, I wasn't even in drama in college. But I studied literature, a lot of Shakespeare and stuff, but never acting as acting.

You always act like yourself, though, don't you?
I think most actors who are successful take from their experience what they can put into a character. I have played so many different roles, from a star in *A Star Is Born*, to a football player in *Semi-Tough*, to a square farmer in *Alice Doesn't Live Here Anymore*. So I'm playing myself, but I'm playing different parts of myself.

What kind of things bother you about life today?
My God, we haven't got that much time! Jeez. Well, it bothers me that I've only talked to two people who are remotely concerned that the House assassination committee was castrated, and that they probably will never try to find out any truth about it. That bothers me. I'm bothered by prejudice, by ignorance, in very vague ways. And I also get bothered by little shitty things, like somebody losing my wardrobe. I should say if there's one thing that bothers me right now, it's lack of privacy. But it's not something I can complain about, when I've forced it on myself. It's like a fighter going back in the corner and saying, "That son-of-a-bitch out there is hitting me."

What kinds of things make you happy?
My wife and kids. People that are great, getting close to people.

Are there any people that you admire?
William Blake is a hero, but he's dead; I have a lot of heroes —Johnny Cash is a hero, Willie Nelson is a hero. I have a lot of heroes, a lot of people that I respect, and the only reason I hesitate to get into them is I'll think of about ten more when I leave—god-dang, I didn't say Jerry Lee Lewis, you know. That's one of my biggest concerns now—amnesty for Jerry Lee. So long as everybody else is finally getting it, why not him and George Jones.

Do you believe in God?
I'm religious. I don't go to church. I would probably state it more like William Blake did than Jimmy Carter, or even Johnny Cash, would. But it's like Blake says: "You who are organized by the divine for spiritual communion, diffuse and bury your talent in the earth, sorrow and desperation will pursue you throughout life, and after death shame and confusion will face you to eternity." I believe that. I think it's the thing that probably distinguishes us from animals.

KARL LAGERFELD
European Fashion Designer

Mr. Scavullo: Are you German or French?
Mr. Lagerfeld: I was born in Germany, but I came to France when I was a child. I can speak German, but now I'm French, I have a French passport, I went to school in France and everything.

How did you first begin designing clothes, and when?
I can't remember when I didn't draw. When I was very, very young I wanted to become a stage designer, but, in fact, I was too attracted by fashion. And when I was sixteen years old, I won a contest that was organized by the International Wool Fashion Society. Two hundred thousand amateurs from all over the world entered that contest. And I got the first prize for a drawing of a coat. That's how it started.

Did you study fashion?
No, I never studied. I started working right after I won that contest. First for Pierre Balmain, who was a big success in the fifties. All the actresses went to him. Dior and Balenciaga had the chic woman, but actresses went to Balmain. I wouldn't say his style is my style, but I was not there to be impressed, I was there to learn. So I told myself, "Shut up, listen to orders and do what you have to do to learn your business, no?" And it was fun. I made dresses for movies with Vivien Leigh, Rita Hayworth, Sophia Loren, Anita Ekberg, everybody of that period. But for that sort of movies then, the dresses were quite tacky.

And then, when I was nineteen, I was asked to be art director of Jean Patou, and I preferred that to being assistant designer to sombeody else because at Patou there was nobody else—Patou was dead. I could do what I wanted. But they had very old clients and the whole atmosphere was—I mean, everybody was very nice, but it was a little too late. Patou was a fascinating house in the twenties, and perhaps in the early thirties, but by then it was quite boring. There was nothing to do. I only had to make fifty dresses twice a year, for the spring and fall collections. I mean, that's not enough to keep me busy. Today I do a hundred thousand dresses a year—I don't even know how many. And that's much more fun because the more I work, the faster and easier I get new ideas.

Do you make clothes for men as well as women?
Yes, but just for my private use. If you get in the men's business and you want to do funny little things, you cannot do them because it becomes too difficult on an industrial level. So I just make funny clothes that I like for myself. Normally, the clothes I wear I make for myself and my friends—I give clothes to them—so nobody else can buy them, nobody else can wear them, nobody else can have them. I don't want to be a shopkeeper . . . that's boring.

How did you get into designing the rather sadomasochist clothes for the movie _The Mistress?_
The director, Barbet Schrader, called me.

Are you interested in S & M?
I am not interested at all. I think it's fun, but I can't believe that people take that seriously.

Can you describe a day in your life in Paris?
I get up quite early, eight o'clock, something like that. The masseur comes very early. And then I do half an hour of gymnastics, and take a bath. I spend the whole morning at home, have lunch at home and go out in the afternoon. I have all my appointments, all my fittings, everything in the afternoon. I come home at seven or eight, and if I have to go

out again, I take two or three hours before for myself. And if I go to bed at two or three, I don't care; I don't need more than five hours of sleep.

Do you have manicures?
Yes, a manicurist comes to me, and I have facials at home.

What do you think are the best fabrics for men's clothes?
Personally, I love to wear cotton all year round because you can wash it, change it every day—cotton pants, shirts, jackets, everything. I must say, the fabric I prefer to wear is cotton. Even in the winter. I wear a fur coat, so who cares if it's cold or warm. And, personally, I nearly never wear sweaters. Nearly never. Every sweater I have designed, I think, This one I will wear—and after a week I give it away. I never keep anything. I have a huge dressing room with mirrors all around, but my closets are almost empty. I give everything away. So I don't have that much at once. I like something for the moment. For example, I have twenty or thirty of this shirt, all different colors—sometimes I wear two of them, one over the other. And when I'm tired of this shirt and change everything, I will give all twenty or thirty away. So I have a lot of drawers filled with scarves and ascots, and I like to play around with those things over a very simple base, that's nearly always the same color—white or ivory— and bright colors nearly never, except very bright emerald green. I don't wear color very much. Sometimes purple. I like to wear purple, very dark red, burgundy, mauve—I hate myself in bright reds, bright yellows—you have to be tanned and I'm never tanned anymore, so it's better to wear other colors.

Why don't you get a tan?
I used to love, like everybody else, to be tanned all year round, and then, suddenly, I preferred to be pale. I don't know why. Now I don't have the patience to stay in the sun anymore. After ten minutes I become an idiot.

Where do you go for vacation?
I have a very, very, very beautiful house in Brittany. But I don't go to the beach. The heat drives my guests to the beach and I stay at home. That's my favorite hour because I'm all alone, it's quiet, there's nothing to do, no one to always look after, it's so relaxing. You know, everybody is always tanned. But I prefer my face pale rather than tanned. I think it's better for the skin. Especially if you are over thirty-five. Because all the men I know who are my age look like old lemons, all wrinkled. They're okay so long as they are tanned all the time. But if they are out of the sun for six months, they look terrible, really tired. Like a drug. You have to keep it up, even though it's ruining your skin you have to keep it up. And I think that, finally, pale is more me than tanned. I'm not especially romantic, so it's not because I think it's more romantic to be pale.

How do you spend that time you have alone when everyone is in the sun?
Doing my favorite thing—nothing. Reading and writing. I am never bored. I don't even have time to look at television, because time goes so quickly. I love to be with people, and I love to be alone. And I work, too, when I'm alone, because I prepare what I have to do in Paris later. But, in fact, I like working only in Paris. And I never use what I prepare in the country. I don't know why. Fashion just has to be done in Paris. It's strange, no? But what I really do best has to be done in Paris and not in a vacation atmosphere. So I don't go

to Brittany very often, and I only stay there for three or four days, never longer than that. Even if my friends stay there for two months, I have to go back to Paris all the time. Very often, and quickly. Perhaps one day I will change, but for the moment I am like that.

You really like working?

Absolutely. And I am a quite well organized soul. Everything is going quite smoothly. But what I love best is to stay at home in the morning. I love the early hours of the day, especially in Paris. I love the Place Saint Sulpice; it is a huge square with a beautiful Italian-looking church, and the light in the morning is very beautiful. From the windows of my workroom you can see the whole square. And the light of the city is stunning. It is an atmosphere I love, and for me these hours are the most creative hours. My best ideas are early in the morning. When I was young, I used to love to work at night. I hated the morning. But now I like morning.

What do you think of couture today?

Couture was important when the women who bought couture were fashion leaders. Today those women are not fashion leaders anymore, and that's why couture is not important. Couture is now as important as good tailors for men. That's all. I don't think it's important for fashion. Because today, before a woman buys an expensive dress, she tries to get an expensive body. I mean, they're all slim today, so there's no problem of fitting anything anymore. And for nothing in the world would today's woman go to a high-fashion house three times to fit one dress. There are no women like Daisy Fellows, who had a dress made to match the blue flowers on her yacht, because they don't have a yacht, so there are no blue flowers there for the clothes to match. Those things don't exist anymore; young, beautiful women have other problems, but not that sort of problem. So there is no inspiration, because the women who can afford to buy cannot inspire, and then there is no life.

I hate the idea of having a high-fashion house, because I like to design whatever I want for an ideal woman. It can be this girl, that girl, it can be inspired by ten different women, but not a woman I'm supposed to sell to. High-fashion designers design for the people they sell to. I don't like that. I am not a couturier. I make dresses—they like them or they don't like them, that is not my problem. I'm not waiting in a high-fashion house to flatter those ladies and say, "Oh, I hope they will like it." That really is degrading, humiliating.

You do one couture kind of collection?

Yes, but it is fun to make twenty or thirty dresses so beautifully that I cannot repeat them. And then to put them in the same shop, and whoever wants them buys them. But they are not made to order, they are just unique items.

Most of your dresses are made of crepe de Chine, probably the best silk there is. Any particular reason for using such incredible silk?

That's why my dresses are all so expensive. And then the prints I design—I design all my prints myself—are very often done in twelve or fifteen colors, and that costs a fortune too. But I think there's nothing more sensual, more beautiful, for colors than silk, and crepe de Chine especially. To me crepe

de Chine is like white paper for an artist. It is the material on which I express myself best. But sometimes you have to put things you like best away and do something new. Everybody has crepe de Chine now. A few years ago nobody else had it. Now they all have it, even if not such a good quality. To people who know nothing about silk it looks the same.

Do you like synthetic fabrics?

I have nothing against synthetics, but I think they are on the wrong track when they try to imitate wool, silk and cotton. That's not interesting. Someday they will make something completely new and different, and I will use it. But there is no reason to use copies of something else.

What do you think of the way American women dress?

There're very chic dressers, well-dressed people, all around the world; there are badly dressed people all around the world too. I have a very international mind. There are people who are beautiful, well-dressed and perfect, and there are others who are not. But they're as much here as in France. The American women look cleaner.

What about American men?

In many ways the American businessman of the higher level looks better than the European businessman of the same level. You have all those important businessmen flying from, say, Paris to Lyons; there will not be one woman on the plane. And they all have the same ugly suits, I don't know where they're coming from. The same ugly shoes, the same ugly ties, the same ugly stockings, all of them, all the same. Italy is where men take the most care.

Do you think a man needs make-up for his face?

I am not against make-up at all. I think it's a great thing. But to bring it out on the market on a large scale is still difficult. So for the moment my line will stick to shaving products and dust powder and fragrance. I like a quite strong fragrance for men. That must be my German part, because German men use a very strong fragrance. It's unbelievable, it smells like Mitsouko from Guerlain.

Do you think modern man is too afraid of his masculinity to buy make-up?

It's so ridiculous. But remember when men had make-up and everything in France in the late seventeenth, early eighteenth centuries. It was fun. Between 1650 and 1850 it was great fun for a man to dress, nearly as much as for a woman. It started to become a little boring, too much just the same suit, about 1840 or 1850. But my favorite period in classic men's wear was 1880. The use of satin, things like this, was very chic. The way the clothes were made was so refined.

What do you think of the classic male uniform?

If you have a uniform, everything has to be of the greatest quality, because it shows more then than in fantasy clothes. I can only accept a uniform when it's really perfection, from the best tailor, beautifully done, with the best shoes, everything top quality. If you wear whatever you want, you can mix everything together. But if you want the uniform, it has to be perfection—if you want to look that way. But who wants to look that way? I don't. I don't even own a dinner jacket anymore. My big problem with classic clothes is that my favorite tailor, who was really a genius, died three years ago. I had my first suit made by him when I was sixteen years old. He fitted clothes like gloves. But I never found somebody else. So if I wear classical clothes, they are all very old; I have black suits that must be fifteen years old now. But if your weight stays the same, they don't look different.

Do you diet?
Once I did and I lost so much weight that I was too skinny for my personal taste. Perhaps it's chic to be very skinny, but I was depressed and tired all the time. I feel better with a little more weight. That's more important. When I was so skinny, I was depressed because I was tired.

Do you ever get depressed for any other reason?
When I don't like my work. When I'm not satisfied with myself, with what I am doing. Even if everybody tells me it's great, I know myself when it isn't.

Does getting older depress you?
Oh no, I never felt better. I hated myself when I was young. I am pleased that I will be forty soon. It's not a problem at all.

Do you have any fears?
I like only good health. It's the most important thing in the world.

Do you do anything for good health?
I don't drink alcohol and I smoke very little. I cannot drink for a very stupid reason. If I have a glass of something I fall asleep immediately, so I have never been drunk in my life because I have always fallen asleep before.

Do you take coffee or tea?
Sometimes I'll have a cup of tea in the morning, but no coffee, no drugs, nothing ever.

What foods do you like?
The worst. Chocolate, American cake, Italian food, Vietnamese food—I don't like French food. I can admit it in America, but if I say it in France they'll kill me. Great French cooking is too overdone. I love Italian food. If I lived in Italy I would be a fat man, I just could not stop eating. And I don't like to have meals at regular hours; I like to eat when I'm hungry. I am unable to have a real social life for a very stupid reason: I am late all the time. Hours late. If you invite me to dinner at nine o'clock, I arrive at eleven. I don't do it on purpose. It just happens that way. I'm late all the time. I was born late. I spend my life running after trains and planes.

Do you like to travel?
I like places I am used to. In New York I always stay at the Pierre; I cannot imagine going somewhere else. It may be better somewhere else, I don't know. I like the same suite all the time. I don't know how the other rooms look.

Your apartment in Paris is Art Deco style?
It used to be Art Deco. But it was like a movie set, it was just too much. Everything was too perfect, I could not live in it.

Do you live alone?
Yes. I prefer it. I have to. My fortuneteller told me to. It's very important for me to be alone for four or five hours a day. And I am unable to sleep in a room with somebody else. In my whole life I have never slept in the same room with somebody else. I could not. I hate the idea of somebody seeing me sleeping. It's as if somebody could see me dead. I hate the idea that somebody could see me without me wishing to be seen.

So you're not afraid to die, but you'd hate for anybody to see you dead?
Oh, death is nothing. I mean, death is the price of life. Millions have passed through life before us and millions will die after. It's not that important.

Do you feel that you have to leave something behind?
That's a joke.

Don't you want to donate any of your clothes to museums?
No. I don't even keep photos of my dresses. I am only interested in what I am doing, and what I will do. What I have done I have done it, I am not interested in it anymore. Perhaps one day when I stop everything, I will start to remember everything.

Would you like to do anything else besides designing clothes?
Oh yes, a lot of other things. My fortuneteller told me that when I stop the fashion business, I will become a movie producer.

Are you from a rich family?
I wouldn't say poor. My father was sixty when I was born, so he would be nearly a hundred today if he were alive. He introduced canned milk in Europe. And then the business became too big and he was getting too old, and I was not interested in that, so he sold the whole thing to the German Carnation Company. I have nothing to do with that anymore. I must say, the milk business is not my dream. If there's something I don't like to drink, it's milk. I *hate* milk!

What do you drink?
Water. And port sometimes; it's the only alcohol I drink.

What kind of people do you like physically?
You know, physically beautiful people are usually plastic. That's the danger. I think personality is more important. I don't like models. And I don't like skinny people. I think it's very *démodé*. It's a nightmare of the high-fashion model from the late fifties and early sixties. I don't like it at all.

Do you like flowers?
I like flowers in the garden. I am not too crazy about cut things or dead in a vase.

What kind of people do you prefer to have around you?
I like creative people. And I like the same people around all the time. I like people I am used to. I'm not a collector of people. And the person whose company I really prefer is an Italian woman called Anna Piaggi, because to talk to her is the most inspiring thing in the world. She is creative in every instant of her life; when she enters a room boredom doesn't exist anymore. She knows how to create magic in a place. And very few women still know how to make a place magic by the simple fact of being there.

What do you think of ambitious working women?
It's good to be ambitious, why not? But it depends on how they look, if they are inspiring or not. If not, they are not interesting for me. And a woman is much stronger if she doesn't compete with men. I think the world would be very boring without women. That's why I don't like women who try to imitate men.

LEO LERMAN
Features Editor of *Vogue*

Mr. Scavullo: Why do you always wear purple?
Mr. Lerman: My real preoccupation with purple began about six years ago. Until then it was limited to purple socks, which I first started wearing twelve years ago. Suddenly one day I saw these perfectly marvelous purple socks. And the color pleased me. I felt so relaxed when I saw that color. So I bought four dozen. And I never bought another color sock after that. Then about six years ago I got to hankering after a lavender shirt, because I thought that since I was getting older, and my whiskers were turning white, and I knew how absolutely beautiful lavender is with silver hair on old ladies, I thought it would work for me, too. Also you can wear practically any other color with lavender. You can wear the loudest colors in the world and they look subdued in some strange way. Lavender caresses, as does the whole purple range.

Then about four years ago I took to writing in purple ink. By that time I had found all shades of purple and lavender handkerchiefs and scarfs. The more I got, the more it pleased me, the more relaxed I felt—"soothed" is the one word for it. But when I took to using purple ink I thought, That's an affection. But it was easier for me to see it. And a year ago I had an eye operation for cataracts and I asked the doctor about purple. He said it was really like a dog eating green grass to get better, because all of that purple range is so kind to the eye. So what I thought to be a fancy, really affected, ultimately turned out to be quite practical. Now my eyes are just marvelous, but why give it up? Also I had this extraordinary revelation after I could see again. You know, for a long time I couldn't see. I groped my way to work. And right after the operation I saw myself in a looking glass. It was a shock, a revelation. When I could hardly see at all I believed that I was actually a madly attractive older man with silver whiskers and that kind of personality. But I looked in the looking glass for the first time after the operation and I saw my mother's father, my grandfather Goldwasser, who was a beast. I have lines in the same places he does. And my beard wasn't silver at all, it was grizzled.

Why do you have a beard?
I woke up in Bellevue with it in 1942. I was in a cab accident. I was knocked out for weeks, and didn't know I had a beard. And, again, I looked in the looking glass and I absolutely hated that beard. In those days nobody had a beard except merchant seamen. Beards were so obsolete that not even old fogeys had beards. But I looked at it again—it was a wild thing, like something Biblical—and I suddenly thought, That's really marvelous, you should keep that beard because it's distinctive and it will give you confidence.

During the first years that I had it, whole busloads of people used to fall into fits of joy when they saw me, especially in the winter, because I always wore fur hats and sometimes you didn't know where the hat began and the beard left off. It's only been off twice in all these intervening years.

Have you always been concerned with your appearance?
No. I thought I was a mighty unattractive boy. I thought I had great charm and could make most people laugh, but I cultivated the ability to make people laugh, since I didn't have the looks. I had an uncle who was most important in men's wear at Saks Fifth Avenue, so most of my clothes came out of the window of Saks Fifth Avenue. I got them because they were sun-drenched, or something like that. But I love clothes. I love women's clothes, I love men's clothes, I love shopping. I feel about department stores the same way I feel about museums. In a department store you see what people want you to have, what you dream about, the whole fantasy life. You can do archaeology there, living archaeology. Think of Bloomingdale's and what you learn about the people of this city.

Where did you get your education?
An enormous amount by myself, and from the kindness of many strangers. I went to elementary school and high school in New York, but I never went to college. I didn't want to—I got in bed and stayed there for almost a year.

Your parents were Russian immigrants?
Yes. I was the first one born here. And I've lived here all of my life except when I lived in London. I've been very fortunate because at a very early age I was somehow able to be around people who knew so much and had such style and aspirations and dreams. You know, when I was about fifteen years old I was sitting with a chum on the elevated station at Third Avenue and Fifty-seventh Street. It was very late spring, and it was that marvelous magical Manhattan moment when you could look the length of Fifty-seventh Street and all the lights were glittering. And my chum said to me, "What do you want to be?" And I said, "The editor of *Vanity Fair*." Because I had organized a lot of kids in my neighborhood to go through the cellars in apartment houses and bring me the magazines they found, as I didn't have any money for magazines. And among them was *Vanity Fair*, this glorious magazine about a world I suspected existed: witty people and wonderful-looking people and people who just knew everything. So that's what I wanted to be. Well, several years ago I sat up in my bed and realized that I had become editor of that section of *Vogue* which is the remains of *Vanity Fair*. I've somehow always had the luck and staying power, the survival instinct, to be with people who are witty, intelligent, great. Marlene Dietrich. Toscanini. Almost all the fascinating people of my time. I love life. I give out. If you give out enough and you're not a slob, it comes back.

Do you find life more fun as you get older?
I've always been very old for my years and now I've caught up. If you're curious, it's always fun. There are no Toscaninis, no Carmel Snows, no Sitwells in my life now. Sometimes I think, Oh, there can't be anybody else who is really going to amuse me, delight me, enchant me—and suddenly it happens, somebody wonderful comes through. Example: Brooke Hayward. I dote on Brooke Hayward and her book, *Haywire*. To measure up to what I've had in my past, which is everything, you have to have echoes of that past, too. Brooke has the whole thing. But she also has her own great individuality, her own views, her own vitality of this time.

Do you worry about death at all?
Yes, it deeply interests me. And it worries me only in that it's very hard to save enough money to leave to somebody you love. That worries me. I've always thought about not being here and people suffering because I'm not. I think of it all the time. I've been very ill in my life so I've had to. It also worries me, because I would simply love to see what happens.

old. I do a great part of my scribbling very, very early in the morning. Anita Loos is my neighbor across Seventh Avenue, and she begins at four o'clock in the morning. Incidentally, one of the things that makes me most proud is that she dedicated her last book to me. That really pleases me a great deal. It's better than getting degrees, because I think Anita is one of the really great people. And I know she's at work across the road there. Ruth Gordon's windows look down on my place and she's up at five o'clock in the morning. There's a circle of charm, we're all up at that time of the morning, working away. I write every morning of my life.

Do you have a routine day?
I suspect it is a routine but I never realized it until recently. I try to scribble from five or five-thirty and that goes on until seven or seven-thirty at the latest. Then I'm up and about like mad, and at breakfast my great friend Gray Foy kindly reads the *Times* aloud to me. That started when my eyes got bad. I do listen to the radio before I go out—music, news. I love hearing things about traffic jams at such-and-such a place on Long Island. It makes me feel so safe on Fifty-seventh Street, it really does. And I always like to hear the weather, so I know whether to put on my long underwear or not. I'm a great list-maker, so that goes on too. Also, sometime before I get out, if I haven't done it the night before, I go through the *Post, Daily News*, maybe *Variety*, the *Village Voice*, the *SoHo News* . . . I read by tearing. I tear out what I think would be useful, what seems to be a trend. It's strange the way you can sometimes spot a trend. But there are very rarely any telephone calls during that time.

I am at my work by nine. If I have a real hot deadline to meet, it's eight-thirty. Sometimes I work until six o'clock, but then, you must realize I usually have a very early curtain, so that means either I've got to eat something before, at home, or I usually go to the Algonquin or one of the Patrick O'Neal's on the way to the theater. Almost every night there's something to do—a play or movie or concert or a party. Or I see three television shows. I try to do almost all of my viewing of the things *Vogue* covers. I do most of my gallery-going on Saturdays. After the theater, I very rarely go to late parties. I go home because I have manuscripts to read, and some telephoning to do, and then frequently before I go to sleep I scribble again for a while. It sounds like an incredibly exciting life and it is.

Sometimes on a Sunday I do nothing. Doing nothing consists of going to visit my mother. She's a very ancient eighty-eight. Very ancient indeed. I'm sure she's older. Perhaps I'm not yet born. Many people would not think this is a relaxing life. To me it's absolute relaxation. I really love writing. Two things are the center of my life: love and work. That's what I'm all about. I'm extremely devoted to my friends and relatives. I love them dearly. The one regret I have is that so many of my friends have died. And they're irreplaceable. There are other kinds that come along, who, as I said, have echoes.

What about your sexual life?
It's marvelous. That's what surprises me, because when I was very young I used to hear older men in the family talk and say that lovely Yiddish phrase, "over the bottle"—I speak Yiddish and think in it quite frequently—that meant you couldn't do it anymore. I sort of understood what they were talking about and there was great fear that it wasn't going to go on. It goes on wonderfully. I sometimes get the impression I'm a very attractive monster, that's all.

Do you diet?
I certainly do. I once lost 160 pounds at one time. I had been an enormously fat man and I loved every ounce of it.

What about your health? *Vogue* is so health-conscious.
Listen, there's a lady at *Vogue* that grows the most glorious basil you've ever seen on her window sill. No, I am conscious of health and diet. When my weight gets to be too much I take it off. I'm very fortunate I can lose it quite easily. And I enjoy getting skinny as much as I enjoy getting fat. But one of my basic rules is never to eat or drink substitutes. I'm not worried about saccharin. I've never had any.

Do you smoke?
I've never smoked in my life. And I don't like people smoking around me, and I don't let them if I can. I just think it's bad for me. I'm selfish about this. But I used to drink a great deal, an enormous amount. I love liquor. I love wine. Now I don't drink any hard liquor at all. I recently did have some cognac, but I didn't frighten the horses in the streets.

Do you ever have a fear, working in fashion where people come and go so, everything is so quick, that you're going to get caught in that shuffle and have to go?
Look, I've been so fortunate in being able to spot the trends before they got here. That may come to an end one day. It's possible that there can be no practical use for me. It's hard to conceive that some part of me couldn't be used, but it happens. I mean, I've seen what happens. And this could very easily happen to me. And deep inside of me I believe it probably will. I'm not going to like it. But I hope I can make the most of it, and I hope I can have a great dignity about it. You know, years ago a young doctor came into my room at Beth Israel and told me what I had said before I went under the anaesthetic. He said, "You said 'I wish I knew how to write this.' " That's very reassuring. It came from something deep inside. I hope in the future I've got the same courage I have now and have had always. Who knows? But I've tried awfully hard. I've worked on my character. It's a very old-fashioned thing, but I've worked awfully hard on it. You must remember that for centuries before Dr. Freud, people had character.

DAVID MAHONEY
Chairman and President, Norton Simon Inc.

Mr. Scavullo: What businesses are you in?
Mr. Mahoney: Norton Simon is an international company, in the sense that it operates throughout the world. And it's diversified. Basically it has four core businesses. The food business, which is made up of Hunt-Wesson, Reddi-Wip, and so on, is the largest. The second largest is Max Factor cosmetics, and along with that is McCall Patterns and Halston. The third largest is Canada Dry, and the fourth is Somerset Importers, the largest importers of liquor in the United States—it handles the products of Johnnie Walker, Tanqueray Gin, Old Fitzgerald and things like that. Our sales are in the neighborhood of $2 billion a year and our profits are about $200 million before taxes, $100 million after taxes.
Isn't it scary to be responsible for such enormous sums of money?
I don't think that "scary" is the correct semantic term. It's always a matter of interest and concern. We have about thirty thousand employees and about the same number of stockholders. But I think it succeeds because we have good management. I'm really the sum total of the people who run the operating companies for me. To substantiate that statement, we operate on the basis of a very small home office, for a company of our size and our diversity. Our home office, in New York, is something like a hundred and twenty people, and that includes switchboard girls and everyone else. We're decentralized; responsibility is out in the operating companies. So that my role, really, aside from overall strategy and direction, is a monitoring job—although I consider that secondary. The primary part of my job is picking the right people, encouraging them, creating an entrepreneurial attitude. I think one of the big problems in America now is the weakness of the whole entrepreneurial idea that got America where it is. The whole direction or motif or ambiance that I'm after is to make these individuals who run the operating companies understand that they are entrepreneurs, that they're in business just like any entrepreneur would be, except that Norton Simon Inc. happens to own the stock one hundred percent. They're rewarded handsomely with large salaries, and a bonus based on the profit of their company, and stock in Norton Simon Inc.

You hear people at the lower levels say they're bored, they're tied down to the assembly line or something. And I think, to a degree, that's true of executives, too. They get too structured, too set. What we're trying to say is that there has to be a genuine entrepreneurial attitude all the way through the company, that's what keeps it going. The fact of the matter is that being entrepreneurial is the willingness to bet on yourself and your own experiences, your own judgment, your own convictions—and it becomes self-fulfilling as you go along. That basically is what Norton Simon Inc. is.
Is there one person who owns most of Norton Simon Inc?
No. There are 50 million shares.
What is your salary?
$400,000 plus an incentive bonus, and so forth.
Do you have a limousine?
I have the use of one.
How does Norton Simon Inc. rank among *Fortune*'s top 500?
About 131.
How did you get where you are today?

My background basically: I grew up in New York City; went to Catholic grammar schools, and so forth; started working when I was about fourteen years old; went to the University of Pennsylvania on an athletic scholarship; went into the service as a private and came out a captain; commuted to Philadelphia for two years and completed my education because the war had interrupted it; got a job in the mail room of an advertising agency; left and started my own advertising agency in 1951; one of my clients was the Good Humor Company and in 1956 I sold my agency and became president of Good Humor, built it up and sold it; became executive VP of Colgate-Palmolive; left that to become president of Canada Dry; we consolidated with Norton Simon Inc. and I became chairman, president and chief operating executive.
Do you spend lots of time at your job?
I think it was tougher for me when I was in school getting my degree. You know, philosophically and psychologically, we talk about what work is. One could say, This is work, but I enjoy what I'm doing, so I don't see it as work. I'm having dinner tonight with an individual on a business matter, and I really don't see it as work. I enjoy the challenge, I enjoy the opportunity, I meet a lot of exciting, bright people—it's hard to really draw the line between what is work and what is not.
What made you do what you're doing?
I don't know. One, I grew up in the Depression, I had to work all my life—that could be part of it. Two, I was around the right place at the right time. Three, I've made the right decisions, or fewer of the wrong ones, as things went along. I do have a certain drive; what brings it about I really don't know. I know that the Lord blessed me with a strong body and a lot of energy. But you can ask, "What made DiMaggio a great ballplayer?" Everybody says hard work, but I assume he liked to play ball. I like what I'm doing.
Is there any social value in what you are doing? Do you do it for anything but your own satisfaction?
It might be self-interest—that's where we all start. But I don't think it's exclusively that. Society has benefited, directly and indirectly from my activities. I serve on the board of directors of three universities: University of Pennsylvania, New York University and University of California at Los Angeles. I'm chairman of the American Health Foundation. And I would be of no value to them unless I had achieved my position.
How do you feel about the future of capitalism?
You're really asking me how I feel about the future of the United States, because I think we are probably the last bastion of capitalism or entrepreneurialism, as we know it. And I think capitalism will come out pretty well. I do believe in the whole entrepreneurial system. I think it's going to go through some adjustments. The pendulum swings back and forth, as it always does; the past is a prologue—it sounds corny, but it is. Most people say that Americans are down on business: it shows at the polls. But if you really take it apart and ask the Americans if they have confidence that America can deliver jobs, food, ammunition—the answer, generally, is yes. If you then ask them, "Do you want the government, the same people who run the Post Office, to run everything else?," the answer is no. And then you ask, "What do you think about

DAVID MAHONEY
Chairman and President, Norton Simon Inc.

businessmen?" Well, they don't like businessmen.

So, the people are fed up, not with the entrepreneurial, capitalist system, but with the conduct of businessmen. I think you have to separate the two things. I think the average American person does believe that whatever happens, somehow the private sector can do it better than the government. And as long as they believe that, I think the capitalist system will survive. Let me give you an example: a British friend of mine told me, "When we're having difficulty with the employees, they pound on my car and say, 'You should be driving a Volkswagen like me.' But in your country, when somebody drives out in a Cadillac, they pound on it and say, 'I should be driving one of those, too.' " There's a significant difference.

Capitalism requires expansion. How are we to expand when countries become Communist and are cut off from us?
Isn't the whole world, isn't your whole life, isn't everything a system of trade-offs, legitimate trade-offs? You're faced with alternatives and options as you go through—you turn left, you turn right, you walk on this side of the street, you walk on that side. I think a businessman is paid for his ingenuity, his decisions, his foresight, his ability to adapt, to find ways to expand. What you say is true. But you tell me when it wasn't true. When were the good old days? Were they the nineteen-twenties, the thirties, the forties, the fifties, the sixties, when were the good old days that I'm hearing so much about? When I grew up it wasn't the good old days— with Dad not working and general despair, those days weren't so hot. In the forties I found myself in the South Pacific fighting the Japanese. Fifties: Korea and the Cold War. Sixties: Vietnam, the student uprising, two stock-market breaks, the threat of nuclear war. Seventies: the Arab-Israeli war, the confrontation on oil. What's new? There'll always be some problem, and there should be. It keeps that blood going, it keeps the adrenalin going.

Is there anyone who gives you power to go on?
I don't think anyone can really give you power. I'm pretty much on my own. But I've been fortunate in my relationships, be they with Norton, who was the founder of our company, or be it with certain people like Gus Levy, the investment banker. I've always had good mentors, and part of the reason is that I've been interested in what they've done. I dissect and value their experience, but that doesn't mean I have to take their recommendations totally, because we are employing different scripts, though the fundamentals may be the same.

Are you married?
I divorced four years ago. I have two children.

What kind of women do you like?
I like women to be attractive, intelligent, honest. You know, when you get to be fifty-three, which I am, you say, "Look, I won't be like you and you won't be like me. Let's put it right out on the table, all the sham. I don't want to kid myself, because I don't have time, and don't you try to kid me, because I've been down that road." Maybe it's a sense of

personal security or a serenity that comes with age. But you say, "What the hell are we playing around with? What do we want? A relationship, an understanding? I'm not going to cater to every one of your whims. I don't expect you to do it to mine. You're independent and I'm independent. You're free and I'm free. If I have a string on you, you have a string on me. Who needs all that?" I'm not speaking about marriage, I'm talking about relationships.

Would you like to get married again?
I probably will. I've been going with one lady principally.

Do you have any dealings with women in business?
Oh, sure. God bless them. You know, the people I really have compassion for are youth and women—both have gone through an extremely difficult period. Some lady who twenty years ago would have been happy living in Greenwich with her two children, and so forth, is now unhappy. I'm not saying either situation is right or wrong, but today's woman has more problems. Kids have it the same way—whether it's the drug culture, the permissiveness, the violence—it's tough, it's a difficult period for them to get through. And men are defensive about this whole thing. Maybe I haven't been exposed to women competing with me from the business point of view. My answer might not be as representative as somebody that's twenty-eight or thirty. We certainly have been way out in front in equal opportunity. But then, I once said in a locker room in Bel Air, "I really like girls. I like women." And this guy says, "Who the hell doesn't?" And it amused me because we were talking on two different levels. I mean, I think women are great, lots of them are good friends. Now, if you can have friendships in that area aside from sexual or romantic relationships, what are we worried about? I think it helps this society. I think it helps industry for men and women to be equal.

Do you have a lot of sex?
I think that's privileged information which would not add anything to this interview.

Do you ever think of retiring?
I'd put it another way: I may take different courses or tangents in my life. What, I don't know. If my job ever got to be real work and I didn't enjoy it, that would be the day I'd leave—that's for sure. I think there are a lot of other things that are interesting. I'd like to become a parapsychologist, somebody who sits back and deals with the psychology and sociology of relationships. We were one of the first companies to use psychologists, sociologists, even anthropologists. I think one of my big problems in business or any large bureaucracy, be it the Church or the government, is communication. And it isn't language; it's relationships, it's feelings, it's blocks, it's failure to level or put it all out on the table. That intrigues me. Or, maybe, running a foundation. If I retired, I wouldn't retire as much as change direction. I always want to feel that I'm growing, expanding, being productive, and happy. But I don't expect it all to happen every day.

Do you think about getting old?

No, and I mean that quite sincerely. Maybe it's because my career has gone along so rapidly, but I don't have any big concerns about that from a humanistic point of view or a business point of view. I do notice that I'm a little slower getting to the tennis ball, I'm missing it completely, that kind of thing I certainly feel, but I don't have time to worry about the fact that I'm getting old.

How do you keep in shape?

I play a lot of tennis, a reasonable amount of squash, and I go to a gym, maybe twice a week.

Do you diet at all?

Oh yes, yes, yes. Sometimes successfully and sometimes not.

Are you concerned about chemicals in foods?

I wouldn't smoke if I was.

You're not concerned about smoking?

I should be. But I enjoy it. I've given it up. I thought I lost a friend. You know, people talk about what they're going to do with their gold watch at seventy. Who said you have to reach seventy? I'm not recommending smoking, I wish in many ways I didn't. I certainly hope my kids don't. But what I'm talking about is fear—that's the biggest thing we have to attack. Almost anything that was a problem to me was the result of my insecurity or somebody else's. Whether it's aggressiveness, competitiveness, unhappiness, sensitivity, bruised feelings, it's all in the area of fear and insecurity somewhere. I'm constantly trying to deal with: How do I keep myself centered? Who am I? What am I about? What am I for? Am I growing? Am I getting smarter? Am I adjusting? Am I handling things better? That's what's important: stability with growth.

Do you get nervous about people liking you only because you are rich?

If that bothers me, it would speak of my own insecurity. But it's true, it's there, forget women, your own kids can do it to you. I, in turn, at times do the same thing. I don't go with homely women, for example. It's a give-and-take, it's a trade-off.

Do you ever get angry and scream at people?

Yes. And when I do I know it's nonproductive and damaging.

What gets you upset?

Lots of things, but most of them come down to either I'm copping out in some way or they're copping out. Any kind of phoniness irritates me. Or anybody trying to give me a con game. Or surprises that could have been anticipated in the business world. For example, our whole position on the energy shortage is not a surprise to me, so I'd blame them all—the oil industry, the ecologists, the government, our great planners. Where the hell is all the planning on energy? What have we done? We have a fifty-five-mile-per-hour speed limit, and we're importing more oil than we did before. The only letter I've ever written to a President was to President Carter, imploring him to take the leadership, regardless of what it is, on energy, because it is a major problem. We

speak about the continuance of the capitalist or entrepreneurist system, but we've got to think about our whole standard of living. Forget under what system it is. The whole standard of living is what's at risk right now. We're a nation that's built on energy.

Are you very nervous?

No, I am a high-strung activist.

Do you take tranquilizers or sleeping pills?

No way.

How do you relax?

There's a million ways to relax. Warm baths are better than any sleeping pill ever invented, or just plain reading.

Do you watch TV or go to movies?

I'm not much of a TV freak. I watch sporting events or special events occasionally. I average two hours a week. Movies, yes. I have a small 16mm projector and I can borrow films, which I do a lot of times and show them at home. But I'm not a big moviegoer.

You seem very speedy, unrelaxed, to me.

I don't think that's a lack of relaxation. It's drive: I speak too quickly and I move too quickly, but it works for me. My energy level is high.

What do you think about cosmetics for men?

I think it's probably going to come in. It's a little early yet; the growth hasn't been there. But you start with the shaving lotion, hair tonics, hair dyes and all of that. I think it'll come in; I think it should.

Do you like the idea of men wearing make-up?

Why not? Whatever makes 'em happy. Max Factor will put it out if we think we can sell it and make a profit on it. But I think there are two ways to look at anything: are you creating a need or fulfilling one? If we find there's a need, we will try to fulfill it.

Would you ever have a face lift?

What the hell do I need it for? That kind of vanity doesn't impress me. If I had a bum knee, I would have no hesitancy about going and getting it operated on. Or a shoulder. But a double chin?

Do you care about your clothes much?

Yes. My suits are semi-made. I get them from Giorgio in California, really off the rack, 42 long, and then they adjust this, adjust that because the thing is tight or loose—it's all done in a couple of days. But I do take pride in how I look because that's something I can control.

Do you have any fears?

We all have fears. Any overriding ones, I hope not.

Do you fear death?

No, I don't think about it. When it happens it happens. And I am not going to use the time I have worrying about it.

Can you sit in one spot for long?

I don't know how to sit in one spot. It's not a hyperactivity, it's enthusiasm. I think we live in a bloody great place. I truly believe that. And I psych myself, because the verb psych means: *you gotta do it.*

NORMAN MAILER
Writer

Mr. Scavullo: I remember your apartment.
Mr. Mailer: It's a great apartment. I wanted it to look like a boat; in fact, it's my little ferry.
Is your environment important to your writing?
Let me get at it in a roundabout way. I didn't know actors well when my play *The Deer Park* was put on, but I got to know them because I was married at the time to a rather good actress named Beverly Bentley, who was in the play. And actors have to have a drink after a show, they sure do, so I drank with the actors every night for three or four months, and I got bored stiff. Actors have very funny preoccupations, and one of the things that drives you mad is that they're always at the stage manager, and most of the conversation we had was not "How can we improve the play in terms of this aesthetic or that?"—there was nothing elevated about the conversation—rather, the conversations were all about: "Norman, for God's sake, do you have any pull with the stage manager? Will you tell that bastard to put the salt shaker in the right place? It was in the wrong place again tonight." For a while I thought they were cretins. And then I began to realize what it was: the salt shaker was important to them because at the given moment the actor would reach for it, he bursts out crying. It's not like movie acting; you act the same part night after night. And you have to make yourself a little factory with little machines in it that are geared to do certain specific jobs. You become a set of conditioned reflexes. You can't just keep using emotions to fuel your tears; you have to adjust yourself to something that will automatically get you crying.

Writing is a little bit like acting. I find that it's better if there are a set of stable conditions about it. Writers are famous for going through these little rituals, sharpening their pencils in a certain way or laying out their paper in a different way. Everybody has his own habits. And I've found there are a few things that are crucial. One of them is that if I'm working on a particular book I like to work in one particular room because the connotation of the book gets attached to the furniture. It can be an attractive room or an ugly room; I much prefer an agreeable room. But there has to be this stability about it. Within reason I go there pretty much the same number of hours after I get up, and I work more or less the same number of hours. If I go to bed one night and I'm planning to work the next day, it's got to be a pretty God-awful day before I won't work the next day.

One of the things I believe is that the unconscious prepares you for a job. In other words, if you go to bed at night and you know you're working the next day, then the unconscious does the work, makes a lot of the fundamental decisions on how you're going to go forward in the work, and if you don't work the next day, then all that material that's been prepared is just sitting in your brain like troops out in the rain. And I know that a day when I don't work when I was planning to is always an awful day for me. I'm incredibly nervous, pent-up, irritable, and have this feeling that I'm spoiling something and can't quite name what it is. And, of course, some of the ideas that I was going to work on that day begin popping out, and that's awful. If you're a professional writer, having an idea come when you don't have a pencil in your hand is bad business.
How many days a week do you write?
If I'm working on two books at once, I'll work on one in New York and the other in Provincetown. I go up to Provincetown and work three or four days in a row. In New York I'll usually work a day or two, then take a day off. But so many things accumulate, there are so many people to see, on my day off. You know, I think between forty and sixty are awful years. One's always overoccupied. In the early years one's trying to get to the point where one's overoccupied, then one gets to that point where there is no real time and it's hard to take time off. I keep thinking that sixty is a magic number.
Do you have many deadlines to meet and contracts to fill?
Yeah. I made the little mistake of getting married five times. My affairs are half as complicated as Tommy Manville's. Seven children, five wives. It takes up an awful lot of my social life. I'm on halfway decent terms with most of my wives.
What do you think about divorce laws?
Considering all the times I've been divorced, I don't think about it too much. I think women's lib ought to live up to a few of its claims and work real hard for a law that would be liberal about alimony. If a woman is able to work, then why is she entitled to alimony? If she's taking care of the children, that's another matter, but I think most of the alimony laws do benefit women much more than they benefit men.

I have . . . oh, ten thousand feelings about women's lib: five thousand are for it and five thousand are against it. It's something I could write about for the rest of my life. I did write a book about it. A lot of different things are going on in women's liberation. On the positive side, women are saying that they were forced to be cowards all their lives, and that's onerous; that they were, to a degree, destroyed by that and diminished by that. They want the right to engage life on the same terms that men do, which means that there's more of a demand on them to be brave. It's interesting as hell because whenever someone says, "Give me an opportunity to be brave" or "Give me an opportunity to take on things that scare me a little," you know that person has to have some substance to say that; it isn't automatic for us to do that. That part of women's lib is fine.

The other part, which I detest, is an ugly—I'll even call it totalitarian—desire to flatten all distinctions between men and women, to say that women are absolutely the equal of men in every single fashion, that the only difference between men and women is that men happen to have approximately from six to twelve cubic inches of meat more than women. That's the only difference. And that, I think, ultimately sets up a kind of totalitarianism because in changing men and women into persons, it diminishes. The next thing is, why use the word "person"; why not call them "units"? Human units. And then it makes it easier to feed people into a machine. The computer can deal with a phenomenon that only has units much more easily than it can deal with a phenomenon that has A and B. There is a tendency in our time to go toward making everybody the same. Androgeny, however, is interesting for what it does positively. Androgeny can be very exciting because it leads us to all sorts of discoveries about ourselves. Some interesting art forms, like Art Nouveau, have come out of androgenous times. Androgeny creates three sexes: men, women and androgens. But the negative side of women's lib is different: it is creating just one sex. And unisex, I think, is far less interesting.

NORMAN MAILER
Writer

What about homosexuality?
What I said in *Prisoner of Sex* came out of what Genet had written about his life in prison. He talked about how the wolves of the prison over thirty years became less and less masculine and more and more feminine, so that finally by the end of their prison career they were taking it up the ass. What I wanted to say is that I felt that there is a peculiar severe logic in sex that one can't ignore, that's there, that's built into it. And I said the same is true for men and women, that when a couple, monogamous and faithful to each other, practice contraception for years, that the strength of the man would go out of him—literally. This is terribly right-wing, if you will, but I did believe it was true and I still think there may be a great deal to it. In other words, if you keep fucking without the thought that you want to conceive, there's a price to be paid. And that strength came from sex only when one was taking the chance of making a child. Now, this notion of course explodes any contentment one can have with sex; it's a very disagreeable and unpleasant notion. And a lot of people just hated it when I wrote that. But I think it's probably true; I think it's more true than not.

It's very close to the position of the Catholic Church.
Yes, of the right wing of the Catholic Church. It's why I call myself a left conservative because on the one hand, I think of myself as a man on the left, but on the other hand, I have very conservative ideas mixed in with it.

What about overpopulation?
Well, in *Prisoner of Sex* I had an idea, but I can't prove it, it's just something I feel is true. I mean, why was there no overpopulation five hundred or a thousand or three thousand years ago? People always say, "Well, because so many children died early." That may be part of it, but I think also that women weren't getting pregnant, from everything we know, at that great a rate. I think that before there were any kinds of contraception, women had the ability not to conceive. There was some signal they could send into their body not to conceive. And they would conceive only when there were great fucks, you know. Which is one of my little thoughts.

Think of it. All the wonders of civilization today didn't come out of us; they came out of the generations before us. You know we're the fuck-up generation. We may be skimming all the human profit that's been developed over two thousand years. We may be obliterating a whole set of instincts that produced the kind of minds that we all have. And so there's that paradox in a lot of life.

Are you pessimistic about the future of mankind?
Yeah. I'm very uneasy. It's a terribly difficult time to assess, it's all choppy water, everything is back and forth. On the one hand, awful things seem to be going on from my point of view. On the other hand, there are more people who really have freedom of mind today than any time I can remember in my life. Kids sort of take for granted things that we fought for years to get to the point where we could believe in our own minds that we had a right to do.

What do you think about drugs today?
Pot, cocaine, alcohol, aspirin, nicotine. I like some and I detest others.

Do you think it's a good or bad force?
Probably bad, but I'm not the one to go around saying that it's bad because I take at least two of the ones we named. It would be great if we could do without whiskey, wouldn't it?

Whiskey's ruined my brain, I think. I used to have a better brain. I had a better head years ago. I think nights of—oh, a couple of drinks—no, but those nights of heavy boozing are tough. Most heavy-drinking reporters or punch-giving prize fighters, they really get punchy when they drink too much. Pot's funny; people who take too much pot end up a funny way, they get drained. I don't know much about cocaine because I've never been able to enjoy it—oddly enough. Just can't get a high on cocaine. And Lady Heroin, I've never gotten there. Smoking cigarettes I gave up ten years ago. I guess because I hated it. I'd light a cigarette and I'd feel as if it were a dagger in my lungs. I didn't enjoy it; I'd retch. And it still took me years to give it up. I made about twenty different attempts to give it up over ten years. I weaned myself away from it very slowly. I can't imagine going back too easily.

Do you think about health?
I have to: I get gouty. I'm a marvelous archetype of the gouty disposition. If I do certain things for two or three days in a row, I'll get the gout. And that's a bitch because then I'm out of commission for three or four days and there's an awful medicine I take to cure it, which works, unlike most medicines. But I go into a vile depression while it works. Vile depression. And feel hideous.

How do you deal with depression not derived from this pill?
There are years you live in deep depression and years you don't. And the one thing about living for years in deep depression is that after a while you come out of it and you don't seem to live in that sort of fashion again, at least I haven't, and I don't think I've been, relatively, that depressed. I haven't had heavy depressions; I can go through periods of a month or two where I'm not necessarily terribly pleased with myself.

How do you feel about money?
I have money problems that are comical, they're so large. I'm the best thing that's come along since Joe Louis in that department. I work every year and I earn large amounts and they just go to pay off the IRS and my five wives; it's a comedy. So I think about money all the time and I hate that. I consider that evil, to spend your life thinking about money. It's all right if you're making it, and then you're debating whether to spend a large sum here or there. But when you're just working to catch up, it's like being on a losing team, just working like crazy to get from four touchdowns behind to three touchdowns behind. Horrible.

If all of a sudden you had a lot of money, what would you spend it on?
My debts. I wouldn't know what I'd do with it. I'd really be at a loss. I might buy a boat. I've got a couple of sons who are getting to the age where they could crew it with me.

Do your children like the fact that you're a writer?
Most of them are too young. The older ones haven't read my books, oddly enough. They find them very hard, very difficult. The oldest one, who's twenty-seven, has read a few of them.

What are you working on now?
A very long novel that'll probably be about . . . oh God, it'll be as long as *Gone With the Wind* when it's done. But not as readable, I fear.

Are there contemporary writers that you admire?
See, I think we have a funny generation of writers. I think there are a lot of us that are really good, but no one that's

really great. There's Saul Bellow, who's a very good writer. There's Nabokov, who's not really an American writer, but certainly an immensely gifted writer on a world scale. There're all sorts of terribly talented people like Barth and Vonnegut and Updike and Cheever and Pynchon and Heller. There are about fifteen or twenty of us who are really pretty good. But there's no one who is really a mountain in the old sense, a literary mountain, a giant.

Don't you think people are looking at television and movies more now?

In the thirties, short-story writers were very important. People cared about them immensely. Literary people got a greater thrill from reading four or five short-story writers than from reading many novelists. After World War II something happened to the short story. There was less and less interest in it. There are still people writing short stories, but somehow it's hard to name a single short-story writer. The same may be said about novels in another ten years. I think people of this generation know more about who's doing and selling screenplays—almost more than who's doing and selling novels. I think an awful lot of publishing has been wiped out by television.

Do you watch television?

I almost don't watch it at all. I hate it. And that's interesting because I'm going to do a piece on TV for *Esquire*. I'm going to sit down and write twenty thousand words—that's a month's work—on TV and I don't know a goddamn thing about TV! Except I hate it. I just felt it was about time somebody said, "I hate TV."

What about movies?

Yeah, I like movies. Love pornies. The sleazos. I get there a couple of times a month maybe.

What kind of women do you admire?

It's odd, but I don't know if I can answer that. I don't know that I can say, "Oh, I'm mad about Golda Meir," "Bring on Elizabeth Taylor" or "Vanessa Redgrave is my true love."

I think beautiful women are always immensely interesting. I don't think a shallow woman can become beautiful. I think beauty contains a kind of courage within it. One has to dare to be beautiful. Virtually all children are beautiful at the age of one. And very few manage to stay beautiful and the reason is it's dangerous to be beautiful. Most people are terrified by the demands and the perils of being beautiful. And so they step down from beauty. There's also always the nightmare of beautiful people, men and women, who discover that beauty is perilous, but they still want to be beautiful. So they lead very guarded lives. They're ringed by police dogs and fences, they're terribly overprotected, and then they begin to have an inner psychic landscape that's overcharged and paranoid and dangerous. Because they live in this terrible relation to beauty, as if beauty is God and God resents what they've done. And so it's a drama, and I'm always fascinated with women who are beautiful, because they're always dramatic whether they're brave or timid about it.

Do you think about your own looks at all?

Ruefully. Ruefully. I look in the mirror and say, "You're getting old." It's getting worse. And it irritates me but at the same time it doesn't . . . you don't get older. Never get older. I don't think I ever felt as old as I felt when I was twenty-nine. When I turned thirty it was the worst birthday of my life. I really felt old. I felt used up inside and, in fact, I was old because my liver burned out about a year later. And

there I was at the age of thirty and in Mexico with a burned-out liver. And so old that it was hard to climb a hill. And I never felt that old again. You get back to the way that you felt when you were twenty except that the inside feels the same, but the outside alters. You realize how odd life is. My mother's in her eighties, and I know the inside of her head is younger than mine.

What about clothes?

It's not a talent, put it that way. I mean, people who know how to wear clothes do it so well that it's a little like being the lowest score on the bowling team.

What about violence?

Well, it's a culture. Unlike other cultures, there's a terrible price to be paid if you know nothing about that culture and you get into it. You can know nothing about opera and go to an opera and the worst thing that's going to happen is you're going to be bored. But violence is the one culture that's altogether different from that. People who are interested in violence very often know a great deal about it, and they learn a great deal about it, and they live with it and they think about it all day long. There are skills in relation to it, and temperamentally they also have weaknesses; in other words, their character is such that they can know certain skills and not know others. And there are maxims in violence.

Jimmy Hoffa is reputed to have said that one must charge a pistol and flee a knife. If I'm holding a gun on you and you come toward me, I have to feel the moral authority that I can shoot you, which is not automatic because it doesn't involve any skill; all I do is press that trigger. *But* the moment you start to run from me, I gain moral authority because you're running away, so it's easier to shoot at you. Whereas a knife is so physical—it involves one's sensitivity and one's ability to move and we all hate not being able to move properly at a given moment—so if you charge a knife, it's a very dangerous business to do. But if you flee a knife, it's very hard, technically, to stab someone who's running away from you. And there's something absurd about running after a man waving a knife.

This is one example of how violence is a culture, where people brood on these matters. It's almost like saying, "Are you conservative or leftist? Do you use a gun or do you use a knife?" They are wholly different approaches to life. So it isn't that I have thoughts on violence as such or that I approve of it or disapprove of it. I feel it's a culture that one goes into on tiptoe and looks around a little, maybe.

What about rape? Murder? War?

They're all immensely different. It's like talking about houses and apples. I mean, rape is one thing; murder's another. I don't go along with the women's lib notion that rape is murder. I think rape in certain conditions can be much worse than murder. Much worse. And war is something else altogether. War is impersonal and it's the worst form of violence. Let me end on this note because I think it's a good point to make: it may be that individual violence is the antidote to war; that where you get societies where there isn't enough individual violence, they'll go to war. It's never the unruly nations where you're in peril walking on the street that start the great wars; it's the terribly orderly countries that really adore law and order that go in for the most monstrous wars, where people are killed by the millions. It's not Kenya that will start a major war, not Zaïre. It will be Russia or the United States or Germany or England or France.

PETER MARTINS
Ballet Dancer

Mr. Scavullo: At what age did you start dancing?
Mr. Martins: I was nine. In Copenhagen, Denmark. My entire family was musically orientated. My mother's a pianist, and my uncle and aunt were both dancers, and my sister was a dancer. Most mothers want their little daughters to be ballerinas, but as we already had dancers in the family, my mother thought—you know, me too. But she was not the type of ambitious mother that you run into sometimes, thank God. She let me do everything in my own way. She never forced me. I didn't really enjoy ballet, because it takes a lot of time. Since I participated in performances when I was young—eight, nine, ten years old—I never had time to play with other kids. It's a time-consuming business.

Are you married?
No, I was. In Denmark. It must be almost ten years ago now. I was a kid, and I had a child—a son, whom I visit all the time. And he comes to visit me. He's ten years old, and also takes ballet. He lives with his mother in Denmark. But I have a wonderful relationship with him and her. It's difficult to be married and live professionally. It's almost impossible. No time, no time. I'm never at home. I'm never at home.

What is a day like for you?
It's a tough schedule. I go to the theater at ten o'clock and take class for an hour and a half, and then I spend six hours, from twelve to six, rehearsing. Then I go have a bite to eat. I go back to the theater and perform from eight until eleven. And that goes on for fourteen weeks, like that. Every day. Two performances on Saturday and two on Sunday. Tuesday, Wednesday, Thursday, Friday, the whole week. Eight performances a week. Rehearsals all day long. Fourteen weeks in a row. After fourteen weeks I'm finished.

Do you take any vitamins?
I should. I will. I will. I'm still young enough to survive on nature. I've decided that when I'm forty years old—when I stop dancing—I'm going to take care of myself. I'm thirty now.

What do you have for breakfast?
I don't have breakfast, since I'm still full from the night before. I take my big meal of the day when the performance finishes at eleven o'clock. Also, when I finish a performance I cannot just go out and eat and go home and sleep. I'm too keyed-up. So that's when I really have my day with friends. I'm never in bed before two-thirty, three, because that's when my life really starts. I eat a big steak, and so on. And by nine o'clock, when I get up, I'm not hungry. I just have coffee. And a pack of cigarettes. And I take a shower. I get up at the last minute so I can get as much sleep as possible.

You smoke?
There's a great Canadian ballerina, a beautiful ballerina. She was once asked by an interviewer whether she smoked and she said, "Yeah, I smoke and I drink and I [bleep] too, honey. Just like everybody else." But smoking is bad, it's really bad. I smoke a lot. I drink wine only. No liquor. It doesn't go with me.

Do you have to wear make-up in the ballet?
Yes. It is a problem. My skin used to be much better. The only thing I miss that I used to do in Denmark is taking long walks, in fresh air that would bite on your skin. I love that. And there's no fresh air in New York. Clean, fresh air I miss very much.

What about your hair?

PETER MARTINS
Ballet Dancer

I have a very good boy who cuts my hair wonderfully. But I never have time to go to him. So our company hairdresser cuts it ten minutes before the performance. It's really hard to get anything fit in. But I've come to terms with the way my life has turned out. It's a mess in one way. I don't have time for me. At all. And I don't like it. I'd like to have more time for myself. When I'm forty and I stop dancing, then I'm really going to have my second life.

What about clothes?

I used to be very into clothes. I can't be anymore. It's impossible. I get up in the morning, I put on clothes and half an hour later I take them off and I don't put them on till midnight, when I go home, so what the hell does it matter what I wear, really, at this point? I used to be so into clothes when I was in Denmark, I used to have suits and nice, matching things. Now it doesn't matter what I wear. I wear what's comfortable.

Do you think you'll ever become "What Becomes a Legend Most?" like Nureyev in the Blackglama mink ad?

They wouldn't ask me. But I have a thing for furs. My apartment is covered in fur. I have suede couches, I have zebra and other furs all over, I love it.

How tall are you?

I am six feet one and a half inches, which is rather tall for a ballet dancer. When I grew up everybody teased me about it because a ballet dancer is supposed to be small. But the funny thing is that it turned out to my advantage. Now there's a shortage of tall boys. Generations are getting taller and the minute a girl gets on pointe you add five, seven inches— and the man has to be tall. He has to be a little taller than she when she's on pointe, for the ideal picture.

Do you ever allow yourself a day of just lying in bed?

No.

Not even on holiday?

I don't have holidays. Last time I had a holiday was two years ago. I went to the Caribbean for one week. I loved it, but I got bored after a week. Not only that, I got stiff. My body can't take it. Even with the sun and swimming and relaxing, which is supposed to be good for the muscles, I got out of shape. When your body is that trained, that refined, you must make your muscles go in a certain direction every day. Dancers are different than athletes. They just build up the size of their muscles. We build them up to look a certain way. We have to build up the power of the muscle, but at the same time we cannot *just* build up the power because it's going to look awful. I have to have power, and yet it shouldn't look bulky. It's very difficult. You have to sculpt your own body. I've looked at my own body in the mirror for twenty years and I know exactly what it needs and what it doesn't need.

Can you improve your body anymore?

I think a body stops progressing around thirty. People always told me that after twenty-five, your body is set and you'll never be able to be better. That never made sense to me, because between twenty-five and thirty I have become so much stronger and better technically that my physical abilities have grown. After thirty, I think you just have to maintain. I think that's the hardest thing—to maintain what you once had.

Are you afraid that your body might change as you get older?

No. I realize that I've got ten, maybe fifteen good years, and I want to get the best out of those years. Then your muscles begin to sag, they begin to lose their juice, their flexibility—you're brought up from when you're a kid to realize this. You realize that your life is really short. But it's not depressing, because I know exactly what I'm going to do: go out and run a ballet company. I'm going to be a director somehow, in some area of ballet. So I'm not worried. At all.

Actors worry and get lines.

But they can always have a face lift. A lot of dancers have them, actually. If it's your profession, why not? But I think it becomes an obsession with people, which is sad. I love lines in the face.

What about working on your mind?

I do. It's very easy to get freaked out or screwed up in the ballet world because the competition is immense. For instance, if I'm injured, or if I do a guest appearance in Europe, and I say to the company, "I'm leaving for three weeks, you have to do without me," when I come back not only have they replaced me in the three weeks—and I'm difficult to replace, I hate to say it myself—but they also are beginning to forget about me. You're out. You have to be there every day. It's really tough.

Do you read?

I used to read a lot more than I have in the last couple of years. I used to read a lot of American literature. I like Steinbeck, I like Hemingway, I'm in love with America. I was in love with it ever since I was sixteen years old. I was in love with the idea. Funny as it may sound, I like the American mentality—if there is such a thing—because it's all influenced by so many different cultures. Americans have an open mind toward everything. I like that very much. You see, I was brought up in little tiny Denmark where people are so stuck, so narrow-minded. They feel that they have the answer for the world. They really think a lot of themselves in Denmark and Sweden; the Scandinavian countries are very much like that. They are a proud people with a great tradition, but they somehow never seem to get any further. I prefer it here because Sweden and Denmark have the highest suicide rate in the world. I go to Denmark and visit my friends and they are so depressed—and they have everything. They live unbelievably well. Everything is paid for by the government. And yet, they complain. They complain because of the high taxes. I prefer it much more over here. You have to work for your own survival here.

Do you make a lot of money?
Yes. I'm interested in money up to a point. I love to live in a beautiful apartment. My ambitions used to be much much higher—because of my upbringing—but eventually, thank God, I got that out of my mind. It's not number one to me anymore. Number one to me now is to keep growing as a human being and to get further in the expansion of my mind. I want to learn all the time. A few years ago the American Ballet Theater asked me to join them. I could have become a huge star and made a fortune every year. But I also had to make an enormous compromise within myself, because I knew I would become a commercial star and I never wanted to be a commercial star. It doesn't interest me. So I decided to stay with Balanchine and learn and grow. And he pays very realistically and I make a lot of money outside. I just want to pay my bills. My luxury is to do whatever I want. It's funny—I never really worried about money in my whole life. But I also have extravagant tastes, in everything. If I want to fly to the Bahamas tomorrow, I want to be able to do it. If I want to bring my son to America for a day for Christmas, I want to be able to do it. I don't want to say, "Oh, I can't afford that." That's all I want out of money. I don't care about the status part of it.

What about the star system in ballet?
Normally in viewers' minds, if you're Russian you're greater. Nureyev and Baryshnikov are fantastic dancers and I have enormous admiration for both of them. And I have to remind the American dancers who are very upset about Rudi and Mischa coming here that they are better than most dancers. They have something special to offer and they did not only become great stars because they were Russian defectors, as most people would like to think. They got a lot of publicity, but they could also, at any given time, back it up. Because they are very, very fine dancers.

When you first danced with Balanchine, was there any problem?
Many problems. I was stubborn and I thought, Who is he, this old man, to tell me anything, how dare he? There was a big personality conflict. But I began to realize: Wait a minute, you know, I'm still a young, spoiled, rotten kid who doesn't really know anything compared to what he knows. I had to go through a whole transformation in my mind. I said to myself, "Just forget your ego a little bit and listen to him. Maybe he has something to offer." He really has a lot to offer young dancers.

What do you think of Twyla Tharp?
I would like to give Twyla another two or three years before

I judge her. She's a fad right now. She's intelligent, she's bright, she has a certain vocabulary. But I want to see her do more and more and more.

Which women do you admire?
My favorite woman is Katharine Hepburn. I've always adored her, I've always loved her. That woman radiates enormous power to me. She does something very strange to me, she gives me goose bumps. I like Jane Fonda. I like strong women. I do. Absolutely. It attracts me, as long as they don't become like Gloria Steinem, don't become castrating.

What kind of women are attracted to you and what kind of women are you attracted to?
I do not attract what I like. The women whom I attract are basically middle-aged, Park Avenue types, who somehow are reminded by looking at me that there's the young Prince Charming that they never had. But the women who attract me can be forty, thirty, twenty, fifteen, it doesn't matter. What attracts me is a frame of mind and, naturally, beauty. That's the first thing you look at, but that fades away immediately, in a way. Physically, I love skinny, skinny girls. I love bodies to be what they were designed to be, no extras. Everything has to be usable. You can't just have something sitting there that you don't use. That turns me off. But women are beautiful. I like American women better than I like any other women.

How do you handle men being attracted to you?
The most difficult thing in the world for me is to say no. I don't like to hurt people's feelings. It's very hard for me to be tough and cut people off, unless I really have been pushed. If somebody hangs on my back, then I cut him off. But I let people get close to me and hope that they will realize that I'm not interested. I give them hints here and there to leave me alone and if they don't take them, I get annoyed and I cut them off. I don't like to do that. But I am not a tease. I've been accused of that. But I'm not at all. I like people. I don't play sex games like that. I don't think so.

Is there time for love for you?
There's only one way for me: to find somebody who is in the ballet—your hours are the same, so at least you get to know each other. I could not have a relationship with somebody who's not involved in the ballet. Impossible. I believe in relationships. I've had a relationship with a person for seven years now and it's been very, very, very volatile. But I'm not the type of person who says, "This doesn't work, the hell with it! Get rid of it! Find something else!" I will try every possibility of making it. I will try forever—it doesn't matter, ten years, fifteen years, I'll try—as long as I see a possibility and think that it's going to be worth it. Yet, if I finally decide that it doesn't work, then it will end irrevocably. I can never go back. There's no way back once I decide, but it takes me a long time to give up.

ARTHUR MILLER
Playwright

Mr. Scavullo: Do you write every day?
Mr. Miller: I go through long periods of just looking around, but when I'm working I write every day early in the morning, about eight o'clock. I get up about six-thirty, seven. I live in the country. When it gets dark I go to sleep.

Do you think it would be possible for you to live in New York and write?
Yes, but I would probably miss the freedom. It's terrible to be stuck in a building. I've lived in the country for so many years now that I can't imagine not being able to go out into the green.

Do you come into the city often?
Sometimes not for months.

Are you married now?
Yes, to a photographer named Inge Morath. She just came back from Japan, as a matter of fact. She was there for about two weeks doing a story on a women's theater troupe.

Do you mind when she goes off to work for a couple of weeks?
Well, we've been raising a girl for the last fourteen years, so this is the first time in many years that she's done that because our daughter is now capable of fending for herself a little bit, so it's no chore for me. But I'm glad she does it. She's a marvelous photographer. She should work wherever it takes her.

What kind of women do you like? Beautiful women?
I think so. But they have to have something upstairs. I think my wife's got more than I do.

How many times have you been married?
Three.

Which was your most difficult marriage?
To Marilyn.

Why?
Partly, I think, because she was an actress. It's a tough career. It's tough on whoever is in it, and it's tough on the people around them.

Do you think it's as tough on men as it is on women?
I read a biography of Montgomery Clift, who was a good friend of mine. In many ways he was like Marilyn—in many, many ways. I always knew that, but I didn't know all this about his nonprofessional life until I read this book. And there are amazing similarities in their personalities and the problems they had. Terrible. I think it's a difficult career. It always has been, probably always will be.

Why do you think people choose it?
For good and bad reasons. The good reasons are that some of them are terrific artists, and they have a capacity for symbolizing and expressing what the rest of us feel. The bad reasons generally have to do with exhibitionism, and when that is too strong an element in the whole thing, I think you have many problems.

Do you think Marilyn was a good or bad actress?
I think she was the best American comedienne of her moment. I think she was that natively before anybody tried to train her. She had a built-in sense of timing and a kind of wit about herself, a sense of humor about herself and what she was doing. It was just delightful.

What do you think about the way the press dealt with her?
They were almost totally destructive when she was alive. There were exceptions, but most of them ranged from simply snide to really vicious.

Do you believe in censoring the press in any way?
I don't believe in censoring anybody.

When you're married, do you generally just stick to that one women or do you fool around with several?
I'm pretty monogamous.

That's good.
I don't know if it's good or not good.

How do you feel about women's liberation? Women becoming stronger and challenging men?
I've always felt that it was necessary. But like every political movement, the women's liberation movement has bred a fringe element which lives or dies for that cause. And there is a monotony to listening to the same ideas over and over again. I think that finally it is self-defeating—not because the ideas are false, but because the litany is repetitious. They're not living in a country where the men are particularly liberated, either, so I have a feeling that this is a social evil that transcends women. However, I'm a husband of a wife and I'm the father of two daughters, and I do think that there are really unjust legal and economic conditions which there is no question that the liberation movement has had an effect on, in terms of conditions of work and pay. Those are real problems, and I think it's criminal that they should still exist.

In what way do you think American men are not liberated?
I don't think that most men I know feel that they are using whatever capacity they have. I think they're serving some sort of machinelike organization which they don't really believe in. In that sense they're not liberated. But all cultures require a conformity that I suppose in the end uses up life rather than supplies it. That's another problem.

You wrote a play called *The Crucible* which was about the Puritanical beginnings of this country. Do you think that the American male, in many ways, still hasn't broken out of the original Puritan patterns?
Our fundamental make-up is Puritan. Maybe the whole of Western Civilization is basically Puritan. It has to do with the work ethic, with discipline, with the male being the breadwinner as well as the soldier. But if you have a civilization based on technology and the fact that most people have to be somewhere at eight o'clock in the morning, then there's got to be social discipline of one kind or another. The most Puritanical society I know is the Soviet Union. So it hasn't to do really with private property; it has to do with the fact that machines have to be tended.

If we didn't have machines, then the fields would have to be tended, no?
Right. I think that it goes with a society based on some kind of rationalization of production. The only kind of society where Puritanism wouldn't work is where a man and a woman were living in the midst of a certain climate like the Bahamas where you could go out any time and pick your figs—where it's not based on time. I think time is the big factor. Our civilization is based on time, as it has to be. Somebody has to be there at that moment and he's got to be motivated to get there.

How do you feel about getting older?
I'll tell you about that in a couple of years. When you're thirty you're learning how to be twenty. And when you're forty you're learning how to be thirty. And when you're fifty you're learning how to be forty. So right now I'm learning

ARTHUR MILLER
Playwright

how to be about fifty. Then you run out of numbers.

How old are you?

I'm sixty-one now.

Do you feel different at sixty-one than you did at thirty-one?

A little more creaky. I tend to wonder why I should get up, instead of getting up and doing it.

You don't look sixty.

I still have a lot of energy.

How do you stay in such good shape?

I play tennis. Mostly I work around my place. I have about four hundred acres of land and I do a lot of work in the woods. It's relaxing. Too much so. I should be more nervous.

Do you watch your diet?

For thirty years I had the problem of trying to put on weight, and then for the last thirty years I had the problem of not getting fat. I could weigh 220 pounds with no problem at all. I love to eat.

Do you care about additives, chemicals, in food?

Yes. I grow all the vegetables that we eat and I don't spray them with anything. We probably live more healthily than most people do. But I still have to drink milk or whatever that's packaged or processed.

Do you drink much alcohol?

A couple of drinks a night.

Do you smoke cigarettes?

I stopped that about a year and a half ago.

How did you do it?

I didn't. It left me. It really did. One morning I just forgot to smoke. I inhaled a pipe for twenty-five years. I was *really a smoker*. I smoked fantastic amounts of pipe tobacco. I *inhaled* it. A pipe goes on for about thirty or forty minutes.

Why do you think you stopped?

I hadn't approved of my smoking for years but I never could get rid of it. I stopped a dozen times. It never worked. This may help others, so I'll talk about it—but it probably won't. One morning about ten o'clock I realized that I hadn't smoked. That wasn't the first time in my life but it was rare. I just had forgotten to smoke and I was doing everything else that I always did. And when I reached for my pipe I realized that I still didn't want to smoke, but that I was doing it as a duty so as not to lose that habit for when I needed it— because pipe smoking is a little different from cigarettes. It tastes nicer. It's terrific. Good tobacco is really a great thing. So I thought, I'll smoke again when I really want to smoke, which will probably be in about three minutes, but I'm not going to smoke as a duty to this habit. Surprisingly, about a half-hour went by before I thought of it again, and once again I thought, I really am doing this because I think I should do this. To make a long story short, that went on right through the day, during which time I really wanted to smoke twice, but I thought that if I really wanted to smoke only twice out of twenty-five impulses, maybe I could defeat the twice. I haven't smoked since.

Do you think about death at all?

I think of it in terms of all the plays I didn't write and the feeling that I better get on the ball. But I've always felt that way. I've always lived at the lip of the grave. When I was twenty-five I felt that I would never live until thirty, that I had a few months left to do whatever it was I wanted to do.

Do you believe in life after death or reincarnation?

Not at all.

Do you believe in any religion?

I have no compulsional ideas of religion. I do feel that there is an area of experience that we don't have any means of rationalizing. As an artist I know that's true because I learn things by simply sitting still—they happen to me and they come from areas that aren't quite within the range of my experience. That's the kind of mysticism that I suppose every artist has that is a sort of religious feeling. I believe in that and in the existence of a universal sense of wrong, which I think is in man's idea that he has to somehow save himself from the waste that life is. But those are hardly religious ideas. They're more psychological.

What made you become a writer? Were you a child when you started writing?

I first wanted to write back in my teens and I've always traced it to the fact that I read, quite by accident, a book by Dostoevsky which I thought was a detective story—I'd never heard of him. But it just swept me away and the idea of being able to actually write such a thing was the most marvelous thought I had had in my life up to that time. I didn't really believe I could become a writer, but it was certain that that was the best thing that could be done, although I didn't know any writers, I'd never met one. And that idea grew. I tried to write and failed many times and then finally I went to the University of Michigan, where they encouraged writing. They had writing prizes for undergraduates. And I wrote plays because—I've said this before—I think that there's a kind of deformation of the mind which is a playwright. It's very rare and it doesn't occur very often in one cultural time. I think a playwright thinks in terms of scenes instead of words. I think in terms of confrontations between people, which is a dramatic way of thinking.

When you hear people talking, do you remember the dialogue perfectly?

Yes. But I don't think that that would be enough for a playwright. Especially in this day and age—with tape recorders you don't need to remember anything.

What do you think of the theater today?

There is a tendency to mistake an anecdote for a play. I think we too quickly accept the explosion and destruction of the form—the form being the integration of each moment into some thematic whole. For twenty years now, the trend has been to simply divert the audience instead of integrating some action into a thematic generalization and making each moment relate and develop that theme in the symphonic sense, the way music is written. All that went by the boards years ago and I suppose it will come back. It will have to, because life is that way.

Do you like movies?

A lot of them.

Do you think they have good scripts?
No, movies are pictures, that's why I don't write them. I wouldn't say that you don't need a good script, but what you need more than anything else is terrific-looking girls and fellows and backgrounds and to keep things moving from one to the other. Movies are a little bit like the dreams we have—there are boring dreams and terrific dreams.

How many movies have you written?
Just one, *The Misfits.* I did another script years ago, about the Brooklyn waterfront, but they never produced it.

How do you feel about business in theater, writing, movies?
I've been lucky. I've had the same producer, Bob Whitehead, for many years now, so I haven't had the problem of having to go and get somebody to raise money for most of my writing life. But I think that the way the theater is set up economically is totally self-defeating and I don't know why they continue with it. I've made one attempt after another to change it, but nobody's listening to anybody. It's quite simple, really. It's not possible to do an adequate job on a serious play in three and a half weeks of rehearsal. It's simply impossible. Consequently, we throw plays on half-assed. They're underrehearsed and not thought out. In European theater of the first rank nobody would think of putting on a show before a couple of months of rehearsal. But you can't do that under purely private enterprise. It costs too much.

Do you think the government should subsidize the theater?
Yes, but I think we have to be very careful about government subsidies. The government should offer a subsidy which would not be controlled by the government. Now, in America that's heresy because the government has got to control what it gives out. But there should be a fund which would be available to responsible people—by responsible I mean they would actually put a play on and not run off to the Caribbean with the money.

Do you like money for yourself?
I do because it's freedom. If I have no money, then I'm the slave of whoever hires me.

What do you do with your money?
It's saved in one form or another. And I spend a lot of it. More than I think I should.

Do you enjoy luxuries like Rolls-Royces?
I have always had a Mercedes car and another car and a third car. That's not what you would call living on a deprived level. We live pretty well. We eat pretty well. We always travel somewhere during the year.

How long a vacation do you take?
I don't call it a vacation. In fact, I come out of these trips with stuff that I've used in my writing. But we're away a month, six weeks, sometimes two months, in the course of the year. I move around a great deal. And unlike most people, I pay for it.

Do you like television?
I have a great time hating it. My daughter is a great watcher of television and I very often have to sit down in the same room with her, so I'm watching the goddamn thing. It's appalling. And it's appalling for only one reason—not the content, which is what everybody's beefing about, but the level of the performances is so often so bad. The comics are so obvious. I was brought up on vaudeville, when you were watching real comics working. These guys had perfected an act in forty-eight states, so when they arrived in New York they were terrific comedians. There aren't many like that today. I was telling my daughter about Jack Benny and Fred Allen, how those men had come up out of the real tradition. It's not easy to find comics like that; it never was. But television consumes so many people. It uses up so many people before they really develop. I suppose there's no way to prevent that, but it's a pity. So a lot of the stuff on TV is just mawkish and obvious. And I look at it sometimes and I think, If this was on stage, I'd tolerate it for ten minutes.

Do you worry about your daughter growing up in an atmosphere that's so violent, with pornography everywhere, drugs available everywhere?
You know, two things can't occupy the same place. The only thing I have against television is that it consumes time that she could use and she does use. She's a good student. She reads a good deal. But when you think of all the stuff you can do nowadays, it's appalling that those hours go dribbling down the sewer watching that drek. Similarly, in the society, pornography occupies a perfectly good movie house and a great projector and all that great film stock. The waste of what might be is terrible. There are hundreds of young people walking around trying to get into film, trying to lay their hands on the means of production. Ninety percent of them aren't any good, probably, but maybe five percent are. It's such a waste, pornography. But I'm not as alarmed by pornography as most people are.

What about drugs?
That is terrible. I have no tolerance for that. I think anybody who really puts anybody on a drug—I have had experiences with that. I can't bear the thought of it.

Including marijuana?
No. I don't regard marijuana as a drug really. Being an old pipe inhaler, I consider marijuana another type of tobacco. What I think is appalling is forcing hard drugs on people by the culture or by others in the culture. I don't like that.

Do you ever take tranquilizers or sleeping pills?
No, I never had the need, but I sympathize with those who do. I just don't have to have them, but that's got nothing to do with my virtue or my will power, because as I said, I didn't have the will power to stop a stupid habit like smoking for a quarter of a century.

Is sex important for you?
Of course. It's the center of any artist's heart and soul. His energies come out of his sexual nature.

Some people say it comes out of the lack of sex almost, that creativity is a substitute for sex.
In a sense, without a lack of sex there is no sex. This argument is so circular there's no way out of it. For me, abstinence from sex has and would reduce my output, if anything. The deprivation turns my mind away from my work.

LUCIANO PAVAROTTI
Italian Opera Singer

Mr. Scavullo: When did you become interested in opera?
Mr. Pavarotti: I was born interested. My family was very musical. My father is still a beautiful tenor. He did not study to become a solo singer, but he sang in the church choir. His voice is quite beautiful and exciting, even now.

Did your mother sing too?
No, but my mother liked music very much. She had a very tiny little voice, but a very good ear and a great sensibility. In fact, my mother is too sensitive. She is the kind of lady who takes care of other people, and suffers because the world is not as gentle as she is. So she is always sad.

Did your father help you?
It depends on what you mean by "help." If you mean that to make an important career, you need somebody who is your judge—and a severe judge—then my father did that for me. He still is my most severe judge. Perhaps because I am the first son. But he was a great help. He did not support my spirit. Never. He always forced me into the condition of being tough, strong, by myself.

Where were you born?
In Italy, in a very little city, Modena, between Florence and Milan. It is very well known because they make Maserati and Ferrari cars there. It is also famous for one of the best restaurants in the world, Fini. And there are others which are as good. I took advantage of these restaurants, as you can see. It's beautiful food, and I can't resist.

Did you start singing when you were very young?
I sang in the church choir when I was a kid, but I was twenty-six when I sang professionally for the first time. For a tenor that's a little late. Of course, I started with a very ambitious plan: no little roles! I never sang a little role. Always, immediately, a big role. My first role was the lead in *Bohème.*

You married almost at the beginning of your career, is that right?
Yes, I sang professionally for the first time, April 29, 1961, and I got married September 30, 1961. At that time I was six months out of work, finishing my studying, preparing scores, and she supported me until I began to work regularly and support the family. But she worked until she had the second child.

I have three beautiful daughters, and a beautiful wife, who tries to divide her time between our daughters and traveling with me. I spend four months with the kids, and six or seven months with my wife. I am going to spend more time with the kids because I think they need me, even if they don't give me that impression when I go home.

How do you take care of your voice?
I decided many years ago that the best way to take care of my voice is to not take care of my voice. I live a normal athletic life. I am a fanatic tennis player. I move myself a lot. I don't wear an undershirt, so I can move freely.

Do you smoke?
I don't smoke and I don't drink. If a lot of people are smoking, I leave the room. That is the only thing I do for my performance. And lots of sleep. It is the best medicine. The dream for a singer is to have ten hours. When I was twenty I never had a problem sleeping ten hours, but now I'm forty, and at a certain age I don't think you need to sleep as long. Now I sleep eight hours, seven, six. But I don't want to take any tranquilizers because I don't think it's necessary. Perhaps it is the diet that I am on now—burning up the fat I have inside. Perhaps it produces a substance in my body to keep me always up and around. I've lost sixty pounds.

Did you stop eating pasta?
No, I eat everything. Generally, I prefer rice, in the Chinese way. I have one hundred grams of rice a day, in which I put some vegetables, white meat, preferably fish. Chicken is not as low-calorie as American people think. Very light veal is not half as fattening as chicken.

Is there any reason why male opera singers tend to be overweight?
I'll tell you the reason in my case. I was a soccer player until I was twenty. And the day I began to study singing I put my soccer shoes in a corner, three scarfs around my neck, and I stopped all physical activity. I thought then that it was bad for the voice, but of course I was wrong. And when you go from eight hours a day of gymnastics to stopping completely, then you begin to gain weight. More than anything, the diaphragm becomes different: larger and heavier. Also, the life of an opera singer is, in one sense, very nervous, so perhaps when we are home alone, the only way to escape is to eat. I am trying to find an explanation to this syndrome, because ninety percent of the opera singers are heavy. But if I thought that by losing weight I am going to lose my voice, I promise you, I will go back to my original weight.

What is your day like when you perform?
On the day of a performance I try to stay in bed as long as I can—before lunch. After lunch, if I feel a little tired, I go to bed, but I try to be sure not to stay more than one hour—to aid the digestion and relax. I try not to speak very much. Speaking is worse than singing, because when you sing you always use your diaphragm. But when you speak, even if you don't know it, unconsciously, you don't support your diaphragm enough and it's more tiring.

After a performance I am totally up; I am never tired. My nerves just stay up. The dream for me would be to drive a car for three hours—with Italian speeding—in the middle of traffic, not on the highway! I don't really work very much in hours, but I take all my power—body power, immense power—and concentrate it in the three hours of the performance. I cannot be down during the performance and up before. I must be up at the right moment. And I have to change myself into another person every night. One night I am a poet, the next a painter, another a killer like the Duke of Mantua. I have to go inside these roles. Even if I have the help of the music, I still have to believe in the role. That means changing myself and it takes even more concentration. Don't talk to me about concerts. I sing twenty pieces of music by ten different composers: I have to go from baroque to modern. But it is exactly what I like and it is not difficult for me, even when I think it is.

Do you have any fears before a performance?
I am always afraid. Because there is the possibility that you are so big, you fall. Like a tightrope walker. If you fall once, it is forever. You cannot make a mistake. And knowing this makes it even more difficult.

What happens if you lose your voice just before a performance?
You cancel. There is nothing else to do. I sang my American debut at the Met. The second performance I canceled in the middle. I had the Hong Kong flu. In fact, I went home and canceled three months of performance. If a singer thinks he is losing his voice, he's a dead person. Panic! It is really like that. Last year my plane crashed in Milan. Everybody was safe but the plane was destroyed. I drove home from the airport in the fog because I wanted to be active immediately. At home, I cried with my family, and then, the first personal thing I did was go to the piano and try my voice. I think at a certain point of our life, singing is like the oxygen we breathe; it becomes part of ourselves. And I understand very well why, even when it is time for somebody to retire, he would not: first, because you have nothing better to do, and second, because you think you are still great. If they don't force you, if they don't kill you, sometimes you don't know when to stop. In a certain way you are like a rock.

How long do you think you can keep on singing?
I'm forty now; around fifty is the time to think about quitting. Unless I am still in good form, like Richard Tucker. He died at the age of sixty-something, and until the last day his voice was fresh.

Do you have any fears about getting older?
I was much older last year than now. I feel much younger with the weight off. Perhaps the reason I lost weight is because I really was afraid of being old. I was feeling old. I was always standing, not moving. If something fell on the floor, I called my wife. I was too lazy, too fat—the two things together don't work in favor of feeling younger. But I am not afraid to die. I think I was ready to die ten years ago when I already had my family and a good career and all that anyone could ask from this life. All these other things are great, and I hope to have even more! But, philosophically speaking, I am ready to die. Of course, if you try to kill me, I will try to kill you first.

Can you make good money singing opera?
We make money, sure. But not like in the past. Caruso, for example, was paid $2,500 at the Met, and over $7,000 outside the Met, a night. You can't make any comparison today, even if you take the biggest stars—Callas, Tebaldi, Sutherland, Sills. But it is understandable because at the time of Caruso, opera was the only entertainment, the big entertainment—not movies, not rock, but opera!

Is there any way you can possibly recommend opera to people who are not familiar with it?
To understand opera they must become involved by themselves and they must, for example, read drama like *Othello*. But opera is a very little world. A big percentage of the people are not interested in opera. Now that the stage director is more important than ever, the opera has made a great improvement, in my opinion. I think even the young generation is interested in it for that reason. And even if you don't understand what is going on, you still get the impression. Even if you can't understand one word of what a singer is saying, even if you don't know the aria, it doesn't matter. Because great singers come to you musically, vocally, they give you the right impression. At certain points you can close your eyes and just hear the music and the sounds: that is already something by itself. If you want to be prepared, you can learn the words and understand the situation. Then you are not a virgin, but a nut of opera. There are people in Italy who speak in opera words. They go home and talk all night long in opera words.

What do you think the future of opera is?
When I was a kid, I remember people were saying that after two years, after five years, the opera was going to be finished. And still now it is very good and very prosperous. Of course, it is mainly supported by outside money. But you cannot make any kind of art without money. I think the opera is not going to die. I am sorry for the people who are waiting for it.

Did you hear the album called the "Classical Barbra" by Barbra Streisand?
I heard some of it on the plane. It's music. If it is well done, I accept even this. There was a big discussion in Italy when Mozart #45 was arranged by "The Swingles." Big scandal! I went home to my daughters, who never wanted to hear Mozart, and they asked me to buy Mozart. Then I decided it was not so great a scandal because now my daughters like Mozart. People don't realize that there are many ways to get to music. I don't think music is something so serious or so active or so sad. It's music.

Besides singing, what do you like in life?
One thing I would like to do very much is to be a painter because it is really creative. In opera we are reading a book. You cannot go very far. The music is already there. A good voice is beautiful, but you are not creating like a painter— from nothing. I'm not complaining about my career. I don't envy anybody. I'm doing exactly what I dream about doing and I'm doing it in the best way, luckily. As my wife says, people love me and I love people. For me this is the most important thing. After that, for myself, privately, I would like to be a painter. It would give a great personal sensation, but not the human sensation I get from singing.

People are always fascinated with singers who can break a glass with their voices. Will we see you break glass one day?
To break glass is so fake.

PHILIPPE PETIT
High-wire Walker, Street Juggler

Mr. Scavullo: Did you really start out in the streets?
Mr. Petit: Yes, ten years ago. I was very well known in the streets of New York before I did my Twin Towers show at the World Trade Center. I would make a circle of chalk in the street and start juggling with torches, with balls. I'd put a little rope between two trees, play with the people. And then I'd escape when the police tried to catch me.
Did you make arrangements with the police before you walked between the World Trade Center towers?
Of course not! I did it without permission. I went to court, I went to jail, everything. The whole story began ten years ago. I got the idea when the building was not even built. Then, in 1974, I came here with the idea of putting my wire up between the towers there, and for eight months I tried to find a way to sneak through the security. I made preparations like those for a bank robbery. I rented a helicopter, made false keys, I made false deliveries, I disguised myself. It involved a lot of money, a lot of time, and a lot of people. And after eight months of preparation I was able to find the little missing link in the whole security system, the way I could bring a whole truckful of heavy props to the top. And then I did it one night—I shot a bow and arrow with a fishing line from one tower to the other—and we spent the whole night putting the cable up there. I'm now doing a motion picture about that whole thing. It was not a stunt for me, it was a show.
When did you start walking on the wire? How old were you?
Around fifteen. In France, as a very young kid, like six, I was doing magic. I still do magic for my friends, but I don't do a magic show anymore. The magic introduced me to juggling; the two arts are very close. So I learned magic by myself, then I learned juggling by myself, and the juggling put me into the circus. I went to see more magic shows, more jugglers, and I discovered these people who walked on lines. And all during my childhood I was climbing trees, making bridges and working with rope, so it came naturally. I learned the high wire by myself.
How do you have such amazing balance?
I don't know if I have good balance or not. If you are very high on a wire, and you must balance, you will not do it with mathematics, you will do it like an animal. I don't think I have the correct balance—I think I'm crazy. I just like to climb trees, you know? Naturally, it does take a lot of work, like every other art, ballet, everything. I don't consider what I do a technical thing, even if technique is a big part of it. In fact, I never speak of balance myself. Balance is a word used by people other than high-wire walkers.
Were you nervous when you walked out there?
I was much more than nervous. This was a very special story: the World Trade Center. I dreamt it for ten years, I organized it for eight months, I didn't drink and eat and sleep for three days before because I was completely involved in it. So I was exhausted, I was nervous, I was mad, I was crazy, I was elated . . . I was somebody else, I was in another world, I was so tired that I couldn't carry the balancing pole. I was checking everything. The wire was not properly tied, and I was afraid that a policeman would touch the wire and I would fall. I was afraid of the wind, and there was so much space, too. All this went through my mind like a hurricane, so I don't know if I was nervous. It was a unique experience.
Don't you have a fear of heights?

Yes, like everybody else. Every time I am very high, I have the same fear, it's very crazy, but I overcome it because I like so much what's going on up there. The height makes me very tense and very aware.
Why do you do what you do in the streets?
Why do you climb trees? It's not as simple as that. If I were looking for a reason, perhaps it is because I am interested in this character that I create, to make him more open, to enrich him—this guy with a top hat and a unicycle. I am a complete character in the streets—I don't talk—and people love me. I love the street, which is where I started when I was seventeen—I dropped school and my family and my country and I went hitchhiking, I traveled. I slowly got my own ideas in the street, and now my act in the street is completely closed, finished—I will not say perfect because it's never perfect—but my character in the street is built. And it's really my life, I will never let go—when I'm ninety-five I will still be in the streets. Nobody can understand it, for in the world of show business, the street is the worst. For other show business people, when you pass your hat in the street it is to beg for money. But for me, when I do it, it is not that idea. The street and the high wire are my two things. Since many millions of people in the world know me as a street juggler, I wanted them to recognize me as such when I performed my feat at the top of the World Trade Center. So I wore the same costume that I wear when I am being chased by the police on Fifth Avenue.
Do you travel alone?
Always, unless I am in a circus or a troupe, but otherwise alone. Because I never know what will happen. It's a day-by-day life. What I am most interested in, besides street juggling and high-wire work, is to go into films. It's a dream I've had a long, long time. I wrote movie scripts, and I never really showed them to people, but now is the time I can really work, because people know me. So I am working on a film about the World Trade Center adventure, and after that I will do a film that I wrote which is about my childhood—you know, this little kid running away from his family and taking his top hat and his unicycle to live in the street. Then I will start what is my real goal in film, which is to create a comic persona and put him in several screen adventures. He will be a new comic character, and I will be the writer and the director of these films, and that's what I want to do. A character like this doesn't exist today. We have comic characters like Woody Allen, but in fact, these comedians give their characters to whatever films somebody wants them to do. They are not people who create with the same energy as the first silent stars did.
Do you do anything to relax?
No. I hate that idea. In America they say, "Take it easy, relax." But there are not enough hours in my day, not enough days in my life, so I grab at everything. But I am not nervous. I know where I want to go, and I know there are a lot of things to do to get there, so I don't relax. I don't go on vacation. I am on vacation all my life. When I work, it's not work to me. It's marvelous that they pay me. It's a nice life, you know.
Are there people that you like to spend time with, or do you like to be alone?
It's a difficult thing to speak about that part of myself.
Do you go out with someone?

"Going out" means you are not really involved in a big love, but in my life, it's a big, big thing. I love someone and then it's finished—it's usually a very serious and true moment. But I cannot live with somebody. I try to sometimes, I get involved, but then I have to go my own way, I have to be left to my own world and work.

Are you attracted by beauty?

Very much. But usually it isn't beauty alone, it's a kind of essence which somebody has. Sometimes people are just fascinating, but they're not really beautiful—the whole personality and body together makes them unique, you know? I am very attracted to people who carry a strong life within themselves because my entire life is my work. I practice all day long. I just like it! Sometimes I go on the beach and try to relax, but ten minutes of that and I find three little stones on the ground and start juggling.

Do you like music?

I like music very much, but I do not, in fact, like music the way other people like music when they sit themselves in front of the stereo and enjoy music. All the music that I like is connected with my work. There is music that I think about for my films, music that I use in my act. So I like Nino Rota's music in 8½, which I use in my high-wire act. And I like very much Paganini, whose *Campanella* I use when I climb the incline wire at the beginning of my circus high-wire act.

Do you eat any special foods?

No. Again, that is not it at all. What I do is not athletic. The high wire is poetry.

But obviously you can't get fat.

I don't even think about it. I love to eat. I go to the best restaurants. I love sugar, I love cake, I love chocolate. I eat whatever I want. And I drink what I want to drink. I'd never drink during a show, of course, but that's normal.

Do you go to a doctor?

What a crazy question! I never go to doctors. I have no time to get ill. I haven't been ill for the last ten years. When I get a cold, I still practice, and the cold goes.

Do you smoke cigarettes?

I do magic tricks with cigarettes, but I don't smoke them.

Do you have a fear of dying?

As far as what is involved in my work, of course, I risk my life, but I never think of it because I am too passionately involved to be aware of the danger. After a show I sometimes realize the craziness of what I just did. It gives me a lot of power, a taste of infinity to be on the high wire. For a few seconds or a few minutes I suddenly live completely, live one hundred percent, because I hold my life, and I carry my life, I'm the master of my life—if I make a false step, I die, I kill myself. It's very rare in life that one has that feeling, and that's what I like very much. I love bullfighting, too; I consider it very close to high-wire walking. I like a guy in front of a bull. I like El Cordobes.

Are there any other people you admire?

I admire a man who has worked in this country for many years, Señor Wences, the father of ventriloquism. He's one friend, I see him often. I have another friend who is very well known in show business. His name is Francis Brun, and he is the greatest juggler ever. I admire Nureyev very much. I like Yehudi Menuhin, because he travels to the end of the world with his violin and shares the instrument—and he is a crazy guy, too.

What do you think of Marcel Marceau?

I don't like mime at all. For me it's a dead art, it's mechanical. It's a school of movement, so when you want to pick a flower, you pick a flower in a certain way, which for me is wrong. There are a thousand different ways to pick a flower. I know Marcel Marceau, he knows me, we are friends; but I never told him how I feel about mime. Maybe what I do is the real mime, like Buster Keaton and Charlie Chaplin were doing. Because they were not performing a school of mime with white gloves and a white face; they were just working with their body without speaking, and it was mime. I cannot relate to the mime of Marcel Marceau. It's amazing to see how a human being can possess and control his body. But then what? Where is the art? Where is the life? Why no speech? Why a white face? Where is the freedom of imagination? Where is the fire? For me, mime is not an art, because there are rules. Break the rules!

If you became very rich, would you still be out on the streets?

I have never had any money, but if you gave me a million dollars, I would rent a theater and practice all day long for the whole year. If you gave me a hundred million dollars, I would make a film. If you gave me a billion dollars, I would make a film and a circus and a traveling show; I would never put money in a little box. I will never become rich. I don't relate to money the way other people do. I never have any money, and I'm living like a king. If one day I cannot eat, I steal food or whatever—it's life. If another day I get a lot of money in my hat, I go into the best restaurant and ask for caviar and chocolate.

Are you doing something at Niagara Falls?

Yeah, that's my big project now. I'm trying to get permission to cross Niagara Falls. In fact, I'm trying to cross where nobody even thought of crossing before. Many people crossed the river, the rapids—it's about four hundred feet across—but, in fact, nobody has ever crossed Niagara Falls because it's impossible. It's two falls: the American Falls, and the big horseshoe, the Canadian Falls. To cross the two falls will take a mile-long wire. I want to cross right above the two falls. I will have to build thirty-story concrete towers on both sides; I will have to use helicopters for four months; I will have to lower the water of the falls. This project will involve a lot of money. I have a major TV network in this country behind me, and also the largest steel company. So I have the possibility of starting it, but I don't have the permission yet. After my book comes out and my film is released, I will feel more positive about seeking permission for this show. That's what I want to do. I want to do the most beautiful show on earth. I want to walk the high wire above Niagara Falls. And, believe me, I have many other "dreams" for my future—and they will be accomplished!

JOHN ARISTOTLE PHILIPS
Princeton Student Scientist

Mr. Scavullo: How old are you?
Mr. Philips: Twenty-one.
How did you come to design an atom bomb?
It was a thesis for school, actually. I needed an independent work project and I wanted to something different. So I thought I'd try to design an atom bomb, mostly because it was a challenge, and partly because I wanted to see if terrorists could do the same thing. I also wondered whether I could do it—if it would take a lot of brains and a lot of money. It wasn't until after I did it and it was publicized that I realized what I had done. And then, when I found out it was being classified, I started getting real nervous.
Who classified it?
Well, when I went to get my thesis back from the dean's department, they didn't tell me anything other than I wasn't going to get back my papers. The secretary had nothing to say to me. So I went back a second time, and I said, "If I've flunked, tell me." The secretary said, "No, you got an A, but your project is being classified, so you are not getting any papers back."
But who realized that you had designed the real bomb?
The professors in the physics department who were my advisers had worked at Los Alamos. They said, "Where did you get this information?" I said, "I found out for myself," and they said, "Pretty good."

There was some math in what I did, but most of it was a conceptual kind of thing, it was just approaching a very difficult problem in a very simple way. It was an educated guess; I guessed right. But I didn't build a bomb. It was a paper design which is simpler, less expensive and easier to build than the way they do it in the Army.
How do you deal with your sudden fame?
The publicity has been neat, kind of fun. Everybody looks at me as if I'm a genius, but I'm not. I know I'm not. But it's a good experience when you're young. It's good to get a lot of people thinking you're really hot shit because you realize how little it means.
Do girls call you up and ask for dates?
That's actually what's happening now. But it's bad, because I don't know why these girls are interested. Before, a girl might come up to me and introduce herself, but I knew she liked the way I looked or something like that. But now I wonder where all these people are coming from and why. I mean, if I get into a car with somebody I don't know, I call the FBI and tell them who the guy or girl is. And they check it out. It's weird. One day in Grand Central Station a guy walked up to me and said, "You're John Philips, aren't you?" He started pressing for the bomb design. He was posing as an Italian reporter. He said, "I want a scoop, I need a scoop." I was having a hot dog and he kept putting a napkin and a pen in front of me, expecting me to draw the design.
How do you feel about people calling you up now just because you designed a bomb?
It's real sad, and it's weird as hell. I wish that I could say something intelligent about it, but it just defies any logical, intelligent thing to say. I can't be flattered because it's not flattering—people asking you for autographs. It's really a stupid thing to do; it's alienating.
Why do you agree to do interviews?

I do it for fun. And I'm also doing it because I think there's a lesson to be learned: the wrong people will get the bomb, if they don't already have it, if we don't stop access to things like plutonium. My case shows how eager everyone is to get the bomb. But at this point I'm using sufficient humor about the whole thing and am enjoying myself. It's not going to lead to any problems.
Were you always considered a really bright kid?
Everybody considered me kind of strange. I was suspended from high school because I was never the obedient little kid.
Do you have a high IQ?
My parents never told me my IQ. They didn't think it would be a good idea. I don't know why.
What kind of family are you from?
My parents are Greek. My middle name is Aristotle.
Do you get good marks in school?
No, I get very bad marks in school. I used to get all A's at Berkeley, before I transferred to Princeton. I have a D average just about every semester. I don't go to classes. But I like school. I want to get into the astronaut training program, and the only way to get in is to get a degree. I've already applied. There's really stiff competition. They want to know how many Ph.D.s you have.
Why do you want to become an astronaut?
I think it's exciting, exciting work. I think I have a good chance of getting to do it.
Do you feel that going to school at Princeton is an unstimulating experience?
No. I'm really enjoying it. If I weren't doing that, I would be sitting on my ass somewhere else. It's not that I don't do any work, I just don't go to classes. I work independently. I'm doing a lot, I'm meeting people and having a good time.
What kind of people?
All types. One nice thing about Princeton is that you meet all types of people, and they're all bright. It's easier to communicate with them. Not that I'm overly intellectual, but I don't have to lower my caliber.
What do you like to talk about?
All sorts of things. One thing I don't like to talk about is the bomb.
Are you interested in politics?
I was, at one time. I was very active in high school. I was class president. But I don't have time for it now.
What's really important to you?
My work. I really do like it. There is something called cosmology, which is beyond physics, beyond astral physics; it's about what happens when notions of time and space don't make sense anymore—which is what really goes on in the universe. It's kind of neat to think about that. For instance, there is something called the tachyon. Tacky-on. It's this tiny thing, we can't see it, it doesn't even exist. It's a negative mass, it's anti-matter. If one was in your hand, you wouldn't know it was there. It's born after it dies. Time is reversed for it. It's backwards. It's a concept in which everything is turned upside down.
Do you think that applies to human lives?
I think it is probably intricately related to human life. Maybe it's not as far out as one would think.

JOHN ARISTOTLE PHILIPS
Princeton Student Scientist

Do you think death is final?
I don't think so. Death is probably just a transition. There's no real end and no real beginning. That's what the universe teaches us. There's got to be some kind of movement, some kind of continuum.

Do you believe in spirits?
I don't know. The more I learn about physics and space, the more I realize how little we understand, and how little I know. I've got a lot to learn.

Do you find being very bright sometimes is a disadvantage, regarding your happiness?
I don't think I'd be happy as a moron. Perhaps it's possible to be too smart to relate to other people, but I'm not that smart. In any case, I don't think that's possible; I think the more intelligent you are—not more educated, but brighter—the more perceptive and sensitive you are to people and things going on around you. I think you can be very, very sensitive and not go to college.

Do you have a girl friend?
It's weird—when you become a public figure you become alienated very rapidly from the people around you whom you previously felt you knew. You get into this whole head trip and you get separated from everyone. It's important to try to hold on to those roots, but I've been unable to hold on to girls or friends. It's hard for them to keep up with me. And it's really important to have good friends at times like these.

What kind of girls do you like?
Tall blond goddess types. I don't mind if she's taller than me, so long as she's sexy . . . unashamed of the fact that she is sexual. And she has to be bright and honest.

Do you like to make love a lot?
As often as possible. I'm convinced it's really good for you. When I go without it I really feel shitty.

Does sex make you feel healthier?
Oh yeah, I feel like a man.

What do you think about career women?
They don't frighten me. If a woman is doing what she wants to do, that's good. But if she's doing it because she feels she has to be a career woman, then she has an overachiever complex, and that's no good.

Do you intend to get married?
Not for a while. I don't really intend to have children unless I meet some woman that I not only dig a whole lot, but also think of as a person with whom I could really have great children. But I never met a woman that I thought I would really like to have stick around in the morning more than for a very short while.

What else do you do besides school?
I'm in the pizza business with a partner. We deliver to the kids on campus. We have thirty-five guys working for us now. It's a big business, a chain now, a sort of big, great machine. But it just runs itself. We have people who manage it; all we do is count the money.

Do you like to make money?
It's not important to me right now. But at the time of my life when it will be important, then I'm pretty sure I'll succeed in making a lot of money. Actually, the fun part of it will be making it, not particularly having it. For instance, with this pizza thing I have all the money I could possibly use. There is nothing that I want that I can't get now. I might want very expensive things sometime, but I don't need them now. I know I have the capacity to do well, to make money. I do. I think the capitalist spirit is in just about everybody, at least everybody in Western society. But everybody is not equally successful at it. I think luck has a lot to do with everything.

Do you think capitalism is good?
I do. But this pizza business has made me realize that I think of people who were formerly friends as cogs in a wheel that just keeps turning. It alienates, it dehumanizes, the people who work for me from my point of view. I pay them enough, but it's just not the same. I think of them as little containers. That's how I think of them in their job. I'm in the situation of hiring them and paying them and expecting a certain amount of work from them—it's just not a very friendly relationship. I don't interfere with them in any way. There are guys who manage them. All I do is count the money, every morning, like a gift from Allah.

How much do you make a week?
I'm making about $200 a week. It's good enough.

Is pizza your favorite food?
I hate pizza. I really hate the stuff at this point. I like really rare, rare steak. I like Hoagies, if they are not cooked too much.

Are you concerned about chemicals in food?
My mother has always been into natural foods, before it was faddy. She reared us on natural foods, so it concerns me a bit. But just about everything has something bad in it.

Do you smoke?
No.

Do you do anything special to take care of yourself?
Yeah. If I want to be by myself, I don't feel bad if I leave whatever I'm doing. I just go away for as long as I want, without telling anybody. I take off, and come back when I feel like it. I don't feel bad about that. I think you're

supposed to feel bad, you're supposed to feel antisocial, but it's good for me.

Do you use any special cologne or soap or shampoo?
Naw. I do like Apple Cider Vinegar shampoo, ACV. It really smells neat.

Are you interested in clothes?
I like fine clothes. Things that feel soft. I like browns, dark greens, blues. I don't like synthetics; they are not warm at all.

Do you like television?
I don't watch television that much. But with all this publicity, I haven't had time to do the things I really want to do, like camping. I like to go out in the woods by myself, bring some books. I had a motorcycle for two years, and I drove it from San Francisco to Princeton.

Do you like any sports?
I played soccer for a year. I like to ski. I like to think a lot. It's kind of enjoyable.

Do you have any hobbies?
Actually, I like to draw cartoons in class, caricatures of the professor, the guy sitting next to me, a dog. I also like to look at pretty girls. I like beautiful women. They have something that is almost eerie, some kind of universal quality. It could be a beautiful woman or a beautiful man—there is something universal and recognizable, and that is beauty. It's good to rest your eyes on something like that.

Do you read magazines?
I read *Newsweek* and *Esquire*. I read the *New York Times* every morning for an hour and a half at breakfast. I only get five hours of sleep, average. I get up early, like six forty-five. In the morning I really take it slow and easy. I take a nice long shower, half an hour. Really hot, steaming hot. I get out of the shower, put on some music and walk around naked until I'm ready to take off. I just putter around. If I feel like it, I sit and watch the sunrise. I just take things nice and easy and think about what I'm going to do that day. Then I go to eat at the Ivy Club, a social club. And I have a really long breakfast. I have poached eggs on English muffins—very bad for you. And I like to have a really good cup of coffee. It's crucial. I like to sit at breakfast, see the sun come through the windows and think about the fresh air.

That's the best way to start the day, relaxed; then I go to class. I only have two days of classes a week now. The university decided to let me do what I do. It was quite a problem, since you are supposed to take so many classes, but they're letting me do my thing. The most productive hours of the day, as far as thinking goes, are during the late afternoon, just before sunset and dinner. In those three hours I can do several chapters of physics. I'm really cruising. I'm awake, I'm alert. And then I have dinner and watch Walter Cronkite, every night. In the evening I'll do some homework, and then around eleven I'll find something else to do, like drinking with friends. I drink Planter's Punch.

Do you ever get depressed?
I'm not the kind of person who is depressed. When I get depressed, I get depressed. But I enjoy it. When I'm down, I have certain kinds of thoughts and a certain kind of introverted insight. I've trained myself not to be unhappy though I'm in that state of mind. I think depression is accurately defined as being angry with yourself. But when I'm angry with myself, that does not make me unhappy; I learn from it. I analyze myself, and try to understand myself better. Likewise, when I'm elated I enjoy that, too.

What makes you elated?
Excellence, that's what makes me elated. For example, I was at the Metropolitan Museum of Art and saw Renoir's "Two Girls Sitting at a Piano"—that made me very happy.

What do you think of the world today?
I'm really optimistic about mankind. We are living in superexciting times. There's so much going on. I think it's really neat. The possibilities are endless, as they've always been—space, for instance, is a new frontier. I think we'll have space colonies in the twenty-first century.

Would you like to move to space?
Not particularly. I'm an explorer, but I like the Earth. I like the ground.

What do you think about the drug laws, concerning marijuana and cocaine?
I think the government interferes far too much in people's lives. The government is lowering itself and involving itself in things that do not concern it.

Do you think our goals should be nuclear disarmament for all the countries in the world?
I think it's a good idea, but I think we have to find something that interests us more, that's more important to us than building bombs. I think that exploration is more important. In every phase of history there is either building armies or exploring. I think we've just passed an era where we've been building armies and now is the time to put our resources, energies and hopes into exploration. And that includes exploration of the arts. I think there is great potential for the arts to flourish in our lifetime.

Are there any big idols on campus now?
Me!

GEORGE PLIMPTON
Writer

Mr. Scavullo: How many characters have you played in your career?
Mr. Plimpton: Among other professions I've tried being a boxer, a football player, a baseball player, a comedian, a trapeze artist, an automobile race-car driver, a photographer for *Playboy* magazine. Did you ever see my attempt at a centerfold? One is required to use a Deerdorf, that huge portrait camera. Very tough to operate. Everything falls out of focus almost immediately, and when you look into it everything's upside down. I was trying to photograph a girl standing beside a horse in a field, a fantasy I have had for years of walking through a wood and seeing this lovely sight. But the horse and the girl kept drifting out of focus, and besides, they were hanging from their heels out there in the meadow. So I found no lust in my heart.

Did you enjoy boxing?
I did it entirely because I hoped to write about the experience. I got pushed around by Archie Moore when he was the light heavyweight champion of the world. Someone once said that sixty percent of the people truly like to hit other people. The other forty percent don't like it at all. I number myself immediately among the latter. I don't like hitting people or being hit. To me, the struggle against Moore was simply a journalistic exercise. But I got to enjoy the profession of boxing as an observer very much. I've just finished a book about Muhammad Ali and boxing—a big long ten-year labor. It's called *Shadow Box*. I watched him fight from the very beginning.

Is it very revealing about Ali?
I don't think he's a very revealable character. He's shy and very hard to get to know. I'm not sure that anybody really knows him, except perhaps Herbert Muhammad, his manager. But he's fascinating to write about. If you're a journalist interested in sports, he's a figure that you have to come to grips with. But my boxing book is really a catch-all . . . a book about Ernest Hemingway, Norman Mailer, Hunter Thompson, reporters, soldiers of fortune, mobsters, heists, the very strange mix that seems to be part of the boxing world. I've used boxing as a departure point for a lot of other things.

Thinking back, though, I'm devoted to the fraternity of boxers. They're perhaps the most interesting of the athletes. Certainly there's no single athletic confrontation as interesting as the heavyweight championship of the world, nor, curiously, as arresting a person as the heavyweight champion. When the heavyweight champion of the world walks into a restaurant, everybody stands up. If the American League batting champion walks into a restaurant, no one stirs.

Are you afraid at all when you participate in sports?
I go through the same emotion almost any athlete does, which, I think, is fear of humiliation. It's not a fear of being hurt. But to go in there and make an idiot of yourself or be shown up or fail at a crucial moment—that is actually what athletes consider when they sit in their locker rooms before a game. They're not praying for victory or praying not to get hurt; what they're praying for is that they get through the afternoon without humiliating themselves.

Do you have any fears?
Enormous numbers of them, but nothing's worse than the fear of humiliating yourself. And, of course, for me it's inevitable, because as an amateur I have no chance of success at the exalted level of professionalism. I have to keep comforting myself by remembering that I am a journalist and that my function, however humiliating the experience, is to find out as much as I can about the fraternity I've been allowed to enter. I'm interested in anything I can get away with and then sit down at a typewriter and write about.

Are you afraid of death?
Well, paralyzed. I've heard rumors about it. This new boxing book I've just finished has a whole series of death fantasies which I asked writers, friends of mine, to contribute. That might suggest my state of mind. The exercise was inspired by Norman Mailer. He was out running with Muhammad Ali in Africa at dawn and he got left behind. He suddenly heard the roar of a lion, and he set off back for the base camp at a terrific speed, as you can imagine, and got there to discover that he had indeed heard a lion, but one caged up in the presidential zoo. We had dinner that night in Kinshasa and he admitted to me that as he ran he kept thinking that if Norman Mailer *had* to go, what a marvelous way it would have been—to be taken by a lion in Africa. He could see this biographical line in the high school anthologies: "Dead, 51, taken by a lion on the banks of the Congo."

The replies from my friends were extraordinary, most of them quite erotic. Bill Styron sees himself coming to an end in a water-polo match against an all girls' team captained by Lee Remick. He suddenly suffers a cardiac arrest. They prop him up on a float in the middle of the swimming pool and minister to him as he dies. His last words are: "I'm dying, Lee, dying . . ." I've written about all this in *Shadow Box*.

Do you have a death fantasy?
I always thought that death would come during some athletic endeavor—beaned by a bearded pitcher in Yankee Stadium.

Do you train before you play a sport or are you always in training?
I ride a bicycle everywhere in New York, which helps. Nervous energy seems to keep me reasonably healthy. I play a lot of tennis and squash. But when one of these assignments comes up, I train very hard at whatever sport it is. I can spend as much as three months going to the gym to learn about that sport so that when I enter the fraternity, its members realize that I'm not just coming in for a gag; I'm really trying my best to find out everything about their sport. I'm trying to be more than an impostor. So they respect that; it makes them feel that I hold what they do at some sort of honorable level. I need their respect to get the material to fill my notebooks.

How do you take care of your health normally? Do you watch your diet?
No. I seem to be able to stay about right without worrying about it.

Do you smoke?
I used to. But when I had to fight Archie Moore my trainer said, "You'll never get a better reason for stopping smoking than because you're fighting this guy and you should be in good shape." That was a long time ago, and I haven't smoked since. So I would recommend to anybody who really wants to stop smoking to challenge the light heavyweight champion of the world.

Do you take vacations?
No, I haven't had a vacation for twenty-five years. I travel all

GEORGE PLIMPTON
Writer

over the world, but I always seem to have an assignment that sends me there. Of course a writer's life, with the exception of actually sitting down and slamming away at the typewriter, seems like a vacation to most people. I'm going down to the Masters' Golf Tournament, for example, and most people would give their eyeteeth to do that. But it's an assignment and I'll have to spend that weekend working.

Do you take notes as you're actually observing something?
When I played with the Detroit Lions I used to keep a notebook in my helmet. I wrote things down and shoved the notebook up into the helmet. The other football players thought I was a rookie with a very bad memory. Then at night I would take the notebook and write things down from it into a big master notebook.

Do you stay up very late at night?
Yes. I sit around restaurants or parties. I go on into the night. If I am at home, I love TV late at night. I find myself watching Mr. Carson. Some of the strange public-channel shows at two in the morning are interesting. I watch those. I read—a lot. Lie in the bathtub and read. I think people sleep too long. I get up at seven and write, usually. There are bad nights after which I don't get up until noon, but I try to get up early because the house is very quiet then and it's a good time to work.

Do you write every day?
I try. What makes me write is an angry editor on the phone saying, "Where is that piece that was supposed to be here last Tuesday?" I don't have very much fun writing; I don't think I'd do it if it weren't for the deadlines.

It seems all of the subjects you've chosen to write about are male endeavors. Would you like to, let's say, become a fashion designer for a week and write about women?
I haven't thought about it. Sports seem to work for me because a very visible confrontation takes place, and writers are always looking for confrontations. I'm not so sure that if I became a fashion designer for a week, I could find that degree of confrontation; at least it wouldn't be as evident as in sports.

Do you think men are more competitive than women?
I don't think I've ever met anybody as competitive as Billie Jean King. She makes up for about six million noncompetitive women right there.

What do you think about women's lib?
Oh, heavens, I'm all for it. I support most of the Equal Rights programs. Certainly there should be equality in hiring practices. I'm a little suspicious about the thought that there must be an absolute equality of responsibility in the household. I don't consider myself equipped to deal with a household and I don't understand why I should be forced to. One does have different responsibilities.

Is having a family important in your life?
The family is very important. I would guess that most social problems finally go back to not having a strong family. Surely the family is the focal point of a comfortable society. There used to be a great deal of emphasis on it fifty years ago; much less so now. As a result, I think we have a much more febrile, nervous, frightened society.

Do you think it's possible to love one person?
I think it's very possible. Whether it's essential or not, I don't know. W. H. Auden said he thought marriages ought to be arranged; he was perfectly congenial to the idea of weddings, but he felt that so often marriages were ruined by being based on a romantic idea of falling in love. Much better to have the parents arrange the whole thing.

Do you think homosexuality is bad for society?
No, I don't see how it can harm a society at all. It doesn't produce a family, but it doesn't destroy it.

What do you think about pornography?
I don't collect or read it very much, but it should be available if you want it. I thought the old Supreme Court ruling on pandering an excellent one. Now they changed the rule to "community standards," which I think is probably going to mean the end of pornography—at least if you have Memphis, Tennessee, calling the shots. I rather like the pandering idea: there could be no display of pornographic advertising where you could see it from the street, but the material would be available if you knew where to go. It was an excessive application of that rule that got Ralph Ginzburg a jail term for mailing copies of *Eros* from Intercourse, Pa.

Times have truly changed. I remember in the fifties when we began publishing the *Paris Review*, my small literary magazine, we couldn't use *any* four-letter words. We printed abroad, and there was a man named Mr. Demcey in the customs office down on Varick Street who reviewed the magazine before letting it in. One of his jobs was to airbrush out pubic hair in sample Danish nudist magazines so that the publishers could see what the restrictions were. You can't believe the arguments that he and I used to have about the four-letter word "crap." I remember an issue with a short story by Alex Trochi, a brilliant writer, who used the phrase "motherfucking spike"—it was a story about a junkie. Mr. Demcey had let the issue off the docks without checking, and when he found out, he said he was going to send out U.S. marshals and seize the shipment. We had to hide the issue in cellars throughout Greenwich Village because of this one word. It would be awful if we got back to something like that.

Are you optimistic or pessimistic about the future of Western civilization?

My mind shifts back and forth. There have been times when I had very small hopes for it, but then I listened to President Carter talking to the people of the United States over the telephone and I thought, He's quite a man. I sensed an interesting intelligence which made me feel much better about things. Then the other day at a lunch with Mr. Kissinger, I heard him say that most of the statesmen he met were mediocre, that the effort of getting to a position of power sapped them in some way, so that when they got there, their minds were exhausted, capable of thinking only about how they were going to *stay* there. If the world is run by a bunch of mediocre people all exhausted by having reached where they've gotten, there's not much hope. Of course, there were exceptions. Kissinger mentioned Giscard d'Estaing.

What kind of people do you admire?

People who take a certain chance, a certain risk. Particularly people who try despite handicaps. I always thought Bobby Kennedy was a remarkable figure because he was a man with very few obvious gifts to run for the presidency. He spoke poorly, he was very shy . . . but he was driven by a type of commitment which made him tremendously appealing, especially to people who also had difficulty—Indians, minority groups—because they could see that somehow he spoke for them.

I admire Muhammad Ali. He has handicaps. He can't read easily because he suffers from dyslexia. He has to learn his speeches. But he commits himself to very rending decisions, such as not to join the Army. Even changing his name. He loved the name Cassius Clay. Adored it. And to change it to Muhammad Ali must have been an awful wrench.

How do you feel about tragic beauties?

I'm doing a book with Jean Vanden Heuvel about a tragic beauty: Edie Sedgewick. She was a child of the sixties who was destroyed by the excessive altitudes and pitfalls of that time. She was from a very old New England family. It's an extraordinary story.

Are you interested in other people more than you are in yourself?

God, yes. Although my books are told in the first person, there is very, very little about me in them, and a great deal about the people I'm given the chance to observe through this device of participatory journalism. My books are not very self-revealing.

Would you ever want to write a self-revealing book?

No. I think it's part of my New England background. One shields oneself perhaps more than other people do, or at least my family does. We're all very nonrevealing people.

Where were you born?

Well, I can reveal that I was born in New York, went to school at Exeter, Harvard, King's College of Cambridge University for a couple of years. I went from there to Paris and helped start the *Paris Review*, which continues to run. I did that for three years; then I came back here, continuing as the *Paris Review* editor, and I taught for a couple of years at Barnard College. Then I began to write, mostly for *Sports Illustrated*, and then began to do these participatory adventures, many of which evolved into books (*Paper Lion, Mad Ducks in Fairs, Out of My League, The Bogeyman, Shadow Box*) and television shows. And that brings us up to the present. Perhaps not too quickly.

Was your family puritanical?

My father's a corporation lawyer and a diplomat. He was Adlai Stevenson's deputy ambassador at the United Nations. He's very much New England in outlook, a stickler for the disciplined life, and many of those splendid virtues. It somewhat puzzles him to see his son dressed in pink tights, soaring through the air in a circus act. In fact, I remember him watching that particular television program. We had a small gathering to watch. He did not look at the television set; he busied himself in the back of the room mixing drinks. I don't know whether he's unnerved by it; it's just that he'd feel the world would be less puzzling if I were a lawyer or a college president.

Do you think it's important to do many different things in your life?

Yes. I'm now doing a book on quests, looking for things. I went to Mexico looking for a bird called the horned guan, a great big turkey-sized thing with a popsicle-like protuberance that comes out of his forehead. Lives high in the cloud forest of Chiapis. Extraordinary expedition. Next I'm looking for a bird in Hawaii which is called the o-o. There are only two of them left, supposedly. The pair live in a swamp where the rainfall is 300 inches a year. The quest doesn't necessarily have to involve birds. I've been to Kenya looking for the bongo, the lovely rare mountain antelope that lives in the Aberdare. Never found him. Doesn't matter. I'm going down to Georgia to look for the species of tree that Benjamin Franklin was supposed to have planted there. Surely won't find it, but the main thing is the search itself. It doesn't really make much difference *what* you look for, a coin or a stamp or a rare book—it's a very good exercise to keep you going, keep you excited. It wouldn't be a bad idea to construct one's whole life out of a series of quests.

THE MARQUIS ANTHONY DE PORTAGO
Stockbroker

Mr. Scavullo: Does your maid wake you up with breakfast?
Mr. de Portago: No, I don't usually have anything for breakfast, though sometimes I have a milk shake. I never drink coffee or tea. I went to boarding school in England, and they shoved so much tea into me for the five years I was there that I hate it. And for me, coffee goes with a brown paper bag. It's like the lunch break in my office. Everyone has a brown paper bag and his little cup of coffee. So if I wake up to that, I've ended the day.

Is this your first job?
This is my very first job, full time, at the brokerage house. I worked one summer for Senator Strom Thurmond. But that's the kind of job you do when you're supposedly a spoiled little rich kid and your parents send you out to work with different people—like a conservative senator. And then the next summer they send you to a farm so you build up some muscle.

Do you like holidays?
Well, I never really worked, so a holiday to me was just going someplace else.

Did you know your father well?
He died when I was three, in a race-car accident.

Did your mother or grandmother tell you a lot about him?
No. My grandmother had a lot of pictures of him, but my mother didn't keep pictures of him in the house. He was never a symbol of what we were meant to become. We never idolized my father, which was fine because he wasn't there. He never meant anything to me. I remember once, when I was about seven years old and in boarding school, someone said, "My father's better than your father," and I couldn't have cared less. Because my father never existed to me, he just didn't exist. I suppose I got a clear picture of him about a year ago, when I was twenty-one. I formed an idea of what my father was because every young male at some point has to have some kind of an identity with a man. I had that in a way, since I was sent to boarding schools from the ages of seven to eighteen. But there were so many different kinds of men whom I didn't like that I didn't want to identify with them, anyway.

Didn't you study with Martha Graham?
Yeah. I studied some dancing. I also studied acting. I went into a lot of arts at one point until I got fairly sick of trying to show myself through an art. A lot of people are very much into self-expression, but I really think that's beside the point. The point is that we *are*. We are living and we are alive. It's irrelevant who we are: we just are. In New York everyone always has a problem. But these people have a problem because they're feeling. This may seem very futuristic, but I have a theory that we should get rid of emotions. I think emotions are bad things. We base our value system on two feelings: good or bad. Everything is usually black or white. Someone asks you how you are, you say, "I'm well" or "I'm not well." You can never just say, "I am." I'm not feeling happy and I'm not feeling sad.

I presume you don't believe in love, then?

I don't anymore, I think. I got married at eighteen and had a lovely, lovely marriage for two and a half years. I was deeply in love and was as high as I think I could ever go in love, but it didn't get me anywhere. I mean I'm sick of love that way. It just gave me a lot of shit in the end. I went through a lot of pain. I grew because of it, but I'm not interested in falling in love. For me, falling in love means deep love. It means giving a lot of my energy. Now, why give away my energy? I really need it for myself.

Do you attract women with this attitude?
A lot of women are more interested when they think that you don't care that much. It's as if you kicked someone and he wanted it again. I've mistreated women, but they were there and they stayed there, so obviously they wanted it. I was having a good time and they put up with it, so why not? They didn't have to stay.

Do you prefer the company of women to men?
I think everything is possible. I feel as if I'm at an age when I can choose my behavioral patterns, but there's no question that I enjoy the company of women, because I like beautiful things and they're very beautiful.

Are you afraid of death?
I don't want to die, but I couldn't care less when I die. I don't believe in death. Every pleasure you've ever dreamed of could come true when you die.

Do you look in the mirror a lot?
No—not until I realized last summer that I was good-looking. I decided then that I should get my act together.

Do you just buy clothes in any store?
I get everything at Saint Laurent—except my shirts, because I like silk. He has silk, but for $250 and they are not exactly the silks I want. I can pay £18 ($50) for a silk custom-made shirt—which is nothing.

Do you care who cuts your hair?
I don't care. I like to be very clean and I like to be neat and I like to be well dressed. I love to shower. I never take baths. I like water falling down on me.

Do you prefer the day or the night?
Night. Because it's quiet. There're many fewer people and you can freak out as much as you want. People are always much more open in darkness because they feel they're hidden. All truthfulness happens at night. Love-making is a form of truth that usually happens at night, because it gives a feeling that is all warm and dark and nobody can see and nobody can interrupt.

Do you have any political ideas?
I believe in a dictatorship. I definitely think a lot of people should be told what to do because a lot of them cannot decide what to do and do not know what to do. A dictatorship doesn't have to be violent. A lot of people want to be told what to do. You're in a group of friends and everyone's saying, "What should we do? What should we do?" They're waiting to hear what to do. People want to be told what to do and are happy following.

ROBERT RAUSCHENBERG
Artist

Mr. Scavullo: When did your interest in art begin?
Mr. Rauschenberg: I'm not sure. It sounds corny, but I nearly
flunked every course I ever had because I was too busy
drawing on the books rather than reading them. But then,
I'm a slow reader, so reading was very boring for me. It's
difficult to know when your interest begins in anything in
Port Arthur, Texas, where I was born and raised. I mean,
you either work for the oil refineries or you don't. And your
father either does or he doesn't.

Did your father?
He worked for the light-and-power company. I remember
hurricanes before I remember anything about art. There
weren't any resources in Port Arthur to stimulate any curiosity
whatsoever about art. All through high school I was on
every publicity crew—I painted all the posters for high school
elections—but I never thought of that as art, it was more
like writing. It wasn't until I was in the Navy that I first saw
some art, but I still didn't associate that with my own interest
in art. And after the Navy I went back to Texas because
there was no other possibility if your family's there and you
go to the Church of Christ and you were only away from
home because of the Navy. It wasn't until I went back that I
was able to even think about the fact that one could make a
decision. Life there was just inevitable.

Did you get a job there when you got back?
Right after the Navy, no. I had some summer jobs there
when I was younger. In fact, it was my idea for the local
store to hire children to sell clothes in the children's
department. And I sold Christmas cards one summer—the
competition was less in July.

When did you make a decision to leave Port Arthur?
I got back to Port Arthur and I knew there were so few
possibilities for my interests to work there. It wasn't until
then that I missed the outside world, so I called a friend and
got a job in Los Angeles as an illustrator for a daily
newspaper. It took me a *week* to do a drawing. That didn't
work out too well. Then I got a job as a packer in a bathing-
suit factory. I lost that job quite quickly because I was so
bored that every time there was a new order I would try to
get a few extra bathing suits in the box—you weren't
supposed to work *that* hard.

Were you influenced by any other artists?
I hope so. But my major influence has just been what happens
during any single day. As far as other art is concerned—I
was walking out of the King Tut exhibition at the National
Gallery in Washington and I was so moved by that show that
I passed a Da Vinci that has always been an untouchable
favorite of mine—it looked flat and simple-minded to me. I
thought, My God, I can't say that about Da Vinci. And then
I went directly back to work and I didn't forget that
experience, it was incorporated, but not in any scholarly way,
not part of the program. But I'm probably more influenced
by what happened today which was a continuation of the
chaos that I've never been able to avoid. I'm supposed to be
three places at seven o'clock today.

Does that chaos always exist in your life?
It seems so. Even on the island in Florida where I live, the
weather changes, and the waves come up and take out the
beach or bring in more sand. Or maybe the wind's too high
for the tomatoes. Or: Where is the other dog? I don't look

for trouble, but when I first went down there it was supposed
to be some kind of paradise. I'm basically a sociable person,
I like one-to-one confrontation with people, and I thought,
What am I doing—I'm living alone and moving to an island.
It was the first time I had the threat of owning property,
because in New York I don't feel like I own my building—I
feel like I'm leasing it from the subway. Even though I paid
for it. But in Florida it's actual land and the idea that I could
own land was fine, and so I began to develop some snob
instincts to protect the trees, the land. I have a whole other
life there—I'm anti-bulldozer, anti-condominium.

Do you have a lot of friends there?
There aren't that many, but they're good because they pretty
much stay on and on. And there's very little to do except
work—you can't run uptown or downtown and see something
that will turn you on—so we spend a lot of time being
highly critical of each other's work and encouraging each
other and sharing ideas, which was pretty much the way it
was in the late fifties and sixties. But we keep our
individuality. Any one of us—there are only six people—can
do something that the other one can't, and we share this.
Though we don't have a plumber. Do you know a good
plumber living in Florida?

What's your day like there?
I tend to sleep late and that's not just because I go to bed
late. I don't really start thinking until about three o'clock, so
I make a bunch of stupid telephone calls and take care of
problems that any idiot could do, like make sure that the air
freight's picked up, that we have enough dog food. And then
at three o'clock I start thinking, Well, here's another day,
what are you going to do now? I do very few projects that
continue along with other projects. Each piece is started at
the beginning and worked on until it's finished. Sometimes I
try to trick myself into going to work earlier, but it rarely
works because I know it's a trick and I don't fall for it. And I
usually work until about three or four in the morning
depending on whether whoever's helping me has to go to
school the next day or not.

Do you usually have an assistant helping you?
Yes. I can't run the litho press really well. It's a delicate
instrument and an essential tool to my work and I wouldn't
want to fuck it up. Plus I like to have someone to talk to
while I'm working.

Do you have dinner all together?
Yep. Actually if you come after dinner, it's about three in the
morning.

Who cooks?
The person who is least busy cooks.

Do you care about food at all?
No, there just should be some. I wouldn't want to get obese,
so I've never had an appetite for a lot of sugar unless under
duress and then I eat some ice cream. But if I have to choose
between hot, home-cooked muffins and another drink, I'll
drink another drink.

Do you ever get really drunk?
I don't seem to, but you shouldn't take a drunk's word. I
know lots of sober people who've fallen right over on their
faces.

Do you have any idea why you drink so much?
I have an idea about it, but I don't necessarily believe it's the

ROBERT RAUSCHENBERG
Artist

right idea. I mean, my drinking could be just a building habit. But it does break down some inhibition and I need to do that because I'm basically very shy and, also, I work with very little confidence in my work. Somehow, after a few drinks the veneer of self-consciousness dissipates and I will do things that I wouldn't do otherwise.

Do you take drugs at all?
I take a lot of vitamins, a little hash now and then, but what do you mean by drugs?

Cocaine?
No, cocaine gives me sinus problems.

Do you like parties?
No.

But I've seen you having a good time at parties.
Oh, that's a major sin—to go someplace and not have a better time than anyone else. That's a real unforgivable one. You go right to hell for that one.

Do you exercise at all?
Not really. I paddle around in the water. I fish. But not too much.

Do you take care of your health at all?
My doctor does.

Do you see him often?
No.

Does getting older bother you?
I would like to make the switch abruptly. The in between bothers me. There are many beautiful old people, that doesn't scare me at all. But there's something about being a middle-aged teen-ager that's most uncomfortable, but I suppose I'll get used to it.

Are you afraid of death?
I've never liked it. My astrologer says that I'll never be killed accidentally, so that gives me some confidence—in fact, you should fly with me.

What sign are you?
Libra on the cusp of Scorpio. One of my problems is that as a Libra I'm basically uncertain and can defend any point of view. But my works seem to be done in Scorpio, which has to do with success and money and power. Sex? No, I straddle that, too.

Do you consider yourself a very sexual person?
Horny, maybe.

Have you ever been in love?
Yes.

Do you think that love has much to do with sex?
I wouldn't want to be very close to anybody that I didn't like.

Do you have some person who pushes you on, who helps you?
Yes, I do—it's me.

What kind of people are attracted to you?
I don't know. I know my blue eyes always get them. Is there any possibility of getting bushy eyebrows?

Why do you want bushy eyebrows?
I just think there's something silly about using your features.

Do you care about your clothes?
Most of my clothes come from the Salvation Army and places like that. Every now and then, for a special occasion, I get somebody to make me a shirt. But lately I've been ordering only from catalogues. I recently ordered some pure-cotton suits made in Yugoslavia that don't fit me.

What do you think about beauty?
It only exists in context. You can't have a concept of beauty without knowing its context. Like compared to what? I mean, how is beauty behaving? What is its function? I would have the same problem with what's ugly.

Do you think women artists are becoming stronger?
There was a lot of resistance which inhibited the development of any successful women artists, but that's changing very rapidly now.

Are you attracted to stronger women?
I'm no more attracted to stronger women that I am to stronger men.

You like to be the strong person in a relationship?
I don't think so. I wish I could make up my mind. Being interviewed can be interesting—it makes me plow through my feelings and responses one more time, and every time I do I think that I find out more than the interviewer. That's not necessarily pleasurable—I mean, I don't always find out what I had wanted to find out. But I don't give the same answers.

Do you think more art was created in the fities and sixties than in the seventies?
I don't think I've been counting. I don't think of myself as like having anything much to do with art. I just like working. I do make art and I do care about artists, but I'm a little confused about what's happening now because I travel around so much that there isn't enough time for me to keep up with what everyone is doing. Also, when I first started working there were five galleries in New York that were showing contemporary American painting; now there must be a thousand galleries that show contemporary art. So I tend to just see what comes to my attention through street talk.

Do you think this tremendous growth in the number of galleries is good for the artist?
I don't know if it's good, but I don't think there's been a proper adjustment made to it because artists still have the same handicaps that they had in the fifties. I started an organization called Change, which helps artists in trouble. The letters are still just as pitiful: "I'm being thrown out of my loft"; "I need an operation"; "I did a project and the people didn't pay me"; "I just broke my foot and I don't have hospitalization"; "I have to pay property taxes on my loft because it's a working space." There's still so much frustration for anyone who takes the profession of being an

artist seriously. And these letters are not only from painters and sculptors, but also from photographers and writers and dancers.

How do you decide whom to help?
It depends on the intensity of the particular emergency. In some cases we have to respond within two hours.

Does your staff interview them?
We have a staff of one person and I'm it.

Does the quality of their art matter?
There's no aesthetic judgment. You know, I recently got some work of mine out of the warehouse that had been stored away and that had almost been forgotten, except that I remembered how bad the work was the last time I saw it. But that was twelve years ago and it was work from twenty-four years ago, so I got the romantic idea that maybe it was better than I thought. You know, maybe it was just a bad day when I last saw it. But it was lousy. And that's why there is no aesthetic judgment when an artist comes to Change for help. Every artist has made really lousy work.

Does selling your work matter to you at all?
Only to the extent that art, not only mine but that of my colleagues, needs financial support to go on. But at this point there really isn't anything I want except dog food and to keep the country from being totally bulldozed.

You wouldn't want a lot of money?
No, I can't fly a jet.

What do you think of art critics?
I don't think of them very much. I think that there are some scholars that might have the same problem I do and therefore, maybe, can understand my work.

Do you collect work by other artists?
Yes. My last purchase was a hand-painted bark—a fertility ceremonial thing from the Amazon that I found in a little antique store. It is absolutely beautiful. And I'm having a case made for a mummy I got about three years ago when I was in Israel. My collection's very erratic. You thought I was going to say erotic, didn't you?

How does publicity affect an artist? You were on the cover of *Time* magazine, for example.
I like it because my interest is in communications and not painting, and that gets to be a problem when your prices go up, up, up, because you aren't sure people can buy it. But possession isn't the whole thing. So I travel with all my shows and make sure that they're hung properly and meet the people who come, and in some cases do a video tape so that when I'm gone they can see that the artist was actually there.

Would you prefer that a museum buy your work rather than individual collectors so that more people can see it?
I'm not sure about that, either. This is the Libra talking. So many things that have been important to me have come as a result of accidents and I don't know why people are even interested in my work. I think I'm just lucky, but I do work hard—so it's a combination of working hard, luck and just trying to be as honest as I can in what I'm doing. And the person that I have to look out for the most is myself, in the sense that I don't gyp myself into thinking some other way. That's not clear, is it? I don't have any kind of planned ideals or destiny, so that to assume a personal program would possibly kill the talent, or at least confuse it. And think how the response to my work is so far beyond anything I ever could have thought of or planned. Therefore I think it's better if I don't have any plans now, too.

Do you read magazines at all?
I do a lot with their pictures.

Do you believe in photography as art?
Oh yeah. I have a portfolio coming out of photographs I took twenty years ago. I haven't taken any since I lost my Rollei, which was some years ago. I had my own darkroom and everything. And then I lost that camera and I haven't found any other camera that I can relate to. Cartier-Bresson told me that he's used the same camera all his life.

Do you watch television?
It's always on. I don't always watch it. If it's really lousy, I turn off the sound and turn on the radio and keep the picture on. It's just like another window. I keep anything around that reminds me that there's more going on than in the room that I'm in. And I keep up with my soaps.

Do you have any favorite color?
No, I was brainwashed by Josef Albers. He taught that each color was better than any other color and that you were only to use colors as a slave to your profession. So I'm a color liberationist, since again, I can't decide . . . I don't see any reason to prefer one color over another, because the situation changes. For the first five years of what's now considered the beginning of my work, everything was monotone. And gradually I went into the reds, and gradually some reds with a little yellow, and finally I broke into a free color sense.

Do you get depressed?
Doesn't everybody?

What do you do to get out of it?
Work, usually.

What gets you depressed?
Bad news, or a sense of inadequacy.

Do you have any religious doctrine that you live by?
Don't hurt anybody that you can avoid hurting.

Do you ever think about the prospect of being remembered in history books?
No. That's their problem. I don't even think the artist makes art.

Do you want your paintings to last forever?
That would be unrealistic, wouldn't it? I don't want them to disintegrate any sooner than they do, but I wouldn't want to censor my responses to materials in any way because of permanence.

HARRY REASONER
Newscaster

Mr. Reasoner: Barbara said you were very kind and didn't have a cruel lens, so I feel comfortable.

Mr. Scavullo: Do you worry about getting older?
Sure. Doesn't everybody? I assume that if you had a choice, most people would choose not to. My traumatic birthday was thirty—I didn't seem to be getting anywhere, I didn't know what I was doing. I was depressed for about six weeks. But forty was no problem, or fifty. I have a pen pal named Bruce Bliven, who used to edit the *New Republic*. In his Christmas letter when he was eighty-three he said, "I don't feel like an old man; I feel like a young man with something the matter with him." But age doesn't make you feel different. I've been disappointed to find out, at forty and at fifty, that I'm no more settled in my attitude about things than I was when I was twenty-five. I suppose that's good, but if you had looked forward to—oh, a time of quietness when passions would disappear and you could live in ease with the world around you, it's a little disappointing to find you get roughed up just as much in your fifties as you do in your twenties.

It may have something to do with the nature of people who go into journalism in the first place. Journalism is a kind of profession, or craft or racket, for people who never wanted to grow up and go out into the real world. If you're a good journalist, what you do is live a lot of things vicariously, and report them for other people who want to live vicariously too. You see a lot of things without ever being completely involved in them. You're like an actor: you touch on politics, you touch on adventure if you do any war corresponding, you touch on all kinds of romantic and portentous activities—but always as a dilettante.

Tell me about your job.
It's obviously a very good job, except that it's kind of a drag. I like to get out once in a while and play reporter, cover something. I think it's not only good to keep in practice, but it freshens me when I come back. Something usually comes up—if the President isn't going to China, it's a convention year or something.

Did you have any idols as a kid?
I suppose my early hero was Elmer Davis. Of course, during and after the war, we all greatly respected and were influenced by Ed Murrow. Davis didn't have the glamour and the great career that Murrow did, but he had just as much influence on American journalism.

Do you watch television now?
Not much, but it's not because I'm prejudiced against it or look down on it. If I get home at eighty-thirty at night, I want a drink and some conversation—I don't want to watch television.

Does your wife stay home or work?
My wife doesn't work, but she's fairly active in volunteer work. She's a member of the board of trustees of the Southbury Training Institute, a school for the retarded in Connecticut, where we live. And she does recording for the blind.

Do you read much?
Yes, but only for pleasure. I made a rule twenty-five years ago that I would not read anything I didn't enjoy.

Do you exercise?
I play tennis. Not because of the recent fad for it; I've been playing since my early twenties. I don't play very well, and I'm not a nut, but I like it very much. I play to keep in some kind of shape.

Do you smoke a lot?
I've smoked heavily since I was young. I did a couple of documentaries early on, when people began to realize the hazards of smoking, so I've been concerned. I've tried to quit—I did quit once for six months—but I was gaining a steady pound a week and that began to seem like more of a health problem than the smoking was. So I decided about five years ago to give up the idea of giving up, and just live with whatever hazards there are. I hate people like my wife, who smoked fairly heavily when she was young, quit about fifteen years ago and can enjoy a cigarette if we're at a pleasant party. That's what I can't do; if I have one, I'll have sixty.

Do you watch what you eat?
I'm a great appreciator of food. I like French cooking. My wife once said that for me travel was just a succession of restaurants. I love food, but I don't think I'm a glutton.

Do you think it's good that women are becoming more career-minded?
I think so. I suppose my daughters were responsible for changing my ideas about women's liberation—several of them are quite enthusiastic about it and well informed. But I don't think I was sexist in the first place. There have always been more women in journalism than most other crafts, and I have worked with them, directed them and worked for them, and I've never found them any worse than men. I think it's a good thing that women who do not want to fit into a pattern now don't have to, but I don't like the unisex idea. I hope there will still be a place for women who want a traditional, possibly flirtatious role in life. I'm glad they have a choice now.

Are you optimistic about society?
Not particularly. I think we've got serious problems that have been building up over a long period of time, and I don't see the country displaying any particular disposition to try to solve them. I think part of it is just being old. This country is the second oldest major continuing government in the world, and like human beings, countries get old, fat, cantankerous, unable to adjust, unable to meet new situations.

Do you have any strong political beliefs?
I believe in democracy and the United States Constitution very strongly. I've never been partisan, because I don't think it goes with my job. I think if I were going to run for office in Connecticut, I would have to do what General Eisenhower did, and decide which party I wanted to be in. It's been suggested that I run for something a couple of times. I'm not sure that I could do it.

CHRISTOPHER REEVE
Actor

Mr. Reeve: I have to make one apology for myself—I'm afraid I'm not much of a dresser. I wear very strange sizes. I'm thin, and yet broad-shouldered, so nothing fits. I have to have everything tailor-made for me, every jacket cut. Frankly, however, clothes have never been that important to me. I go around in jeans, in sweaters. I've had this sweater since I was fourteen. I've just been cast as Superman, and one of the PR guys said they wanted me to make one of the Ten Best Dressed next year. I said, "You're going to have to do a lot of work."

As far as I'm concerned there is Superman and then there's Christopher Reeve, and I'm not interested in having them merge. What I'm interested in is acting.

I'm twenty-four; I've been working since I was fourteen; I studied at Juilliard. I wasn't Superman before and I don't plan to be Superman after.

Mr. Scavullo: Were there any feats you had to accomplish as Superman in your screen test?
No. Didn't have to knock anybody down or leap over any buildings. The hardest thing I had to do was jump off a balcony at about four feet while keeping my hair in place and speaking at the same time. But in the film there will be an enormous amount of stunt work—flying and fighting especially—much of which I will do myself.

What do you do when you get up in the morning?
Take a shower, shave. I use soap and a brush. Just from habit I've always used Ivory soap. I use Head and Shoulders shampoo. I brush my teeth with whatever I find at the drugstore. Then I face the day.

As an actor you have to wear make-up. Does your skin suffer?
I was on TV for two years on *Love of Life*—I quit when my contract was up. But the make-up didn't bother my skin at all. I would just clean it really well afterwards. Soap and water, then Albolene cream—let that soak for a while—and then soap and water again. In terms of my skin condition, I have no regular program of lotions or treatments. Every now and then I look at my face and say, "My God, it's getting really dry," and hunt all over the place for a bottle of skin cream, that Vaseline Intensive Care stuff, and just slop it on.

Do you like to drink?
I don't really care about drinking, though I will have a couple of drinks. Now, last night I really tied one on; that's rare for me, but it was somebody special.

To relax I play the piano. I've played for about ten or twelve years. I can do an hour every night, and sort of drain away the day. I also find that a nap in the afternoon is essential. I come home every day—I don't care what happens. If I have to be at the theater at seven-thirty, I take the phone off the hook and I sleep from four-thirty to six. I need to recharge my battery. I want to go to the theater feeling that it's the beginning rather than the end of the day. I get to the theater very early, and basically I do an Alexander technique, which I studied with Judy Liebowitz at Juilliard. It is a way of releasing tension in the body, through the joints. If you think of the body as a well-oiled machine that runs on very precise ball bearings, it gets them functioning smoothly. It gives you a kind of liquid freedom from muscle tension. What tension does is restrict the joints from moving naturally; you can see it in the way people sit sometimes with their

neck jammed down or stand with their knees locked.

What I do every day before the performance is lie down on the floor, widen the back and lengthen: you know, the head gets back up on the shoulders, the shoulders drop down into place, the voice settles, and you get ready to go! The first time I did Alexander I stretched out about an inch and a half. I used to have a psychological thing about being tall; I was sort of apologizing for my height. I've gotten over that.

But other than that, for my head, I fly glider planes to relax. I also have my own airplane. I simply drop out of life, seven or eight thousand feet up in the sky. I go wherever I want to go. I usually take friends, though when I'm really down and out I go up solo. Otherwise I like to share it with people. I usually take a friend and a thermos full of chicken noodle soup. There are little tiny airports all over the country, where you can just drop in. I flew back from California this summer, just puddle-jumping from place to place.

I find the same release in sailing. I've sailed all my life; I'm very grateful to my father for teaching me to sail from the time I was four or five. I grew up racing in international competitions. I'm very lucky—you see many people who don't have ways to get out—I've always had the means, I've always known people, there always has been a way out for me.

Are your parents rich?
No. My father's a professor, a novelist and a translator. My mother's a newspaper reporter. My stepfather's a stockbroker, which is not exactly the most secure business these days. It probably sounds like I play with a lot of toys, but I don't spend a lot of money. I have a tiny apartment. I live like a squirrel, because sailing and flying mean more to me. The two years I spent in the soaps has pretty much given me the means to do what I want to do.

Do you have a girl friend?
I'll pass on all that. There's something going on, but it's very private.

What kind of people attract you?
I certainly don't like fat women. I do have a preference for tall women; they just make me feel more comfortable. I don't like to feel like a giraffe. I also tend to be attracted to people who aren't wasting time in their lives, those who have figured out something that they want to be. I have very little patience with people who just lie back and let life happen to them. The opposite can also be a problem. I remember one of my early girl friends, who will probably end up as the first woman Justice on the Supreme Court. She didn't really leave me in the dust, but what happened between us was that we were too competitive.

Do you agree with the statement that Truman Capote made once that actors are stupid people?
I think that you can't be a good actor and be stupid; to be an actor is to understand enough about other people so that you can represent them.

Do you want to be a star?
Not a star. I'm sure you've heard this eight million times, but I want to be an actor first. If I become a star, terrific. But that hasn't entered my head yet. In a year I might be sitting here with a mohair jacket and cigarette holder and a driver waiting outside—talk to me now before I turn into complete schmuck.

Could you?

CHRISTOPHER REEVE
Actor

No, though last year it might have been possible. Last year I was really a pretty insecure person. If life is a roller coaster, I was on the downgrade. But this break came very early in my life. I've always secretly thought that I would get a break, but I didn't think it would hit until I was around thirty. I really feel ready for it.

Does anything worry you?
No. The only thing I'm afraid of is . . . I would hate to be a really old man. I would hate to have my second childhood. I don't want to be reduced to eating Gerber's Baby Food, attended by a nurse around the clock. My grandfather is in that state. He's in a nursing home, just hanging on. All he can remember is World War I. As far as I'm concerned, he doesn't exist anymore. It may sound callous, but I don't want to see that person. When I see very old people I get a very uneasy feeling in my stomach. I'm also afraid of anything that has to do with blood, and dissection, and medical things like that.

I'm afraid of . . . I used to be afraid of, I'm doing better now—one major fear is: I want to really make sure that my professional life and my personal life meet in a happy place. I don't want to be a successful person who has to compensate because he can't keep his personal life together, and at the same time I wouldn't give up what's going for me now for somebody else. I'm going to have to find out how to put those together. That's one major, central anxiety—how's it going to work out? I used to think that in a few years I'd get married, and I'd want a little place in the country. Now the whole possibilities of my life are different. So I wonder, how am I going to keep it together? Am I going to believe in different things? I would rather look forward and think positively and accept the experience than back into it. I've got a choice to dive in and find out how the water is, or to stand at the end of the pool, dipping my foot in, backing into it. I've backed into a lot of situations in my life. I backed into the soap opera. I backed into the play—*A Matter of Gravity* —wriggling and squirming all the time. I could have backed into Superman, too, but I feel better just to say, "Here we go!"

Do you fear death?
I do. It's funny, when I was a kid, around eleven or twelve, I was so afraid of dying that I wanted to die so I wouldn't have to die. It hits me every now and again—I'm buying cookies in the grocery store or I'm talking on the phone or looking out the window, and suddenly a little voice inside says, "You're going to go away one day, you're not going to be here, so take a good look." And I just shut him up, and he goes away.

Do you watch television?
I'm really pretty allergic to television. I used to watch myself on the soap opera: I loved to do it and then go home and watch it. I learned a lot from it.

What do you think of soap operas?
I don't want to put them down, because the training for the actor is terrific. My reservation about the soaps is the blandness, their calculated inertia, the way in which they move nowhere.

What about *Mary Hartman, Mary Hartman*?
I think *Mary Hartman*'s a disgrace. It's ludicrous that it's so close to the reality of American life that it can be that important. I get physically ill when I watch that show.

Are there any men or women you admire?
One of the things that's had the most to do with my life is a tremendous respect for my father, with whom I've gone through the whole gamut of feelings. Starting from intense hate and competitiveness—he used to treat me as if absolutely nothing I could do was right, whereas my mother treated me like everything I did was right. I knew they were both wrong. You know, I'm between two families; I have a Princeton family and a Connecticut family, and it's great. When the water gets too hot in one tub I'll go to the other, back and forth. My father's my best friend in the world. He's like my brother; we are just yin and yang.

Also, I respect Richard Chamberlain for what's he's done with his career, for getting out of *Dr. Kildare* and going to work on himself as an actor.

Do you have any secret desire for a particular role?
I think the world can be spared my Hamlet. The first thing I'm going to do after *Superman* will be totally nonheroic, nonwonderful, not larger-than-life, because I've always been allowed to play those parts before. In the theater in New York I played a very frail, introverted, shy grandson of Katharine Hepburn; the leader of Hitler's personal bodyguard in a play about Hitler; and a young farmer from Wisconsin. In the same year, in the same city.

Do you ever take drugs?
Absolutely never. There's a psychological connection there; of three very important people in my life one died and two were very, very badly messed up because of what they went through with drugs when we were growing up together. I'm pretty much a balanced person, anyway; I don't tend to be sucked into what other people are trying.

Do you have a lot of friends?
Yes. I used not to—not their fault, my fault—because I couldn't accept them. A lot of people offered me friendship, and my reaction was, "What's it going to cost me?" And I realized that what I was doing was saying, "I like who I am, so I'm going to hold on to it. I'm not going to give any away." And what happens is, friendship dies; it dries up and dies. I've since realized that the more you give away, the more you have.

RAVI SHANKAR
Indian Musician

Mr. Scavullo: Is it an honor in Indian society to play the sitar?

Mr. Shankar: No, it is like playing the violin, it depends on how good you are. If you are bad, there is no honor. Many, many, many people play the sitar, but again, you have thousands of violinists, but how many Jascha Heifetzes do you have?

How old were you when you started playing the sitar?

I was nine when I started, but I didn't take it seriously until I was fifteen. And at the age of eighteen I gave up absolutely everything for the sitar. I was a dancer—maybe you have heard of my elder brother, he was a famous Indian dancer, Udi Shankar. I was with his group, touring all over the world, the States, Paris . . . so I was more of a dancer, and singing, playing the sitar but not seriously. Then I met this great man, my guru, who joined my brother's group when I was sixteen. And that's when I became more interested in music. But it still took me some time to decide to give up dancing and other things completely. So it was in 1938, when I was eighteen, that I left my brother's group, everything, and went with my guru and stayed with him almost seven and a half years. It was like a hermit's life—a complete surrender to the guru, and the whole style of his life.

Were you born in India?

I was born in Benares, in Bengal, and we belong to the Brahmin caste.

Is that a high caste?

It was considered so, but now it is not important, no one bothers about the caste system anymore. I cannot say that it is *completely* gone in small villages, but we don't think about it.

When you spent seven and a half years with your guru, what did you do?

Nothing. Nothing but learning music twelve to fourteen hours a day, seven days a week. The whole concept is mental conditioning—when we go to a guru we take it very seriously. A guru is not only a teacher but also a master. You surrender your life completely to him. And he doesn't just teach you an art of technique; he passes on a whole way of life, a tradition, everything. That's the old system and that is what I went through.

What is the popularity of the sitar today as compared to what it was in the sixties?

I want to make one thing very clear. The music I play is the traditional classical music of India. It is as classical as classical Western music, which comes from the Church. Our music also started from the scriptures, thousands of years ago, and little by little became a performing art. And ours is an oral creation; it is not a written document like yours. So as it was passed down, it developed, it never stood static. And improvisation is important in our music. But one has to learn the base, the classical system, the whole concept, and one has to memorize it to learn sitar music. Now, that's my background and I'm basically a traditional classical musician when I perform the sitar at Carnegie Hall or Avery Fisher Hall or any of the big halls. And I came to the United States four times in my childhood, with my brother's dance group. Solomon Hurok was our impresario. So I had an orientation to the West and I could communicate here in later years and then, after I closed myself off with my guru for years, I became established as a top-rate sitar player in my country. I

didn't come to the West to be known. I was the highest-paid musician performing in my country.

But my childhood experiences prompted me to come here—it was like a self-appointed duty that I took because at that time no one had any idea in the West of Indian classical music. So that's why I came in 1956 for the first time, as a sitar player, to the United States and Europe, and I started touring. In the beginning there was a very small audience. I used to play small places all over the country, giving concerts for six hundred people, seven hundred people, eight hundred people. I used to come every autumn, year after year, and by 1960 I was playing to larger audiences, mostly regular classical music lovers, and also to jazz lovers—they took to my music right away. And by 1964 I was playing to full houses everywhere—Albert Hall in London, Philharmonic Hall, Carnegie Hall.

Then a new period came . . . George Harrison heard me a few times and was very interested in performing sitar. He became my student at the end of '66; he came to India for a very short while. Until then I had never heard of the Beatles, or any pop musicians. I gave him as much training as possible, but I could not teach in six weeks what I spent seven and a half years of doing and nothing else. He was a very sensitive boy, and he understood the seriousness of it. He was very inspired by me and my music, but he sounded like himself, he made it a part of him. But because of him, all of a sudden I found myself like a superstar. All over the world, all the young kids became my fans. It was very good in a way because overnight it brought my music and the sitar a lot of attention. But I paid the price for that and, frankly, I was not very happy. These kids came to me through George Harrison or Donovan or other pop musicians that were playing the sitar, and they took the whole spirit of my music in a very light vein; they took it as rock or pop. They came to my concerts drinking beer or Coca-Cola, necking with their girl friends, high as a kite on drugs—and it was terrible. For me, it was sacrilegious because it is a very sacred thing to us. And I started from the very first day of my superstardom to protest. I would stop playing. I said, "Please don't smoke, please behave yourselves," and many walked out. And films immediately took it up—they always used the sitar sound behind orgy scenes, pot parties and drug sequences.

Had I been twenty or fifteen years younger, I might have enjoyed myself, but with my maturity and background, I was not at all happy because they were taking my music in the wrong sense. And my followers in India thought that I was selling myself, commercializing myself, jazzing up my music in America, while it was the other way around. Believe me, my friends, for nearly seven or eight years I have gone through a terrible strain. Today I am very happy because I am no longer in that stupid superstar position on the pop scene. They have crossed me out; naturally, they did not like my telling them not to smoke or drink Coca-Cola. So this superficial group has walked away from my music, and I have come back again to my own forte like a circle. I'm back to my classical programs. And I'm very happy about it. And out of those kids, I'm sure that five to ten percent have stayed with me. They are the ones who are really beautiful. Because they know the seriousness of my music.

Do you prefer to live in the West or in India?

I have built a beautiful house in Benares, my birthplace and

RAVI SHANKAR
Indian Musician

my city, so I'll be spending more time in India—seven or eight months a year, and touring in the West only three or four months.

What do you do in India?

Whenever I'm there, I give many benefits for different charity organizations, hospitals, things like that. And I have a lot of students there and I teach them as well as I can. I want them to learn in the same manner that I learned. Of course, I do a lot of composition work for my records there. My latest recording is one side with Yehudi Menuhin, the violinist, and one side with Jean-Pierre Rampal, French flutist. I have a number of things I am going to do: write music for a ballet, some chamber music—that is another side of me.

I like to say I have two identities, one is as a classical sitar player, and the other is as a composer who does a lot of things. It seems contradictory to many people; they ask, "Why are you doing all this?"—like my record called *Shankar Family and Friends*, which George Harrison produced. It is a ballet on one side and all types of songs on the other: Western classical, Indian classical, folk songs, rock songs, jazz songs, electronic songs, Moog synthesizer songs. I do a lot of compositions.

Is your sitar ever electrified?

Absolutely not. I have to use an amplifier when I perform because sitar has a very soft sound. The moment you go beyond thirty-five to forty feet, you don't get the nuances—the sustaining notes are lost.

Your rings are beautiful.

You won't believe this, but both of these rings came out of nowhere. Have you heard of Satya Sai Baba, the great yogi? He materializes things. He gave me this diamond ring about five years ago. And he gave this ruby ring to me when I was last with him. He can make anything—whole diamonds, watches—he squeezes it out of him. But that's nothing; that is just to attract people and then he gives you his highest spiritual guidance. He's fantastic.

What do you do with him? Meditate?

Yes, that's part of our training program. The yoga that you know in the West is a physical yoga, which is good for the body. I do very little of that anymore. I do more breathing and meditation now, and the mantras. By the way, Satya Sai Baba is a person I respect and love very much and he has great affection for me, but I have my guru from many years ago—my spiritual guru, I'm talking about, not my musical guru. He entered my life in a very strange way when I was twenty-three and wanted to commit suicide.

Why did you want to commit suicide?

Because of a terrible situation, mostly financial, but also I was going through a lot of emotional problems. I was really completely suicidal. And then one morning this guru walked into my life. He just walked into my room and said he was passing by and needed to go to the bathroom very badly. That's how he came. And then we sat and I was impressed by his look and later on he became my guru. You see, the mantras that we learn from our gurus are the important thing. They are secret words and you have to meditate and pronounce them in your heart and in your body.

Does that help your health?

I think so. I was a very sickly child. I was always sicker when I was young, and now I have become better.

Are you on a special diet?

I don't eat beef or pork. But it's hard to be a vegetarian, the way we travel. So I do take chicken and fish, and sometimes lamb, but that's all.

When you eat just vegetables at home, do you feel much better?

Definitely. I don't like very rich food. I like vegetables, nice and fresh and cooked with a little seasoning, a little spicy.

When you travel, what do you do with your sitar?

I have to buy a seat because they don't permit you to carry on anything that big, so I strap the seat belt around it like a person. That's why, when people ask me the price of my sitar, I say, "Hundreds of thousands by now." It is a unique instrument. It was made especially for me by a friend who travels with me. I cannot be found in a shop. The ones you find in shops are not good.

Do you exercise?

Not too much. I wish I did. I love to walk, but the burden of travel tires me.

Are you a very sexual person?

I think every man likes to see himself as that, but I don't know if I'm normal or what. I love women, though. Very much.

Are you married?

Separated. My wife is the daughter of my guru. I was married when I was very young. I have a son, who is in California, married to an American girl, works in commercial art, but plays the sitar quite well. I just became a grandfather.

Are you faithful to one woman?

My record shows that I have not been able to be, but somehow, basically, I feel that I am.

What kind of women do you like?

I have been attracted to all different sorts; I mean physically they have been all different types. But they have to be superintelligent, that's the basic quality I like. And they have to be very—sexual is not the word—very sensitive. If you are quite intelligent, you are usually too sensitive and emotional, so you have to be very sexual.

Do you like a modern sort of women who is strong and has her own career?

I have always been fond of women who are feminine. That doesn't mean they have to be weak. I like strong women, but they should have a surrendering quality. They don't have to be slaves. That's not what I mean. That's a very Eastern way of thinking, to keep a woman passive or feminine and weak, but that's not exactly the type I like either.

Can you describe a normal day in your life?

When I'm traveling it's catching a little sleep, traveling to another Holiday Inn, and performing. But when I have time to myself in Benares, I like to be as lazy as possible. I get up as early as I can, but I relax more. Even if I try, I cannot sleep more than to seven or seven-thirty. And the first thing I do is to take my bath and do my meditation before taking breakfast. And then I have my students come to me, and I teach, and I practice for a couple of hours, and read as much as possible. I like to read anything I get—classical literature or light novels. And I like to see good films. I've always been a film addict. I do music for films.

What do you think of the violence in films now?
I don't like it very much, unless it's such a good film as *The Godfather* or *Taxi Driver*.

Do you watch television?
I love American television. That's one of my weaknesses. When I come to the States, it's just like having an orgy, but after a month or two of constant TV I become normal again.

Do you paint?
I used to, but somehow I got out of it. I used to write poems too, but my talent was divided, it was not channeled. Since my musical hand took over and said, "You cannot be jack of all trades," I put all my energy into the sitar.

Do you think a guru could help American young people?
One thing that is good is that some kids who were into drugs have given up drugs and are now into their guru. I think this is good unless it becomes fanatic, like Hari Krishna. But even that, physically, is better than hard drugs. But having a guru is not a joke. One must approach it with a maturity and seriousness. Most kids go out of vanity, and they overdo things.

What kind of clothes do you like?
I hate to wear ties—I've always felt strangled in a tie. Otherwise I'm comfortable. But, of course, in India we wear loose pajamas, cotton things. I love cotton. And pure silk. I don't like synthetic fabrics, but, unfortunately, we have to wear quite a lot of them touring because they travel easier. But I don't really like them.

What things do you really like?
I feel that I am, as an Indian, as a Hindu, more of the past than the present. And one belief or thought that we have in our past is that there is a very thin borderline between spirituality and sensuality . . . that people who created the *Kamasutra* were very spiritual people. And that is something I feel in my music and my way of life; that's one pattern that I think of always.

I don't understand why you objected to young people necking while your music was being played. Maybe they felt very sensual?
We don't shit outside—it is one of those rules which have been written by logic. Of course, I'm not comparing the two —necking is a beautiful thing, but if it is exhibitionism it's not beautiful. I mean, I've seen some beautiful necking and kissing in Paris in a park—it looks very beautiful and fantastic. But I've seen some things at rock concerts—they just get up and start masturbating or fornicating, and it's not beautiful, it's animal. There's a thin borderline. There are places and times to do things. Classical music has to be listened to with respect. Love and respect. And also, our music can make you feel sort of high, so I feel cheated when the audience is already high on their own and they hear the music from a different dimension. They can do that in their own rooms playing the tapes; they are doing that, in fact.

Do you find modern society depressing?

No. I have always been very optimistic, and that's what's kept me in good humor. And I believe in humor. We should never lose it. Naturally, the generation gap is something which we all have to live with. Sometimes I feel that I cannot understand the new type of music or the way of life, but at the same time, because I love young people I try to understand, and I feel hopeful.

Do you involve yourself in politics at all?
That is one thing to keep away from. I think it is so dirty. And what is today changes tomorrow. So how could I be involved with any party or person? A great person today is no one tomorrow. I've seen it. And the way I traveled—today America, tomorrow a Communist country or a dictatorship —I see all sides of it and that has cleansed me of any interest in politics.

Are you rich?
I could have been very rich. I have earned lots of money, but I've spent very much, and not on horses or diamonds, but on foolish ventures—like bringing a group of musicians to this country and trying to present them, or making a movie or producing a ballet. I've done it four or five times and each time I lost money miserably. However, I am comfortable and I am grateful for that.

Do you ever take vacations?
I have started to, after long time not. I am going to have two months in Los Angeles when I come back from Japan. I like Los Angeles because of the climate, dry, not too hot, not too cold. It's very inspiring. And now I also have the inspiration of my grandson there.

When you became a grandfather, did that bother you? Did you feel you were getting old?
Not really. I have to remind myself sometimes that I'm getting old because I have not felt that yet. I do worry about my health, because of the way I have been pushing myself. From the age of ten I have been in show business, working hard, from fourteen to sixteen hours a day, and it has not been easy for me. I have worked step by step for whatever success I have had. I've worked hard. So sometimes I do feel tired and exhausted. That's when I worry a little. I have to take it easy and not overdo.

Have you ever been to a psychiatrist?
No. As far as I am concerned, my guru serves as one.

Do you think religion is important in today's society?
I believe that one has to have faith in something. Faith in yourself is the greatest thing, but religion helps one in being strong. If you don't believe in anything, you are blocked and confused. Unless you are very wise.

What do you think about dying?
I am not frightened of it. It is sad to see a fantastic creative person, whether young or old, die—a person who has given so much and is still giving. But if one has done it all, seen it all, and is not productive, I feel that's good for him, to die.

Do you believe in reincarnation?
Absolutely.

What would you like to come back as?
I would like to come back as a better musician.

RAMON TORRES (TUPACC AMARU)
Teacher of Mind-Expansion Techniques

Mr. Scavullo: What kind of training do you have?
Mr. Torres: No formal training. I was apprenticed to a great Inca medicine man whose teachings awakened me to the spiritual path of my ancestors.
Where do you come from?
I was born in Peru and I grew up in Ecuador. My original name is Tupacc Amaru, which my mother gave me in honor of a famous Inca hero. At the present time I prefer to use my original name.
What is your function?
My function is to train people to develop their full potential, to bring about the utmost of themselves. I train creative people to develop a superb performance in any realm of creativity, whether a person is an actor, an actress, a dancer, a painter, a sculptor, a photographer or an athlete, a basketball player, a tennis player.
Do you help businessmen as well as artists?
Yes. The whole objective is to show a person how to overcome stress, how to master the psychosomatic-condition syndrome that the person has developed. I have developed a technique that I call unlearning—and it's basically the ability to overcome the psychosomatic conditions that we get from our childhood, our parents, society.
What kinds of tools do you use?
The tools are basic techniques or systems that I developed from living with the Yajua Indians in the Amazon region of Peru. I lived with them when I was about nine years old. It was a marvelous experience—being able to relate to nature, to live in harmony with nature with no restrictions, no clothes. And I was able to relate to the tribesmen as if I was one of them. And I observed them and learned how they deal with pain, with illness.
How do they deal with pain?
To begin with, they are not afraid of pain, so it is modified for them. In other words, they do not react to it; thus, by their very nature they have an extraordinary healing ability.
Do you have that same ability?
I developed the same ability by observing them. Later I had the opportunity to live with an African tribe and I was able to corroborate those same feelings. To them, pain is nothing to fear, it's just like death. They do not fear death. Not like us. We have a negative reaction automatically just to the thought of it.
What do they do in particular not to fear pain?
It's ingrained in them not to fear pain. In terms of their knowledge, fear of pain is something that they haven't learned. When I teach these concepts to others I say, "I'm not going to teach you anything. Most to the contrary, I'm going to show you how to unlearn." There is nothing to learn. What we are trying to do is unlearn what we have been taught. And the process of unlearning, like any form of self-healing, any form of understanding or taking responsibility for yourself, must be done with self-ecology. You must detoxify yourself. And that is a mental process, too. We must detoxify our minds because we suffer from the computer concept of garbage in, garbage out. Our heads are programmed with a great deal of toxins, rubbish, unnecessary things that are lurking, that are somehow cornering us and putting us in closed spaces.
Does self-ecology include a special diet or not drinking or not smoking or not taking drugs?

I believe the best diet that one can find is learning to respect the body. Everybody knows exactly what is best for himself, and just common nature will tell you not to abuse yourself and what to intake and what not to do. Obviously, we abuse ourselves with any form of toxins like chemicals, alcohol, tobacco and drugs. Anything that is unnatural will create an unnecessary overtaxing of our system. That is the main reason why one has to be extremely selective in the food that one eats. I avoid eating regular food as it is offered in the marketplace. I'm very particular about my own cooking, I'm a vegetarian person by nature. And, also, I avoid any form of drugs, including any form of conventional medicine. I prefer pure water. I drink tea a lot—not ordinary Lipton tea, just herbal tea. I prefer honey instead of sugar. And I avoid any form of unnecessary chemicals. I utilize olive oil in my cooking as a natural cleanser for the body. I think simplicity is the key to any kind of a healthy living, whether of mind or body. I think we very often have a natural tendency to complicate things.
You learned how to control pain in the jungle, where you lived in harmony with nature. But how do you deal with people living in New York?
I teach that this is a different form of jungle—a modern jungle. And we begin by questioning ourselves, questioning our own values, trying to understand our own very nonsensical nature. And in that way we begin breaking through barriers that we, along with our parents and society, have created. I believe it's extremely important to learn any form of mind-device to clear through that barrier of thick thinking that we have, to open our inner world. I feel that we are blinded by the outer world without realizing that the basic objective we need to come to terms with is our inner world. Sometimes our stability or internal balance is in constant struggle with the outer world. And we are the victims of that stress—with headaches, with ulcers, with colitis, with arthritis, with no end of psychosomatic illnesses and allergies.

I think self-inquiry is a commitment, an *individual* commitment, that each person has to make openly. And the first thing one does is kind of like taking a mental laxative by fasting—to review things, to try to make some order of the internal disorder. I think anyone can begin by reading the tremendous outpour of books on Eastern philosophies, and by understanding how to breathe, how to stop these internal disorders—how to regulate our velocity—because we often go at tremendous speeds with no sense of direction. I feel we can learn to regulate this velocity, learn to take full command and control ourselves. In some cases we are lucky and come into contact with someone who can relate this knowledge to us on a person-to-person basis or, maybe, through a program. I think that can be very interesting as an introductory format, but I believe that it's very much up to the individual to take the full load of responsibility as each advances along the way to knowledge. In the beginning it's *their* responsibility that *I* take. In the beginning I try to understand their mental age—in other words, their age in terms of years of light— just as you would consider the distance from here to a particular star in terms of years of light. I consider their ability, their development in terms of light-years.
By "mental age" you mean that someone may be twenty-nine physically but only fourteen mentally?

RAMON TORRES (TUPACC AMARU)
Teacher of Mind-Expansion Techniques

No. I'm talking about the velocity of the mind. The great masters have been able to develop many light-years, and that doesn't necessarily mean in terms of their mind or energy. It's very easy to feel where a person is just by their own vibrations, the aura that they project.

But we don't even live as long as a light-year.
I think that we can transcend this earthly life and we can live several lives by one degree of evolution.

Do people come to you at an office?
I have some individual students. I charge $25 a session, which lasts an hour. It usually takes a person about three sessions to begin to assimilate and to try to understand some of the introductory levels. At the Vilcabamba Institute, I conduct an introductory program of four hours on a group basis. It does different things for different people. It's like utilizing a mental form of acupuncture. Each person responds differently; some understand the meaning of the teachings, the meaning of unlearning. Others get a totally relaxed feeling; they have an outer body experience through the teaching. Others understand the whole concept intellectually. Some people will experience what the great masters call a first degree of enlightenment. And they will proceed.

Do you practice acupuncture at all?
No, but I'm very familiar with it. I practice mental acupuncture.

What about the needles you put through people's faces?
That is a mind-opening device to allow the person to break certain barriers.

Once you get past unlearning, then what?
Then you begin. A cyclone has an eye, right? The eye is the basic acknowledgment of the cyclone. And the whole objective is to get to the eye of the cyclone, the yolk of the self—to pierce through many layers until you have found a level of a stability, of balance. Then you have made some sort of peace with yourself. You have found a system of self-regulation which will help you relate to this modern jungle.

Can you cure diseases with your treatments?
The whole idea is not only to recondition people to the fear of pain, but also to show them that they have the ability to self-heal—and in the process of self-healing to blossom. Most people have not learned how to blossom. They remain repressed. They haven't really allowed themselves totally to fulfill themselves.

Are you fulfilled?
I would say very much so. That doesn't necessarily mean that I have reached my pinnacle. I'm moving in that direction. As a teacher, and as a person, too, I feel very much fulfilled. Of course, nothing comes easy. No one can tap this reservoir of knowledge without having to work hard. Anyone who thinks that it is easy is in for a great surprise.

Is love important to you?
I think that I have already grown beyond it. Not that I don't know how to love. On the contrary, I believe that I've learned how to love much more—but not to focus in on a specific person, but the world, everything.

Do you like sex?
Very much. I think sex is like putting water into flowers. We're very repressed and afraid to express our feelings; it's because of rejection or hurt. But we have to rise above those things, we have to learn to express our feelings clearly, especially with people that we feel we can be open and receptive to.

Do you think there's any such thing as a sexual perversion?
I think sexual perversion is only in the eyes of the beholder. It's just like beauty. Beauty is in the eyes of the beholder. I feel that sex is simple, and it's something for the individual to deal with. I don't believe that there is any room for limitations or for even labels. I think we're very much accustomed to putting labels onto things: perversion, sadism, masochism. I think that everything is in everyone.

Is money important to you?
It's important, but I consider myself extremely wealthy inwardly. Sometimes I have a lot of money and sometimes none—either way, I am able to enjoy life to the utmost. As a matter of fact, I have great difficulty in trying to make some sense of the business world, the whole idea of dollars and cents in this society.

What is your life style?
Trying *not* to conform, trying *not* to fit into any particular mold.

What is your apartment like?
Very bare, full of books, articles, nothing extraordinary or fancy. As simple as it could possibly be.

What do you think of airplanes, cars, buses, trains?
I think they have contributed to our world progress, and yet, they have also contributed to a lack of unlearning ability. According to our Western thinking, we can say that they have been indispensable tools to our progress. But in terms of our own individual selves they have only contributed to our mental pollution and physical pollution.

Why do you shave your head?
I feel more comfortable for one thing, and for another, it's a person reminder of overcoming any form of egoconsciousness or vanity.

Do you think you would look better with hair?
We have a cosmetic concept of hair and beauty. I think that is the main reason why many Buddhist monks thought about the concept of shaving to learn some form of self-detachment. I feel that if we were all blind, we'd have a much more meaningful society because we would go beyond external looks. We would look for the inner beauty of the person.

But if you see a beautiful woman, don't you turn your head?
That is a conditioning process—we are so concerned with external beauty. I myself am above that. In my early *Latin* years I would twist and turn in a thousand different directions. But as I have developed I have learned to focus on the internal beauty of the person. I do think that there is a limit to physical intercourse between any persons. But I think that one can have long-lasting, unlimited mental intercourse

with a person who has a beautiful mind or a beautiful soul.

And let me add something—I'm very down-to-earth, in a sense. When I feel that I need to experience something—a beautiful flower, a fruit, a person—if conditions or circumstances allow, I have no sense of repression.

Do you practice any religion?
My own living religion. I am a living form of spirituality. I do not conform to any organized concept. I believe that the more one believes in oneself the more one evolves, develops a very strong sense of self, a great sense of self-respect—and also, a respect for all living things.

Do you believe in God?
The idea of God is within oneself. God is expressed in every living thing. God is a living force as it exists within me, as it is expressed in the flowers and the trees and the animals—nothing higher, nothing lower.

What do you think about style and the way you dress?
To convey a point of view to a society, I must integrate into society rather than become apart from it because of the way I dress.

Do you feel that you have to prostitute yourself to be accepted, to wear a suit and a tie instead of a robe?
It's not necessarily prostitution; it's compromise. My objective is to put a point across, and I'm not going to do it with an odd costume or by detaching myself from the norm. I have learned that I have to look like the norm, to show that I'm just like anyone else, that I'm not different—that the only difference is my desire, or perhaps responsibility, to reach a plateau.

Do you have feelings of hate?
I used to, but I've learned to overcome any feelings like that. I've learned, for instance, that any kind of anger, any kind of negative feeling, is not doing anything to whomever we are against—it's only damaging to ourselves.

If someone slapped you, would you slap him back?
I would try to communicate with the person, and if I felt that the person didn't want to communicate, then there won't be a second slap—for sure.

Are you an aggressive person?
No, not in the normal sense of aggressiveness. I am inquisitive. I am a pioneer in my desire to understand the mind itself.

Do you have any goals?
The only goal I have is to convey my feelings, my ideas and my knowledge to as many people as I possibly can in this lifetime. But, personally, for myself, I think that I have reached my basic goals.

How old are you?
Thirty.

What do you think about age?
There are no limitations whatsoever. I think that if I have to depart from the earth tomorrow, it would be perfectly all right. I have seen what I have to see. I feel much better now than when I was younger because I have seen things. I have seen my own conquest. I knew that I possessed knowledge,

but I didn't know how to deal with it until I reached that point.

What things really turn you off?
Nothing turns me off except my own lack of awareness.

What about violence, rape, murder, war?
I think that before we can pass judgment on somebody else, we have a lot to judge in ourselves. And I think that if we raise our level of awareness, we will rise above hatred and violence and wars. I believe there is good and evil in every single person.

What do you think about innocence?
Innocence is a form of enlightenment. It is, perhaps, the full blossoming of unlearning.

Do you have any innocence left in you?
I think we all have, no matter how much we have been exposed to the callousness of the city.

Do you watch television?
I prefer not to. I enjoy seeing documentaries once in a while.

Movies?
Very select movies—movies that have a message, that contain a central theme.

Are you optimistic or pessimistic about the future of the world?
Very pessimistic, because we have a very destructive nature to begin with, and it would take many light-years of evolution for the majority of us to reach a degree of equanimity and peace among all human beings. There is too much self-interest, too much egotism. I think we're moving toward a very destructive end, as we have already done with the ecology of the earth. I think nature is now reacting toward our own lack of consideration.

Does that bother you?
I just don't let it bother me. I have the ability to transform the things that bother me into positive experiences that I can learn from—no matter how bad the situation is.

Do you ever worry?
I have learned how to dissolve worrying—to neutralize it so that it won't engulf me. We have a tendency to engulf ourselves in worry and self-pity. We allow the headaches to take place. But as soon as I feel that feeling, I automatically neutralize it.

Do you think language is enough to express ourselves or are we too screwed up even to talk?
Language is very stereotyped. I think that we can learn to express feelings without even talking. A marvelous beginning exercise would be to try to relate to another person without talking. I think we need to experience love and kindness and affection and tenderness just by touching. We have such a fear of touching another person, of saying hello and shaking hands with warmth. We have a false concept of masculinity even in the process of shaking hands—we need to clasp hands very strongly to prove that we are men. I think we have to go beyond proving. There are so many stereotypes that we have created in our own minds. If we could just stop to think and unmold ourselves, we will grow.

SAMUEL J. WAGSTAFF, JR.
Collector of Photographs

Mr. Scavullo: Where were you born?
Mr. Wagstaff: New York. I grew up here, went away to school, went into the Navy during the war, then I was in advertising a little bit, hated it, went back to school—NYU Institute of Fine Arts—got a fellowship from the National Gallery in Washington, went abroad on that for two years, came back and became Curator of Paintings at the Wadsworth Atheneum in Hartford, was there about eight years, then went to the Detroit Institute of Art as Twentieth-Century Curator—it sounds as if I were a mechanical automaton. About five years ago I dropped out. I had a little bit of cash, enough, if I husbanded it right, to keep me going. I decided that I was able not to have to punch the other guy's time clock. That meant that I had to find my own time clock to punch.

I met a photographer named Robert Mapplethorpe and was quite amazed by his photographs. He photographed in series. I've been taking photographs actually since I was a child and I had color pictures in series I had taken on the beach in Cannes a couple of years before, and I was amazed that he was doing series, too. I very much admired what he was doing in photography. Until then I had always hated contemporary photography, it didn't seem very interesting. Then I saw a show called "Painterly Photographs" at the Metropolitan Museum of Art—mostly turn-of-the-century—and it knocked me out. From that moment on I decided that I wanted to get involved in photography; it was something of great quality that I had overlooked, a whole medium that I didn't know anything about at all. I've been collecting ever since. I started with nineteenth-century photographs because I thought the supply would dry up fastest. I'm beginning to be more interested in contemporary photography, though I think it's incredibly hard to distinguish gems from paste in contemporary photography. There's incredible craft in photography today, but art isn't a matter of just craft—it's made with intelligence and imagination and magic. I think what has passed for good photography in the last forty years has become worn-out and lackluster, but there are a few people who have added something new. It takes a little something different to make the magic come alive.

Is collecting photographs work for you?
I work in spurts and starts. I have a lot of paperwork that I put off, letters and things like that; I have had someone help me catalogue the collection. I read extensively about photography and look at it quite a lot; I look at the things I own quite a lot. I'm in the process of putting together a show which will open in February 1978 at the Corcoran Gallery of Art in Washington, D.C. Then it will travel to five other museums around the United States. That presents a lot of problems, like: How many photographs can you get somebody to look at without boring him to death? What should they be? How many should there be by each photographer? How should they be hung?

I consider myself a propagandist for photography. I'd like to see a lot more people turned on by it. And I think it's very natural for people to be turned on by photography, in a way that the international art world is not cognizant of—if they are, they put it down. Steichen's "The Family of Man" show broke all attendance records at the Museum of Modern Art. You'd think they might do it again . . . it's nice to have a lot of people come in and be pleased. The Seattle Museum recently had a show of the private collection of Joe Monsen. Broke all attendance records there. Never had so many people come to an exhibition. Asia House had a show of photographs from English Empire India. Broke all attendance records. They couldn't believe how many people they had coming. Sixty thousand people saw the Nadars at the Met.

What does that mean?
It means that people come naturally to photography. They've been trained to look at photographs by the picture books they had as kids, by the daily newspapers, by the magazines they read, but they haven't been shown photography as an aesthetic consideration. Photography is the purveyor of information to most people, but I think it also has its aesthetical side. That's what I'm most interested in. I don't care about the socio-politico-economico-historical side. I am interested in the scientific side of photography: astronomical photographs, microscopic photographs, photographs of stress in metals under polarized light, that kind of thing. They're very beautiful. I have quite a few medical photographs, of skin diseases, etc.

Sometimes it seems everyone today is a photographer.
In the 1850s Thomas Carlyle's wife said something like, "The invention of photography is as important as the invention of chloroform." Imagine what it must have been like to live before the invention of chloroform. Everyone on earth was scared that at a certain moment in their life they would have to be operated on while conscious. And this one incredible discovery put that fear out of everyone's mind. Mrs. Carlyle said that photography is equal to that gift because it puts the ability to make art into the hands of the average man.

Does it also make us more aware of ourselves than is perhaps natural?
Mirrors have always existed. The Mayans made mirror out of black volcanic glass, the Romans, Chinese and Egyptians made mirrors out of bronze. Mirrors are very important. If there was only one mirror in the world, how many people would get there? Almost everybody. I don't think there's anything tricky, inhuman, modern or atypical about mirrors. People want to see what they look like. I think vanity is incredibly interesting. Once, in the middle of a party, a hostess began arguing with one of the guests: she said men are vain and he said they are not. So she said, in a rather loud voice, "The necktie of the most attractive man in the room needs straightening"—and every man in the room started to straighten his tie.

Do you care about your clothes?
Unfortunately, I don't. I'm not that interested. I like to look well, but I'm lazy about it. And I'm not trendy, it takes me a couple of years to pick up something that everyone has been wearing for that length of time. Like Saint Laurent. I used to wear ordinary, preppy clothes, Brooks Brothers.

What about your hair?
My hat's off to a good haircutter. A good haircutter can change your life. Every time I have a really good haircut I feel like a million bucks. It does a great deal for me.

Do you have a special cologne you like?
No, I never use cologne. I like the smell of perfume, but I don't use it myself. I like it on a woman, not on a man.

Do you exercise and take care of yourself?
I used to swim a lot, I love it. Arica, which I did a few years ago, had a half-hour exercise every morning, not a build-up-

SAMUEL J. WAGSTAFF, JR.
Collector of Photographs

your-muscle exercise, but a flow-of-energy-through-the-body exercise, which is very good—stretching, toe-touching, things like that. I still do a little of that. And I think water is a great necessity. Look at the French: they're a blueprint for inner complications and they never drink water. I don't like ice in the water, particularly at mealtime. I drink about two quarts of water a day.

Are you interested in living to an old age?
You know the story of Tithonus, who asked for eternal life but forgot to ask for eternal youth, and he just got older and older and older—it's a nice poem by Tennyson which starts: "The leaves decay, the leaves decay and fall . . . and after many a summer dies the swan." I think the next line is: "Only I keep on"—with one tooth falling out after the other. I think it would be fantastic to live to an old age if one could keep one's health, if one could keep active . . . and if one could keep up to date.

Do you know any men like that?
I recently met the photographer Lartigue. He's eighty-two and he's in incredibly good shape, wears sneakers—that'll give you an idea of his bounciness. And he's very quick-witted, takes beautiful photographs, and seems to be in pretty good shape. I think it's very largely mental.

What do you feel about death?
The only answer that makes sense to me is reincarnation. I *hope* that's what happens. We'll never know until it hits us. But it seems sad that the ecstasy, knowledge and ability that accrues in a lifetime is lost, that one can't come back in some subliminal form to increase one's ecstasy, one's knowledge and one's ability in another state. Buckminster Fuller once said that we can't really do much about civilization, because civilization is doing it to us. He said that it's taken care of us until now, so there's absolutely no reason to think why it's not going to continue to do so. And that doesn't mean that half the world may not be blown up; maybe that's civilization's way of taking care of us, so that the other half can continue. Who knows?

Do you have any idols?
I've always been impressed by certain people, but I haven't consciously patterned my life on anyone else's example. Actually, New York City is my hero. I think it's the greatest hero alive. If you like civilization, which I do, New York seems to be the center of it. I love to travel, I go abroad a few times a year, particularly for photography sales, but I've always felt edgy when my base wasn't New York.

Do you like TV?
I hate TV. I've never owned one. I only watch it when famous people get shot.

Movies?
I do like movies, but I don't go very often. I've never thought of cinema photographically. I get carried away by storylines and people, so I don't really look at it. I think of it as an art, but not a photographic art, which I know it is. I suppose I haven't seen enough Jean Renoir movies. I think of movies as *the* medium. You have to be a great general to be a moviemaker.

Are there any magazines that you like?
I don't buy any magazine regularly. I read the *New York Times* daily and on Sunday. I can't think of any photographic magazines that I look at. As a child I used to read *The New Yorker*, but I don't want to now.

What do you think about women today? Feminists?
I think people ought to do their thing. I don't think you always know what you're getting when you ask for it. Chief Justice Oliver Wendell Holmes once said a very beautiful thing: "The minute a woman exerts her female prerogative, she loses it." Women are going to lose something, but it's up to them to decide whether what they gain is equal.

What kind of women are attracted to you?
I know exactly what kind of women are attracted to me: the bad ones. The really bad ones.

Do you find women more attractive today or less?
I rather enjoy the fact that women seem to feel more equal and able to meet one on one's own ground. And I like that. But I don't think that's part of the feminist movement, I think it's just part of the way things are going. I'm an optimist and I like the direction in which civilization seems to be taking us. It's nicer to be alive today for more people than it was fifty years ago, and therefore the hope is that it will be better for even more people fifty years hence.

You're not afraid of shortages of resources?
As a night-school demographer, I think the world is overpopulated. But I know nothing about it whatsoever. I assume there are a lot of people having too many children today who can't cope with bringing them up properly.

Do you get depressed?
Being one-quarter Polish, I get Polish miseries. I have them occasionally and I go out and take a walk. If I change my physical place and move, it helps. Something seems very concrete until you change your scene and then it seems that it must have been some kind of illusion.

What was the greatest compliment someone ever paid to you?
Well, there was one I just happen to have in mind. It was the actress Leueen McGrath and I guess it was just about the time she was getting divorced from George Kaufman and she was very beautiful in a Broadway play. I had never met her; someone had invited me to dinner and asked me to pick her up and bring her. There were about ten of us, I guess; it was a rather fancy Park Avenue apartment. In the middle of the dinner several men were talking to her and the whole table was directed at her, asking her wasn't it difficult to be the subject of so much adulation? And she said, well, it sort of was at first but she had gotten used to it and she said, "You know, you begin to take it in your stride." And very offhandedly she said, "Sam would understand what I'm talking about," and then went right on. I was left there speechless with pleasure. I thought it was great, and the way she tossed it off, like a great actress, was fantastic. I dug it.

I don't know whether I've talked enough about photography, which really is my life. I'd like to be a photographer eventually—and perhaps collecting is a school for that.

HENRY WINKLER
Actor

Mr. Winkler: One of the first things I ever wrote down in my actor's notebook is that I must be healthy. I have to take care of my body because it is my instrument, and if I'm going to play it, I have to keep it well tuned. And when you make a movie, you are so many feet high; there is very little room for error. The camera just sits there and it does not lie, and if you lie, the camera will tell it. So I always must be the most lucid that I can possibly be when I'm working. I've got to keep myself real calm and rested so that when I'm projected on that screen my energy comes out positive and I don't look like I'm all beat. When I'm working on a movie I don't go out at night. But doing the TV series, *Happy Days*, is a whole different story. There's a routine. I rehearse four and a half days; I shoot in one night. So Saturday through Wednesday I can socialize; Thursday and Friday (the day I shoot), I cannot.

Mr. Scavullo: Do you eat special food or do you not drink because of your work?
I don't drink any liquor whatsoever. I don't really eat special foods, I just eat very little of what I'm eating. I try to stay away from meat, but I'm not a vegetarian. I enjoy my work, so I don't mind directing all of my energy into my work. I will never do anything that I think will take energy away from my work.

What are you going to tell your fans when you finish being the Fonz?
Catch me on reruns. Really. My responsibility is to grow; my responsibility is not to live my life for the public, because if I do that, I'll imitate myself—I'll live one day behind myself.

Why do you combat the image of the Fonz?
I don't see it as combating an image, because I really believe that if I'm good, if I know what I'm doing, then people will go and see me, no matter what I do. The more human one is, the more magnetic one is. The same thing with a character. The more human I make my characters, the more magnetic they are. My latest film, *Heroes*, is a monumental movie in my life because it is really graduation. The other two films I did, *Lords of Flatbush* and *Crazy Joe*, were like going to school. And this one is now going to catapult me into another level, another step.

Has success changed you as a person?
If I've changed, I've tried to channel the change into a positive force—I minimize my success and I always put some new goal ahead of me so that I don't start to think that I am what other people say I am. Because, actually, after everything is said and done, I'm only Henry, the son of Harry and Elsa, and that's the bottom line. And if I were to get cocky, if I were to assume the power that I'm supposed to have, if I were to toy with it, I would be cut in half. I would be destroyed. Now, it's more fun to be successful than not. When I was first starting acting in New York, I couldn't get arrested, you know. I made thirty commercials—that kept me alive. I did plays for free, but I couldn't get hired doing legitimate stage or movies. I always came close, but no cigar. And, of course, that's a bummer.

What do you think about stars who come up fast, hit the top, and then go down fast?
Well, they've made their bed. I don't want to be a flash in the pan. I don't want to be small potatoes. I want to work until I'm put in a box. And so every decision that I make is toward that—the overall theme is longevity.

Do you worry about getting older?
I think about getting older, but the age I am is the age I am. I cannot get any younger. That's true, so I have to get into the age I am at the moment, and I don't worry about it. What I do worry about is that I don't want to be old and look back and feel empty. Or alone.

Have you ever been married?
Never. I will be married someday, when I am able to take full responsibility for my own actions. I really believe there is a great strength in twos, and I am convinced that a couple will only work if each individual has shaken his or her own hand, has taken possession of himself or herself. Because then you do not live *off* the other person, you live *with* the other person, and that distinction is very important.

What kind of woman would you marry?
A woman who has her own life, her own course. A woman with a sense of humor. A woman who is open enough to be in love with me. And a woman who drips dirt, who deep down has a dirty soul. The Talmud says it very well: "A whore in the bedroom and a lady in the living room." And a cook in the kitchen. If she does not cook, that's all right, too, because if I don't, I can't expect her to.

Why do you feel that you're not ready for marriage? Do you feel that you haven't shaken your own hand yet?
I'm just beginning to. I'm just reaching out for my own hand now. That I know is true.

Is sex very important to you?
I have found that if I don't make love for a while, sexual tension certainly adds a lot to my performance. Supposedly Mae West talked a lot about it but did less than she talked about, because she understood that sexual tension absolutely comes across.

Wouldn't it be fun for you to have that punky Fonzie attitude in real life?
I don't think of him as a punk. He's built on a morality, on loyalty, he has his own values. But there is no way that I could live up to that attitude. That man is one step out of reality. There is no way that I could pretend I'm him. I must be the most me I can be in order to center myself. It is a fantasy to think that I could be the Fonz. For me it is a very serious business. It is *my* photograph, it is *my* cover of a magazine.

Does being short bother you at all?
I don't think of myself as short. I'm five foot six and a half. I got out of a limousine at a personal appearance in front of twenty-five thousand people, and a woman said, "Oh, he's so short!" I said, "Fuck you, I'm short!" I was just so cool. Really, when people are hostile to me I'm hostile back at them. On TV I'm only twenty-five inches tall.

What don't you like?
People's attitudes sometimes turn me right off because I think all we've got are people. And it's very easy to be nice, and it's very easy to be civilized. Pushy people just kill me; I'll go right through their throat—I'll bite their jugular right in half. You know, I try to respect other people's space, and someone invading my space pisses me off.

What turns you on?
Commitment to something. Janis Joplin *needed* to sing those songs. And therefore she turned yelling into commitment. Good performances, good food, being relaxed when I am able to get myself relaxed. I live with great intensity.

HIS EXCELLENCY AMBASSADOR ARDESHIR ZAHEDI
Iranian Ambassador to the United States

Mr. Scavullo: Could you tell us how you became ambassador to the United States?
Ambassador Zahedi: When I first came to the United States in the latter part of 1946, I went to Columbia University. I did not know a word of English, and it was rather difficult for a person who didn't know the language at Columbia because there were so many GIs studying there at that time. So I decided to move to California and go to UCLA, where my cousin was. I found myself with quite a few friends with whom I spoke in Persian; as my English was not improving and the campus was very crowded, I decided to go to Berkeley for the next semester. At Berkeley I met a gentleman called Dr. Franklin S. Harris who knew another one of my cousins. Since he had this feeling for Iran, he came and told me maybe I should go to the University of Utah, where he had been appointed president. I was there from 1948 until 1951, when I got my degree.

During holidays and summer I travelled. I worked, for instance, for two months in Gary, Indiana, in a distillery, and then I went to Arizona, where I washed dishes. I went back to California and worked as a mechanic in a factory close to San Francisco, and also as a fruit picker in Fresno. I went to Alaska in the summer of '49 and worked on the railroad. In this way I was able to work and also see different parts of the United States. I had a car, and in those days if you had transportation, those who traveled with you would pay you one and a half cents per mile expenses. So I traveled with one of my fraternity brothers and two of my close friends, one of whom was my cousin. We went to a military store in Salt Lake City and bought a special liquid that you put on your hands and face to protect you from mosquitoes, and we also bought two sleeping bags. Every night we pulled off onto the side of the road, and two of us would sleep in the car and the other two would get into the sleeping bags. And the next night it was vice versa. At about eleven in the morning we would go to a hotel which everybody was checking out of, and for $1.50 to $2.50 use a room for a shower and a shave. This is how we actually visited, in three years, about forty-six states.

Then, about the time that I graduated, Dr. Franklin Harris was asked by President Truman to go to Iran and start a Point Four program there; it was known as the Iran–United States Commission. Dr. Harris asked me if I would go too and work with him. At that time I thought I would not work for the government or any organization—I wanted to be on my own. But after a few weeks of talk I was convinced that I could help my country because this commission was helping Iran in the areas of education, malaria control and agriculture. I was with the commission until 1953, during which time the organization grew from three of us working in a small room in the American embassy to a staff of almost fifteen hundred Americans working with us.

Then we had a political problem in my country—a man called Mossadegh was Prime Minister; he used to cry all the time. In the beginning I was among the people who worked for him; so was my father, who was a general and the Minister of Interior. Mossadegh told the commission that either they throw me out or he would close it down. I certainly did not want anything like that to happen, since they were doing a wonderful job, so I decided to resign voluntarily and become politically involved against Mossadegh. I was taken to prison twice, but I escaped and helped make the Revolution of '53 with my father, who then became Prime Minister.

And then I was asked to be Chamberlain to His Majesty, the Shah. I was only twenty-six or twenty-seven years old. I traveled everywhere with him. I also was an adviser to the Prime Minister, my father, so I became involved in foreign affairs. And in 1959 His Majesty asked me to come here as ambassador. I was here until 1961, when my father, who at that time was living in Switzerland, had two heart attacks and a stroke. He and I were very close; we were like two brothers, two friends. I found it very difficult to be here and do my job the way I wanted, so I resigned and was appointed ambassador to England. I used to go back and forth from London to Switzerland to see my father, but in 1964 my father died.

I was appointed Foreign Minister in 1966 and I was involved with the discussion of the Arab-Israeli conflict at special sessions of the United Nations General Assembly. I resigned from the government about six years ago and went to Switzerland to write my father's biography. And then, again, His Majesty asked me to take this post, which I have held every since.

What do you think of the government in America?
I think the system of democracy in this country is a unique system in the world—about the best, I would say, but not necessarily so for other countries. But for the United States, a country which is so vast and contains so many different creeds and nationalities, I think it's the only system that could have survived. I admire your democracy, the freedom of the press, the kind of brakes you have between the courts and the legislature and the executive, and the system of independent states under the central government.

Do you think that monarchy is becoming outmoded in this day and age?
I do not think so at all. I think the best example of this is Spain, which had been run by a dictator for almost forty years, and ever since the new king came to power, Spain has taken steps toward democracy. I think in many countries a king would bring stability. Let's take a look at a country like Great Britain—the monarchy brought unity and stopped division. Or let's take a look at a country like mine—we celebrated our 2,500th anniversary of monarchy a few years ago. And look at our neighbor Iraq—ever since the collapse of the monarchy in that country in 1958 there has been a series of coups d'état that cost the country quite a lot not only in money, but also in leadership, because in each coup so many people got killed or went to prison that very few people with know-how are left—and this ended the development of the nation. Developing nations need know-how more than money, because money you can get from the developed countries by either credits or loans. But know-how takes a long time to get.

What is your typical day like as an ambassador?
It depends on where I am and what I'm doing. If I'm in Washington, I get up in the morning, have an hour and a half of briefing, then have visitors or meetings or read telegrams, or call on some of my colleagues or on officials of your government. Since our countries are very much engaged with each other in agriculture, education and health as well as defense, economics and business, there are many different people in your government that I see. Then, of course, I have

HIS EXCELLENCY AMBASSADOR ARDESHIR ZAHEDI
Iranian Ambassador to the United States

social functions to attend—cocktail parties, which give me a chance to see many different people in a short time. And I go to dinners—again there are many different people I deal with, each dinner involves a different group I need to be in contact with. Tonight, for instance, is the White House Correspondents' dinner, but at six o'clock I have to go to a charity benefit of the Brooklyn Museum and then fly to Washington to be at that dinner at eight-thirty.

Each day is completely different from the next one. Last Sunday I went to Valley Forge for a ceremony, and last Monday I was in Notre Dame to make a speech at the university. This morning here in New York I saw the Chase Manhattan group. Last night I was at a function to help a hospital—the one Frank Sinatra sponsored. Before that I had a meeting with King Hussein of Jordan who happened to be here, and another with the Prime Minister of Spain. And today I was able to cancel a luncheon and go to see my dentist instead. Then I met with a gentleman who's helping me write a speech because I am receiving two honorary degrees, from Harvard and Westminster. I usually talk off the cuff, but when I have to make a commencement speech I would rather have it written. And I want it to have a conclusion. What is our big problem as human beings today in the world? Hunger, disease, drought, energy—is it these things? Or is it how to work together? Can we live alone? Can we isolate ourselves and say the hell with the others—the 1.270 billion people who are dying of hunger and disease? Can we say we don't give a damn what they think or what they do as long as I'm happy? If we do that, there is going to be a third world war, because the rich will become richer and the poor poorer and you will have to have the violent dispersal of power.

And what are the problems of energy today? Is this the only problem we are going to face in the next ten or fifteen years which we have ignored for the last twenty-five or thirty years? Or is it food? What if we have no food to eat? What is going to happen to you as an individual or all of us? And how are we going to help the starving countries? Just talk to the newspapers and television and ignore the reality? Or put our efforts together as one, because today the world is like a human being—we need your right arm as much as we need your left arm. The whole world has become one body. These are the things I want to talk about in my speech. I'm sorry I went off the subject. You asked me what I do each day as ambassador, and I gave you my philosophy.

Do you think that women should have power?
Whether I think so or not, we don't have any choice. There are many things women can do better than men. I don't think we should exaggerate this, though, because you have to judge each person individually. You really cannot separate women and men or black and white. Some people are talented to do some things, other people are talented to do other things—and it doesn't make any difference what religion or color or sex they are. I think women today are part of our society. Whether we like it or not, this is the reality of our lives.

Do you enjoy making love to women?
Well, if I didn't, I wouldn't do it.

Do you like beautiful women?
Naturally, the way I like beautiful paintings or beautiful flowers or beautiful suits. It's always nice to see beauty.

Are you attracted to strong women personally?

I am attracted by women who have more than beauty. If they have only beauty, my attraction is very temporary. In fact, a woman could be ugly or at least not very beautiful, and if she had personality, naturally I would have more interest in a relationship with her.

When did you marry the Shah's daughter?
In 1957.

Was that the only time you have been married?
Yes.

Would you consider getting married again?
Since I have not been married for the last eleven years, I think that is probably my destiny. I really hope to see my daughter educated and carry on with life. I have lived my life. Whether I have done good or bad, I have done what I could. And, actually, when you get used to being a bachelor for a long time, it's not very easy to find the right kind of partner. I think the best word for "wife" is a Persian word—*hamsalid*, someone who is equal to you. And to find somebody that equals you takes quite a lot of time. Now I work about eighteen, nineteen hours a day, so I have very little time to be with someone. You need time to understand each other. And we come to an age when just attraction and falling in love are past. You want to have understanding, you want to be with interesting people with whom you can talk and discuss and fight and argue. It takes time to find whom you want and what you want.

How do you feel about getting older?
I get used to it. Maybe I fool myself or maybe I don't want to be young anymore. Or maybe it's the selfishness in my mentality that makes me think that now is better than yesterday, although yesterday will never be forgotten. I always have had wonderful memories of my youth, of the days I was going to school. But I don't think I'd like to go back to those days. I look to the future.

Do you worry about dying?
Not at all. My philosophy of my life is that death is something which is out of our hands. It's going to happen sooner or later, and when it has to happen it will happen. This is why I believe that we should finish everything we have to do each day and not put it off till tomorrow. If I died at this moment, there is nothing left on my desk. Everything is clean. There is nothing I wanted to do that I have not done.

Do you get upset if people criticize you?
No. I would get upset if they said something which is not true. It would make me more sad than upset. I like being criticized because receiving criticism is like seeing yourself in the mirror.

Have you ever gone to a psychiatrist?
No. I'm interested in psychology, so I talk with people who have knowledge or I read books about it, but as far as my belief in psychiatrists goes, it depends on whether you have a very good one or not—if not, they can make a fool of you. In the Catholic religion you go to the priest, and whatever you have inside you put out. Going to the psychiatrist has the same effect for many people, as long as you go to the right one and as long as you don't become an addict to it. A good psychiatrist is like a philosopher—they are very hard to find.

Are you a religious person at all?
I don't think I'm a very good religious person—maybe I'm not fanatical. I believe in God very strongly, but—and I feel

that all religions are the same—Christianity, Judaism or Islam are all really talking about the same things in different languages. I am Islamic, but I respect all religions.

Did you relate to the Hanafi Moslem terrorists in Washington last year on a religious basis? Is that how you helped negotiate the release of the hostages?
Yes, I think that our religion helped us to come close to each other, to trust each other. The leader believed that we were not going to storm that building, so he gave us his word that he would not do anything wrong with the hostages. From the early morning I was convinced that a face-to-face meeting was necessary and everyone thought that I was crazy. It came to my mind and I said it because I always say what I think. So eight hours later everybody thought that maybe I was right, and I had no choice but to have the face-to-face meeting. And I think that face-to-face meeting worked because of our personal understanding, because of our trust, because of our religious philosophy, because of all of these things together.

Is money very important to you?
Money comes and goes. I have another philosophy. I think if you have a good friend, you are the richest person in the world. And if you haven't got a friend, no matter how rich you are, you are the poorest. You can buy anything in life— jewelry, a house and a car, but you cannot pay five, ten, thirty billion dollars for one good friend who would come and sit with you and talk to you or share a piece of bread and a little wine with you. I am used to money, but it's not necessary. I have lived many, many days on a loaf of bread and cheese and a little fruit compote. After the second bite I have exactly the same feeling as if I had steak or chicken. And how many suits can I wear?

Are you concerned about your health and diet?
I try not to become fat. I try not to do anything unhealthy. But I love my job so much . . . actually, I'm in love with working. If I didn't work I would get sick and die, just like a candle fading away. Because of that, I don't pay much attention to myself. I do my early-morning exercises, I try to walk as much as possible. I don't do much of the exercise I used to do—horseback riding, tennis and swimming—because I don't have the time, unfortunately. However, for my age—I'm fifty-nine—I think I'm healthy and don't have any complaints.

Do you smoke?
I used to smoke about a hundred and fifty cigarettes a day. One day I decided to quit and I did. And I carried half a package in my pocket for three months to see whether I would have the will to quit, and I did. Now I only smoke one small Cuban cigar after dinner, sometimes one during the day if I eat lunch out. Usually I do not eat lunch at all—I prefer to work during my lunch hour.

How many hours do you have to sleep?
If I have a good five hours' sleep, I'm all right. *If* I sleep— because sometimes when I am too tired or I have something on my mind, I can't sleep. That's why I would rather stay in my office until three in the morning and finish my work than go to bed at twelve and leave it till the next day, because then my mind would work continuously. But if I am relaxed and have a good five hours' sleep, it's enough. If I am not relaxed, I just roll and roll and roll.

Do you ever take a sleeping pill?

Never.

Do you ever take vacations?
I haven't been able to for the last few years, but I would enjoy it. I would like to be able to always have short vacations so I wouldn't get bored.

Do you read a lot?
With books I'm rather lazy. From childhood it would take me a long time to read a book. I could not finish a book. In school I used to spend the whole night reading one book. But I have quite a lot of reading in my work, a lot of reports to read and write—I dictate them—and newspapers to know what's going on.

What do you think of the press in America?
The press in America is very interesting because you find so many different mentalities and personalities and ideologies. I cannot really judge them, but generally speaking, I think that in this country if you feel a person is doing something wrong, you can discuss it in the press, which is unique to this nation. And, also generally speaking, I think if you have the understanding and trust of the press, there is no problem. I have had no problem personally with the press.

Do you care about your clothes much?
I do. I am moody—I am not artistic—but I like to have different colors and styles of clothes for different moods or different places.

Do you have your suits made?
I have my suits made in Paris at my father's tailor. It's much cheaper for me there because it's kind of a family tradition. Since he knows me, I don't have to go and try on my suits. One look at my face, and he knows whether I have put on five pounds.

Why do you like to give so many parties?
I believe if you want to find friends, you have to make contact; and you cannot make contact by standing on a street corner or isolating yourself in your room. But I think my party-giving has been exaggerated. The parties I give are only for people that I like and their friends.

Do you collect anything?
I like to collect books, pictures—I don't have enough money to get good pictures—watches, coins, antique pill boxes. It depends on my mood. I like china very much, so I collect whatever I like—broken or not—that makes no difference. I don't care about the value as long as I like to look at it. Once I bought a lovely painting for about £18 in London, and it is now worth many thousands of dollars. But when I bought it I didn't *understand* it—I *liked* it. I still have it and I would not sell it for even ten thousand dollars. I have it in my bedroom and every morning I look at it.

Do you have a house of your own other than the embassy residence?
I have a house in Montreux, Switzerland, and I have a house in Iran which has been added onto my family's house, which is about 408 years old. I like old houses, so I've tried to keep it. It has so many additions which I designed myself that it may not look beautiful at all. It may not even make any sense, but I feel comfortable in it. The old building has walls of sun-baked clay that are two and a half meters thick in some places. They're very good because in winter they keep out cold and in summer they keep out heat. Of course, the architects today don't think thick clay walls are wise because they take a lot of space, but I like them—it's cozy.

DR. C. L. ZOIS

Psychiatrist Specializing in the Treatment
of Drug Addiction

Mr. Scavullo: Can you tell me something about yourself, your background?
Dr. Zois: I'm thirty-seven. I was born in Newark and I still live in New Jersey. I was twenty-five and still in medical school when I got married. We have one boy, eleven.
Have you ever taken drugs?
I have a martini with dinner. I have smoked pot on two occasions in my life. I've done a lot of work at a drug-addiction inpatient facility—and I've treated and evaluated over a thousand addicts to this point.
Addicts of what?
All drugs, pills, cocaine.
Does anyone come for treatment who just smokes marijuana?
No. I don't consider that a treatable entity. I think it's less debilitating than alcohol, if anything.
Many people say that cocaine helps them socially.
That's just it—it helps them socially—that's the key. I maintain that drugs substitute a sense of well-being that we usually get from meaningful relationships. When we are interacting with other people and it's going well, then that sense of well-being is really the end result of what it's all about. But a drug gives us that sense of well-being when we don't feel capable of obtaining it in a straightforward way with another human being. It's a false sense of well-being, but still it's there.
Do you prescribe drugs for your patients as part of therapy?
I do, in some instances, but in the long run, just as the body heals itself, the individual has to heal himself. The individual has to draw on his own resources.
Can heroin addicts be treated?
I believe that heroin addiction is the product of an emotional disorder. It's not a character disorder. These people are alienated, isolated, they really lack the ability to relate, so they use heroin to achieve the high which gives them the sense of well-being, the feeling they would have if they related. And you see this in encounter groups with addicts using the group itself, even the institution they're being treated in, as a vehicle to experience the sense of well-being. And it's very common to have two addicts then pair off and say, "We've made it. We've found it, we're going to leave here now, and things are great. She has feelings for me, I have feelings for her . . ." And they leave and a few days later they're shooting up and they're back within a week! What I'm trying to say is that in an existential sense the addict is dead. He's totally abandoned. I'm talking about severe heroin addicts. Although I'm tempted to put the multiple-pill popper even beyond the heroin addict. The kind of abandonment I'm referring to takes place probably before thirty-six months of age. It can be a real abandonment or it can be emotional abandonment. The majority of times it's an emotional abandonment.
What do you think about our drug laws?
I think the drug laws on marijuana are unfortunate. I think the cocaine laws are also excessive.
Do you think it's crime if you choose to take drugs?
I think it's a crime to allow someone to do what he does to himself with heroin. I don't feel that strongly about cocaine. I certainly don't about marijuana. But I think heroin is in a different ballpark. You know, certain psychiatrists have said people can kill themselves if they want. My reply is, "If you want to kill yourself on Monday, that's terrific, but what if on

Friday you felt like living?"
Do drug addicts need a lot of money to come see you for treatment?
I don't treat heroin addicts outside of an inpatient facility. There is no ability in outpatient treatment to contain the impulse to use drugs. I do not treat multiple-pill users outside of an inpatient facility. And the drug-addiction facility that I'm the medical director of is free. It's in the South Bronx, so it serves an indigent population.
Do you find many people come to psychiatrists for sexual problems? Or love problems?
When you talk about love problems, you're talking about the ability to relate and the ability to separate—the ability to say goodbye, as well as the ability to maintain a relationship. When you talk about sexual problems, to a large degree, you're talking about the same thing. Some of my patients do have sexual problems, but usually they stem from a basic issue that they're dealing with.
Do parents send their teen-agers to you because they're promiscuous or homosexual?
Not really. Most of the time, parents will send young adolescents for therapy because the child is not behaving in a way that is acceptable to the parent. In most instances, what the parent considers acceptable is usually not what's in the best interests of the child anyway. The parent wants the child to be dependent, an extension of his or her own personality. So most of my experience in that area is that finally the parents feel very negatively about me because I refuse to fulfill their expectation of what treatment should be, which is that I should tell the individual to behave as the parent wants.
Be good.
Right. Be good means don't separate, don't individuate, fulfill my expectations. In general, that's called engulfment, i.e., it requires the death of an identity. It's the same thing as abandonment, which is also an emotional death.
Do you ever feel kind of useless, that you never know if you helped a person or not?
Well, there are barometers . . . I once treated a writer who was missing deadlines, and in a period of months he was making deadlines and started on a book he had been contemplating for years. That I would call progress. But what you are talking about is a very philosophical concept. I don't feel I'm helping someone if I don't feel someone is working in therapy. Then I call in question what's going on. A patient might come to me and say, "This is what I want." And then two months later I say, "I hear what you say, but I see what you do. And I wonder if this is what you want, and I wonder if I'm for you and you're for me." I won't work with people that I can't be intellectually honest with. I don't believe that everybody can treat everybody. I think you have to be able to make a connection. Usually from the first couple of sessions you know whether you can make a connection with the individual or whether he can make a connection with you. When someone comes in to see me, I never make a contract with him immediately. I say to him, "We'll meet a few times and we'll see how you get along with me and how I get along with you, and at that time together we'll make some determination as to whether we should continue and then we'll formalize it." The only thing I ask from a patient is what I ask from myself—honesty with each other.

FRANCESCO SCAVULLO was born on Staten Island, and was raised and educated in New York City. He began his career as assistant to the photographer Horst. In 1948 he photographed his first cover for *Seventeen* magazine and opened his own studio in 1950. Mr. Scavullo has done covers for every major magazine in America: *Women's Home Companion, Ladies' Home Journal, Redbook, Charm, Today's Woman, Glamour, Life, Newsweek, Harper's Bazaar, Town & Country, Vogue, Playboy, People,* in addition to *Seventeen.* He has been taking photographs for the cover of *Cosmopolitan* magazine for the past ten years. He also does commissioned portraits, and photographs celebrities and artists for record-album covers and book jackets. He is the author of *Scavullo on Beauty.*

Francesco Scavullo uses a Nikon camera with a 105-millimeter lens. He shoots with Tri-X film and develops with Acufine. The printing is done on Kodak polycontrast F paper. All photo printing for this book was done by Robert James Cass, Jr.

The text of this book was set in hot metal in a face called TIMES ROMAN, designed by Stanley Morison for *The Times* (London), and first introduced by that newspaper in 1932.

Among typographers and designers of the twentieth century, Stanley Morison has been a strong forming influence, as typographical advisor to the English Monotype Corporation, as a director of two distinguished English publishing houses, and a writer of sensibility, erudition, and keen practical sense.

The book was composed by Maryland Linotype Company, Baltimore, Maryland. It was printed on 70 pound Casco gloss by the Murray Printing Company, Forge Village, Massachusetts, and bound by American Book-Stratford Press, Saddlebrook, New Jersey.